Coloniality, Religion,
and the Law in the
Early Iberian World

HISPANIC ISSUES • VOLUME 40

Coloniality, Religion, and the Law in the Early Iberian World

Santa Arias and Raúl Marrero-Fente
EDITORS

Vanderbilt University Press
NASHVILLE, TENNESSEE
2014

© 2014 Vanderbilt University Press
All rights reserved
First Edition 2014

This book is printed on acid-free paper.

The editors gratefully acknowledge assistance
from the College of Liberal Arts and
the Department of Spanish and Portuguese Studies
at the University of Minnesota;
and the Department of Spanish and Portuguese
at the University of Iowa

*The complete list of volumes in the
Hispanic Issues series begins on page 279*

Library of Congress Cataloging-in-Publication Data

Coloniality, religion, and the law in the early Iberian world /
eds. Santa Arias and Raúl Marrero-Fente.
   pages cm
   Includes bibliographical references and index.
   ISBN 978-0-8265-1956-6 (hardcover : alk. paper)
   ISBN 978-0-8265-1957-3 (pbk. : alk. paper)
   ISBN 978-0-8265-1958-0 (ebook)
   1. New Spain—History—16th century. 2. Spain—
Colonies—History—16th century. 3. Spain—Religion—16th
century. 4. New Spain—Religion—16th century.
5. Law—Spain—History—16th century. 6. Law—Spain—
Colonies—History—16th century. 7. Law—New Spain—
History—16th century.
I. Arias, Santa, editor of compilation.
II. Marrero-Fente, Raúl, editor of compilation.
F1231.C647 2013
946'.04—dc23   2013013895

HISPANIC ISSUES

Nicholas Spadaccini
Editor-in-Chief

Antonio Ramos-Gascón and Jenaro Talens
General Editors

Nelsy Echávez-Solano, Adriana Gordillo
Luis Martín-Estudillo, and Kelly McDonough
Associate Editors

Cortney Benjamin, Megan Corbin, and Scott Ehrenburg
Assistant Editors

Advisory Board/Editorial Board
Rolena Adorno (Yale University)
Román de la Campa (Unversity of Pennsylvania)
David Castillo (University at Buffalo)
Jaime Concha (University of California, San Diego)
Tom Conley (Harvard University)
William Egginton (Johns Hopkins University)
Brad Epps (University of Cambridge)
*Ana Forcinito (University of Minnesota)
David W. Foster (Arizona State University)
Edward Friedman (Vanderbilt University)
Wlad Godzich (University of California, Santa Cruz)
Antonio Gómez L-Quiñones (Dartmouth College)
Hans Ulrich Gumbrecht (Stanford University)
*Carol A. Klee (University of Minnesota)
Eukene Lacarra Lanz (Universidad del País Vasco)
Tom Lewis (University of Iowa)
Jorge Lozano (Universidad Complutense de Madrid)
Raúl Marrero-Fente (University of Minnesota)
Walter D. Mignolo (Duke University)
*Louise Mirrer (The New-York Historical Society)
Mabel Moraña (Washington University in St. Louis)
Alberto Moreiras (Texas A & M University)
Bradley Nelson (Concordia University, Montreal)
Michael Nerlich (Université Blaise Pascal)
*Francisco Ocampo (University of Minnesota)
Miguel Tamen (Universidade de Lisboa)
Teresa Vilarós (Texas A & M University)
Iris M. Zavala (Universitat Pompeu Fabra, Barcelona)
Santos Zunzunegui (Universidad del País Vasco)

Contents

Introduction:
Negotiation between Religion and the Law
Santa Arias and Raúl Marrero-Fente   ix

PART I
Politics

1   José de Acosta: Colonial Regimes
for a Globalized Christian World
Ivonne del Valle   3

2   Conquistador Counterpoint: Intimate Enmity
in the Writings of Bernardo de Vargas Machuca
Kris Lane   27

3   Voices of the *Altepetl*: Nahua Epistemologies
and Resistance in the *Anales de Juan Bautista*
Ezekiel Stear   51

4   Performances of Indigenous Authority in
Postconquest Tlaxcalan Annals: Don Juan
Buenaventura Zapata y Mendoza's *Historia
cronológica de la noble ciudad de Tlaxcala*
Kelly S. McDonough   71

PART II
Religion

5   Translating the "Doctrine of Discovery":
Spain, England, and Native American Religions
Ralph Bauer   93

6   Narrating Conversion: Idolatry, the Sacred,
and the Ambivalences of Christian Evangelization
in Colonial Peru
Laura León Llerena   117

7   Old Enemies, New Contexts: Early Modern Spanish
    (Re)-Writing of Islam in the Philippines
    Ana M. Rodríguez-Rodríguez   137

8   Art That Pushes and Pulls: Visualizing Religion
    and Law in the Early Colonial Province of Toluca
    Delia A. Cosentino   159

PART III
Law

9   The Rhetoric of War and Justice in the Conquest
    of the Americas: Ethnography, Law, and Humanism in
    Juan Ginés de Sepúlveda and Bartolomé de Las Casas
    David M. Solodkow   181

10 Human Sacrifice, Conquest, and the Law: Cultural
    Interpretation and Colonial Sovereignty in New Spain
    Cristian Roa   201

11 Legal Pluralism and the "India Pura" in New Spain:
    The School of Guadalupe and the Convent
    of the Company of Mary
    Mónica Díaz   221

12 Our Lady of Anarchy: Iconography as Law
    on the Frontiers of the Spanish Empire
    John D. (Jody) Blanco   241

    Afterword
    Teleiopoesis at the Crossroads
    of the Colonial/Postcolonial Divide
    José Rabasa   263

    Contributors   271

    Index   275

◆ Introduction:
Negotiation between Religion and the Law

Santa Arias and Raúl Marrero-Fente

Coloniality, Religion, and the Law in the Early Iberian World reexamines the crucial role that the Catholic Church and newly created legal and colonial institutions played in the production of coloniality by directing attention to discourses that emerged from this experience of human inequality.[1] Most scholarship investigating the ties between religion, law, and conquest tends to emphasize the intellectual and legal debates that took place during the sixteenth century regarding the methods of conquest. This volume, on the other hand, takes a broader view that incorporates how other sectors of colonial society engaged with the political engineering legitimated by Spain's laws and the Church's doctrine of salvation, examining, beyond legal texts, a wide range of colonial discourses generated from the sixteenth to the eighteenth century. The essays also emphasize the role of colonial subjects in the establishment, contestation, and reconfiguration of the colonial apparatus through the laws that ordered society. The discourse produced by this intra-imperial dialogue significantly altered the influence of the evangelization project and divine right embedded in the texts that legalized the Spanish conquest. Moreover, the existence of this dialogue represents a redefinition of "New World" coloniality (Maldonado Torres), the key element in the production of Europe's modernity

(Dussel). Maldonado-Torres explains the impact of this change: "Se da un cambio en la visión de mundo que hace de la acumulación una indicación de la salvación, lo que abre las puertas para que el capitalismo pasara, de modo de producción solo en algunas zonas, al modo de producción dominante de un emergente eurocentrado sistema-mundo" (684) (There was a change in worldview that transformed accumulation into a sign of salvation, thus opening the way for capitalism to pass from the mode of production only present in certain regions to be the dominant mode of production of an emergent Euro-centered world-system). According to Enrique Dussel, religion and the law in the Spanish Americas had a pivotal role in the making of Spain as the first "modern" nation unified and strengthened by the Inquisition, military power, Nebrija's *Gramática de la lengua*, and, more importantly, "the subordination of the church to the state" ("Europe" 470). In the process, these discourses contributed to the creation of new identities and ideologies, which reacted against the exploitation of people and the natural world for the acquisition of power and wealth. For many critics this is a point of origin of the postcolonial mentality.

Rethinking Colonial Law

In order to fully understand the pervasive force of the colonial/modern roots of domination in the Spanish global empire, it is crucial to examine the significance of two unique legal documents: the series of papal bulls issued by Alexander VI (1493–1494) and the *Requerimiento*, authored in 1513 by jurist Juan López de Palacios Rubios. These texts reveal the complicity of Catholicism with the beginnings of modern empire building, which for Spain meant the legal justification for territorial expansion and the overpowering of indigenous societies for the sake of expanding the frontiers of Christianity, and the development of its modern imperial economy. These central documents provide ample space for an interrogation of the role of textuality, representation, and the rhetoric of the law in early modern transoceanic colonial/religious projects.

Pope Alexander's Bulls of Donation represent an inaugural act, asserting a right to conquest that tightened the bond between secular and spiritual powers. From a geopolitical standpoint, these decrees reasserted a foundational tenet of Christendom that God owned the globe and that the Pope had the power to oversee his domains. This geopolitical ideology took its colonialist form in the medieval reconceptualization of the notion of *imperium* and the millenarian theology that saw Catholic empires as "agents of God providential plan" (Muldoon 17). Influenced by this medieval doctrine and the original classical connotation of *imperium* as a form of power, popes played a prominent role as the legitimating authority of conquests and appropriation of territories by Christendom, both inside and outside of Europe. Alexander VI in his *Inter caetera* bull of May 4, 1493, conferred to Spain rights of conquest on the basis of a line of demarcation that assigned to Spain and Portugal territories and oceans to the west and south of Europe.² With this foundational colonial text, the Pope established a geography of coloniality instated by the controversial Treaty of Tordesillas (June 7, 1494).³ These rights of conquest had a price: Spain and Portugal became financially responsible for all evangelization efforts in this vast territory. L. C. Green explains that the language of the first bull makes evident that Alexander VI was highly cognizant of his legal authority to define the bounds of *imperium* since he wrote the document as a "legal grant giving the Spanish and Portuguese monarchs full power of sovereignty and jurisdiction" (6). Carl Schmitt underscores the idea that the conquest's legal foundation was rooted in a history of territorialization, in *the writing of the earth*, not in the usual way we conceive of geography, as a description of the territory, but as the drawing of borders and imposition of order within them as an instrument used to define and reinforce sovereign power. Schmitt explains, "In this way, the earth is bound to law in three ways. She contains law within herself, as a reward of labor; she manifests law upon herself, as fixed boundaries; and she sustains law above herself, as a public sign of order. Law is bound to the earth and related to the earth" (42). Ultimately, earth and law are God's creation enacted by his appointed servants.

These papal bulls provided the legal basis for another foundational document, the *Requerimiento*, and the establishment of the Patronato Real de Indias (Royal Patronage of the Indies). The *Requerimiento* "the purest expression of writing that conquers" (Rabasa, "Writing Violence" 54) was a response to the 1511 polemical claims by the Dominican Antonio de Montesinos about the mistreatment of indigenous populations in Hispaniola, and to the 1512 *Leyes de Burgos*, which sought to regulate the institution of the *encomienda* and its requirement to provide Catholic doctrine to indigenous subjects. Its companion document, the Concordat of Burgos, gave local parishes governmental authority in the collection of taxes, in return for granting the Crown the legal right to present candidates for ecclesiastical positions and participate in the administration of the Church (Schwaller 48). The *Requerimiento* magnified Spain's hegemonic authority and decisively compelled Indians to peacefully submit themselves to Spanish royal authorities. If immediate obedience did not follow, the *Requerimiento* explicitly warned of punishment: "las muertes y daños que de ello se siguiesen" (par. 8) (the death and harm that from it will follow). Such harm involved being deprived of their land, property, and freedom. Rubios's *Requerimiento* extended further the legal fiction of legitimacy of the conquest of the newly opened Atlantic world, as part of the uninterrupted and pervasive set of practices underpinning coloniality.[4]

Previous scholarship demonstrates that the *Requerimiento* intertwined secular and religious privilege by reworking earlier legitimations of just war employed by both Christians and Muslims against so-called infidels. Similar to the Bulls of Donation, its immediate reference can be found in medieval theocratic theory, with the corollary that "the Christianization of the natives is the only valid end for legitimate Spanish sovereignty" (Rivera Pagán 40–41). Through the authority of Church doctrine and the law, these two documents legalized colonial violence and cleared the way for the subordination of indigenous societies and centuries of racial and ethnic conflict that persists today.

The law did not legislate a stable relationship between Church and state; in fact, during the fifteenth and sixteenth centuries the Spanish monarchy gradually got the upper hand in most matters dealing with the "new divine" possessions on the other side of the Ocean Sea.[5] The Patronato Real de Indias, a deeply rooted institutional affiliation between the monarchy and ecclesiastical authorities, further empowered Spain in its acquisition of a world empire. This papal-imperial agreement was also established by the 1493 Bulls of Donation and modified in two decrees by Pope Julius II: *Universalis Ecclesiae regimini* (1508) and *Eximiae devotionis* (1510). Through the *patronato real*, the Spanish ruler acquired control over secular church appointments and received the right to tithes from American mineral production to be used for missionary activities and building ecclesiastical infrastructure (Schwaller 47). Since the *patronato* only dealt with one part of the clergy, this empowerment of civil government did not stand in the way of the reinvigoration of religious orders, which also began competing for the spiritual conquest of new territories. Thus, the history of the *patronato real* illustrates how civil authorities engage in constant negotiation for power with the Holy See.

In the Spanish Americas, the privileges and limitations of the ruler and the religious orders were continuously contested and negotiated as geographical explorations offered up unknown territories to Spanish possession. One must remember that Columbus set sail west and south just as theological and legal thought were flourishing in Spain like never before. At the University of Salamanca—dominated by the mendicant orders and influenced by Thomistic and Augustinian political thought—geopolitics and the violence of conquest fueled some of the most important scholastic debates of the era, of such influence that they have been labeled a "second scholasticism" (Boland 129).[6]

Such engagements produced a philosophical apparatus concerned with ethics, morality, individual freedom, natural law (*ius naturae*), and the law of nations (*ius gentium*), as they were applied to colonial practices. With regard to the relationship between spiritual and secular powers, Muldoon explains that canon law "was the vehicle by means of which abstract moral principles would be transformed into the basic rules according to which an entire society would operate" (64).[7] Important actors, such as Francisco de Vitoria, Melchor Cano, Francisco Suárez, and Bartolomé de Las Casas, engaged with canon law to debate the rights of Amerindians (once they became vassals to the king), including individual rights that were conveniently ignored on the other side of the Atlantic. While some Church agents sponsored empire building, these brokers of morality and justice sat in a constrained space pressed upon by Church-state agendas in need of legitimation. These political theologians took advantage of the institutional shift in legal purview over these issues from common law to canon law to develop theories on government and arguments on how to conquest the Indies. Inside or outside the law, this body of rules determined the colonial condition and exclusion of subaltern subjects.

If religion and the law sat at the core of the polarized hierarchy and archaic version of the "civilizing mission" that Spain imposed on its territories, Christian principles also provided grounds for a critique of the colonial project, while the law became instrument of reform. Missionaries were among the first to attack excessive labor demands complicit in the demographic decline and extinction of indigenous groups. Bartolomé de Las Casas, the most prominent Dominican advocating Amerindian rights, had a well-known role in the elaboration of new legislation against coloniality. His polemical arguments about the mistreatment of Amerindian populations centered not only on first-hand testimonies that he collected as their legal protector but also on the priestly abuse of the rite of absolution granted to those who had repeatedly confessed to heinous crimes. His treatises and letters systematically refute the full cadre of legal advisors to the Spanish emperor and provide a celebrated example of legal intervention against the excesses of the colonial project.[8] In fact, the debates on the Spanish rights of dominion and Amerindian rights of freedom and property underpin most of the literature of the colonial period up to Independence and continue to be recounted in the literature of contemporary writers (Adorno).

This political and social context is crucial for the interpretation of colonial texts and the body of laws of the Indies. However, these sixteenth-century debates and their production of "anticolonial" texts should by no means be viewed as the climactic moment of this conjuncture between religion, the law, and coloniality. Rather, they should be seen as a midpoint in a long and tortuous history that begins with the Iberian *reconquista*, and reaches in space and time to the distant Philippines and Marianas and the anticolonial wars of the nineteenth century.[9]

A central thrust in the study of colonial laws in the Iberian world has been to study them not only as a set of rules put forward by institutions but also as a discursive practice vital to imperial domination based on a genealogy of ideas (Marrero-Fente 248). That is, laws are not reducible to a set of abstract principles in their application, because legal discourse is itself a social construction founded in the hierarchical nature of empire. Moreover, one must take into account the fact that behind every law and its application is a context and a set of unwritten rules that respond to conventions, protocols, and uses of power (Baxi 540).[10] In the colonies, laws and decrees were often rewritten with official expectations in mind. It is vital to read contestations and resistance to the law within this context. The main legacy of European colonial law was the creation of colonial societies that promoted assimilation of indigenous and mixed race groups, while ensuring their exclusion from most positions of power, including the very offices charged with maintaining legal and religious institutions.[11]

Persistent Global Negotiations

Scholarship on coloniality and religion has shown that patterns of royal patronage, methods of conversion, extirpation of idolatries, and cultural practices developed differently across imperial space and time (Charles; Díaz; Kirk; Mills; Schwartz; Schwaller; Tavárez; Klor de Alva; Díaz Balsera). Indeed, coloniality was constituted by a wide array of situated practices that justified Hispanization of Amerindian societies, environmental degradation, violence, and dispossession. The study and critique of coloniality is a hermeneutic act that interrogates political, cultural, and religious realms. More importantly, it reveals silenced histories that survived in the interstices of colonial discourses, oral traditions, and forms of non-verbal representation. In these discourses one can find cultural resistance and accommodation, and evidence of the ambivalent and unstable character of colonialism. By re-thinking colonial and visual texts from an interdisciplinary perspective, these essays unveil different ways in which coloniality was reproduced, rejected, and renegotiated within the legal and religious apparatus that gave meaning and legitimacy to colonial projections of the Spanish state as it plunged forward toward modernity.

Underpinning colonial practices were constant negotiations between colonial administrators, members of the clergy, new Spanish settlers, emerging

Creole elites, and indigenous and *casta* groups. The archives of the Inquisition and ecclesiastical histories of the Orders, as well as census, baptism, and sacramental records, document the manner in which Amerindian groups engage with missionary efforts (Cline). One of the assertions of this volume is that the legal otherness inscribed in Amerindians did not leave them devoid of legal power, as has been argued (Subirats 401–63). From the very beginning, the body of the law and the instruments of Church and state were persistently negotiated and often supplanted, as Jody Blanco asserts (in this volume) with regard to the Philippines. In the Spanish Americas, natives became important actors in urban centers and remote peripheries, demonstrating their intellectual capacity and audacity to accommodate and shape new colonial conditions and laws. In the struggle for landholdings, often with priests involved, native elites challenged the rule of the law when they made their claims heard at the viceregal courts. As Ethelia Ruiz Medrano argues in her important study *Mexico's Indigenous Communities*, in central Mexico some of them successfully used written documents of pre-Hispanic provenance to claim legal rights to their lands. Some of the essays in this volume dwell at length on Amerindian political agency and demonstrate that subaltern subjects were not passive victims of the body of the law or the force of coloniality (Blanco, Cosentino, McDonough, Stear).

Sabine MacCormack reminds us that native actors also played a role in the spread of the new Christian faith by interpolating their own histories and cosmologies into Catholicism. More recently, José Rabasa has made a crucial contribution to the understanding of indigenous agency and modernity by rereading the Codex Telleriano-Remensis as a central document of colonial history written from an *elsewhere*. He introduces the notion of *elsewhere*, which constitutes the habitus from which the *tlacuilo* defied the traditional binaries of modernity and reaffirmed her memory and worldview of colonial order. For Rabasa, regardless of the imposition of Western structures, the indigenous mind remains ungraspable; this site of knowledge production constitutes the limits of empire (*Tell Me the Story* 193).

The imposition of Catholicism on indigenous groups should never be interpreted as a finished project. Indeed, Spain's global colonizing mission had to figure out ways of adapting to cultural difference and forms of resistance, notwithstanding what was warranted by discourses on religion and the shifting text of the law. Most scholarship in colonial studies has focused on the Americas, however the violence of coloniality was felt globally, and the European conquest of the Pacific provides another vantage point for examining the range of articulations of coloniality. The case of the Spanish Philippines presents an opportunity to examine intercoloniality, as its colonial government was under the direct jurisdiction of the wealthier viceroyalty of New Spain, which controlled its important trade and the annual *situado* after 1571 (Bjork 27). This borderland on the margin between the trading empires of Asia, the Indian Ocean, and the vast Pacific World sustained 333 years of Spanish colonial rule and played an important but unheralded geopolitical role in early modern history. The Pacific Ocean, where Spaniards competed with the Portuguese, the Dutch, and the Chinese, became a site for hegemony that invites an interrogation of Spanish imperial identity and, simultaneously, one that tests the validity of apparently well-internalized perceptions of the Other.

Politics, Religion, and the Law

This volume acknowledges the strong complicity between secular government and the Catholic Church in laying the legal foundation of coloniality, a relationship that was nonetheless tense and changeable. It also underscores that the study of how colonial laws were put into effect needs to consider ideological shifts that compelled agents of empire and subaltern groups to strategically reposition themselves as lawful subjects of the Spanish global empire. Furthermore, as Ralph Bauer suggests (in this volume), Spain and its colonies did not act alone in these matters, and had a strong and lasting influence over other European empires within the transoceanic circuit.

The essays included in the first section of this volume (Politics) explore the engagement between colonial structures and practices in the writings of the Jesuit José de Acosta, colonial administrator Bernardo Vargas Machuca, anonymous indigenous authors of the *Anales de Juan Bautista,* and indigenous intellectual Don Juan Buenaventura Zapata y Mendoza. These essays focus on how laws were thought out, reconfigured, and contested by subjects representing divergent colonial ideologies.

Spanish officials and clergy were especially concerned with imposing colonial order in the aftermath of the chaos of the conquest. While race played a major role in the production of coloniality, as Aníbal Quijano has argued (1992), perceptions of different degrees of barbarism also influenced methods and practices leading to the Hispanization of Amerindian cultures. Ivonne del Valle (in this volume) focuses on one of the key figures of Spanish colonial thought, the Jesuit José de Acosta, who in his *De procuranda indorum salute* (1588) introduced a plan for ordering difference. In this treatise on Amerindian conversion, Acosta sets out a critique of dystopic conditions and proposes a series of reforms that would replace violence and chaos with order. For Del Valle, Acosta's program of missionization represents the first full-fledged theory based on the necessary mutually self-sustaining expansion of Christian civilization and the colonialist economy.

The issue of order and control maintained its relevance in urban and peripheral regions under Spanish rule. By the mid-sixteenth century, the largest urban settlements in the Americas had fallen to Spanish conquerors; yet, as David Weber has persuasively argued, many smaller indigenous groups remained recalcitrant or independent until the eighteenth century or beyond. In this volume, Kris Lane explores this theme by revisiting the work of Bernardo de Vargas Machuca of Simancas, who in 1578 proposed an aggressive plan for "western conquests" from northern Mexico to Chile. The reception at the imperial court of Las Casas's critique of the practices of "conquest" compelled Philip II to make a "paternalistic, 'post-conquest' rhetorical shift," resulting in the ordering of the so-called pacification campaigns. As a result of this new culture of colonialism, Bernardo de Vargas Machuca wrote his *Defense and Discourse of the Western Conquests*. In his semi-legalistic *Defense*, Vargas Machuca offers a justification for his plan for conquest based on his personal appraisal of Amerindians. In the text he articulates his own predicament, reminiscent of what Ashis Nandy has called the "intimate enmity" of the colonial condition. Colonial consciousness, that psychological realm shared between the colonized and the colonizers, influenced codes of conduct, ideologies, and projects, which defined coloniality.

In opposition to the Eurocentric perspectives of Acosta and Vargas Machuca, indigenous and mestizo intellectuals introduced their own reactions to the logic of possession. While indigenous elites often accommodated themselves to the Spanish political, economic, and theological structures of cross-cultural domination, their writings reveal their own reasons for such ideological positioning. An important document that demonstrates accommodation and resistance is the *Anales de Juan Bautista*, which depicts sixty three years (1519–1582) of colonial rule in central Mexico and elucidates on indigenous reactions and rejection of the imperial imposition of monetary tribute. Ezekiel Stear (in this volume) explains that the author misinterprets Spanish ideas on political and economic organization and ritual, and projects Amerindians' own cultural expectations onto the Spaniards. By uncovering what James Lockhart calls a "double misunderstanding," Stear sheds light on motivations behind the composition of the *Anales*. The Nahuatl-language annals of seventeenth-century Tlaxcalan elite statesman Don Juan Buenaventura Zapata y Mendoza offer another important example of how local elites negotiated their political and social power in colonial Mexico. Kelly McDonough (in this volume) argues that Tlaxcalans publicly asserted their political authority, legitimacy, and rights via productive and at times contradictory discourses and performances focused on noble indigenous lineage, and loyalty to the Spanish Crown and Catholic Church. From the political theology of Acosta to the unveiled responses of indigenous agents, this group of essays on interethnic politics suggest that the law was not only a dominant presence in all domains of colonial life but a constant reference in Spanish and indigenous discourses.

The second section (Religion) focuses on Spanish religious practices and their influence on the English colonial enterprise, the recovery of ancestral myths, and the paradoxical reconfiguration of the colonizers' identity. Ralph Bauer (in this volume) grapples with the question of diabolism and its influence on European legal claims of territories for Spain and Britain. Spanish images pointing to the violation of natural law that justified the extirpation of idolatries circulated among English historians of the period, particularly Protestants who manipulated these representations in their own writings.

In central Mexico, Nahua leaders developed strategies for protecting their autonomy and influence in the face of aggressive legal repression by institutions aimed at the extirpation of indigenous religion. As Patricia Lopes Don demonstrates in *Bonfires of Cultures*, in the Andean region including the Viceroyalty of New Granada, indigenous elites followed suit. The campaign to extirpate idolatries underlay the creation of the Huarochirí Manuscript, the only indigenous book-length text written in Quechua in colonial times. It used the creation myths of the people of Huarochirí to interrogate their persistence in worshiping ancestral deities. Laura León Llerena (in this volume) analyzes the significance of the political and social context of the text and highlights the importance of the marginalia and intertexts in the manuscript by the extirpator of idolatries, Francisco de Ávila. Her essay lays out the complex representation of Christian conversion, one that did not conform to post-Tridentine reforms.

It has been stated that the history and legacy of colonialism in the Philippines was limited mainly to European missionary efforts (Rafael 18). Ana M. Rodríguez-Rodríguez (in this volume) brings this theme to the foreground as she untangles the abiding preoccupation with the construction of cultural difference and its role in the reconfiguration of missionaries' self-identity. Francisco de Combés's *Historia de Mindanao y Joló* (Madrid 1667), a Jesuit historical account of the missionary experience with Muslims reveals how the imposed "official" ideology does not always provide an appropriate mold to contain the process of apprehending and understanding both Self and Other in this new space.

Refuting the idea that indigenous subjects were passive entities in colonial situations, Delia A. Cosentino (in this volume) highlights another instance of indigenous agency within the walls of the Church by analyzing two images produced by native artists in the Toluca Valley. Indigenous visual inscription of territories and ancestral symbols provide evidence of the prominent role of visuality in natives' entanglements with the Church and the law and demonstrates that local artists and patrons used genealogical imagery as a strategy of inclusion, to legitimate their claims to land and political power.

In the last section of this volume (Law), David Solodkow and Cristian Roa explore the political instrumentality of early ethnography on legal and humanistic discourses. Solodkow reexamines the debate on Amerindian "nature" in Juan Ginés de Sepúlveda's *Demócrates segundo* and Bartolomé de Las Casas's *Apologética historia sumaria*. According to him, ethnography served as the basis upon which these legal and theological debates were formulated. On the other hand, Roa identifies human sacrifice as a central concern among early chroniclers of the conquest of Mexico. Their interpretation of sacrifice influenced colonial legislation and inquisitorial processes while creating a new idiom of colonization based on its own ambivalence. Of key importance is his argument regarding the supplementary relationship between human sacrifice and colonial law, which demonstrates their reliance on ideas of order, symbolic autonomy, and cultural meaning.

Subaltern subjects' perspectives on the law are emphasized by Mónica Díaz and Jody Blanco (in this volume). Díaz explores the role and agency of indigenous women at the Colegio and Convent of Nuestra Señora de Guadalupe y Enseñanza in Mexico City at a moment when Bourbon policies were addressing the integration of Indians through education reforms. Díaz demonstrates that although "integration" was the ultimate purpose of the convent, the long-standing division between the two Republics (Indian and Spanish) fostered a clear ethnic consciousness among Indian women and their families, which in turn reinforced a racialized division. Díaz engages with the difficult and polemical area of postcolonial legal studies to analyze the shifting logic of exclusion/inclusion in European law and its effect on and responses from Indian women participating in conventual life.

Certainly the relationship between Catholicism and colonial law was unstable and kept changing during the period of conquest and settlement. While evangelization efforts made the Catholic Church the most important instrument of conquest, paradoxically it also undermined colonial law as indigenous societies empowered themselves in a newly found spirituality. This different take on the relationship between the law and religion is the focus of Jody Blanco's essay (in this volume) on the display of images and devotional cults in the Philippines. In a twofold argument, he demonstrates how the display of images in devotional cults supplemented, substituted for, and even challenged coloniality. More importantly, he shows that the iconography of law allowed for the survival and reaffirmation of native customs.

As a group, these essays are overwhelmingly concerned with the crucial role of writing and representation in the production of coloniality. The authors demonstrate the conflictive entanglements between the Catholic Church and the law in discourses that legitimated and destabilized the ideologies and institutions that sought to produce colonial subjects in unequal social conditions of existence. From a European perspective, Spain played a leading role in the development of a code of laws for colonial rule and in the evangelization of non-Christian peoples around the world. However, when assessing the history of colonialism from the perspective of the colonized, it is evident that the articulation of policies, establishment of administrative institutions, and exercise of domination was not an easy task. Subaltern discourses, oral traditions, and iconography show the imprint of a subaltern consciousness that responded to and contested imperial laws and colonial practices of domination. These texts and images not only described social reality, they also shaped it a way that reconfigured the history of how Spain and the Catholic Church conjoined efforts and pulled vast regions of the Atlantic and Pacific into the modern world.

Notes

1. The adoption of the notion of coloniality, also referred to as the darker side of modernity (Mignolo), has been the subject of much interpretation revolving around Peruvian sociologist Aníbal Quijano's contributions to colonial studies. Coloniality and power entanglements are reunited in his idea of *"coloniality of power," an important point of departure for understanding the historical legacy of early colonialism, the emergence of modernity, and geopolitics in the construction of knowledge (see Mignolo "Preamble" and Quijano).*
2. In *Tropics of Empire*, Nicolás Wey Gómez emphasizes the importance of southern regions (i.e., the tropics) in the colonizing ideology underpinning this act.
3. The Treaty of Tordesillas established an imaginary line located 370 leagues west of the Cape Verde Islands. This contentious line protected Portuguese possessions in Africa with wide ocean space for navigation. However, it gave the upper hand to Spain, which was entrusted with all territories to the west of the line. The line of demarcation remained a subject of dispute with further explorations that placed Brazil,

Newfoundland, and the Spice Islands under Portuguese domain. On the political significance of the Treaty of Tordesillas, see Philip Steinberg.
4. The *Requerimiento* served as an instrument of conquest until the early eighteenth century through several written versions responding to local histories. On the *Requerimiento*, see Patricia Seed, Luis Weckman, Silvio Zavala, Luis Rivera Pagán, and Demetrio Ramos.
5. There has been much discussion of the perceived unfairness of the bulls against Portugal, which before the Columbian voyages was in the lead on exploration. At issue is how these papal decrees opened competition for the oceans and further exploration of the Pacific; on this topic, see Blair (6).
6. While much of the discussion of sixteenth-century political theology has been dominated by inquiries into the School of Salamanca and the role of the Dominicans, it is crucial to bring to the fore other schools such as the Jesuit University in Coimbra, which had an enormous influence on the ethics of missionary work (Marinheiro).
7. Las Casas's ideas were incorporated by sixteenth-century theologians and canon lawyers such as Melchor Cano, Domingo de Soto, Bartolomé Carranza de Miranda, and others (Cárdenas Bunsen).
8. On Las Casas's role as a political broker of the New Laws, see Mauricio Beuchot, Santa Arias, and Larry Clayton.
9. Magellan reached the Philippine archipelago in 1521, but it was not until 1565 that Miguel López de Legazpi established the first permanent settlement in Cebu. On the colonial history of the Philippines, see Nicholas Cushner and John Leddy Phelan.
10. In terms of context, Antonio de León Pinelo's decades of work compiling the original scripts of the laws of the Indies (*Recopilación de las leyes de las Indias*, 1681) highlight the existence of secular/religious tensions as inspiration for their promulgation. Juan de Solórzano y Pereira's magisterial political commentary on these laws in his *Política indiana* (1648) reveals the preoccupations of canon law experts about the juridical status of Amerindians and the justification for the war of conquest.
11. Darian-Smith and Fitzpatrick refer to this "assimilation/exclusion antinomy" as the philosophical foundation of the injustice of conquest (1–2).

Works Cited

Alejandro VI. "Segunda bula Inter caetera de Alejandro VI." 4 May 1493. Bulas de donación del papa Alejandro VI a los Reyes Católicos. *Rincón castellano*. Web. 31 April 2012.

Adorno, Rolena. *Polemics of Possession in Spanish American Narrative*. New Haven: Yale University Press, 2008. Print.

Arias, Santa. *Retórica, historia y polémica: Bartolomé de las Casas y la tradición intelectual renacentista*. Lanham: University Press of America, 2001. Print.

Baxi, Uprenda. "Postcolonial legality." *A Companion to Postcolonial Studies*. Ed. Henry Schwarz and Sangeeta Ray. Malden: Blackwell, 2000. 540–55. Print.

Beuchot, Mauricio. *Los fundamentos de los derechos humanos en Bartolomé de Las Casas.* Barcelona: Anthropos, 1994. Print.

Bjork, Katharine. "The Link That Kept the Philippines Spanish: Mexican Merchant Interests and the Manila Trade, 1571–1815." *Journal of World History* 9.1 (1998): 25–50

Boland, Vivian. *St. Thomas Aquinas.* London: Continuum, 2007. Print.

Bourne, Edward. Introduction. *The Philippine Islands, 1493–1806.* Ed. Emma Helen Blair. Teddington: Echo Library, 2006. 4–31. Print.

Cárdenas Bunsen, José. *Escritura y derecho canónico en la obra de fray Bartolomé de las Casas.* Madrid: Iberoamericana / Vervuert, 2011. Print.

Charles, John. *Allies at Odds: The Andean Church and Its Indigenous Agents, 1583–1671.* Albuquerque: University of New Mexico Press, 2010. Print.

Clayton, Lawrence. *Bartolomé de las Casas. A Biography.* Cambridge: Cambridge University Press, 2012. Print.

Cline, Sarah. "The Spiritual Conquest Reexamined: Baptism and Christian Marriage in Early Sixteenth-Century." *Hispanic American Historical Review* 73. 3 (1993): 453–80. Print.

Cushner, Nicholas P. *Spain in the Philippines, from Conquest to Revolution.* Quezon City: Ateneo de Manila University, 1971. Print.

Fitzpatrick, Peter, and Eve Darian-Smith. "Laws of the Postcolonial: An Insistent Introduction." *Laws of the Postcolonial.* Ed. Eve Darian-Smith and Peter Fitzpatrick. Ann Arbor: University of Michigan Press, 1999. 1–17. Print.

Díaz, Mónica. *Indigenous Writings from the Convent: Negotiating Ethnic Autonomy in Colonial Mexico.* Tucson: University of Arizona Press, 2010. Print.

Díaz Balsera, Viviana. *The Pyramid under the Cross: Franciscan Discourses of Evangelization and the Nahua Christian Subject in Sixteenth-Century Mexico.* Tucson: University of Arizona Press, 2005. Print.

Dussel, Enrique. "Europe, Modernity, and Eurocentrism." *Nepantla: Views from South* 1.3 (2000): 465–78.

Don, Patricia Lopes. *Bonfires of Culture: Franciscans, Indigenous Leaders, and the Inquisition in Early Mexico, 1524–1540.* Norman: University of Oklahoma Press, 2010. Print.

Green, L. C. "Claims to Territory in Colonial America." *The Laws of Nations and the New World.* Ed. L. C. Green and Olive P. Dickason. Edmonton: University of Alberta Press, 1989. 1–139. Print.

Kirk, Stephanie L. *Convent Life in Colonial Mexico: A Tale of Two Communities.* Gainesville, FL: University Press of Florida, 2007. Print.

Klor de Alva, Jorge. "Spiritual Conflict and Accommodation in New Spain: Toward a Typology of Aztec Responses to Christianity." *The Inca and Aztec States, 1400–1800: Anthropology and History.* Ed. George A. Collier, Renato Rosaldo, and John D. Wirth. New York: Academic Press, 1982. 345–66. Print.

León Pinelo, Antonio, and Bella I. Sánchez. *Recopilación de las Indias*. 3 vols. Mexico City: Porrúa, 1992. Print.
López de Palacios Rubios, Juan. "Requerimiento." 1513. *Ciudad Seva*. 10 Nov. 2010. Web. 3 Jan 2012.
MacCormack, Sabine. *Religion in the Andes: Vision and Imagination in Early Colonial Peru*. Princeton: Princeton University Press, 1991. Print.
Maldonado-Torres, Nelson. "El pensamiento filosófico del 'giro descolonizador.'" *El pensamiento filosófico latinoamericano, del Caribe y "latino" (1300–2000)*. Ed. Enrique Dussel, Eduardo Mendieta, and Carmen Bohórquez. Mexico City: Siglo XXI, 2011. 683–97. Print.
Marrero-Fente, Rául. "Human Rights and Academic Discourse: Teaching the Las Casas-Sepúlveda Debate at the Time of the Iraq War." *Human Rights and Cultural Studies in Latin America*. Eds. Ana Forcinito and Fernando Ordónez. Minneapolis, MN: Hispanic Issues Online, 2009. 247-57. Web.
Marinheiro, Christóvão S. "The Conimbricenses: The Last Scholastics, the First Moderns or Something in Between? The Impact of Geographical Discoveries on Late 16th Century Aristotelianism." *Portuguese Humanism and the Republic of Letters*. Ed. Maria Berbara and Karl A. E. Enenkel. Leiden: Brill, 2011. 395–424. Print.
Mignolo, Walter. *Local Histories/Global Designs: Coloniality, Subaltern Knowledge and Border Thinking*. Princeton: Princeton University Press, 2000. Print.
———. "Preamble: The Historical Foundation of Modernity/Coloniality and the Emergence of Decolonial Thinking." *A Companion to Latin American Literature and Culture*. Ed. Sara Castro-Klarén. Oxford: Blackwell, 2008. 12–32. Print.
Mills, Kenneth. *Idolatry and Its Enemies: Colonial Andean Religion and Extirpation, 1640–1750*. Princeton: Princeton University Press, 1997. Print.
Muldoon, James. *Empire and Order: The Concept of Empire, 800–1800*. New York: Palgrave Macmillan, 1999. Print.
Phelan, John L. *The Hispanization of the Philippines: Spanish Aims and Filipino Responses, 1565–1700*. Madison: University of Wisconsin Press, 1959. Print.
Quijano, Aníbal. "Coloniality of Power and Eurocentrism in Latin America." *International Sociology* 15. 2 (2000): 215–32. Print.
Rabasa, José. *Tell Me the Story of How I Conquered You: Elsewheres and Ethnosuicide in the Colonial Mesoamerican World*. Austin: University of Texas Press, 2011. Print.
———. "Writing Violence." *A Companion to Latin American Literature and Culture*. Ed. Sara Castro-Klarén. Oxford: Blackwell, 2008. 49–67. Print.
Ramos, Demetrio. *La ética en la conquista de América: Francisco De Vitoria y la Escuela de Salamanca*. Madrid: Consejo Superior de Investigaciones Científicas, 1984. Print.
Rivera Pagán, Luis. *A Violent Evangelism: The Political and Religious Conquest of the Americas*. Louisville: Westminster/John Knox Press, 1992. Print.
Ruiz Medrano, Ethelia. *Mexico's Indigenous Communities: The Lands and Histories, 1500–2010*. Boulder: University of Colorado Press, 2010. Print.
Ruiz Medrano, Ethelia, and Susan Kellogg. *Negotiation within Domination: New Spain's*

Indian Pueblos Confront the Spanish State. Boulder: University of Colorado Press, 2010. Print.

Schmitt, Carl. *Nomos of the Earth in the International Law of Jus Publicum Europaeum*. Trans. G.L. Ulmen. New York: Telos Press, 2003. Print.

Schmidt-Riese, Roland, and Lucía Rodríguez, eds. *Catequesis y derecho en la América colonial: Fronteras borrosas*. Madrid: Iberoamericana/Vervuert, 2010. Print.

Schwaller, John Frederick. *History of the Catholic Church in Latin America: From Conquest to Revolution and Beyond*. New York: NYU Press, 2011. Print.

Schwartz, Stuart B. *All Can Be Saved: Religious Tolerance and Salvation in the Iberian Atlantic World*. New Haven: Yale University Press, 2008. Print.

Seed, Patricia. *Ceremonies of Possession in Europe's Conquest of the New World, 1492–1640*. Cambridge: Cambridge University Press, 1995. Print.

Solórzano y Pereira, Juan, and Brun M. A. Ochoa. *Política indiana*. Madrid: Ediciones Atlas, 1972. Print.

Steinberg, Philip E. "Lines of Division, Lines of Connection: Stewardship in the World/Ocean." *Geographical Review* 89. 2 (1999): 254–64. Print.

Subirats, Eduardo. *El continente vacío: la conquista del Nuevo mundo y la conciencia moderna*. Barcelona: Anaya, 1994. Print.

Tavárez, David E. *The Invisible War: Indigenous Devotions, Discipline, and Dissent in Colonial Mexico*. Stanford: Stanford University Press, 2011. Print.

Weber, David. *Bárbaros: Spaniards and Their Savages in the Age of Enlightenment*. New Haven: Yale University Press, 2005. Print.

Weckmann, Luis. *La herencia medieval de México*. Mexico City: Colegio de México, Centro de Estudios Históricos, 1984. Print.

PART I
Politics

1

José de Acosta: Colonial Regimes for a Globalized Christian World

Ivonne del Valle

Hay algunos tan patrocinadores de los indios que afirman seriamente que se les hace injuria grave si se les fuerza [a trabajar y pagar tributos]; y de los españoles dicen que se sirvan a sí mismos, como se hace en España, o si todos quieren ser nobles que no coman ni beban; como dice el Apóstol, el que no trabaje que no coma. Y a quien esto se le haga duro, dicen, que deje la tierra que ocupó por codicia y no por conveniencia de sus habitantes originarios, y se vuelva a la estrechez de su terruño en España. Opinión que, aunque en el dicho aparece liberal y honrada, de hecho es puro disparate y llena de dificultades. —José de Acosta, *De procuranda indorum salute* (1984: 515)

(There are some who are so solicitous of the Indians as to claim in all seriousness that grave injury is done them if they are forced [to work and to pay tribute]; and of the Spaniards, they say that they should serve themselves, as is done in Spain, or that if they wish to be nobles, they should neither eat nor drink; for, as the Apostle says, he who labors not, should not eat. And whosoever objects to the harshness of this, they say he should leave the land he took out of greed, rather than for the benefit of its original inhabitants, and return to his paltry plot of earth back home in Spain. A viewpoint that, for all that it appears generous and honorable, is in fact utter nonsense and plagued with difficulties.)

There is always something arbitrary in the assignation of historical origins, and yet at least from European and Latin American perspectives, the "modern" world unquestionably begins in 1492 with Spanish colonialism.[1] Previous attempts to spread and impose a single *universal* truth, in the form of political and metaphysical premises that would guarantee the sovereignty and power of one nation or ethnic group over others, as in the Greek and Roman Empires, or the discriminatation against certain groups based on religious differences, as in medieval anti-Semitism, come together in the experience of colonial Spanish America. From the political premises that underlie the relations between Spain and its American colonies emerge both the possibility of a *global* order that would assign each nation a place in a descending hierarchy, and the underpinnings of the internal colonialism of the future independent nations of Latin America.[2]

The development of racial categories, nationalist sentiments, bureaucratic governments, and nascent capitalism are elements that come together and are spread internationally in the Spanish colonial experience. We may also add to these converging elements the mobilization of cultural, legal, and religious policies for the formation of new subjects on a massive scale, as occurs in the imperative to create *Indians* as a homogenous group that, regardless of language or ethnicity, would participate, voluntarily or by compulsion, in the colonial, religious project.

De procuranda indorum salute (1588), by the Jesuit José de Acosta, is a paradigmatic text that reflects the totalizing will of Spain's Christian Empire. This work on missions represents what is perhaps the first theory of this new world order based on the expansion of Christianity, "civilization," and a particular economy. Acosta examines the situation in colonial Peru during the sixteenth century, and based on his diagnosis he proposes the complete rationalization of colonial life. Although intended as a practical manual whose primary goal was the evangelization of indigenous Americans, *De procuranda* exceeds this objective in establishing the principles by which the dystopia prevailing in the new territories could be corrected. It is important therefore not only for its overall character (the desire to regulate every aspect of colonial life) but also because Acosta recognizes the illegality of the conquest. Yet he abandons the intellectual rigor that leads him to this conclusion. In a move typical of Jesuit thought, Acosta decides to displace the conquest and to construct a less monstrous universe upon a foundation he has judged to be unacceptable.[3] Felipe Castañeda argues that by deeming the violence of the conquest alien to his generation—as a historical fact—Acosta closes the debates on the justice of the enterprise and thus establishes the basis for a new, colonial regime. As if violence were a "given" condition, Acosta decides to sidestep questions about legitimacy in order to tackle the most immediate problems, and to lay down "los principios incuestionables de un orden colonial" (Castañeda 135–51) (the unquestionable foundations of a colonial order). In the following pages, I will examine the premises of this Christian and global colonial order.

The Impossibility of Other Worlds: Universal Truth as an Irrational Foundation

In the prologue of *De procuranda*, Acosta outlines both the objective of his text and its limitations. If one wished to achieve the "salvation" of the Indians, posits Acosta, the main challenge resided in the difficulty of finding a method that would be universally applicable to the innumerable indigenous groups whose customs were so diverse. Despite the difficulties, Acosta takes on the challenge analytically. Given that a single method for evangelizing such disparate groups was unthinkable, he begins by classifying the "barbarians" (all those who, like the Indians, deviated from "la recta razón y de la práctica habitual de los hombres" [1984: 61] ["right reason" and the common practices of men]) into three overarching categories according to what today we might call their stage of development.[4] Thus, the method of evangelization employed with a particular group would depend on the category to which it belonged.

The first category included the Chinese, Syrians, and Japanese, who, according to Acosta, did not diverge too far from the "recta razón" ("right reason"), as they possessed stable governments, laws, cities, commerce, and letters. Given that Acosta does not specify what constituted the barbarity of these groups that had a high level of social organization and whose societies had achieved a great flowering, and given that conversion to Christianity is the final end of this classificatory system, one can infer that their "barbarity" was entirely attributable to their not being Christian.[5] The second category included "barbarians" who did not possess written script, laws, or science, but did have governments, resided in fixed settlements, and had military leaders and religious authorities. This group, which included the Incas and Mexicas, encompassed all non-nomadic peoples of the Americas. Lastly, the third category consisted of nomadic groups that, according to Acosta, lacked any recognizable form of government or laws and essentially lived as "beasts."

Due to the level of civilization attained by the peoples of the first category, their conversion should be achieved through the use of reason and never by the exercise of force. Members of the second category, for their part, must be subjected to the jurisdiction of a Christian authority that would ensure, through the use of strategic violence if necessary, the propagation of the faith but would allow them to maintain possession of their territories and material goods. With respect to the third category (people Acosta equates with the groups of whom Aristotle claimed that "se les podía cazar como a bestias y domar por la fuerza," (1984: 67) (they could be hunted down like beasts and domesticated by force), it was first necessary to compel them to become "true" men, that is, to abandon the nomadic life of the wild and settle in cities where they could be educated. Only after this coerced transmutation from what Acosta described as "mediohombres" (half-men) into fully realized human subjects could the work of evangelization begin (1984: 61–71).

This framework, though ostensibly simple, has broad political implications. In the expansive philosophy of history proposed by Acosta, Christianity and a developmental doctrine comprise the two components of a unique teleology that would apply to every human community, even those that Europeans had yet to encounter. Ideally, all civilizations would someday share not only Christianity but also the same cultural models and technologies, e.g. written script, urbanism, specific institutions, and a specific form of government.

The centrality of Acosta for what Jennifer Selwyn has termed the Jesuits' "global civilizing mission" (1) shows that his all-encompassing system to evaluate the "barbarians" (culture, religion, government, technology) was immediately understood as an instrument for expansion. *De procuranda* became the theoretical foundation for the whole Jesuit missionary enterprise (El Alaoui 18)—that is, for the Jesuits' integration of the world into the fold of Christianity and Western civilization.[6] *De procuranda* sets the basis for the evangelization of insufficiently Christianized populations in Europe and of pagan peoples all over the world. Even though the missionary endeavor of the Jesuits was not new by the time Acosta wrote (their work among "backward" people in Europe, and among the Moriscos in Spain, had been important precedents), from the time of its publication *De procuranda* provided a flexible and wide-ranging methodology for missionaries everywhere.[7]

Acosta's universalist project establishes decreasing degrees of sovereignty for the non-Christian nations of the world. According to him, only members of the first category had the right to preserve their way of life and possessions; the second group could keep their material goods but would be subject to the sovereignty of Christian princes; and the third group would have no claim to any rights over themselves, their territories, or their property. His empirical knowledge about Amerindians and peoples in other parts of the world is structured by philosophical thought to create a rational, evolving framework that is sufficiently broad to encompass any non-Christian human group. The scientific nature of his method of general classification (Anthony Pagden considers it the origin of comparative ethnography) is founded on a mixture of religion and the study of "policía" (police), the term used at that time to refer to general forms of government. Christianity then called forth not only a universal system for the classification of civilizations, but also for a differentiated exercise of power over populations that *had* to become Christians.

This line of thought leads to the supposition of a future with no *outside* possible, unless we consider the Muslim world (the enemy of Christianity par excellence) or apostasy (another mortal adversary). Acosta's scheme envisioned that all peoples would eventually attain the same state of civilization, either voluntarily through the use of reason or by force. This developmental Christian teleology was totalitarian. Without even mentioning the concept of sovereignty, the degree of self-determination ascribed to a given group within Acosta's system would determine the proper method of evangelization to be employed. In this sense, the sovereignty of any group was directly proportional to its power and organization; that is to say, a group was sovereign insofar as it could demonstrate it militarily. When Acosta speaks of the first category, for example, he maintains that Chinese, Japanese, and Syrians must be reached through the use of reason, not only because of their considerable learning but also because they were "powerful" nations. By contrast, the absolute defenselessness of members of the third category is assumed in Acosta's quotation of Aristotle concerning those groups that could be hunted down like beasts. Perhaps the greatest irony of this proposition is the fact that it is posited as a means of "saving" the Amerindians in terms of religion and civilization. In other words, Acosta prescribes a campaign of violence for which the "barbarians" should be grateful. Acosta's model is disconcertingly closed: to resist this violence offered as assistance would mean that the Indians were ignorant of the "recta razón" ("right reason") or, worse yet, that they voluntarily chose to reject this self-evident truth and, as a consequence, would be doubly subject to violence.

The cornerstone of Acosta's global program is the imperative to Christianize. If Christianity had been simply one possibility among many, then Acosta's hierarchy of civilizations would have served only as a tool for the study of human diversity and not as a project for imperial expansion. Classifying "barbarians" was an exercise that made sense not for its own sake but as a means to understand how they should be dealt with to make them abandon their barbarity and accept the truth of the gospel. Thus, the project posited by Acosta encompassed those who were already Christian, those who were in the process of conversion, and those who had the potential to convert. There were no other possibilities except for the enemies mentioned above. Consequently, it was important to quickly and summarily silence alternative doctrines that had begun to emerge in the colonies.

Francisco de la Cruz, a Dominican friar burned at the stake in Lima in 1578, sentenced by a tribunal that included Acosta, is a case in point. De la Cruz's "heresy" consisted of asserting that the salvation of the Indians did not necessarily depend on their being Christians—believing in Christ or knowing of Him—but rather in simply leading a virtuous life. The thesis of this Dominican heretic, whom Acosta alludes to, without naming him, as the "pseudo-Pablo" (1987: 215), assumed that other worlds were possible: if the Indians could achieve salvation without knowing Christ or without following the precepts of Christian life as outlined by the Church, then Christianity itself was unnecessary either in Peru or anywhere else.[8] Accordingly, the Spanish Empire was also superfluous.

The ideas put forward by de la Cruz and the reality of the Indies brought Acosta face to face with the irrationality of the Christian myth. In the case of America, Christ was not an origin already present in the cultural and linguistic horizon of its inhabitants; in America, he had to be fabricated. This logical impasse confronted the evangelizers with the fact that Christ was an empty signifier for the Andean peoples. And yet Spain's sovereignty over the territory and its inhabitants was founded upon this void. Consequently, in Acosta's text, Christianity is an irrational proposition transformed into law. Furthermore, Christ as a comprehensible and significant message does not figure in *De procuranda*, despite the many chapters that Acosta dedicates to the matter. Only as a command does he appear on the horizon of the New World. "El misterio de Cristo," avers Acosta, "no obligo a comprenderlo nadie, porque es de pocos; pero digo que deben creerlo todos" (1987: 219) (I don't require anyone to understand the mystery of Christ, as that is only for a few; but I say that everyone must believe in it). Once this premise is established, without which it was possible to imagine (just as both de la Cruz and Bartolomé de Las Casas, each in his own way, had done) a world in which the inhabitants of America could continue to live in their territories without the need (and much less the obligation) to know Christ or to follow the preaching of his "emissaries," Acosta outlines his reforms for the domestication of a grotesque colonial reality.[9]

The Heart of Darkness: The Origin of Sovereign Power

According to Acosta, evangelization in the Americas had yielded such meager fruits not only because of the obstacles inherent in the enterprise (the persistence of Andean religious beliefs, for example) but also due to the methods employed up to that point (1984, Book 1: XI). The violence perpetrated by soldiers and the abuses committed by missionaries and bureaucrats were impediments to the establishment of a government that could promote a true conversion. Thus, an important objective of his text is to proclaim the imperious need to discipline the corps of officials charged with the colony's political, religious, and military administration. The danger for the Spaniards of falling into a moral abyss was linked to the perversion of the will to power in the absence of oversight.

Furthermore, this descent seemed assured by the small numbers and fragmentation of the colonizers, who were an isolated minority in the new territories. In contrast to the experience of the Apostles, writes Acosta:

> entre nuestros ministros del Evangelio, [es] sorprendente la soledad. De ella va brotando, en primer lugar, poco a poco la desgana; después la permisividad, al no haber testigos de su pecado ni temor alguno de reconvención; finalmente tras la caída la enmienda se retarda y se hace difícil, al carecer de médico. De ahí el hábito de pecado, a continuación el olvido de toda obra buena, finalmente la pérdida de esperanza en una enmienda de vida. (1987: 105)

> (among our ministers of the Gospel, the solitude [is] surprising. From it springs first, little by little, tedium; then permissiveness, there being no witnesses to their sin nor any fear whatever of being called to account; finally, after this debasement, reform is delayed and becomes difficult, there being none to doctor to the spirit. Thence the habit of sin, then the abandonment of all good works, and in the end the loss of hope for a rectification of one's life.)

The absence of *fellow* witnesses to the actions of the subject immersed in the colonial experience (considering that the Indians whom the priests lived among did not count) could result in the relaxation of all discipline and morality.

In addition, Acosta claims that the very nature of the Indians contributed to the colonizer's steady slippage into the darkest corner of his soul. Coexistence with the barbarians, contends Acosta, presented the colonizer with little incentive for virtuous conduct and many enticements for just the opposite:

> El abismo de toda clase de impudicia es inmenso, nulo el temor de los hombres, sorprendente la desvergüenza y procacidad de las mujeres, desconocida en absoluto toda idea de pudor, la ocasión de lujuria frecuentísima, no hay que ir a buscarla, es más bien ella la que va en busca de la lujuria. (1987: 107)

> (The abyss of all manner of depravity is immense, the dread felt by men negligible, the indecency and lewdness of women shocking, any idea of shame utterly unknown, the occasions for lasciviousness frequent; there is no need to go in search of it, rather it is opportunity itself that ventures out in search of lewdness).

Thus, the absence of a true Spanish *polis* led to the weakening of morality in subjects who possessed little aptitude for such an important enterprise to begin with, to which Acosta adds the Indians' lack of morality as another peril. The Spaniards who found themselves in this unregulated space, and in the face of the constant temptations of the indigenous world, were in danger of descending to the very limits of human baseness. And if this was the case for priests, it is easy to imagine what Acosta thought of the secular members of the colonial enterprise. The latter, for example, were more inclined to greed and to the exploitation of the Indians, which was a crucial problem for Acosta:

> Existe también otra fuerte tentación, a la que no se puede hacer resistencia sin una gran fortaleza del alma: la de ejercer el despotismo sobre los indios; la natural y acostumbrada sujeción de éstos y su nula valentía para la resistencia, engalla fácilmente al que los manda, hasta el punto de no vacilar en llevar a la práctica cuanto le viene en gana. . . . De ahí también el dejar flojísimas las riendas de la codicia para ejercer cuanto se quiera el lucro sin contradicción de nadie, con los servicios de los indios a su disposición para cualquier cosa. (1987: 109, 111)

> (There is also another powerful temptation, one that cannot be resisted without great fortitude of the soul: that of exercising despotism over the Indians, whose natural and habitual subjugation, and whose lack of the valor to resist, easily puff up the pride of him who rules over them, to the point where he does not flinch to carry out absolutely anything that may strike his fancy. . . . From this comes, too, an utter loosening of the reins of greed, a pursuit of lucre to the heart's content and with contradiction from no quarter, having the Indians at their command for whatever thing they might wish.)

In the Indies *any* Spaniard could become a sovereign, insofar as he could wield absolute power over Amerindians, dictate their life or death "para cualquier cosa" (for whatever thing they might wish). In the colonies, power was not centralized and embodied in recognizable institutions to which one could appeal. On the contrary, according to Acosta, in every relationship between Indians and Spaniards, this fragmented power was total and was always weighed toward one side of the scale. Any Spaniard had power over the life of any Indian that he came across. There were no controls to curb this power, and any colonizer (secular or religious) could easily fall into the abyss of greed and violence, demanding from the Indians "cualquier cosa" (whatever thing they might wish) that came to mind.

An interesting issue concerning the formation of subjects in the colonies arises from the foregoing passages. In this new environment, the European struggled with his own demons, with the most degraded side of himself. The "heart of darkness," or "the night of the world," was not experienced by every human being—or at least this is what is suggested by Acosta, who documents the degeneration of Spanish colonizers at the moment of affirming their power over subjects who, at least according to the Jesuit, did not resist this authority.[10] In the colonial world, the European subject could be reduced to an infra-human state that required multiple disciplinary procedures to return him to the place in the *polis* that he had abandoned. In name of a "proper" colonial administration, the reincorporation of "normality" required restricting the power exercised by every Spanish colonizer in his encounters with Indians, through the transference of this power to institutions and rules laid out by Acosta.

Acosta's disapproval of the majority of the participants in the colonial enterprise reminds us of Las Casas's attitude in the *Brevísima relación de la destrucción de las Indias*. Given that the problem originated not from any one *conquistador* or *encomendero* but rather from the system itself, Las Casas felt it unnecessary to publish the names of those who had orchestrated massacres or destroyed entire populations. Violence was ubiquitous. However, while Las Casas argued that accidents had taken the place of substance (the system *was* its application), Acosta maintained that the problem was not the system itself but the way in which men had carried it out. For Acosta, the system could remain in place so long as its "accidents" were corrected (1984: 493).

Nevertheless, faced with the impossibility of reforming every Spaniard who traveled to the Indies, Acosta lowers his expectations. If it was not possible to form militias of virtuous men to replace those who were "perdidos y facinerosos, aficionados a cometer infamias y crímenes" (1984: 421) (lost and delinquent, friends of committing infamies and crimes) an attempt should at least be made to exclude "los peores y más infames" (the worst and most despicable)—although Acosta recognized that for many even this modest petition was so improbable as to be more worthy of derision than of serious consideration (1984: 421).

Time after time, Acosta's desire to correct the history of the Indies inevitably encounters the improbability of the project's success: perhaps it was impossible to change the vicious cycle of a fallen history. An enormous distance separated the theory of evangelization and good government from its practice in the Americas. Curiously, in a very distinct way, this paradoxical distance foreshadows the rupture between words and things that, according to Michel Foucault, led to the emergence of literature in the seventeenth century. Cervantes's Don Quijote discovered that the words of chivalric novels were empty because their referents did not exist in the real world, but this incongruity would lead to the freedom of a language that had the potential to create new universes instead of simply repeating what existed (53–56). In the transatlantic experience of half a century earlier, however, the disconnect between text and reality culminated in a dystopia that appeared impossible to correct.

Acosta claims that the obstacles to conversion came first and foremost from Spaniards, whose deeds contradicted what was being preached to the Indians. Christianity and all laws, says Acosta, were absolutely negated by the deeds and facts. This led to the absurd situation in which one group toppled with its actions what the other group attempted to build with its words, rendering all efforts at true conversion useless: the "barbarians" would never come to know Christ and his religion but through the models of Christian conduct they observed, yet the example set by the Spaniards constituted the total negation of the evangelical message, a fact that is central to his arguments (1984: 371). According to Acosta:

> Difícilmente se han cometido jamás tantos y tan enormes crímenes por ningún pueblo bárbaro y fiero o escita como por esos defensores del derecho natural y por los propagadores de la fe cristiana, que dominados por la opinión y el aplauso del pueblo y por su ambición desenfrenada desprecian a cada paso las leyes de Dios y las Ordenanzas de los Reyes Católicos. (1984: 281)

> (It is difficult to believe that so many and such monstrous crimes have ever been committed by savage barbarians or by Scythians as those committed by those defenders of natural law, those evangelizers of the Christian faith, who, ruled by the esteem and applause of the people and by their own unchecked ambition, scorn at every turn God's laws and the Decrees of the Catholic Monarchs.)

To correct this, Acosta proposes a system of "buen gobierno" (good government), one of the basic principles of which is the reform of the intolerable practices of those who exercised control. Even though he recognizes that this would be impossible, he still insists that it is necessary to keep going (1984: 419).

Indigenous Languages and Time: Habits or Consensus

Although Acosta eschews the political segregation of "un mismo pueblo y comunidad" (a single people and community), in many ways *De procuranda* establishes the foundations for distinct forms of governance for dealing with these different communities (1984: 485), that is to say, a people and community composed of Indians and Spaniards. In some cases Acosta defines two distinct bureaucratic apparatuses (for example, there are no *encomenderos* for the Spanish); in other cases, a single institution functions differently with each group. In one form or another, the distinctions regarding how to deal with each sector of the population cover practically all aspects of existence (religion, labor regimes, legal recourse, etc.), which brings us to the centrality of bureaucracy in giving differentiated forms to life in the Spanish colonial project.

The political objective of Acosta's program was to create, on the one hand, subjects and docile workers who over time would also become Christian and civilized (Indians), and on the other, citizens who were competent to run the colonial government, or at least not undermine it with their reprehensible conduct (Spaniards). In the case of the Indians, this political program becomes a transformative project to be carried out primarily by the Church and by economic institutions such as the *encomienda* and the distribution of tributes.[11]

The historical Indian represented an enormous challenge to the goal of creating civilized, Christian subjects. Acosta is always ambiguous about the nature of the Indians, and this ambiguity defines the colonial project itself.[12] Although Acosta frequently portrays them as infantile subjects who require an approach similar to that of a schoolmaster with his pupil, or that of a father toward his children, on other occasions the Indians seem to merit the most severe treatment. Thus, the portrayal of the Indians oscillates between one of puerile but reformable subordinates and, contrastingly, one of enemies who must be combated.

To the Indian as an epistemological problem, Acosta adds the Indian as a moral problem, inasmuch as, even though they were capable of fully embracing the gospel, they were unwilling to do so. "Son de voluntad muy refractaria a las cosas de la religión cristiana" (They have a very resistant will to anything related to Christian religion), he indicates, and for this reason their memory of any Christian teaching was fleeting (1987: 23). They were, on the contrary, completely consumed by their "idolatrous" practices. Recounting John of Damascus's catalogue of idolatries in the Ancient World, Acosta observes that the indigenous peoples of the Andes, like all barbarians, adhered to all of the practices that were to be condemned in the Greeks, Egyptians, and Chaldeans (1987: 255). Among the Indians, Acosta complains, there is no love "so mad" or "imprudent" as that of idolatry (1987: 247–49). This panorama presented the missionaries with a monumental task:

> Para dar a entender cómo están los ánimos de estos desgraciados, no se me ocurren palabras bastantes. Más que imbuidos, están trastornados totalmente por sentimientos idolátricos. Ni en paz ni en guerra, ni en el descanso ni en el trabajo, ni en la vida pública ni en la privada, nada son capaces de hacer sin que vaya por delante el culto supersticioso a sus ídolos. . . . Es cosa que asombra, pero que apenas puedo explicar de palabra. (1987: 249)

> (I cannot think of the words to convey the state of the spirits of these wretched people. More than imbued, they are completely stupefied by idolatrous sentiments. Neither in peace nor in war, neither in rest nor in work, neither in public nor private life are they capable of doing anything in which superstitious cults to their idols are not in the forefront. . . . It is something truly astounding, but I can hardly find the words to explain it.)

This statement casts doubt on Acosta's optimism regarding the possibility of establishing Christianity among the Indians, since he frames this endeavor as a struggle against life itself and each one of its features. The magnitude of the problem seems to overwhelm Acosta. Nevertheless, just as in the prologue he had addressed the difficulty of supplying a single method of evangelization, here Acosta also takes on this challenge by proposing a program for the suppression, substitution, and creation of *habits* among the Amerindians.

Acosta suggests various parallel methods: for example, education to demonstrate the error of the Indians' practices, along with the territorialization of their senses, of their temporal orientation and daily schedule, and of their annual celebrations, with Christian rites and customs that would leave no space or time for idolatrous practices (1987: 271, 277). Although Acosta recognizes that the creation of new subjects out of people who seemed impermeable to the teachings of Christianity would be a long-term undertaking, his optimism derives from historical precedents. Time, maintains Acosta, would end up converting the irrational into the rational. Even a mistake could end up becoming law, as had happened in the ancient world in an example cited by John of

Damascus: what had begun as paying homage to a dead person had become a civic and familiar memory that over time evolved into a profane cult (1987: 257). Time could erase the origin of a certain practice and turn it into something altogether different; it could even transform situations that were originally scandalous into anodyne and conventional truths simply through their reiteration.

This is what Acosta had in mind with respect to the sacraments: for instance, the Indians would be made to participate in what could at first be a "lie" (that is, a practice that they neither understood nor embraced) that would become "true" with the passing of time (1987, Book VI). Acosta's recognition of the artificial and fictitious foundation of culture, religion, and subjectivity does not weaken his ideological system; on the contrary, it represents the very possibility of this system's expansion. It was possible to spread Christianity among the Andean Indians precisely because it was a fabrication.

The Church would be at the center of this massive transformation, establishing and overseeing new activities that would fill the time of the Andean Indians in a manner distinct from the ways of "idolatry." In addition, and echoing the civilizing hierarchy put forth in the prologue, this project would not only create Christian Indians, or replace idolatry with Christianity, but also instill social discipline. These two goals were not just related; in a sense they were one and the same. To be a Christian meant a particular way of "loving oneself" and one's peers, which translated into a series of norms that went beyond the acceptance of a faith and were related to the most intimate aspects of life. The missionary was to take on issues such as suicide, "deviant" sexual practices, and the abandonment of reason through drunkenness. Christian dogma was thus linked to a particular regime of social hygiene, a social discipline.

Nevertheless, for Acosta, the problem of Indian languages and their relation to a non-Christian universe took precedence over time as a magical force that would someday transform the irrational into rationality. Recognizing the importance of indigenous languages in the process of conversion, Acosta argues that missionaries had an obligation to preach and hear confessions in these languages, whose comprehension was necessary in order to cross the epistemological barrier separating one universe from another. It was imperative that the Indians understand and accede to Christian interpellation in their own language:

> Quien, pues, esté inflamado por el celo de la salvación de las almas de los indios, convénzase en serio que nada grande puede esperar, si aprender el idioma no es primera e incansable preocupación. Porque si el que ocupa el puesto de simpatizante

no puede responder *amén* a tu acción de gracias, que no entiende, pues aunque tu acción de gracias esté muy bien, pero al otro no le ayuda, ¿cómo un pueblo de idioma desconocido y lenguaje misterioso a ti, aunque le prediques maravillas y le hables de Cristo divinamente, en su corazón te va a responder *amén*, esto es, cómo te va a presentar su interior asentimiento? (1987: 49)

(Whosoever, then, is inflamed by the zeal for salvation of the souls of the Indians, must be persuaded with the utmost seriousness that nothing great can be achieved unless learning the language is the paramount and tireless undertaking. For if he to whom you preach cannot respond *amen* to your thanksgiving because he does not comprehend it (though your thanksgiving be very well, yet it does not help the other), then how can a people of language unknown, of a tongue mysterious to you, though you preach marvels and speak divinely to them of Christ, respond *amen* to you in their innermost heart—that is, how can they provide their interior assent?)

These arguments suggest the necessity of a Christian empire that would evolve and be intelligible in the language of the Indians. In this sense, the "amen" referred to by Acosta is not the same as the affirmative in Spanish; rather, it implies an assent that would be meaningful in the universe contained in and named by the indigenous language in question. Acosta's logic is impeccable: the total acquiescence of the indigenous peoples was only possible in their own languages and in accordance with their own understanding of the universe. Thus, it was essential for Christian priests to learn indigenous languages in order to extract this most intimate of affirmations from the Indians.

And yet Acosta also insisted on the ubiquity of superstition among the Amerindian:

Por lo que se refiere a las supersticiones de los egipcios están tan extendidas entre nuestros bárbaros que no se puede llegar a contar las clases de sacrificios y de guacas: da igual que sean montes, cuestas, rocas prominentes, manantiales que brotan suavemente, ríos que corren con rapidez, picos altos de rocas, montones ingentes de arena, torbellino oscuro de un abismo, talla gigantesca de un árbol milenario, vena indicadora de un yacimiento de metal, forma menos usual o un poco elegante de cualquier piedrecita. (1987: 257)

(As regards the superstitions of the Egyptians, they are so widespread among our barbarians that there is no counting the types of sacrifices and guacas among them: it is all the same to them if it be a hillside, a slope, a prominent rock, a soft-flowing spring, a fast-flowing river, high rocky peaks, a great heap of sand, the dark whirlpool of an abyss, the gigantic trunk of a thousand-year-old tree, the vein indicating a deposit of ore, or the somewhat unusual or attractive form of any ordinary pebble).

Both spaces—the linguistic space related to a particular cognitive and affective universe, and the space of a natural world overpopulated by sacred objects—are related in a way that escapes Acosta, and their convergence represents an insurmountable obstacle for any missionary, regardless of the time he may have at his disposal. Despite the agency Acosta concedes to the passage of time, despite its ability to convert any falsehood into truth, the indigenous languages are paradoxically both a prerequisite for achieving an affirmative response to Christian interpellation and also the medium that would continue to produce associations contrary to those contained in evangelical preaching. Unless made to disappear along with its speakers, any language is uncontainable, and because of this, its poetic and ludic capacity ensures the continuity of old and new relations between the worldly objects it names and makes intelligible. Thus, indigenous languages made possible the existence of a world outside of the Christian imperative. Given that Acosta doubted the evangelizing corps's ability to totally conquer indigenous languages, he appears to settle on a partial evangelization reduced to the most basic tenets, such as the obligation to recognize a name (that of Christ) and make room for the sacraments, which may not be either understood or truly accepted.

Cynical Reason as the Shock Absorber of History

Enrique Dussel argues that the factor determining the emergence of the modern subject is not Descartes's *cogito* but rather the Spanish *conquisto*. For Dussel, the conquest historically and ontologically precedes the subject of thought, since for this subject to identify himself as *res cogitans*, there must have existed a world understood as difference. That world needed to be displayed for the thinking subject to apprehend it.[13] In this light, Acosta and not Descartes should be considered the first thinker to postulate the world as a differentiated extension to be reflected upon and planned, and the violence of conquest as the prerequisite for a universal philosophy of history. As Acosta asserts:

> Dos cosas que parecían entre sí tan dispares, como son la difusión del Evangelio de la paz y la extensión de la espada en la guerra, no sé por qué nuestra época ha hallado no sólo la manera de juntarlas, sino aun de hacerlas depender necesaria y legalmente una de otra. (1984: 247)

(Two things that would seem irreconcilable one to the other, namely the diffusion of the Gospel of peace, and the extension of the sword of warfare, it is beyond me how it is that our age has found not only the manner of conjoining them, but even more, of making one depend necessarily and juridically on the other.)

Therefore, the thinking that proposed an epistemology and a philosophy that would make it possible to integrate the world and all "barbarians" into universal reason, and would create institutions and disciplines in order to achieve it, depended on the violence that provided spaces and bodies for expansion. Notwithstanding the fact that *De procuranda* is an a posteriori reflection, this violence must be duly understood through its justification as a providential and civilizing mission. As the previously cited passage demonstrates, means and ends might be not only disconnected but even diametrically opposed, yet they maintain a relation of mutual dependence. There is a necessary alliance between violence and Christianity. In that sense, *De procuranda* is the text that poses the difference as well as the contiguity between violence and thought. About this, Acosta says:

Así que conciliar cosas tan contrarias—como libertad y violencia—y hacer que la propia inteligencia halle caminos para unirlas y que la caridad diligente y activa las torne coherentes, es una empresa que supera con mucho mis fuerzas e ingenio. (1984: 247–49)

(Thus, to reconcile things so contrary—such as liberty and violence—and to drive one's reason to find the path by which to unite them, and that diligent and active charity render them coherent, is an enterprise that far exceeds my powers and my ingenuity.)

However, his text vacillates between reforming the dystopia or simply making it "coherent." If indeed one of Acosta's objectives is to rein in the unmitigated and pervasive violence, the previous passage would actually seem to point to the need to create a body of thought (the "path" which intelligence should find) that would give violence a justified, logical function. Just as with anything related to the "buen gobierno" (good government) of the Indies, to accept that war and the gospel were irreconcilable was also to recognize the corrupt origin of history.

Nevertheless, this corrupted origin had at its disposal a program that would transform it into a coherent whole. While Acosta's program may have begun as an attempt to breach the gap between text and reality by providing the rules whereby conquerors and colonizers could carry out their duties within the dictates of Christianity and the laws of the Indies, the Jesuit ended up choosing to remain halfway to his goal. Thought was thus circumscribed by the impositions of a grotesque reality. After the conquest had yielded territory for expansion, the new violence of economic reason guaranteed the prospects for Christianity and civilization. In a characteristic about-face, and without seeing how to do without the labor levies that were a "cementerio de indios" (a graveyard for Indians), Acosta opts to think of them productively (1984: 527). His distress at the grim work conditions in the mines is dispelled by the following certainty:

> si se abandona la explotación de minas de metales y, como se dice en el libro del Santo Job, si no se arranca la plata de las venas de la tierra, descuajando de raíz las montañas; si no se saca oro de las escolleras de los ríos y se deja al margen los demás metales, entonces se acabó: toda promoción y organización pública de los indios cae por los suelos. (1984: 531)

> (if the exploitation of the mining of metal is abandoned, and if, as is said in the Book of the Blessed Job, the silver is not yanked from the veins of the earth, pulling up the mountains by their very roots; if gold is not extracted from the breakwaters of rivers, the remaining metals left to the side, then all will be lost: any progress and public organization of the Indians will crumble to the ground.)

Given that the exploitation of indigenous territories and the exploitation of the Indians themselves were indispensable to the project of evangelization, they would have to be accepted and made instrumental by "humanizing" them through less devastating working conditions.

Consequently, Acosta's teleology of history has three complexly intertwined axes: Christianity, a particular idea of what civilization should be, and economic development. Regarding the first two, which are ostensibly the objectives Acosta has in mind, it appears that Christianity slips toward a form of social hygiene and a civic order that is both less and more than religion. His ideas on self-love and his theories about the technologies and characteristics associated with a certain degree of civilization are related to the necessity of creating a social order within which Christianity could be inculcated. Nonetheless, none of these cultural or religious potentialities were possible without the continued expansion of economic interests.

Acosta's explanation of the problems that led the Pope to cede the propagation of the faith to the Catholic monarchs (1984, Book III: II) is turned upside down when he accepts that the execution of the conquest had passed from the King of Spain into the hands of private merchants whose investments had to be compensated with privileges related to the exploitation of the Indians and the new territories (1984, Book III: IX). This political realism of Acosta, who is resigned to accepting the restrictions imposed by the way things are yet at the same time disposed to intervene optimistically, can be interpreted as a resolve to take part in and modify an unacceptable situation.

In this sense, it could be said that there is no "amen" in *De procuranda* other than the one giving assent to the colonial system it attempts to create. The most intimate affirmation of the evangelizing enterprise, whatever the cost, is Acosta's, above all because it is pronounced with greater force insofar as it is the product of the clarity of a vision that critically evaluates the situation: one must press on, identifying errors, but at the same time brushing them aside. Acosta asserts that the polemics concerning the right to sovereignty and dominion over the Indies:

> conduce sin duda, a que se abandone el dominio de las Indias, o a que se debilite al menos su prestigio. Por poco que se ceda una vez en este asunto, difícilmente podrá contarse la destrucción futura y la ruina universal que se seguirá. Y no es que yo me ponga ahora a defender las guerras y títulos de guerras pasadas y los resultados de ellas, ni a justificar las destrucciones, represalias, matanzas y demás disturbios de anteriores años en el Perú. Pero sí advierto, por razones de conciencia e interés, que no conviene seguir disputando más en este asunto, sino que, como de cosa que ya ha prescrito, el siervo de Cristo debe proceder con la mejor buena fe. (1984: 333)

> (will doubtless lead to the abandonment of our rule over the Indies, or at the very least, that its prestige shall be tarnished. For if we so much as begin to relent in this matter, it will be difficult to imagine the future destruction and universal ruin to follow. And it is not that I now defend the wars, nor the titles of past wars, nor their results, nor do I justify the destruction, reprisals, massacres, and other upheavals of past years in Peru. Yet I do caution, for reasons of both conscience and interest, that no good purpose is served by continuing to dispute over this matter, but rather, as if in the face of a title prescribed in effect by the passage of time to as if in the face of a debate already prescribed, the servant of Christ must proceed in the best of good faith.)

There was no point in insisting, as Las Casas had, on the illegality of the enterprise; rather, one must simply begin from the fact that it is there, in a situation that, despite its irrational foundation, must be continued in the name of a more transcendent purpose, which made it necessary to overlook the horrors produced by the universalization of a single truth.[14]

In an example meant to distance the Christian empire from that of the ancient Greeks, Acosta states that because there was no justification for Alexander the Great to carry his flags throughout the world, it was evident that when Aristotle asserted that war was justified against barbarian nations that refused to accept slavery, he must have written more to adulate his emperor than "as a philosopher" (1984: 285). Yet the limits Acosta sees in Greek philosophy constrained by reasons of state have their parallel in his own inability to think beyond the reality on the ground. While slavery was not justified in the name of a pagan empire, it was justified, according to Acosta, in name of the economic reason that sustained the possibility of the Christian universe.

One must highlight this reading of Acosta in which the violence of the conquest is transformed into a complex administrative and technological program for the formation of new subjectivities, new labor regimes, and new religious practices. Acosta's "third way," midway between brutal exploitation and the radical justice demanded by Las Casas, did not represent an alternative to naked violence; on the contrary, it is the work of an organic intellectual of the empire who reinscribes violence into rationalized and functional norms such as the obligation to stop questioning the sovereign's dictates. Violence is therefore normalized. As Acosta points out:

> a pesar de que la acumulación de grandes riquezas y los derechos, sobre todo, de los imperios la mayoría de las veces se han introducido con injusticia, sin embargo vemos que la Sagrada Escritura respeta a los príncipes su poder, y manda a los súbditos que les presenten obediencia. Así, *haya sido usurpado injustamente el dominio de las Indias, o—lo que más bien hay que creer y proclamar* por lo que toca al menos a la administración de los Reyes—con derecho y debidamente, de ninguna manera es conveniente hacer que abandonen los príncipes cristianos la gobernación de las Indias, que por lo demás es utilísima para su salvación eterna. (my emphasis, 1984: 335–37)[15]

> (despite the accumulation of great wealth and of the prerogatives, above all, of empires, most of which have imposed themselves unjustly, nevertheless we observe that the Holy Scriptures defer to the power of princes and command their subjects to show them obedience. Thus, *whether dominion over the Indies was unjustly usurped or rather—that which must be believed and proclaimed*, at least as regards the Crown's rule—justly and duly, it is in no way proper to bring about a renunciation by the Christian princes of their rule over the Indies, which in any case is exceedingly useful for bringing about its eternal salvation.)

With this claim, Acosta neutralizes the force of all criticism. The word of Saint Paul and the other Church fathers, indeed all philosophical inquiry, is cast aside in the name of a perspective that dictated ("hay que creer y proclamar") (one must believe and proclaim) a way of thinking and acting that refused to see the original violence, hoping it would be forgotten or transformed into something else with the passing of time.

The Jesuit program in general, and particularly that of Acosta, have been associated with this "third way" that aimed to soften a process that would have otherwise devolved into the pure violence of unfettered capitalism. Undoubtedly, Acosta proposes that the Jesuits and the clergy of all other orders serve as mediators between the Indians and the abuses of the other Spaniards. Nor can it be denied that Acosta sought to reform the brutality of the extraction of the Indians' labor. Yet, the realism with which he accepts the state of affairs in the colonies turns his project into a kind of shock absorber for a deformed history that would continue to be, though attenuated, brutal and iniquitous.

On the other hand, it is also true that Las Casas's radical proposal to restitute the property usurped from the Amerindians and withdraw from the continent never yielded any real change. This is why, as Rolena Adorno has indirectly demonstrated, Las Casas's project continues to resonate in its constant repetition and in varied forms in Latin American historical and literary works. It is in this sense that a complex dilemma emerges from the panorama inaugurated by the relations between Europe and America. On the one hand, the only real justice possible appears to be the assortment of "disparates e imposibles" (nonsense and impossible tasks), which Acosta alludes to in the epigraph, while on the other hand the only realistic option appears to be the persistence of violence made functional and coherent. With regard to Las Casas's proposal, Acosta counters:

> aun concediendo que se hubiese errado gravemente en la usurpación del dominio de las Indias, sin embargo ni se puede ya restituir—pues no hay a quién hacer la restitución ni modo de efectuarla—y sobre todo porque aunque se pudiese, de ninguna manera lo sufriría ni la evidente injuria que se haría a la fe cristiana una vez aceptada ni el peligro a que se expondría la fe. (1984: 333)

> (even granting that grave errors had been committed in the usurpation of the dominion of the Indies, nevertheless, restitution is no longer possible—as there are no persons left to whom such restitution could be made, nor do there exist any means by which to carry it out—and above all because, even if it could be accomplished, neither the evident harm that its realization would do to the Christian faith, nor the dangers to which the faith would be exposed, could be permitted.)

For Acosta restitution was impossible, and the ideas about the Spaniards' returning to their own land unless they were willing to work without depending on the Indians were pure nonsense. Seen from another perspective, however, these "disparates" (nonsense) were in reality nothing other than the very possibility of justice.

Acosta could accept the impossibility of a real reform of the brutality of the conquerors and colonizers, and he could accept that the evangelization and civilization of the Indians would never be fully carried out. What Acosta refuses to accept in the name of a transcendent goal is the possibility of the loss of sovereignty over the Indies. For his part, Las Casas, invoking each people's right to self-determination, advocated for a withdrawal from the Indies, a proposition that obviously lacked resonance in his day, which is precisely why it is still visible on today's horizon. This is the colonial legacy for both the internal politics of Latin American nations and for the diverse nations of the world organized according to a hierarchy of civilization and participation in global capitalism: the dilemma of demanding necessary yet impossible justice or being resigned to a cynical and corrupt, but realist, version of history.

Notes

1. This is still a Western, and Christian, perspective. History certainly follows other rhythms if seen, for instance, from the world of Islam or the experience of other Asian countries. Adopting alternative points of view that do not take for granted Christian historicity would be a way of denaturalizing this uniquely Western perspective.
2. Carl Schmitt argues that Spanish colonialism was crucial in the creation of an interstate system in which Europe set itself as the center that dominated and exploited the rest of the world.
3. In response to the political and religious crisis of his times, Ignacio de Loyola, the founder of the Jesuits, opts to intervene at the level of the subject and not at the level of the system. Instead of breaking with a problematic institution (the Church), Loyola attempted to create subjects that would personify a new institutional form. In this sense, the Jesuits would continue to be part of the institution while maintaining with it a relationship of difference. René Descartes, another important reader of Loyola, lays out a similar long-term reformist project (the old institution would change once there were enough "new" subjects in its ranks). In *Discourse on Method*, Descartes begins by transforming himself and inviting others to change with him, an attitude that entails a serious questioning of the institutions of knowledge without a radical rupture (sections II and III).
4. In his introduction to *De procuranda*, Luciano Pereña employs an ahistoric, but not

inaccurate, vocabulary to describe how Acosta discovers "the roots and causes" of the Indians' "underdevelopment." According to Pereña, Acosta is optimistic in proposing a "cultural indoctrination" that would enable the Indians to "progress" (7). Regardless of what one thinks about Pereña's position, his vocabulary (typical of the discourse on the supposed "Indian problem" in Latin American nations during the twentieth century) is correct in considering that a civilizing teleology lies at the core of Acosta's program. In this sense, Acosta foreshadows Enlightenment thought. One could claim that the classifying system proposed by Acosta, minus his Christian faith, is the foundation of Enlightenment ideas on progress.

5. "Recta razón" ("right reason") is a tautology insofar as it is derived from the practices of the group that Acosta has in mind as his model (Christian Europe). That is, civilized Christian groups acted according to "la recta razón" ("right reason") because they were Christian and civilized, and they were Christian and civilized because they acted according to "la recta razón" ("right reason").
6. Selwyn says that early in the sixteenth century Francis Xavier had become a model representing a heroic stance for other missionaries to emulate. Later Acosta provided the model for the institutionalization of a global missionary agenda (17, 117–18).
7. As Youssef El Alaoui reminds us, Alonso de Sandoval's *De instauranda Aethiopum salute*, written for the evangelization of slaves in Africa, is a ramification of Acosta's text (20), which was also central in the evangelizing and "civilizing" efforts among southern Italy's unruly populations and is behind the main texts produced in the early seventeenth century to Christianize Moriscos in Spain (Selwyn 137; El Alaoui 16). In this last case, it is very telling that Ignacio de las Casas, himself a Morisco and author of the manuals to Christianize the Moriscos, would go back to Acosta as the basis for his work since he exhibits a detailed knowledge of the populations he worked with that is lacking in Acosta's appraisals of the Indians. Nevertheless, it was the theoretical character of *De procuranda* that allowed it to become a central piece in the Jesuits' global designs.
8. The ideas of Francisco de la Cruz are much more complex, and problematic, but what concerns me here is how the Dominican compelled Acosta to recognize the fictitious nature of Christian belief.
9. Las Casas's texts affirm the possibility of other worlds, or, in other words, the idea that Christianity did not represent, nor did it have to be, the *only* possible universe. According to Las Casas, Christianity was a doctrine that should guide Christians, and, in the name of this doctrine, Christians should respect the right of others not to be Christians if they so wished ("Treinta proposiciones").
10. For Acosta, the most inhumane and horrific aspects of the subject emerge in the colonies, where all desires are given free reign without the limits imposed by a moral life in society. For Hegel, by contrast, a similar experience explained the formation of all subjects. "The night of the world" is Hegel's term for the terrifying experience of the undifferentiated as direct access to the real. According to Hegel, neither society nor knowledge could emerge from this darkness. Due to the terror of this experience,

the subject withdraws from himself and from the "natural" world and takes refuge in the symbolic and social order. In this sense, for Hegel all subjectivity arose from the violent suppression of this chaos inherent in every human being (Žižek, "The Cartesian Subject"). Ironically, the experience described by Acosta also called for a suppression, not in order to bring forth subjectivity but rather to improve colonial dominion. The colonial experience perhaps points to one of the blind spots in Hegel's ideas on history.

11. I will set aside the labor question to focus on the religious aspects of Acosta's program.
12. Brian Whitener demonstrates how Acosta is able to inscribe a certain ambiguity in the concept of "indio" that would permit colonial authorities to determine on a case-by-case basis whether to apply procedures related to sovereign authority (pure violence) or else mechanisms of authority more akin to biopower (institutions). According to Whitener, this ambiguity allows Acosta to propose an institutional regime without renouncing the possibility of violence when dealing with the Indians.
13. Quoted in Moreiras 349–50.
14. This lack of interest in the real subject that would be forced to perform exhausting and inhuman labor is indicative of what Slavoj Žižek has termed "the perverse core of Christianity"—that is, the putting into practice of the logic of Christian love, whose objective is the transcendent mystery hidden in the immanent: "I love you but, inexplicably, I love something in you more than yourself, and, therefore, I destroy you" (*The Puppet* 145).
15. In this sense we can think of Acosta as a product of a triumphant process of subjectivization (i.e., becoming a Jesuit). Acosta addresses the uncertainty before the question of what God wants, the great puzzle to be resolved in the *Ejercicios espirituales*, by emphasizing Loyola's identification between divine and royal design by which God's will is subsumed in the will of the monarch (54–55). For Acosta's view on the necessary alliance between civil and ecclesiastic power, see 1984: 519–31.

Works Cited

Adorno, Rolena. *The Polemics of Possession in Spanish American Narrative*. New Haven: Yale University Press, 2007. Print.

Acosta, José. *De procuranda indorum salute. Pacificación y colonización*. Ed. Luciano Pereña. Madrid: Consejo Superior de Investigaciones Científicas, 1984. Print.

———. *De procuranda indorum salute. Educación y evangelización*. Ed. Luciano Pereña. Madrid: Consejo Superior de Investigaciones Científicas, 1987. Print.

Castañeda, Felipe S. *El indio: Entre el bárbaro y el cristiano. Ensayos sobre filosofía de la conquista en Las Casas, Sepúlveda y Acosta*. Bogotá: Alfaomega Colombiana, 2002. Print.

Casas, Bartolomé de las. "Treinta proposiciones muy jurídicas." *Las obras del obispo fray Bartolomé de las Casas o Casaus, obispo que fue de la ciudad Real de Chiapa en las*

Indias, de la Orden de Santo Domingo. Barcelona: Casa de Antonio Lacaballería, 1646. 1–60. Print.

———. Brevísima relación de la destrucción de las Indias. Ed. André Saint-Lu. Madrid: Cátedra, 1996. Print.

Descartes, René. "Discourse on the Method of Rightly Conducting the Reason and Seeking Truth in the Sciences." Trans. John Veitch. The Rationalists. New York: Anchor Books, 1974. 35–96. Print.

El Alaoui, Youssef. Jésuites, Morisques et Indiens. Étude comparative des méthodes d'évangélisation de la Compagnie de Jésus d'après les traités de José de Acosta (1588) et d'Ignacio de las Casas (1605–1607). Paris: Honoré Champion Éditeur, 2006. Print.

Foucault, Michel de. Las palabras y las cosas. Una arqueología de las ciencias humanas. Trans. Elsa C. Frost. Mexico City: Siglo XXI, 1993. Print.

Loyola, Ignacio de. Ejercicios espirituales. Madrid: Ediciones Atlas, 1944. Print.

Moreiras, Alberto. "Ten Notes on Primitive Imperial Accumulation. Ginés de Sepúlveda, Las Casas, Fernández de Oviedo." Interventions 2.3 (2000): 343–63. Print.

Pagden, Anthony. The Fall of Natural Man. Cambridge: Cambridge University Press, 1982.

Pereña, Luciano. "Proyecto de sociedad colonial, pacificación y colonización." De procuranda indorum salute. Pacificación y colonización. Madrid: Consejo Superior de Investigaciones Científicas, 1984. 3–46. Print.

Schmitt, Carl. The Nomos of the Earth in the International Law of the Jus Publicum Europaeum. New York: Telos Press Publishing, 2006. Print.

Selwyn, Jennifer D. A Paradise Inhabited by Devils: The Jesuits' Civilizing Mission in Early Modern Naples. Burlington: Ashgate Publishing Company, 2004. Print.

Whitener, Brian. "'Pero a mí este libro no me dice nada': Colonial Power in José de Acosta's De procuranda indorum salute." (unpublished manuscript).

Žižek, Slavoj. "The Cartesian Subject versus the Cartesian Theater." Cogito and the Unconscious. Durham: Duke University Press, 1998. 247–74. Print.

———. The Puppet and the Dwarf: The Perverse Core of Christianity. Cambridge: Massachusetts University Press, 2003. Print.

◆ 2

Conquistador Counterpoint: Intimate Enmity in the Writings of Bernardo de Vargas Machuca

Kris Lane

Es gente de behetría toda ella, sin consideración ni valor, y así, si se ven presos se dejan morir miserablemente en dos días; y si notablemente ha habido algunos valerosos y que en sus infortunios han mostrado fortaleza, han sido y son muy contados, como lo fue aquel Araucano de quien cuenta Alonso de Ercilla que antes y después de cortadas las manos por nuestros españoles prometía grandes daños, con grandes oprobios que les decía, si con vida le dejaban, como así sucedió, cosa que el caudillo debe excusar, dejando libre de sus miembros al que derechamente no mereciere muerte, y al que la mereciere dársela con la ley en la mano, y al que se hubiere de soltar, obligándole con buenas obras a la amistad, porque al que le cortaren la fuerza de las manos se la multiplican en la lengua, que en viéndose tan lastimado, cualquier sabe bien persuadir y mover los de su bando a coraje y lástima, como en este se vio ben el efecto que hizo con sola su lengua, que con sus parlamentos y exhortaciones alcanzó aquella nación tantas victorias y nombre, consiguiendo su gentilidad arrebatados de una cólera bárbara. Y si mostró discurso y valor aquel famoso Lautaro con tan memorables hechos, se puede atribuir al tiempo que cursó entre nuestros españoles sirviéndolos; y no es mucho que entre tan gran número de gente se hallen algunos como yo los he topado en el discurso de mis conquistas y jornadas. (Vargas Machuca, *Milicia* 58)

(They are all a leaderless and disorderly people, with neither a sense of merit nor value, and thus, if they find themselves imprisoned, they let themselves die in two days. And if there have been any notably valiant ones who have demonstrated strength amid their misfortunes, there have been and are but very few, such as that Araucano told of by Alonso de Ercilla who, before and after having his hands cut off by us Spaniards, promised great harm (telling them with great opprobrium) if they left him with life, as it so happened—something the commander should avoid, leaving without limbs he who does not directly deserve death, but to the deserved, give it [i.e., execute him] with the law in hand; and to him who should be released, oblige him to friendship with good deeds, for he whose strength is cut from his hands will multiply it in his tongue—that being seen so wounded, anyone well knows how to persuade and move those of their band to courage and pity, as was well seen in this case of the effect he made with only his tongue; that with his speeches and exhortations he gained for that nation [the Mapuche] so many victories and renown, so much to our ruin and damage. There have been other valiant ones, but they have been few and unpersuasive, and following their false religion they are taken by a barbarous rage. And if that famous Lautaro demonstrated discourse and valor with such memorable deeds, it can be attributed to the time he spent among our Spaniards serving us; and among such a great number of people, not many are found, such as I have encountered during my conquests and expeditions.)

Thus did a luckless Indiano militia captain named Bernardo de Vargas Machuca blend blanket condemnation, backhanded praise, and a typically long-winded didactic aside in his 1599 manual for conquistadors, *The Indian Militia and Description of the Indies*. This essay examines this and other writings by Vargas Machuca, a self-styled champion of colonial Spanish American arms and letters in the era of Cervantes, that focus on his seemingly contradictory views of native American peoples. Such self-contradictions may be typical of racist rants, ancient and contemporary, but this essay argues that, at least in the case of Bernardo de Vargas Machuca's writings, inconsistent characterizations or stereotypes can provide insights into an emerging Indiano consciousness—a deeply conflicted and often disenchanted one—and also shed light on the larger Spanish colonial relationship as it matured in the first generations after conquest. This essay asks what Vargas Machuca's self-contradicting views may reveal about his intimate—sometimes allied—and hostile relationships with native Americans beginning in 1578, and what he felt compelled to make of this long, shared experience in the course of his instructional and polemical writings, stretching from 1599 to 1618. The point is not to put Vargas Machuca on the analytical couch, but rather to use his case to consider some of the less acknowledged side effects of early modern Spanish colonialism in the Americas on the so-called colonizer, in this case the Spanish "neo-conquistador" of the immediate post-Lascasian era. As a contemporary of indigenous polemicists such as Felipe Guaman Poma de Ayala, what does Vargas Machuca have to say by way of defensive counterpoint, and what might his sometimes puzzling utterances mean for our understanding of the colonial predicament in the seventeenth century?

The Incomplete or Never-Ending Conquest

> Con la espada y el compas, mas y mas y mas y mas . . . (original unaccented)
> (With sword and compass, more and more and more and more . . .)
> —motto of Bernardo de Vargas Machuca, beneath his portrait in the frontispiece to *The Indian Militia and Description of the Indies*, 1599

It is hard to say if in Spanish America the pen (and possibly compass, or map) had outdone the sword by the time Vargas Machuca published his *Indian Militia and Description of the Indies* in Madrid in 1599, but there were still many opportunities to take up arms. Indeed, although the most densely populated regions of the Americas fell to Spanish conquerors between 1519 and 1538, many peoples in lands claimed by Spain remained independent or recalcitrant for decades and even centuries afterward. The Mapuche of Chile, as Vargas Machuca would have agreed—he even wrote a plan to conquer them in 1599, separate from his military manual from the same year (Vargas Machuca 1961)—were the archetypal example of "indomitable Indians," but there were many others, including the Caribs met by Columbus in the Windward Islands, and the Charrúas who forced the Spanish to abandon Buenos Aires soon after it was founded. Late-arriving conquistadors such as Bernardo de Vargas Machuca of Simancas (c.1555–1622) proposed plans to finish the job of conquest from northern Mexico to southern Chile. Some such men were motivated by cyclical rumors of Eldorado, usually leading them to financial ruin or death in the Amazon or Orinoco basins, but others were more realistic about their prospects. They would conquer small bands of forest peoples, mountain peoples, desert peoples—and perhaps find gold or precious stones besides.

"Conquest," however, had been made a bad word in lettered Spanish circles thanks to the writings of preacher-critics such as Bartolomé de Las Casas and Domingo de Santo Tomás, compelling Philip II to license only "pacifications" of unconquered peoples and "punishments" of rebellious ones by the early 1570s. This paternalistic, "post-conquest" rhetorical shift reflects a deeper tension or dilemma that emerged in the immediate post-Lascasian era: how to justify the conquest and consolidate the resulting overstretched claims while still acknowledging "excesses" and avoiding new ones in the struggle for the backlands. The task of justification/codification was eventually taken up by the Lima-born jurist Juan de Solórzano Pereira (1629; Muldoon), but there were others who came before, including the simpler but no less self-confident Indiano soldier Bernardo de Vargas Machuca. Rather than offer an original legal defense of Spanish imperialism, Vargas Machuca struggled to formulate an almost personal one, juxtaposing righteous Spanish conquistadors, among whom he counted himself, against mostly evil native Americans. His 1599 militia manual offered a generally prescriptive rather than programmatic approach to "conquest, continued," but it too was at root personal and autobiographical.

As a self-styled colonial enforcer in the era of pacification and punishment, Bernardo de Vargas Machuca grew so outraged by the continued success of Las Casas's *Brevísima relación*, particularly in Protestant Europe, that he decided to write a rejoinder, the *Defense and Discourse of the Western Conquests*, first drafted in 1603 in the fortresses of Portobelo, Panama, and finally denied publication and shelved in Madrid in 1618. As Flores Hernández has shown, it is an odd document in many respects, far easier to dismiss than to take seriously and analyze (1991). An Indiano's "conquest counterpoint," one that might be profitably read alongside Guaman Poma de Ayala's contemporary and similarly ignored *Nueva corónica y buen gobierno* as well as Las Casas's much earlier *Brevísima*, Vargas Machuca's *Defense and Discourse* offers not only a shrill, semi-legalistic justification for conquest and a series of bitter attacks on "the Indian character," or "nature," but also a perplexing jumble of contradictory examples and occasionally confessional anecdotes drawn from the author's personal experience in "the Western Indies," primarily in the rugged backlands of New Granada, roughly modern Colombia. As can be seen in the opening quotation, similar contradictions, and hints of the same argument in germ form, appear in the earlier (and successfully published) *Indian Militia and Description of the Indies*. It is in Vargas Machuca's self-contradictions and personal asides that one senses the psychological struggle and entanglement entailed by what Ashis Nandy famously termed "intimate enmity," that space or condition in which colonialism was experienced day-by-day and cheek-by-jowl, steadily challenging the limits of tolerance and eating away at the souls—or selves—of all parties.

Intimate Enmity

> que si el primer intento que los conquistadores tuvieron en sus poblaciones se considera no fue otro que reducir almas al cielo, vasallos a su rey, como para sí propios honor y hacienda." (Vargas Machuca, "Apologías" 33)
>
> (the primary intention of the conquerors in their settlements was none other than to bring souls to heaven and vassals to their king, as well as for their own honor and estate.)

If today the Spanish conquest hardly seems like the heroic enterprise that it was for Bernardo de Vargas Machuca and many of his contemporaries, anticolonialism (if not "reconquest") certainly retains its halo of sanctity. With few exceptions, anticolonialism—at least as a political struggle—remains a phenomenon painted in black and white, with heroes and villains in clear-cut roles. After the horrors of WWII, even twentieth-century conservatives came around to agree that conquest and colonialism were bad, not just in execution, but as ideas. If you wanted to be on the "right side of history," "liberation" from any sort of colonial oppressor was universally good. There were no more benevolent empires.

In 1983, Ashis Nandy, in *The Intimate Enemy*, challenged readers to discard some of the most cherished dichotomies bequeathed by the twentieth-century anticolonial struggle. As if to negate Albert Memmi's famous 1957 formulation, Nandy argued that the only way to face down the persistent demons of colonialism—all too evident in the India (and broader world) of his day—was to stop thinking in terms of binary opposites such as colonizer/colonized, colonialism/anticolonialism, collaboration/resistance, west/non-west. He also asked readers to invert old notions of powerful oppressor and powerless victim and realize that colonialism entailed the moral degradation of the so-called colonizer as well as the incidental if not ironic empowerment of the so-called colonized (inverting what was then generally assumed).

For Nandy, colonialism generated a whole spectrum of possibilities along which a person might move over time before hitting upon a "true self," often worked out or at least partially articulated in polemical writing. The colonial relationship, in this new rendering, was not simply (or really ever) about conqueror and conquered, although these were powerful tropes because they managed to freeze a highly dramatic moment of violent domination—*The Conquest*—and make it emblematic of colonialism itself (less true in most of British India, perhaps, than in Spanish America or the Philippines, but with violent episodes such as the Sepoy Rebellion playing iconic roles not unlike that of Cajamarca).

Rather, for Nandy colonialism was something far more ambivalent and processual, and far more personalized, even internalized, centered on the compromised, struggling, entangled self of the colonizer as individual and the compromised, struggling, entangled self of the individual as colonized. Whereas Memmi and Fanon developed virtual physician's manuals documenting (with actual patient files) colonial pathologies that readers assumed would be magically cured by political independence, Nandy's colonialism was a nagging and more persistent condition characterized by shared loss, with humans playing mostly tragic roles even as they thought they were engaged in heroic (or neutral) projects. But Nandy's colonialism was also about shared recovery, in large part recovered dignity, the hard struggle to escape from humiliation both as perpetrator (or enabler, or even bystander) and victim (or stooge, or "gray zone" collaborator). Examining colonialism in this personalized way required a sort of "deep biography," one that sought to encompass the full life cycle of pro- and anticolonial authors and activists such as Kipling and Gandhi, not just homing in on their young adult "awakenings" and (usually) later, conservative reactions to them, but analyzing them as full, "exemplary" lives.

Locked in this interior struggle from childhood, Nandy's historical personalities, British and Indian (tricky categories, he acknowledged) were all "colonized" in the sense that colonialism was the one shared predicament from which they all had to extricate themselves—or, in reverse, embrace and champion—in order to retain or recover their dignity, their "selfhood." Such an approach to colonialism offered a new means to understand seemingly contradictory figures such as Gandhi, Kipling, and even Orwell, raised betwixt and between, and finally falling—as mature adults—on either side of the pro-/anticolonial dividing line. We might declare Nandy's approach helpful for understanding British colonialism and anticolonialism in nineteenth- and twentieth-century South Asia, but could this approach to the colonial predicament as an essentially internal, more or less psychological struggle fit or be adapted elsewhere, and should it be? Might something be gained by examining similar individuals from Spain's Golden Age (or Dark Age?) of colonial rule? Might we learn something new about complex and sometimes contradictory sixteenth- and seventeenth-century figures such as Bartolomé de Las Casas, Felipe Guaman Poma de Ayala, or Bernardo de Vargas Machuca by applying a similar set of analytical criteria?

For current academic tastes, the last of these Spanish American colonial figures is arguably the least sympathetic. More or less by his own account,

Bernardo de Vargas Machuca was an unapologetic, Spanish-born "Indian fighter." In a 1604 merit report to the Council of the Indies, he called himself a "caudillo general" whose job had been to "desbaratar las ladroneras de los yndios" (AGI Panamá 45: 49). Unlike Guaman Poma, he never presented himself as a complex or conflicted person, someone caught "betwixt and between," somehow victimized or degraded by colonialism yet also anxious to see it reformed. If anything, Vargas Machuca was one of Spanish colonialism's most ardent and consistent, if not optimistic, champions, this at a time of considerable doubt and reflection among Spain's prolific literati. Yet his world, as we find both in the documentary record and between—and sometimes within—the lines of his published work, was not so simple or clear-cut. Despite his strident claims to the contrary, I would submit that Bernardo de Vargas Machuca *was* deeply compromised by colonialism, degraded by it and frustrated by his degradation—defensive about it. He was, I suggest, not so different from his "latinized" native Andean counterpart, Guaman Poma. The more loyally Vargas Machuca served in Spain's many colonial American conflicts and the more dangerous the location or foe, the more he seems to have felt ignored, disdained, even mocked. Worse, his long service in what he called the Indian militia caused others (he strongly suggests in his defense of himself and those of his class) to question his morality, his Christianity, even his manhood. What sort of man would want to be a conquistador after the denunciations of Las Casas?

Like Las Casas and Guaman Poma, Vargas Machuca's energy as a writer seems to have come principally from rage, rage over how Spanish colonialism, or Castile's imperial project, had gone wrong, or had at least lost its way or purpose. Vargas Machuca, a conservative critic, wrote in support of conquest as it had been accomplished up to his time or as he believed it had been accomplished by the likes of Cortés, his one true and perfect hero. But beginning with the *Indian Militia*, Vargas Machuca was also defending his self-nominated continuance of the conquest, his desire not only to see or witness its completion, but also to be one of those responsible for taking on so many of the backlands' "indomitable Indians" and getting the job done. The shame that enraged him came from how the project of conquest had been misrepresented, even betrayed, by fellow Spaniards such as Las Casas, whose criticisms he took as a personal libel, an attack on his honor as an individual and self-styled conquistador. What makes Vargas Machuca different from other defenders of the conquest and of the Habsburg colonial order, and why he is worthy of examination here, was his personalizing of such alleged misrepresentation in print that recalls another unsung conquistador, Bernal Díaz del Castillo, treating his response to Las Casas's *Brevísima* literally as "self-defense," or as Nandy might have it, "self-recovery." How had Vargas Machuca come to internalize Spanish conquest and colonialism to such a degree when unlike Bernal Díaz he had not participated in anything so historically momentous as the fall of Mexico?

The Indiano Latecomer

> "si acertare a satisfacer atribúyase a la divina providencia, considerando que soy soldado y que sigo un intento bueno y descargo cristiano, que para en este caso bastará considerar la razón pues con ella no habrá criatura que no le juzgue por tal, y, como dice el consulto, que basta por ley y desta lo es el alma." (Vargas Machuca, "Apologías" 34)

> (If I should manage to satisfy, may it be attributed to Divine Providence, considering that I am a soldier and follow good intentions and Christian duty, that in this case, considering my reason will be sufficient, for with reason there is no creature judged as such; and as the wise say, the law is sufficient and by law goes the soul.)

Born in about 1555 in the Old Castilian village of Simancas, outside Valladolid, Vargas Machuca grew up in the wake, if not the constant presence, of royalty. His father had served in the retinue of Charles V as a footman, but by the time Vargas Machuca was born he had settled into a position as constable of the new Royal Archive. After serving with his father as a teenager against the Alpujarras Moriscos around 1570, Vargas Machuca went to Italy, where he apparently joined a Spanish militia for a few years but never saw combat. Word of Protestant corsair Francis Drake setting out on a new raiding voyage to Spanish America drew Vargas Machuca's attention, and he was approved for passage overseas to serve against the arch-pirate. Drake proceeded to circumnavigate the world, and Vargas Machuca never faced him, nor any other "Lutheran heretic" corsair, as far as we know. Instead, he became an Indian fighter, an Indiano militiaman, a neo-conquistador. This was precisely the identity he would struggle to explain in his writings, principally the *Indian Militia and Description of the Indies*, or *Milicia Indiana* (1599), and the *Defense and Discourse of the Western Conquests* (1618).

Vargas Machuca "the soldier" arrived in the Americas in 1578, far too late to participate in any major conquest campaign, and he died in 1622 in Madrid, while at court seeking a promotion in return for his services against a variety of non-sedentary or semi-sedentary Amerindian "rebels," mostly Carib speakers from the rugged interior of New Granada. A variety of records in Spain and Colombia show that none of his acts, with the possible exception of harsh "punishments" meted out to several Muzo caciques of Colombia's emerald belt, yielded lasting results (AGN Bogotá Historia Civil 22: 887–972; AGI Patronato 164:1; AGI Panamá 45). The allegedly incorrigible Carares of the middle Magdalena River basin and the mountaineer Pijaos of the Central Cordillera, about whom Vargas Machuca has much to say, both in his published work and in manuscript merit reports, continued to resist conquest well after their "conqueror's" time, and the town he founded and named for his birthplace in the Upper Magdalena Valley was abandoned almost immediately due to the aggressive Andakí (Friede).

After several years spent begging at court in Madrid, Vargas Machuca was named castellan of Portobelo, on Panama's north coast, a position he claimed nearly killed him. A local official asked that such Indianos not be sent to jungle posts, as their constitutions were not suited to it (AGI Panamá 45). Next came a longer stint as governor of the pearling island of Margarita, off the Venezuelan coast. Here Vargas Machuca thrived, despite having no significant enemies to fight (he dispatched one Carib "punishment," but his tenure lined up with the Twelve Years' Truce between Spain and the Netherlands). A last trip to Madrid won him the governorship of Antioquia, in northwest New Granada, but he died of some unnamed illness in Madrid before taking up the post (Martínez de Salinas).

Vargas Machuca may have been a failed conquistador, but he left a substantial published and manuscript legacy that seems to suggest otherwise. If we may trust his writings, he did not consider himself a failure, and in fact he felt qualified to write not only a manual for neo-conquistadors but also a defense of the conquistadors as a maligned social class against no less an opponent (though long dead) than Bartolomé de Las Casas. Vargas Machuca presumably could not have known it, but he was attempting to justify the Spanish conquest, and also personally embody it in a new and regenerated form, at precisely the same time that Peruvian critic Felipe Guaman Poma de Ayala sought to denounce it in a far more categorical and imaginative way than had Las Casas. Like Guaman Poma, Vargas Machuca wrote from the margins of empire to defend his pride and his peers, as well as to inform the monarch and to offer recommendations for reform. Both writers deployed rhetorical strategies drawn from their years of personal struggle within the notorious judicial bureaucracy of the Habsburg state—and indeed one might argue that this was where they sounded most confident, as alternately individual plaintiff and defender of a corps or constituency before the monarch as judge.

"Love" does not figure much in these more or less fictional pro- and counter-conquest narratives, unlike in Cervantes as examined by Roberto González Echevarría (2005), but "law" certainly does. What we see in both authors is not a use of Castilian law and legal language to explore the ambiguity or irony of criminality by way of exemplary stories, but rather the adoption of a stiff, uncompromising, legalistic tone of authority used to deliver decree-like statements, including numbered declarations and proofs meant to exonerate individuals and larger groups accused of crimes. Guaman Poma plays lawyer and legal scribe to exonerate the Incas and his ancestors, as well as himself and his kin, and Vargas Machuca does much the same to exonerate the conquistadors (among whom he rather unconvincingly counts himself).

Although both writers prided themselves in their staunch Catholicism and faithful service to the crown (or at least they did not neglect to make these legally necessary "autos de fé" as subjects of a jealous God and merciful king), their interpretations of Spanish colonialism c.1600 read almost like inverse images. One may be tempted to apply simple, opposing labels to them: Spanish "colonizer" versus Andean "colonized," but for me such labels hide rather than explain their many and sometimes overlapping predicaments. In reading Vargas Machuca closely, it becomes clear that, like Guaman Poma, he struggled to make sense of conquest history and its aftermath in a very personal way, a way that kept it in a limbo-like present. Writing about it, and comparing the experiences of many predecessors with his own as first detailed in his merit reports, forced him to contemplate, and finally to construct (thanks to Las Casas) a defensive, an embattled colonial self. Where did Vargas Machuca fit into this great drama of conquest? If he was a hero (as, indeed, he had to be), then who were the villains? Did they include his present-day enemies in the rugged South American and Caribbean hinterland?

The Indiano vs. "the Indians"

> Siendo como es cosa natural la propia defensa, no he podido excusar de volver por mi particular honor y por el común de nuestra nación, que con rostro y apariencias pías le pretendió deslustrar el docto Obispo de Chiapas don fray Bartolomé de las Casas, o Casaos, en el discurso que escribió año del 1552 con aquel indigno título Destruición de las Indias, en que pretendió probar por crueldades los castigos jurídicos en todas las [Indias] Occidentales que los conquistadores ejecutaron y ejecutan en los indios por enormes delitos que cometieron y cometen cada día. (Vargas Machuca, "Apologías" 33)

(Self-defense being, such as it is, a natural thing, I have not been able to avoid defending my own honor and that common to our nation, which with pious countenance and appearances the learned Bishop of Chiapas, don Fray Bartolomé de Las Casas, attempted to tarnish in the discourse he wrote in the year 1552, with that contemptible title *The Destruction of the Indies*, in which he tried to depict as cruelties the legal punishments in all the West, which the conquerors executed (and presently carry out) in the Indies for heinous crimes that were (and are) committed every day.)

Here again the conquest past is also the conquest present, and the learned bishop's conquest victims are mirrored by "today's" native criminals, justly punished by just conquistadors. There seems to be no room here for opposing Spanish views, much less indigenous perspectives, so what might Bernardo de Vargas Machuca, a committed if not eloquent defender of the Spanish colonial project, have to tell us about anticolonialism, or subaltern concerns of any kind? Even if he offered something, would not such an unapologetic colonial "perpetrator" be too biased, too blind or blinkered, to tell us anything of value beyond his own hard views and prejudices? I believe there is considerably more than simply uncompromising racist opinion in Vargas Machuca's writings, and there is also much about the compromised colonial self, his own conflicted, angry, frustrated self. It is perhaps difficult to see beyond statements such as the one above, but I am convinced there is more. What Vargas Machuca tells us about his indigenous foes (and occasional allies) and what he tells us about himself are wound up in the same skein.

If we were to judge Vargas Machuca's various arguments as rhetorical exercises, we would find—as Rolena Adorno did in examining Guaman Poma's *Nueva corónica y buen gobierno*—that they often suffer from a core problem: failing to reconcile contradictory evidence. Both authors make blanket generalizations about large groups of people that repeatedly crash into "exceptions to the rule." Both rely on historical authorities as touchstones, only to discover that these "official" narratives too often fail to conform to the needs of their arguments, which are focused—ultimately—on the present, or rather, the writer's sense of "a present," the moment of writing.

In both Vargas Machuca's 1599 military manual and especially his c.1603–18 defense of the conquistadors, contradictions arise particularly as regards "the essential Indian character." In both books Vargas Machuca needs "Indians" to look universally bad in order to sustain his claims, yet his own experience and his historical understanding of the conquests will not allow it. It may be for this reason that he chooses to preface his *Defense and Discourse of the*

Western Conquests with Juan Ginés de Sepúlveda's "Twelve Objections" to Las Casas's arguments (published in 1564 as the *Tratado de las doce dudas*) at Valladolid in 1552. It serves as an impenetrable legal screen behind which he feels more free to improvise and extemporize.

In his 1618 *Defense*, Vargas Machuca has the opposite problem of Las Casas, who needed the conquistadors to be universally bad—essentially straw men. Las Casas in the *Brevísima* (a sermon disguised as an epistle) solved the problem by painting both "Indians" and "conquistadors" with the broadest of brushstrokes despite his seeming attention to reportorial, region-by-region detail, his alarmingly precise and "statistical" account of atrocities. He leaves no room for ambiguity, crowding it out at every turn in order to convince his readers that Spaniards in America did only bad things, very bad things, to innately "good," docile, tractable Indians. Men who should have known better, should have restrained themselves, should have followed their consciences and acted like Christians, instead robbed, raped, and slaughtered innocent natives. Worse, they robbed God of so many thousands—no, millions—of souls, and in the process wagered and lost their own.

How to counter this and similarly exaggerated charges, or claims? Vargas Machuca, particularly in his *Defense and Discourse of the Western Conquests*, is at pains to show that the conquistadors were in most cases virtuous men, honorable men, Christian men, measured in their approach to Amerindian societies, not driven by greed or lust but rather by a sincere desire to spread the faith and extend the king's realm. The real problem with the conquest was the Indians. Vargas Machuca has to make clear to his readers that they were the real villains, and he has the firsthand experience from having lived among them and fought them to prove it.

Noble conquistadors, Vargas Machuca claims, perfectly inverting the characterizations made by Las Casas, found themselves trapped, faced with an innately duplicitous, vicious, and otherwise incorrigible indigenous population, a horde of infantile but also malicious and even deadly potential subjects whose pacification was demanded (but never paid for) by king and pope. It was the ungrateful Indians who deserved blame for any "excesses," or violent outbursts, or exemplary punishments, not their well-intentioned guides to civilized living, the conquistadors. The conquistadors were doing their duty, but they were betrayed—the Indians simply failed to be good, honest, Christian subjects. They rebelled and therefore had to be crushed, but even so, according to Vargas Machuca, the Spaniards had been quick to extend the olive branch and forgive, only to be betrayed again.

It is notable that Guaman Poma, as Adorno has shown, rewrote the conquest of his native Peru in an entirely different way, neutralizing it by claiming that it was a non-event, a ritualized act of mutual submission (29). The problem for Guaman Poma was that he and his fellow Andeans were being treated as a conquered people when in fact they had accepted both king and pope without a fight. Was there any middle ground between the authors on this matter, or were they seeing things from perfectly opposite directions? Put more simply, could native Americans be anything but incorrigible rebels for someone like Vargas Machuca? Well, yes and no. He did praise former Inca subjects such as Guaman Poma and his cohort for their industry and relative docility, and he had nothing but good to say about the Tlaxcalans of highland Mexico who aided Cortés, and also the stout Guayquerí fishing folk whom he got to know during his tenure on Margarita Island. Mostly, however, he finds himself compelled to make blanket claims that are entirely derogatory. The demands of countering Las Casas's *Brevísima* seem to require it:

> Pues viniendo a su trato y comunicación es cierto que no dicen verdad ni jamás supieron guardar fe ni palabra ni término bueno a quien de ellos se fió, y obliga a creerlo ver en general gente sin honra ni estimación, y verificarse esta verdad saber por cierto que venden la mujer, la hija y la hermana a cualquier español para que use torpemente de ella, de donde se infiere ser gente sin razón, viciosa y sin honra . . . pues siendo todos sus actos malos síguese que no tienen honra, y a quien le faltare lo mismo será la virtud, y a gentes que estas dos cosas falta considérese cual podrá ser; y no sé para que me canso en disponer más la materia, pues sabemos que comen a sus propios hijos y vasallos. (Vargas Machuca, "Apologías" 64)
>
> (As for their trade and communication, it is true that they do not tell the truth, nor have ever known how to keep faith, nor word, nor promise with those who have trusted them. One is forced to believe they are a people with neither honor nor esteem, and this truth is verified in knowing for certain that they sell wife, daughter, and sister to any Spaniard to make use of lasciviously. One may infer that they are a people with no reason, depraved and without honor. . . . As all of their acts are evil, it follows that they have no honor, and whoever lacks this lacks virtue as well, and for peoples who lack both, one wonders who they might be. I know not why I tire myself with presenting the material further, as we know that they eat their own children and vassals.)

So there you have it in a nutshell: American natives range from faithless cheats to lascivious cannibals who eat their own children. The urge to fight Las Casas's fire with fire is clearly strongest at the beginning of the *Defense*, but even later on Vargas Machuca argues that unsavory Amerindian character traits, like persistent infections, demanded (and still demand—his constant reminder that the conquest is ongoing) "a strong caustic." Such was the justification for the *castigos* or "punishments" of his own time, the sometimes-rough handling of rebels, subversives, and backsliders. How could Las Casas have got it so wrong, Vargas Machuca seems to ask, when the evidence for Amerindian "badness" was so overwhelming, and so obvious?

In virtually all his writings, Vargas Machuca speaks of Amerindians as white masters once spoke of African slaves. As a rule, he says, "Indians" are pusillanimous, lazy, conniving, hateful, disease prone, stupid, even self-destructive. What kind of people, he asks, commit suicide for trifling reasons, seemingly just to spite their masters? As Nandy would perhaps have noted, Vargas Machuca takes a hyper-masculine view of the Spanish colonizer and attaches a feminized "passive-aggressiveness" to the Native American colonized (extended also to the unconquered). He further emphasizes male Amerindian depravity by claiming all native men pimped "their" womenfolk, an act that perfectly negated all possibility of their possessing honor (centered on male protection of women from other sexually predatory males). But here and elsewhere Vargas Machuca is not representing some abstract "Indian," but rather is drawing a composite image taken directly from his specific experiences with male hunter-gatherers who continued to resist Spanish hegemony (i.e., him) in the jungle and desert backlands of New Granada.

The effeminate or feminized Native American male was of course an established trope or characterization long before Vargas Machuca came along, but his rendering, again drawing from personal experience, is somewhat different from earlier iterations. Vargas Machuca openly personalizes and internalizes what he regards as this fundamental, gendered difference between him and "them." He repeatedly casts himself as the manly conquistador, à la the western chivalric tradition: resolute, courageous, but also wise and concerned with the protection of his men. His enemy, by contrast, is the effeminate Indian guerrilla, running from him, hiding from him, sneaking up on him, poisoning him, unwilling to face him in broad daylight and fight him "like a man." In both the *Indian Militia* and *Defense and Discourse*, Vargas Machuca's is not the voice of a passive observer, viewing "Indians" from a safe distance, but rather that of the seasoned backwoodsman, the decorated Indian fighter. He is also a horseman, but he downplays equestrian advantage in the *Indian Militia* and in the *Defense and Discourse of Western Conquests*.

The "essential" Indian, then, is a feminized inverse of himself, but Vargas Machuca does not leave it at this. Instead, he reuses and expands on examples of what he regards as cowardly or duplicitous behavior to demonstrate Indian ways of war, which now also—ironically, one might say—become Indiano, or "Indian militia," ways of fighting Indians. Effective counterinsurgency entails tactical convergence, which is to say not only adapting to "effeminate" indigenous methods of fighting, but also adopting them, at least in part, learning to set and anticipate ambushes, learning to march all night and hide by day, learning to travel light, to "leave no trace," and to improvise in the wilderness. Even Vargas Machuca's bush medicine takes key pointers from his allegedly effeminate enemies, who skulk and poison their attackers with "twenty-four hour venom." He recommends fermented maize plasters for a sore behind (Vargas Machuca, *The Indian Militia* 66). Two problems emerge here as things get detailed: the author's failure to acknowledge what he has learned from indigenous allies (always unnamed) and his reluctant acknowledgement of his enemies' cleverness and determination. The blanket generalizations suddenly lose force.

It is mostly in the *Indian Militia* that Vargas Machuca praises or at least compliments his native foes. When determined to find and vanquish an enemy, they are, he says, the best hunters in the world (referring to the Carib-speakers of interior New Granada, such as the Carares and Pijaos). They do not even have to eat when in hot pursuit, and will not lose a trail for days on end, jungle or desert conditions notwithstanding. These are not simply backhanded compliments, in the end, but an acknowledgement of considerable skill, wile, and will—in other words, of full humanity. And the enemy thus becomes not only "worthy" as an opponent of the Spanish militiaman but also worthy of mimicry. Counterinsurgency means fighting Indian guerrillas like an Indian guerrilla, which also means finding native allies who already know and practice this way of war and learning from them. Vargas Machuca is loath to admit contradictions here, even as he himself becomes drawn into a new, "Indiano" world, a world of self-remaking. Here indeed is where the struggle to find or articulate a true self comes out from behind the smokescreen of racist-style ranting and stereotyping. The jungle Indian fighter has to make sense of his own tangled narrative, as his enemies, too, are jungle Indian fighters.

More striking is a case that Vargas Machuca cites in both the *Milicia Indiana* and the *Defense and Discourse of the Western Conquests*. At some point in a late 1580s campaign against the Carares of the Middle Magdalena basin in central New Granada, Vargas Machuca ordered a captive indigenous child drowned in order to enforce silence. He claimed that his camp was surrounded by Carare warriors who were being encouraged by crying babies whose captive mothers were pinching them in order to goad their husbands, brothers, or other men-folk to attack. Vargas Machuca claims he sought the council of an indigenous chieftain who was his ally, and this unnamed chieftain told him to have one of the babies drowned so that the other mothers would keep theirs quiet. Vargas Machuca ordered this done, and it seemed to have the desired effect. He later claimed that his camp would have fallen victim to the Carare warriors had this sacrifice not taken place. It was necessary, he said, to save his people.

Ordering the murder of a child, albeit the child of sworn enemies, was possibly the most compromising act of Vargas Machuca's life, at least as a colonial enforcer. Whatever else he may have done, this act appears to have weighed heavily on him as he says (in detached third person) that it prompted "the commander" to consult a theologian. Vargas Machuca seems anxious to report to the reader (to posterity) that he, the commander, was absolved. But behind the mask of confidence and absolution, one senses him wondering aloud whether this was an act of heroism or of "Indian-style" villainy. If he was ordering babies to be drowned by their own mothers, what had he done? In taking on the role of "caudillo general" in a backcountry "castigo," what had he become? One of Las Casas's "tyrannical" conquistadors? Or perhaps something quite different: an Indian? Could he have become somehow much like the "thing" he claimed to detest so much, the skulking, effeminate, duplicitous "rebel"?

The Recovery of Self through Writing

> Cuales sean las partes de que ha de ser compuesto nuestro caudillo, cuanto a lo primero, buen cristiano, noble rico, liberal, de buena edad, fuerte, diligente, prudente, afable, determinado: otras partes que penden de éstas, que se pudieran reducir a ellas, quiero declararlas, porque el que siguiere o tratare de esta milicia, advierta a sí mismo que el caudillo ha de ser dichoso, secreto, cauteloso, ingenioso, honesto. (Vargas Machuca, *Milicia* 67)

> (Our commander must be composed of these qualities: first, a good Christian, noble, wealthy, generous, of good age, strong, diligent, prudent, affable, and determined. Other qualities that stem from these I should like to declare, for he who should join or address this militia observes that the commander must be happy, discreet, cautious, resourceful, and honest.)

Vargas Machuca shared another trait with his contemporary, Guaman Poma, in the use of writing, or "discourse," as Vargas Machuca consistently calls it, to fashion and present—and, I would argue, "recover"—the self. Both did so directly if sometimes awkwardly by inserting their persons and lineages into the historical dramas they narrated. But both also did so more subtly and ahistorically, in the form of self-congratulatory exempla. If Guaman Poma can be understood to have used himself as the model of the "good cacique," an honest Christian and faithful subject, but also a noble worthy of command and *merced*, then Vargas Machuca must be seen as the source for his own idealized "good commander," a figure he describes in detail in the first book of the *Indian Militia*.

Why do this when the historical self ought to suffice? Quite simply, because the historical self did not suffice. In the Indies, fame, like its inverse, Aguirre-like infamy, was a do-it-yourself affair. One had to write oneself into history if one wanted to be taken seriously. Certainly no one else was going to do it on these men's behalf, and even "valiant Cortés" had been forced to become his own best promoter and agent at court. Both Guaman Poma and Vargas Machuca were marginal figures in their day and age, if not "failures." Both certainly felt slighted and overlooked, and their anger prompted them to write. But their writing also may be understood as psychologically compensatory. Vargas Machuca claimed that his authority as a writer of a conquistador manual derived directly from his long and distinguished experience fighting Indians in the backlands of South America, but since his twenty-eight years of fighting produced no lasting results, and certainly no bona fide conquests (although he may have argued otherwise), his surest means of compensating for this "inconvenient truth" was by fashioning an imagined militia leader who happened to be a spitting image of himself. No better "espejo del héroe" appears than that of Vargas Machuca in the frontispiece to the *Indian Militia*.

Yet even the post of militia commander has to be defended, as Vargas Machuca notes:

> Aunque es verdad que la milicia ennoblece al que viene de baja estirpe, ejercitando las armas en servicio de su rey, sirviéndole lealmente, por ser el arte más honrado y sublime de todos, aunque el día de hoy está desfavorecido, ya casi no hay ciudadano que no se ría del que sigue la milicia y no solo se ríen, pero aún le tienen por falto de juicio, y no tienen razón, porque cuando no hubiera otro premio más del que de la virtud propia a quien la sigue, es bien seguirla y servir a su Rey y señor. (Vargas Machuca, *Milicia* 69)

> (Though it is true that the militia ennobles the one who comes from low lineage, exercising arms in the service of his king and loyally serving him, this most sublime and honored of all arts is in disfavor these days. There is hardly a citizen now who does not laugh at him who joins the militia and not only laughs but deems him lacking in judgment. But they are mistaken, for when there is no other prize than

that which imparts its own virtue to him who joins it, it is good to join and serve his king and lord.)

Ever defensive, Vargas Machuca weaves these abstract insults from colonial (and possibly metropolitan) townsfolk into his point-by-point description of the ideal commander of militias in the Indies. In several asides, he goes farther, clearly boasting of his own exploits in the same abstract, third-person way:

> Y así digo, que ha de tener edad para poder caminar a pié de noche y de día, por la quebrada, loma y sierra de invierno y verano, donde ofende bien el sol por estar debajo de la equinocial y trópicos; y tras este gran calor, cargado de armas, sufriendo un aguacero o turbión de agua, que en aquellas partes es muy ordinario, llegando mojado al rio caudaloso, donde le es forzoso balsearlo a nado, por las corrientes, ayudando a pasar su gente y bagaje, como se dirá adelante. Lo que sucede de esto es un pasmo o resfriado y otras enfermedades, pues la noche que se le ofrece es bien trabajosa, cansado y mojado, sin tener abrigo ninguno. Pues decir las calamidades que padece en la tal jornada, son muchas, porque aquel marchar tan cotidiano de noche y de día, cayendo en una parte y despeñándose en otra; recibiendo la herida y caminando con ella por no perder la ocasión. Pues aquel ordinario dormir vestido y calzado y armado en toda la jornada y en un pié como grulla, velando todas las noches el cuarto del alba, que le es forzoso porque a esta hora el enemigo siempre está encima . . . (Vargas Machuca, *Milicia* 73)

> (I say that he must be of an age to walk night and day through the ravine, mud, and mountain range in winter and in summer, where the sun offends, being under the equinoctial line and the tropics; and through this great heat, laden with arms, suffering a tempest or downpour, which are very common in those parts, arriving wet to the mighty river, where it is necessary to swim across because of the currents, helping to pass his people and baggage across, as will be told of later. What occurs from this is a chill or cold or other sicknesses, for the night offered to them is also laborious, tired and wet, with no protection whatsoever. Speaking of the calamities that occur on such a campaign, they are many, such as: constant marching, night and day, stumbling in one part and falling headlong into another, receiving a wound and walking on with it so as not to lose any opportunity; constantly sleeping clothed and shod and armed during the entire campaign; and, on one foot like a crane, keeping the dawn watch every night, which he cannot avoid, for at this hour the enemy is always near . . .)

The text goes on to detail the ideal commander's need to face the problems of bridge building, path finding, avoiding venomous snakes, battling mosquitoes, and much more. If this is a boast, it is, like Guaman Poma's vivid descriptions of abused Andeans at the hands of brutal *encomenderos*, priests, and majordomos, a means of informing the king of the harsh realities of the Indies, what it is about the vast and different Americas that renders this kind of service so special, so worthy of praise and reward. Having explicated the many difficulties of campaigns in the tropical American backcountry, Vargas Machuca is compelled to return to the matter of his foe, "the Indian," and more specifically, the Indian commander. Having repeatedly called his enemies leaderless, weak, stupid, even self-destructive, he finds himself forced to admit that none of these blanket terms in truth applies in the field:

> La calidad de los indios es como de aves nocturnas, que andan toda la noche sin reposar un punto cuando traen las armas en las manos, y en esta parte no hay nación en el mundo que les gane y no sé si diga que les iguale porque el caudillo de ellos anda en el aire cuando previene las cosas de la guerra, porque ni come, ni para, ni duerme; y sus soldados aún se le aventajan, porque entre ellos jamás rehusó ninguno mandato de su cacique y capitán, ni tuvo orden en el trabajo y riesgo, porque aquel que primero topa a ese ocupa: de tal manera son que, si ponen una centinela, la dejan estar dos días con sus noches y en todo este tiempo no duerme obedeciendo en pié o sentado, mascando una hoja de árbol que llaman Coca y por otro nombre Hayo, sin que haya falta en su modo bárbaro. Y esto no parezca ponderación, que muchos son los que lo han visto. Es gente que en la oscuridad de la noche, con truenos y relámpagos caminan para dar un aviso a sus vecinos y prevenir casos de guerra, no estorbándoles la aspereza y maleza de la tierra, el largo camino, el grande aguacero, el caudaloso río, la sed y hambre, ni el sueño y trabajo, todo lo rompen, por todo pasan, contándonos los pasos, trayéndonos siempre al ojo, de día y de noche, notándonos el descuido en que caemos. (Vargas Machuca, *Milicia* 76)

> (The quality of the Indians is like nocturnal birds, who travel all night without resting a bit even when they carry arms in their hands, and in this respect there is no nation in the world who can defeat them, nor, can I say, equal them, for their commander walks on air [*anda en el aire*] when he prepares for the things of war; he neither eats nor stops, nor sleeps; and his soldiers even surpass him, for among them was never refused any command from their cacique and captain, nor were any orders to work and take a risk, for the first to come upon it occupies himself with it. They are such that, if a sentry is placed, he is left for two days and nights and in all this time does not sleep, obeying, standing or sitting, chewing a leaf of the tree called coca and by its other name, *hayo*, lacking nothing in his barbarous way. And this should not seem an exaggeration, for there are many who have seen it. They are a people who walk in the dark of night, with thunder and lightning, in order to warn

their neighbors and prevent affairs of war, bothered neither by the ruggedness nor the undergrowth of the land, nor the long road, the great flood, the mighty river, nor thirst, hunger, fatigue, or work, breaking through everything, passing everywhere, counting our steps, always keeping us in sight, day and night, noting the carelessness into which we fall.)

The Unrecovered Self

It may be too much to say that Bernardo de Vargas Machuca suffered any sort of crisis of conscience, and he likely would have vigorously denied having become anything like the "wild Indians" he had fought for so long while cooling his heels at court in Madrid. Furthermore, he was not only an Indian fighter; he was also, or wanted to be recognized as such, a *"soldado indiano"* in the fullest sense of the term. In his merit reports, Vargas Machuca claimed experience fighting against Panama maroons in the 1570s, some of the Americas' earliest and most successful runaways, and he later criticized their 1603 resettlement near his post at Portobelo. He also ordered an enslaved African belonging to him killed on Margarita after an alleged murder—to show that he did not play favorites. (He also exiled his own son to Flanders for dereliction of duty against the Island Caribs.) Like Guaman Poma, and mostly unlike Las Casas, Vargas Machuca saw that Africans increasingly played key roles in the emerging colonial Spanish American world. Their resistance had also to be dealt with, he might have argued, and harshly. This, too, was a specifically "Indian," or American, reality—the growing multitude of restless subalterns.

But whereas Africans and their descendants could be broadly classified as more or less recalcitrant auxiliaries of the Spanish, indigenous Americans were, as Guaman Poma went to great lengths to emphasize, "natural lords," a more complex problem in legal terms. By Vargas Machuca's time, the majority of Andeans and Mesoamericans were conquered if not fully colonized, ruled indirectly by native middlemen (and occasionally women) in the form of caciques, *capitanes*, and *gobernadores*. Guaman Poma was a striving, disgruntled one of these. Fringe-dwelling peoples, however, were a different story. Acosta had even applied categories to account for them, most being seemingly incapable of adjusting to colonial rule, except perhaps through the gentler yoke of mission life—and even then only after many generations. In terms of Spanish imperial policy, what had emerged by Vargas Machuca's time was convergence here, too, of unconquered Amerindians and maroons falling under the same rubric: backlands rebels, guerrilla challengers to crown authority, subversives to be rounded up and punished, criminals to be made examples of, put in their proper place, exiled, resettled.

Such a task, such an unglamorous "police" job (distinct from the conqueror's), was what fell to Bernardo de Vargas Machuca from the time he arrived in the Americas until his death. Although he tried desperately to cast himself alongside Cortés, Pizarro, and Jiménez de Quesada, he could not possibly join their league. Vargas Machuca's frustration at not being able to fully identify with these illustrious men was palpable, and in part it was this that led him to collapse time in his *Defense and Discourse of the Western Conquests*. As an Indiano knight-errant, he tilts against the phantom giant of Las Casas, seeking in vain to win back the honor of a generation of conquistadors long since dead and by this time unlikely to be helped by his "parallax view" interpretation of their acts. Vargas Machuca is in the end left struggling, as in the *Milicia Indiana*, to define himself as a colonial actor of some account.

Perhaps he was, even if we do not much sympathize with him. Like Guaman Poma, Vargas Machuca represented something new, something "Indian" and "colonial," and like his Andean inverse, he found that the everyday work of colonialism, whether construed as ongoing conquest or rebel "punishment," made him a victim as well as a perpetrator, a colonizer who was also colonized. In their writings, and through the act of writing, both men seem to have struggled to determine how best to collaborate with their shared king and pope even as they advanced disparate projects and saw the colonial world in almost perfectly opposing terms. Our natural sympathy for Guaman Poma may help us see beyond his complex and (to us) contradictory colonized self, his seeming myopia and self-obsession, whereas most of us are less likely—thanks to our "pro-anticolonial struggle" prejudices—to grant the same latitude to someone like Vargas Machuca.

Las Casas had succeeded in making the conquistadors and their successors suspect when they returned to Spain, and Vargas Machuca hated this fact—yet he could never undo it. The Indiano soldier was forever tainted by the charge of tyranny, and volunteering to fight new "Indian wars" would do nothing to help erase the stain. What were such alleged "baby-killers" to do? For Vargas Machuca, escape from this trap proved finally impossible. All he could do was try to defend himself like a self-made lawyer while also writing himself into history, hoping against hope to convince a distant monarch, if not us today, that it had all been worthwhile and that it all made perfect sense. At the risk of falling into the same traps that killed psychohistory in Nandy's day and before, I hope this essay has served to help explain how Spanish colonialism's defenders, too, were caught in moral and ethical binds, degraded and often left searching for a means to recover and redeem damaged and compromised selves.

Works Cited

Adorno, Rolena. *Guaman Poma: Writing and Resistance in Colonial Peru*. 2nd ed. Austin: University of Texas Press, 2000. Print.

Archivo General de Indias (AGI) Panama 45.

Archivo General de Indias, Patronato 164, Ramo 1: Probanzas de méritos y servicios de don Bernardo de Vargas Machuca.

Archivo General de la Nación (Bogotá, Colombia), Historia Civil.

Flores Hernández, Benjamín. "Pelear con el Cid después de muerto: Las *Apologías y discursos de las conquistas occidentales* de Bernardo de Vargas Machuca, en controversia con la *Brevísima relación de la destrucción de las Indias* de Fray Bartolomé de las Casas." *Estudios de Historia Novohispana* 10 (1991): 45–105. Print.

Friede, Juan. *Los Andakí, 1538–1947: Historia de la aculturación de una tribu selvática*. Mexico City: FCE, 1953. Print.

González Echevarría, Roberto. *Love and the Law in Cervantes*. New Haven: Yale University Press, 2005. Print.

Las Casas, Bartolomé de. *An Account, Much Abbreviated, of the Destruction of the Indies*. Ed. Franklin Knight. Trans. Andrew Hurley. Indianapolis: Hackett Publishing, 2003. Print.

Las Casas, Bartolomé de, and Bernardo de Vargas Machuca. *La destrucción de las Indias* and *Refutación de Las Casas*. Ed. Juan Guixé. Paris: Biblioteca Económica de Clásicos Castellanos, 1913. Print.

Martínez de Salinas, María Luisa. *Castilla ante el Nuevo Mundo: La trayectoría indiana del gobernador Bernardo de Vargas Machuca*. Valladolid: Diputación Provincial, 1991. Print.

Menéndez Pidal, Ramón. *Bartolomé de Las Casas: Su doble personalidad*. Madrid: Espasa-Calpe, 1963. Print.

Muldoon, James. *The Americas in the Spanish World Order: The Justification for Conquest in the Seventeenth Century*. Philadelphia: University of Pennsylvania Press, 1994. Print.

Nandy, Ashis. *The Intimate Enemy: Loss and Recovery of Self under Colonialism*. New Delhi: Oxford University Press, 1983. Print.

Poma de Ayala, Felipe Guaman. *The First New Chronicle and Good Government*. Trans. David Frye. Boston: Hackett Publishers, 2006. Print.

Solórzano Pereira, Juan de. *Política indiana*. 1629. Madrid: n.p., 1648. Print.

Vargas Machuca, Bernardo de. *The Indian Militia and Description of the Indies*. Ed. Kris Lane. Trans. Timothy Johnson. Durham, NC: Duke University Press, 2008. Print.

———. *Defending the Conquest: Bernardo de Vargas Machuca's Defense and Discourse of the Western Conquests*. Ed. Kris Lane. Trans. Timothy Johnson. University Park: Pennsylvania State University Press, 2010. Print.

———. *Apologías y discursos de las conquistas occidentales*. Ed. and trans. María Luisa Martínez de Salinas. Ávila: Junta de Castilla y León, 1993. Print.

———. "Carta de don Bernardo de Vargas Machuca a S.M. y discurso sobre la pacificación y allanamiento de los indios de Chile." *Colección de documentos inéditos para la historia de Chile*. 30 vols. Ed. José Toribio Medina. Santiago: FHBM, 1961. 5:119–32. Print.

———. "Apologías y discursos de las conquistas occidentales." *Colección de documentos inéditos para las historia de España*. 112 vols. Ed. José Sancho Rayón and Francisco de Zabalburu. Madrid: Miguel Ginesta, 1879. 71:201–309. Print.

———. *Milicia y descripción de las Indias*. Ed. Mariano Cuesta Domingo and Fernando López-Ríos Fernández. Valladolid: Seminario Iberoamericano de Descubrimientos y Cartografía, 2003. Print.

3

Voices of the *Altepetl*: Nahua Epistemologies and Resistance in the *Anales de Juan Bautista*

Ezekiel Stear

The clash of cultures in sixteenth-century Mexico produced multifaceted discourses that captured the stark reality of coloniality. Among those, Nahua historical codices have contributed to our understanding of native ways of knowing among the precontact and postcontact societies.[1] To the same end, the increasing study of early alphabetic texts in Nahuatl yields significant insights about the material and symbolic effects of the imposition of a new religion, culture, and economic order. This essay focuses on the *Anales de Juan Bautista*, a key yet understudied text that offers a distinctive portrayal of the complex perception of and reactions to the imperial mission and the acculturation of indigenous people in central Mexico. I am interested in how Nahua elites writing under the tutelage of the Franciscans were able to document conflict and accommodation to Spanish political control and religion in the postconquest urban setting of the Mexica capital. This important text demonstrates that indigenous agency against colonial power could not escape the colonizer's legacy, one that already ran deep by the mid-sixteenth century. The complex dynamics of resistance are particularly clear in the episodes I will discuss here in which indigenous leaders—Juan Tetón and Miguel Tecniuh—confront baptism and tribute respectively. These accounts offer a clear indigenous perspective on religious conflict and a critique of economic demands.

The *Anales de Juan Bautista* is comprised of 420 entries that recount events spanning 63 years (1519–1582) in the viceregal capital of New Spain and its surroundings.[2] Pages filled with vivid imagery set out details of urban life and of Amerindian material culture and religious practices. Significant events include the arrival of newly appointed officials, large festivals and religious processions, and notable offenses against colonial law. It is precisely in the narrations of these events—and in their intersections with the law—that the *Anales de Juan Bautista* communicates not only how the Mexicas survived Spanish rule but also how they understood and resisted colonial policies and the imposition of a new religion.

The year 1564 was a defining moment for native residents of the conquered city. In addition to the labor and agricultural produce required of the natives, the Spanish monarchy imposed a new monetary tribute. This event sent shockwaves through the Nahua community, whose economy was only partially monetized.[3] Luis Reyes García and Camilla Townsend argue that the central theme of the *Anales* is the struggle against this new economic imposition (Reyes 27–28; Townsend 639). Examples of disagreement with authorities abound in the text, which focuses on the first five years of the implementation of this tax policy, 1564–1569. Although efforts to overturn the monetary tribute failed, the native writers considered the dissent worth remembering. In order to fully understand in what light the indigenous elites cast public unrest against Spanish authority, I focus on their critical evaluations of the meaning and value of European cultural forms.

My reading places importance on the complex interactions between mistaken cultural attributions, the limits of public behavior that Spanish authorities imposed, and the Nahua response to Spanish rule, which while drawing upon Western cultural forms still succeeds in defying them by destabilizing their control. The fact that the Spanish and a sector of the Nahuas came to terms with each cultural form—an effect James Lockhart calls the "double mistaken identity"—leads to erroneous perceptions of cultural alterity (445). When the Nahuas misconstrued organizational features of Spanish religion and law, they often projected their own culture onto the invaders. This kind of misconstruing of Spanish ideologies becomes the immediate cause of what can be perceived as the failed opposition to colonial administration recorded in the text.

However, this "double mistaken identity" does not alone account for the distinctly Nahua responses to the adoption of Spanish cultural values and ways of life in the text. Key to identifying these misattributions are deployments of political power that signal the limits of what the supreme authority of the Spanish court, the Council of Indies, and its colonial administrators considered acceptable. The tacit and arbitrary preference on the part of conquerors for their own cultural forms—Homi Bhabha's "rules of recognition"—is the assumed mode the Spaniards use to justify further repression of the indigenous population. In this way, confrontations, censure, and other forms of violence that the Spanish direct against the Nahuas allow their victims a greater self-understanding of native ideologies and innovative cultural forms used in resistance to Spanish power.

Nahua Intelligentsia, the *Anales*, and Rotating Authorship

Considered in an isolated manner, the name of the manuscript (*Anales de Juan Bautista*) itself points to its potential usefulness as a testimony in a legal situation. In contrast to its 419 entries written in Nahuatl, only one is written in Spanish, identifying one Nahua writer as "Juan Bautista, *alguacil*," a position roughly equivalent to "constable" or "bailiff" (Reyes 136). The title suggests that colonial authorities may have used these *Anales* to help record violations of the law.[4] However, the organization of the text, its varied topics not directly related to any tribunal or to legal questions, and the circumstances of its production signal complexities not present in legal documents of the period.[5] On the other hand, we are faced with a text that, though its title identifies it as *anales*, corresponds directly to neither European nor traditional Nahua categories.

A European writing genre, annals first appeared in the Middle Ages. They document local events from the perspective of a writer or various writers over a number of years (White 4–8). The practice of the textual preservation of local events also has deep roots for the Nahuas. Postconquest evidence attests to the importance of a traditional Nahua pictorial genre known as *xiuhpohualli*, used to provide yearly accounts of the actions of local political figures and memorable events in general (Lockhart 378–80). The Spanish invasion and evangelism also included efforts to teach alphabetical writing to the *tlacuiloque*, the Nahua painters of traditional pictorial texts. Places meant for this kind of teaching and conversion—such as the Colegio Imperial de Santa Cruz de Tlatelolco—allowed for the Nahua appropriation of alphabetic writing and methods of preserving local events, such as annals.[6] Thus, the preconquest xiuhpohualli yearly account was combined with the annals genre, resulting in a uniquely Nahua way of capturing local events on paper (Reyes 24).

Whereas the lettered city of Ángel Rama is comprised of intellectuals from the dominant sectors of society, the indigenous elites writing the *Anales de Juan Bautista* had native readers in mind. The *Anales* takes its place among other sixteenth- and seventeenth-century annalistic Mexican texts, including the *Anales de Tlatelolco*, the *Anales de Cuauhtitlan*, and Domingo Francisco Chimalpahin's *Relaciones*. Annals written in alphabetic Nahuatl from this period connect preconquest history to contemporary events. Moreover, annalistic literature responded to local needs of the *altepetl*.[7] In its organization, the *Anales de Juan Bautista* reflects a pattern of rotating authorship, allowing for many scribes over sixty-three years to offer their perspectives on events in their altepetl (Townsend 642).

Details in the text identify San Juan Moyotlan—the southwest quarter of Mexico City in the sixteenth century—as the altepetl of its authors. Luis Reyes García, editor of the Spanish and Nahuatl bilingual version of the *Anales*, supports the idea of corporate authorship, narrowing down the group of Nahua writers to a workshop in the barrio of Nacaltitlan in San Juan Moyotlan. He links this group of scribes with the Franciscan friars' literacy project but argues that they maintained preconquest *tlacuilo* forms of knowledge keeping (Reyes 27–28).

The *Anales de Juan Bautista* represents another form of history making for those trained in the alphabetic writing in Nahuatl introduced by the Franciscans. These authors use the text as a means to marshal the power of their *altepetl* by employing a wide array of genres and forms of representation such as annals, testimony, legal discourse, and visual elements. Multiple narrative perspectives thus become key to understanding indigenous views of resistance in the text. As Camilla Townsend observes, the use of multiple genres and vantage points follows Nahua preconquest rhetorical strategies. The combination of genres written from different perspectives within the Nahua population would have strengthened the text's arguments for the intended native readers (642). Lockhart and Reyes García have both commented on the sense of immediacy that characterizes the *Anales de Juan Bautista*, suggesting that much of it was written as the events unfolded.[8]

The pressures placed on the Nahuas by colonial rule, in both a quotidian sense and on the plain of collective metaphysical imaginaries, form a powerful impetus for community action in the *Anales de Juan Bautista*. The episode of the counter-evangelical preaching of Juan Tetón illustrates native opposition to Christianization, while on the economic front, a public protest against Spanish tribute policy also shows how an indigenous elite was able to proclaim their rights as they resisted the new economic order. Both of these episodes bring to light indigenous engagement with colonial power structures. The perceptions of and reactions to Spanish rule emerge from the tensions and negotiations between the colonizers and the colonized. Nothing is clean-cut in this ideological contact zone in which indigenous intellectuals employ the episodes in a manner that reveals their views on the Spanish and their adaptation to their culture. As I will demonstrate here, writing in the *Anales* cannot be disentangled from indigenous agency and persistent cultural negotiations.

Juan Tetón: Nahua Prophet of Rebellion

The multiple genres present in the text recall the preconquest role of the tlacuilo as a preserver of local indigenous lore and spirituality. The tlacuilo acted as both the painter and the interpreter of images and glyphs communicating important information on the cosmos and the dealings of supernatural beings with humans. In the production of codices, he was, above all, a keeper of ancestral myths and symbols (León-Portilla 172–74). Indeed, even after the conquest the Franciscan friars inadvertently supported this religious role when training the Nahua scribes in alphabetic writing (Lockhart 332).

In the *Anales*, the presence of the disgruntled Juan Tetón highlights the continuing importance of the tlacuilo as interpreter of the sacred. Tetón, a *macehual* (commoner) from Michmaloya, an altepetl south of Mexico City, communicated a message critical of the evangelization and dietary changes brought by the Spanish. Juan Tetón challenges the colonial religious establishment and draws attention to native anxieties about the abandonment of traditional Nahua beliefs and practices. By recording this important account of a critical stance toward Christianity, the amanuenses indicate that religion is a crucial intellectual topic for the members of the community. In fact, as Reyes García points out, it is religious conviction itself that here becomes a mode of indigenous resistance in the *Anales de Juan Bautista* (45).

Amid what appear to be reaffirmations of imperial authority, at least two kinds of subversive content appear in this passage: apocalyptic warnings and spiritual remedies. At the beginning of the account, the narrative voice explains how Juan Tetón's message led the people astray in Cohuatepec, a community outside of Mexico City: "quintlapololti quimiztlacahui" (157) (he caused the people to err, he lied). In so doing, the officious voice seems to reaffirm orthodoxy and imperial authority. Curiously, this opening does nothing to censure the details of Juan Tetón's subversive communication, even though the authors know their manuscript will circulate among their fellow Nahuas. This suggests that the indigenous authors have deemed Tetón's speech worth circulating as a way to voice their own disagreement with aspects of Christianity and new dietary customs. The free indirect discourse of the narrator and the complicity of native listeners reinforce the idea of the writers' implicit support for Tetón's message (Arias 43).

Juan Tetón calls for the people to remember the ways of their ancestors, reminding his listeners that Nahua religion has always foretold that at the end of the Age of the Fifth Sun, demonic beings would come to devour humanity. To this he adds that due to the rampant abandonment of traditional beliefs, all those who had become baptized Catholics would be transformed into the European animals they had been consuming since the invaders' arrival:

> [T]laxiccaquican yn ame huantin quen anquitohua ca ye anquimati yn quitotihui in tocolhuan yn iquac toxiuhmolpiliz ca centlayohuaz hualtemozque yn tzitzimime in techquazque yhuan yn iquac necuapaloz. Yn omoquatequique yn oquineltocaque yn dios mocuepazque. Yn huacaxnacatl quiqua çan no yehuatl mocuepaz. Yn pitzonacatl quiqua çan no yehuatl mecuepaz. Yn ychcanacatl quiqua çan no yehuatl mocuepaz yhuan yn ichcaayatl quiquemi. (Reyes 156–58)

> (Listen, all of you, and tell me your opinion. You know what our grandparents said, that when the end of the year count was tied, that all would become dark and the tzitzimime[9] would come down to eat us. Then many people would be transformed. Those who were baptized and believed in God will be transformed. Those who ate the meat of cows will become cows. Those who ate the meat of pigs will become pigs. Those who ate lamb shall turn into lambs, and likewise those who wear woolen cloaks.)[10]

The consumption of these domesticated animals and the use of their products are presented as metaphors for harmful native assimilation of European customs. In addition, these warnings reveal cultural and spiritual anxieties. Foreign goods have displaced local dietary traditions and dress. Nonetheless, Tetón does not consider the presence and use of these European animals to be threatening because of the accompanying economic changes. Rather, this prophetic voice stresses the ritual damage that these elements cause to society. Tetón critiques these aspects of European culture for their effects on the body and, by extension, on every individual's relationship to the gods. Sustaining one's body with foreign food represents a rejection of the metaphysical order, which prescribes traditional Nahua dietary customs. The prophet describes the shift from Nahua domesticated animals and food consumption to those of the Spaniards—a process of both imposition and appropriation—as a loss of humanity. The zoomorphic transformation, as a disaster that Tetón forecasts, may thus be understood as a spiritual punishment for abandoning native dietary customs, dress, and agriculture.

Of greater urgency to Juan Tetón, however, are European forms that are explicitly ceremonial. As a remedy to the impending apocalypse and to avoid the punishment of being transformed into European livestock, Tetón offers his listeners solutions in ritual form:

> In axcan amohicpa ninoquixtia aocmo huecauh ye mochiuaz yn tlamahuiçolli yn tlacamo anquineltocazque yn namechilhuia ca ynhuan anmocuepazque ynic anpatizque ca namechpaquilliz ynic oanmoquatequique ca namechpopolhuiz ynic amo anmiquizque ye huel polihuiz. (158)

> (Now I have done my duty and it is up to you, because there is not much time left before these wonders happen. If you do not believe, I tell you that you will be transformed with the rest of them. In order that you may recover, I will wash away what they baptized you with; I will give you forgiveness so that you will not die in the coming destruction.)[11]

As has already been argued, Tetón's discursive medium and his message are hybrid in nature and show the effects of syncretism in textual form (Arias 43). This written account presupposes an oral message to be conveyed widely to Nahuas in the region. A religious counterdiscourse is preserved and communicated in alphabetic Nahuatl, which appropriates the idea of a holy writ as the preferred means of communicating beliefs.

After his first address to a crowd in Cohuatepec, he sends a written copy of his preaching to Atlapolco, which recalls the importance of geographical expansion in evangelization projects. Both of these locales are near present-day Xochimilco, in the southern part of Mexico City. For this reason it is also clear that the native annalists express agreement at least with parts of this religious rebellion. Not only have they preserved it for posterity, but they have also mentioned another written copy of Juan Tetón's preaching intended to do the same and spread his message beyond their locale. The medium of alphabetic writing in this case is a carrier of common characteristics of apocalyptic discourse: the use of fear and a sense of immediacy used to inspire religious conviction. This passage shows appropriations from Spanish evangelizers including a written prophetic discourse, itinerancy, and a rhetoric of apocalyptic fear. Yet the content of Tetón's preaching radically departs from that of the friars.

Certainly, it is reasonable to assume from this account alone that the authors of the *Anales de Juan Bautista* have already encountered similar strategies in friars' sermons. However, what is notable in this case is that Tetón has appropriated these techniques in order to *de*-evangelize converts. This prophetic voice carries a message of duty to undo Spaniards' evangelical efforts through a series of counteractive rituals intended to reverse the effects of the invaders' religion. Representing such opposition in textual form requires consciously appropriating aspects of Catholic ritual while at the same time rejecting its doctrinal teaching. This process of negotiation becomes evident as the text weaves elements of mimesis and subversion together to continue Tetón's denunciation of foreign spirituality.

In fact, many of Tetón's predictions, warnings, and instructions parallel elements of Catholicism, attempting to engage and resist the colonizers' beliefs in kind. In this approach, Juan Tetón's invective incorporates values and beliefs from traditional Nahua religion.[12] In the final analysis, this native preacher's vision is neither preconquest religion nor a simple set of parallels with Catholicism, but rather a product of intentional choices alternating between the appropriation and the rejection of European cultural forms.[13] The armature of this prophetic denunciation is itself revealed to be Christian ritual.

The cornerstone of Juan Tetón's discursive representation is the Catholic sacramental system. To undo baptism, he requires listeners to partake of an adapted traditional purification ceremony in which the participant receives a ritual washing of the head. To save oneself from death and destruction, it further becomes necessary to obtain Juan Tetón's absolution for the transgression of following non-native ways. These alternatives to Catholic baptism and confession are in this case neither European nor part of preconquest Nahua practices. Rather, they are new ritual measures designed to appropriate the rhetorical and institutional powers of the conqueror, question Catholicism's validity for the Nahua, and offer a form of spiritual cleansing intended to assure the community's survival.

With an appearance that makes use of what he considers the optimal elements of preconquest religion and Christianity, this native leader attempts to seize back official religious power from the Church. A spiritual movement expressed through forms familiar both in terms of the past and present of the newly converted indigenous readers and hearers of this text would satisfy their need for continuity on a ritual plain. In spite of any differences from Nahua religious practices before the conquest, the native spirit is preserved in a reverence for traditional gods, ancestors, and dietary customs. Tetón offers pardon for the sin of conversion to Christianity and reincorporation into a remnant of those who follow traditional beliefs.

The Christian underpinnings of this nativist eschatological discourse are unmistakable and have been correctly linked to themes present in the Book of Revelation. For example, there is no coincidence in the names: the Apostle John was traditionally held as the author of Revelation; Juan Bautista bears his name, as does the *barrio* of San Juan Moyotlan, mentioned sixteen times in the text. To this we add the name of Juan Tetón himself (Arias 45–46). While the concurrence of names and themes between the flagship of Christian apocalyptic writings and this text are intriguing, the parallels between the two run much deeper. The manner in which these themes have been imbedded in this discourse sheds light on its rhetorical power for the Nahua reader. Indeed, cultural accretions from European sources have passed through the evangelizing friars' discourses to the native scribes of this text. It is equally useful, however, to emphasize not just content but the common processes that lead to the composition of prophecy. This draws attention to parallels—intentional or not—that show how indigenous mimesis of Christian apocalyptic discourse carries with it a mimesis of the mechanisms that generate the prophetic genre itself.

As Soren Kirkegaard observed, life can only be understood backwards, although it must be lived forward (111). Tetón's summary of how the Nahua have gone astray gives voice to collective memories of the conquest. In recalling the ways of the ancestors, he literally bases the authority of his discourse on eyewitnesses' accounts of the invaders' arrival. The anxieties of this discourse at the same time are forward-looking as Tetón predicts future calamities for those who do not repent and follow his advice. In addition to his warnings about the transformation of human beings into livestock, in the majority of his sermon Tetón bemoans the infamous events that have led to the Nahuas' current state of affairs. The retrospective formation of prophecy, as Tzvetan Todorov has observed, certainly fulfilled the function of providing a satisfying explanation for the Spaniards' arrival and military conquest in Mesoamerica (84–86). Todorov has shown how Moctezuma consulted the Mayan *Chilam Balam* to help him understand the Spaniards' arrival, and how Bernardino de Sahagún, Diego Durán, and Toribo de Motolinía noted the indigenous premonitions of the loss of their civilization.[14] The postconquest gathering and interpretation of these sources, however, remains affected by the conquest itself. Juan Tetón's predictions of crisis can therefore be understood as reflections on events that had already happened.

In light of this, the threat of future calamity in the *Anales de Juan Bautista* only enhances its power to convince the Nahua reader based on that which has already been established. In the formulation of this eschatological speech, it is thus necessary for some of the events to have already occurred; otherwise, the prophet loses credibility. Historical criticism of the Book of Revelation itself has noted this fact. Juan Tetón's warnings are therefore consciously directed toward a Nahua audience that has already experienced the agricultural and demographic disasters he describes.[15] Both future punishments for Nahuas who refuse to return to traditional ways and divine retribution against the Spaniards have thus been given a sense of imminence. The threat of these consequences—directly perceptible to listeners—strengthens Tetón's argument.

A similar argument drawing upon the lived experience of a faith community and its anxieties about the future forms an axiological pillar of the Book of Revelation. Written at the close of the first century and addressed to seven congregations in Asia Minor, this prophetic text recounts a great persecution against Christians. According to the account, anyone who does not bow to the "beast" (an anti-Christian governor) and take his mark on his or her forehead and right hand will be barred from buying or selling (Rev. 13:17–18).[16] Rather than considering this prediction a simple projection into the future, many critical scholars of the New Testament have linked the veneration of the beast figure and the economic sanctions levied against Christians to customs and policies present during the Roman emperor Domitian's reign (Collins, *Crisis* 104–05). The negativity directed against Christians based on his policies reached a notable level of intensity in Asia Minor, the precise region where the first recipients of this text resided. While the temporal economic levies against Christians are one preoccupation in the book, the future consequences of venerating the beast are of greater concern. According to the text, those who worship the beast and take his mark for the sake of material security will suffer unending punishment in a lake of fire and brimstone (20:10, 21:8). Yet, just as Tetón proposes solutions to the Nahua, so the writer of the Book of Revelation assures his faith community that unbending Christian belief and refusal to worship the beast will save them (22:3–5).

The parallels between the Book of Revelation and Juan Tetón's prophetic discourse have roots in similar circumstances behind their composition. Both texts are produced by marginalized writers in the shadows of empires who face negative economic pressures on the basis of their religion. Audiences of both are encouraged to reject dominant societal economic practices through highly visible and subversive actions. While it remains uncertain to what extent the scribes of the *Anales* manuscript were aware of these similarities, clearly both texts call for this kind of seditious conversion. Thus, one result of these discourses is to provide the people with concrete methods of resistance to their respective governments, along with the hope of attaining spiritual purification.

Apocalyptic discourse—an aspect this nativist discourse shares with early Christian writings—outlines specific means for group survival. Both Catholicism and the religious rebellion of Juan Tetón require the renunciation of present misdeeds and promise the return of mythic ideals. The moral demands of this discourse reject the imposed Spanish economy, promoting instead the revival of local preconquest agriculture. The denunciation of European domesticated animals recalls to listeners the grandeur of the highly productive *chinampa* agriculture practiced in Tenochtitlan, which sustained the entire city.[17] In the face of the radical destruction of the Nahuas' former way of life, accompanied by a drastic decline in traditional agriculture, this call to action uses religion as the means to repair a ruined economy. A return to traditional food customs restores humanity and spares the community from a grim zoomorphic punishment.

Undoubtedly, apocalyptic discourse uses fear of the threat of punishment to influence its audience. However, in order to mobilize community action, this fear has been coupled with hope. The confidence based on ancestral beliefs is here communicated in the form of an open-air sermon. From observations of Franciscan friars preaching in open air chapels, the Nahua scribes of this manuscript surmised that such an action would not draw negative attention or reprisals from the Spanish soldiers. Hence, preaching is proposed as a method of peaceful resistance in the *Anales de Juan Bautista*. This peaceful approach rings true to Tetón's postapocalyptic vision: the nonviolent restoration of a Nahua economy with the collective voluntary exclusion of Spanish animals and commerce. The oppressor now faces the strident appropriation of his own theological and metaphysical principles, poised against him.

Problematic to the Spaniards, nonetheless, is the idea that another sacramental system could replace that of Catholicism. For Spanish agents, only Catholic sacraments are valid, meaning that any non-Church-sanctioned parallel to baptism and confession is blasphemy and must be swiftly punished. Juan Tetón, along with seven of his followers who have taken the ritual washing in order to efface their Christian baptism, are imprisoned and subjected to the Inquisition.

The apocalyptic rebellion of Juan Tetón, albeit a failed attempt to appropriate Church authority and foster the widespread resurgence of traditional beliefs, remains incorporated in written form in the *Anales*. The Nahua audience of this text has been warned to use less publicly visible ways to preserve traditional religion and values. By testing an explicit discourse against Spanish repression of native religion, the *altepetl* learns the futility of such direct modes of religious resistance.

Juan Tetón's rebellion points to how social mobilization fails when the Spaniards refuse to recognize its resonances with Christian prophecy. However, it succeeds as a precedent for future resistance. In retrospect, we also observe that this rebellion serves as an early instance of Christian-inspired rhetoric at the service of indigenous rights. Yet this text is unique in that it appears to do so without a Bartolomé de Las Casas or Bernardino de Sahagún mediating between cultures. Direct protest against civil authority also appears in the *Anales* as a collective cry of opposition to the new tribute. When the city reaches a crisis point, the politics of indigenous writing as a form of resistance become transparent.

In Vain We Contradicted Them: The Riot of Miguel Tecniuh

On the evening of February 18, 1564, Miguel Tecniuh, a *pilli* (noble), enters the Royal Audience with a group of other Nahuas of his rank. The purpose of their visit is to pay their tribute to the Spanish-appointed native governor who will in turn give it to the Spaniards. Yet the narrative voices of these annals present this as a unique opportunity to tell high-ranking Nahua authorities what they truly think about the newly imposed policy. The governor receives their tribute and explains that he and his aides have done their best to dissuade the Spanish from this policy, but that their influence has been in vain. To this, Miguel Tecniuh abruptly replies:

> [C]a otoconcac in timexicatl in titenochcatl ynic tonmotequitiliz yn iuh oquimotlalili yn totlatocatzin in Magestad cuix çan nican omoyocox cuix no ceceme tlatoque nican oquitlalique ca ye ixquich cahuitl yn ticnemitia ye axcan chiquacentetl metztli yn oc nen titlacuepa aoc hueliti aocmo titlahuelcaquililo auh onehuatica yn amotlatocauh cuix aoctle amopan quichihua cuix oamexiccauh cuix oquixicauh yn icuitlapil yn iatlapal auh ye cuel iquac on ye axcan chiquacentetl metztli yn nican anquimocaquiltico auh yn axcan maximotetlahuilli yn timerimo maxiccaquilti yn motlahuilanal maximotecalpanhuilli yn nican ticmocahuilia yn meliotzin. (Reyes 214)

> (You, from Mexico Tenochtitlan, have heard that you will pay tribute as our Lord and Majesty has decreed. Was this conceived here? Did each one of the local indigenous rulers decree it? For a long while now we have negotiated, for six months now and in vain we contradicted them. It's impossible; our petition was rejected. Now your governor is present here. Does he no longer do anything for all of you? Has he neglected you? Has he abandoned his vassals? You have come here to listen to what has happened for the last six months. And now, since you are governor [merino], you tell the people; inform those who depend on you; you go from house to house, you who turn in the money.)

In this case, Tecniuh articulates a series of rhetorical questions to underscore the force of the answers his listeners already know. This cathartic discussion with the native governor allows the nobles to vocalize the imperial subjects' collective dissatisfaction. Tecniuh and the other nobles, as representatives of the entire altepetl, set off a chain of events with unexpected consequences.

After six months of lobbying in vain against the tribute, the release of frustration in Miguel Tecniuh's battery of questions unleashes a riot in the governor's patio. As one of the most vivid spectacles of these annals, the commotion continues for seven entries, indicating the importance the writers place not only on Tecniuh's speech but also on the rioters' own words:

> Auh yn iquac otzonquiz ytlatol niman ye ic neacomanallo auh in goernador oc nen quihualito matlapitzallo niman ye ic netenhuiteco tlacahuaco niman ye hualtemohuac tlatzintla netenhuiteco yhuan mochi tlacatl quito can ticuizque auh ixquich çihuatl yllamatzin in chocaque yhuan cenca quallanque auh ce tlacatl quito ytoca Huixtopolcatl Amanalco chane quito aquinon tlatohua cuix tlillancalqui cuix quauhnochtli cuix hezhuahuacatl tle mochihua tlapaltontli achac momati. (215–17)

> (And when he had finished talking, the people began to riot and the governor cried in vain, "Play music with flutes and wind instruments." Then the people came out from the meeting yelling and beating their mouths. They ran down to the foot of the palace yelling. The people shouted: "How will we handle this problem?" And the elderly women were crying and getting very angry. A man from the neighboring Amanalco called Huixtopolcatl cried, "Who of authority is speaking? Perhaps it is Tlilancalqui. Perhaps it is Quauhnochtli. Perhaps it is Ezhuahuacatl. What has happened to the peasantry, and what are we to think?")

Here, Nahua perspectives on due process conflict with and decenter the imposed Spanish legal system. A *tlilancalqui* was a lower-level judge who began a trial, while the terms *quauhnochtli* and *ezhuahuacatl* have a meaning similar to "executioner" (215). Huixtopocatl, the man from the neighboring Amanalco, uses terms from the Nahua's preconquest legal system with the expectation that a trial would settle the people's grievances. However, the expectation that the native has taken for granted is entirely lost on the Spanish. Suddenly, officials arrive with drawn swords to disperse the crowd. They manage to restore order only after threatening the crowds with bloodshed and arresting Miguel Tecniuh along with nine more nobles. They establish a curfew with the warning that any "mexicano" found in the street will be arrested and join the incarcerated indigenous leaders.

For the swordsmen, the scene is simply unintelligible shouting stemming from an internal native affair. The Nahuas, for their part, recognize the Spaniards' authority, yet the application of their own legal culture remains inscrutable to the Spanish. As Homi Bhabha comments, "it is not that the voice of authority is at a loss for words. It is, rather, that the colonial discourse has reached that point when, faced with the hybridity of its objects, the presence of power is revealed as something other than what its rules of recognition assert" (121). The Nahua projection of the indigenous legal system onto the Spaniards fails and is interpreted by authorities as a justification for the use of violence to enforce their law. By recounting the repression of an individual, Miguel Tecniuh; a group, his fellow tribute collectors; and the entire community of protesters in the courtyard, the scribes attempt to show an altepetl-wide effort of resistance to monetary tribute. In this crisis, everyone—from nobles to commoners—collectively shows nonconformity and attempts to physically reclaim formerly native-controlled urban space.

One of the most telling aspects of this episode is the demonstrators' occupation of the patio and palace vicinity. Taking for granted their right to assemble in an area familiar to them, the indigenous find they are no longer in their home city. *Tenochtitlan* seems to have disappeared within the Hispanized *Ciudad de México*. Even so, they force colonial authority to reckon with the indigenous capacity for reclaiming spaces. By imposing a curfew in response, the Spanish confirm their control over the places that the Nahua can access and the hours they may be in public. The band of swordsmen effectively signals the erasure of the authority of the indigenous nobles. Instead, the Nahua distinction between noble and commoner has been suspended and reduced to the conqueror's simple opposition of *castellano* or *mexicano*.

The riot of Miguel Tecniuh also shows an implicit projection of the cellular model of altepetl organization with its rotating leadership, extending it to the whole of the Spanish empire. Although the indigenous authorities of Mexico-Tenochtitlan consider themselves on equal footing with authorities in Spain and viceregal Mexico, clearly they are reduced to vassals. The misunderstanding of Spanish political organization, together with the religious discrimination and other essentialist strategies arrayed against the indigenous, make it impossible for them to successfully relate their altepetl of Mexico with the larger imagined altepetl of "castellan" of the invaders (134). Nahua attempts to participate in Spanish politics from their altepetl paradigm are incompatible with the quasi-feudal system of the Spanish under which they now live.

Miguel Tecniuh begins his speech to the governor with a different sort of projection: by addressing one of the nobles in collusion with Spanish authorities as a *tenochca*, a resident of Tenochtitlan. In this sense, when the Spanish soldiers suppress the riot, it not only affects the bodies of the protesters but also tells of colonial authority's disavowal of native civic identity. The Spanish guards, who pacify the crowd, would not call any indigenous resident of the city a tenochca, since in their minds Tenochtitlan no longer exists. In his harangue against the Spanish-appointed native governor, Tecniuh reminds his superior of their Nahua traditions and ethnic identity; and based on these affiliations, he demands solidarity. Similarly, the governor's indifference to his own altepetl highlights the imperative of loyalty: according to the scribes, protest against unfair imperial policies is one mark of the true Nahua.

The native projection of their cultural expectations onto the Spanish combined with the Spanish disavowal of indigenous culture makes this opposition to the Crown ineffectual. Nonetheless, for the Nahua such events are not without their instructive elements. Future protesters may take a number of observations from this account as useful knowledge for continued opposition. The fact that the rest of the altepetl joins Miguel Tecniuh's confrontation could persuade readers of the *Anales* that the majority of the altepetl still opposed tribute. In addition, this episode could be used as a sort of summary of the counter-tribute actions native leaders had taken up to that point. By recording the riot, the authors of these annals wished not only to perpetuate this message of solidarity but also to suggest the possibility of mobilizing the entire altepetl to defy imperial policy and preserve traditional ways.

(Con)textualizing the Voices of the Altepetl

Failed protest does not eliminate native epistemological processes. In terms of how the *tlacuilo* reveal their resistance in the *Anales de Juan Bautista*, we read small successes between the lines of apparent failure. The use of free indirect discourse allows the compiling scribes to express views contrary to those of colonial authority. This same technique gives them a safe personal distance from the critique articulated in the *Anales*. The approach makes possible a wider distribution of anti-imperialist material without risking the writing project altogether. While ostensibly in this manuscript the Nahua are unable to reform imperial policies, they manage to recover significant examples of cultural survival for posterity.

The Nahua participate in complex strategies of rejection and appropriation of Spanish cultural forms, testing their viability through trial-and-error experimentation. Juan Tetón's religious rebellion shows resonances between the Nahuas' situation of oppression and the persecution some early Christians faced. Beyond a simple appropriation of saints' names and ritual forms, the scribes at this point betray the same mechanisms of the retroactive formulation of written prophecy also disclosed in the New Testament. Nahua discourse, in conjunction with the over-appropriation of sacramental appearances of this movement, caused the immediate censure of the prophet. Yet the scribes have accomplished the long-term preservation of a subversive message and a valuation of the sanctity of traditional agriculture and diet.

Similarly, the riot of Miguel Tecniuh, while achieving no immediate advances for the anti-tribute cause, shows its success as an unintentional action of reconnaissance. These native intellectuals have demonstrated through this confrontation that the Spanish give validity neither to their legal claims nor to their ethnic and toponymic distinctions. The world has shifted, and those who will survive must adapt. Yet this realization stands alongside a record for Nahua contemporaries and their posterity demonstrating that all avenues for negotiation and revolt against the tribute had been exhausted. Through the fires of experience, the text still proposes at least two kinds of viable resistance to imperialism. The text encourages the indigenous appropriation of alphabetic writing, which did prove useful for the dissemination of their protest. Likewise, there is an insistence on defending tradition in the face of mandated Spanish technological and economic changes.

By uncovering the causes of failed resistance to imperialism in the text, this reading of the *Anales de Juan Bautista* offers ways to understand the motivation behind some of the first voices of native opposition to colonial policies in sixteenth-century Mexico City. In the recounting of Juan Tetón's prophetic discourse and the riot of Miguel Tecniuh, we see protests against both evangelization and the Crown's tribute policy. Yet the text also contains criticism of ecclesiastical authority and of the Spanish treatment of indigenous women and the elderly. The wide-ranging nature of the *Anales de Juan Bautista* contributes to its relevance in studies of Nahua epistemologies. It documents how indigenous intellectuals critically engaged imperial policy as they also sought accommodation to new ways of life. Beyond recovering Mexica memory, it records key power struggles in the first years after the conquest, helping to provide a more nuanced understanding of cultural, ethnic, and textual *mestizaje* in the region.

Notes

1. See Boone and Mignolo, Brotherston (*Painted Books*), and Rabasa.
2. The Biblioteca Lorenzo Botourini de la Basílica de Guadalupe in Mexico City holds

the earliest copy of the manuscript. It consists of 30 folded *fojas* bound along their creases into a single volume of sixty well-conserved and legible pages (Reyes 19–21).
3. Ruggiero Romano provides a comprehensive study of the colonial economies of New Spain with attention to the different means of exchange used among Spaniards and the Nahuas.
4. James Lockhart concludes that one of the authors, who was in close relationship with the cabildo, asked for a written report of how tribute law had been enforced (382).
5. Tavárez and Lopes provide two important studies on the Inquisition in sixteenth-century Mexico City and their indictment of indigenous leaders for their beliefs. Both scholars make extensive use of testimonies from tribunal archives.
6. José Jorge Klor de Alva and Rocío Cortés are important sources on the role of power associated with the Franciscan literacy project. Klor de Alva describes how alphabetic writing was a tool of religious conversion used by editing friars to mask their interlocutors' true opinions of Christianity. Cortés explains how the Colegio de Tlatelolco managed to teach alphabetic writing and Latin to indigenous intellectuals. Ironically, the institution contributed to its own decline when the Crown deemed its activities subversive and decreased its funding (93–94).
7. For the Nahuas, the basic unit of organization is the altepetl, a settlement comprised of neighborhood-like groupings, which in turn were made up of individual households. Fernández and García Zambrano's edited volume *Territorialidad y paisaje en el altepetl del siglo XVI* offers an excellent introduction to Nahua territorial and political organization.
8. Reyes García maintains that the text is a compilation from many scribes who recorded events from their communities (27–28). He also describes the collection of tribute (29–40). On the style of the manuscript, Lockhart claims, "No annals entry has ever given me as full a sense of immediacy, of drawing the writer and the reader into the observed action, as when this author [wrote] for May 28, 1568" (382).
9. Reyes García cites the *Códice Magliabechi* to explain the meaning of *tzitzimime* as supernatural beings of death and destruction that appear at the end of a cosmic age to kill humanity (157).
10. I am grateful to John Sullivan (Instituto de Docencia e Investigación Etnológica de Zacatecas), who assisted with the translations.
11. Juan Tetón also gives instructions on how to prepare for the coming famine by gathering wild turkeys and other native plants (158).
12. For example, archeological evidence exists that the Mexica used water in ceremonies of moral and spiritual purification. See Miller and Taube (183–84).
13. Rather than understanding syncretism as an accidental mixture of beliefs and religious practices, I agree with anthropologist Richard Haley, who posits an intricate system of negotiations, affirmations, and negations that result in a constantly evolving spirituality among the Nahuas. Haley describes aspects of this ongoing relationship with Catholicism with special reference to an isolated Nahua community's veneration of saints. Serge Gruzinski in the first two chapters of *The Mestizo Mind* also provides

a nuanced understanding of how *mestizaje* leads to conscious rather than incidental innovation.
14. Todorov (1992) argues that indigenous groups reinterpreted the *Chilam Balam* and Tarascan prophecies in light of the Spaniards' arrival in Mesoamerica. Similarly, he points out how the indigenous people interviewed by Durán, Motolinía, and Sahagún would have necessarily provided information about pre-Hispanic prophecies transformed by the experience of conquest. Pithily, Todorov concludes, "Prophecy is memory" (85).
15. It would have been credible to Tetón's listeners that some people had already received their punishment. He cites examples of well-known local figures—the children of one "don Alonso" and other community leaders—who have already turned into livestock (85).
16. Adela Yarbro Collins and Elizabeth Schussler Fiorenza both offer well-documented and balanced examinations of economic, political, and theological currents key to the composition of the Book of Revelation.
17. These island plots, constructed of reeds and silt from Lake Texcoco, produced harvests several times per year and supported the dense population of Tenochtitlan. See Lockhart (61–68) and Gruzinski (*The Aztecs* 22).

Works Cited

Arias, Santa. "La visión Nahua ante la conquista espiritual: Milenarismo e hibridez en los *Anales de Juan Bautista.*" *Ensayos de cultura virreinal latinoamericana*. Ed. Luis Millones, Takahiro Kato, and Ulises Zevallos Aguilar. Lima: Fondo Editorial de la Facultad de Ciencias Sociales de la Universidad Nacional Mayor de San Marcos, 2007. 33–52. Print.

Bhabha, Homi K. "Signs Taken for Wonders." *The Postcolonial Studies Reader*. Ed. Bill Ashcroft, Gareth Griffiths, and Helen Tiffin. New York: Routledge, 1995. 29–35. Print.

Boone, Elizabeth Hill, and Walter Mignolo, eds. *Writing Without Words: Alternative Literacies in Mesoamerica and the Andes*. Durham, NC: Duke University Press, 1994. Print.

Brotherston, Gordon. *Painted Books from Mexico: Codices from UK Collections and the World They Represent*. London: British Museum Press, 1995. Print.

Collins, Adela Yarbro. *Crisis and Catharsis: The Power of the Apocalypse*. Philadelphia: Westminster Press, 1984. Print.

———. *Early Christian Apocalypticism: Genre and Social Setting*. Decatur: Scholar's Press, 1986. Print.

Cortés, Rocío. "The Colegio Imperial de Santa Cruz de Tlatelolco and Its Aftermath: *Nahua* Intellectuals and the Spiritual Conquest of Mexico." *A Companion to Latin American Literature and Culture*. Ed. Sara Castro-Klarén. Malden: Blackwell, 2008. Print.

Fernández Christlieb, Federico, and Ángel Julián García Zambrano, eds. *Territorialidad y paisaje en el altepetl del siglo XVI*. Mexico City: FCE, 2006. Print.
Gruzinski, Serge. *The Mestizo Mind*. Trans. Deke Dusinberre. New York: Routledge, 2002. Print.
———. *The Aztecs: Rise and Fall of an Empire*. New York: Harry N. Abrams, 1992. Print.
Holy Bible: Revised Standard Version. New York: World Publishing, 1962. Print.
Klor de Alva, J. Jorge. "Sahagún's Misguided Introduction to Ethnography and the Failure of the Colloquios Project." *The Work of Bernardino de Sahagún: Pioneer Ethnographer of Sixteenth-Century Aztec Mexico*. Ed. José Jorge Klor de Alva, Henry B. Nicholson, and Eloise Quiñones Keber. Austin: University of Texas Press, 1988. Print.
Lockhart, James. *The Nahuas after the Conquest: A Social and Cultural History of the Indians of Central Mexico, Sixteenth through the Eighteenth Centuries*. Stanford: Stanford University Press, 1992. Print.
León-Portilla, Miguel. *Aztec Thought and Culture: A Study of the Ancient Nahuatl Mind*. Trans. Jack Emory Davis. Norman: University of Oklahoma Press, 1990. Print.
Lopes Don, Patricia. *Bonfires of Culture: Franciscans, Indigenous Leaders, and the Inquisition in Early Mexico, 1524–1540*. Norman: University of Oklahoma Press, 2010. Print.
Miller, Mary, and Karl Taube. *An Illustrated Dictionary of the Gods and Symbols of Ancient Mexico and the Maya*. London: Thames and Hudson, 2004. Print.
Rabasa, José. "Thinking Europe in Indian Categories, or, 'Tell Me the Story of How I Conquered You.'" Ed. Mabel Moraña, Enrique Dussel, and Carlos A. Jáuregui. *Coloniality at Large: Latin America and the Postcolonial Debate*. Durham, NC: Duke University Press, 2008. 43–76. Print.
Rama, Ángel. *La ciudad letrada*. Hanover, NH: Ediciones del Norte, 1984. Print.
Reyes García, Luis. *¿Cómo te confundes? ¿Acaso no somos conquistados? Anales de Juan Bautista*. Mexico City: Ciesas, 2001. Print.
Romano, Ruggiero. *Mecanismo y elementos del sistema económico colonial americano, siglos XVI–XVIII*. Mexico City: FCE, 2004. Print.
Schussler Fiorenza, Elizabeth. *Invitation to the Book of Revelation*. Garden City, NY: Doubleday, 1981. Print.
Tavárez, David Eduardo. *The Invisible War: Indigenous Devotions, Discipline, and Dissent in Colonial Mexico*. Stanford: Stanford University Press, 2011. Print.
Todorov, Tzvetan. *The Conquest of America: The Question of the Other*. Trans. Richard Howard. New York: Harper Collins, 1992. Print.
Townsend, Camilla. "Glimpsing Native American Historiography: The Cellular Principle in Sixteenth-Century Nahuatl Annals." *Ethnohistory* 56.4 (2009): 625–50. Print.
White, Hayden. *The Content of the Form: Narrative Discourse and Historical Representation*. Baltimore: Johns Hopkins University Press, 1987. Print.

◆ 4

Performances of Indigenous Authority in Postconquest Tlaxcalan Annals: Don Juan Buenaventura Zapata y Mendoza's *Historia cronológica de la noble ciudad de Tlaxcala*

Kelly S. McDonough

In recent decades, we have witnessed a remarkable florescence of scholarship in the field of Latin American colonial studies that attends to indigenous perspectives and modes of knowledge production. In the case of New Spain—today's Mexico—the analysis of indigenous sources along with European and *criollo* texts and visual vocabularies has added exponentially to our present-day understandings of complex colonial cultures in contact. My own interest lies in how Nahuas, native speakers of the Nahuatl language, have participated in modernity as writers and producers of knowledge, agents of their own discourses and agendas. Along these lines, this essay focuses on the writings of a seventeenth-century Nahua intellectual, don Juan Buenaventura Zapata y Mendoza, an elite-class indigenous statesman and annalist who wrote the history of his *altepetl* (city/state), Tlaxcala.[1] A noble son of Quiahuiztlan, one of the four sub-altepetl of Tlaxcala (along with Ocotelolco, Tizatlan, and Tepeticpac), Zapata was born to rule. Like other high-ranking members of the Tlaxcalan noble class, he held a variety of political positions in the indigenous *cabildo* (municipal council) of Tlaxcala, including *regidor* (council member), *alcalde* (judge), *gobernador* (indigenous governor), treasurer, and notary (Townsend, "Don Juan" 153). Besides being a life-long politician, Zapata is also responsible for the richest extant Nahuatl-language history of Tlaxcala.² Providing a window into the world of indigenous "negotiation within domination," his writing paints a dynamic picture of how Tlaxcalan elites—the embodiment of the altepetl—shaped and responded to the rapidly changing social and political landscape of colonial Mexico.³

Commonly referred to as *Historia cronológica de la noble ciudad de Tlaxcala*, Zapata's manuscript contains—as the postconquest Nahua annals genre dictated—a yearly record of the territorial and political disputes, transfers of power, public works, and natural/climatic phenomena as they affected the altepetl. Yet beyond these expected topics, our protagonist also left us with an unprecedented insider's view of the cabildo's political activities during the seventeenth century, offering a vivid firsthand record of seventeenth-century Tlaxcalan elites' acute understanding of the relationship between colonial politics, religion, and the law. This essay will focus on episodes in Zapata's text that exemplify the ways in which Tlaxcalan elites promoted their legitimate political authority and rights, as these were being restricted and undermined. I argue that the performances and subsequent written records of what can be considered the Tlaxcalan discursive pillars of political authority and rights served as critical tools in the affirmation and defense of Tlaxcala's right to continue to enjoy its privileged status established in the earliest days of European conquest and colonization.⁴

The manuscript, presently housed at the Bibliotèque Nationale de France, consists of one hundred and twenty folios of Nahuatl alphabetic text. The first five make up the "Origen de la nación tlaxcalteca" (The Origin of the Tlaxcalan Nation), a migration story copied, presumably, from a pre-Hispanic document (Reyes García and Martínez Baracs 38).⁵ The remaining folios narrate a year-by-year account of Tlaxcala since its origins in 1310, through 1692. The elaboration of the text would have included a compilation (and perhaps editing) of earlier texts (oral, pictorial, or written), to which the annalist would add new events accumulated and/or witnessed during his lifetime.⁶ We can imagine, for example, Zapata sifting through *xiuhpohualli* (painted pre-Hispanic year-count codexes), transferring visual data to an alphabetic narrative, copying and compiling other alphabetic texts, building consensus through conversation with elders of the altepetl, and exchanging sources with other annalists. As a genre, the corporate histories did not require a single authoritative voice, and as products of multigenerational collaborations, most Nahuatl-language annals do not identify a specific author; instead they tend to be anonymous projects (Lockhart 376). There are, however, exceptions to this rule: Hernando de Alvarado Tezozomoc (Tenochtitlan), the great Chimalpahin (Chalco), and our protagonist Zapata, give themselves away on several occasions. The "somewhat anonymous" Nahua annalists were usually elite-class members of what Krug and Townsend have identified as a closed circle of intellectuals (3). They tended to be well educated and politically active (or affiliated with the church in some manner), and were able to navigate both indigenous and Spanish cultures, in the political sense as well as on linguistic and cultural planes (Lockhart 376). Nahua annalists in general are notable for the patriotic zeal in their reports of the glories of their altepetl, and Zapata is no exception. Yet his manuscript stands out for being especially concerned with constructing a "Nahua" kind of history for present and future generations of Tlaxcalans. Along these lines, ethnohistorian Camilla Townsend has noted what she calls a sense of "ethnic patriotism" in Zapata's manuscript. That is, the style, structure, language, and sources consulted admit a conscious favoring of indigenous forms over European ("Don Juan" 154–57). This is in contrast to the procedures of other annalists—for example Chimalpahin, who is known to have regularly consulted both Nahua and Spanish sources (Lockhart 380; Townsend "Don Juan" 157). That Zapata seems to have been intent upon writing a Nahua-centric text in a Spanish-dominated context makes sense if we consider Tlaxcala's long tradition of understanding itself as distinct, unique, or special.

Tlaxcala Is Special

It is common knowledge that Tlaxcala routinely petitioned for privileges as reward for their instrumental role as indigenous allies to Hernán Cortés in the conquest of the Aztec Empire, and for their services as loyal subjects to the Spanish Crown. Diplomatic missions to Madrid began in 1527 when four high-ranking nobles from each of the Tlaxcalan sub-altepetl made a voyage across the Atlantic Ocean to petition and secure rights and protections.[7] Shortly thereafter, in August of 1529 a royal mandate was issued stating that the Tlaxcalans would never be given in encomienda; they would not be obligated to provide tribute or draft labor to a conquistador (Baber 23–24).[8] Instead, Tlaxcala was to retain a direct tributary relationship with the Crown, and throughout the sixteenth century Tlaxcala lobbied for, and was granted, varying degrees of territorial autonomy as a *república de indios*. Furthermore, Tlaxcalans were authorized to formally exclude all but elite Nahuas from their local government.[9]

The Tlaxcalan cabildo members, charged with serving both their indigenous constituents and the interests of the Crown, were elected from some two hundred and twenty representatives of the noble houses of the four sub-units of the polity. Bridging the political, economic, and religious spheres of New Spain, the primary responsibilities of the cabildo members—who, like Zapata, rotated through most, if not all, of the cabildo positions during their lifetime—included labor organization, supervision of public construction, trade regulation, and the organization of religious ceremony and ritual (Lockhart, Berdan, and Anderson 1). As formal representatives of Tlaxcala to outsiders (Spaniards, Church officials, other indigenous groups), the cabildo members served as key intermediaries representing, ideally, the interest of the altepetl before all others.

Regardless of Tlaxcala's initial "exceptionalism" in the colonial order, by the seventeenth century elite Tlaxcalans were at risk of losing their hard-won privileges and status, as well as their control of the cabildo.[10] As the Spanish Crown consolidated power, tributary relationships were modified in a way that was not to the advantage of indigenous elites or their subjects. According to Charles Gibson, the renowned historian of Tlaxcala, shifting imperial policies and an increasingly powerful class of European and criollo colonists were the primary causes for which the once stubbornly independent altepetl slowly became subsumed into the "colonial scene" (x–xi). During this time, the Nahua elite's political control of the Tlaxcalan cabildo was undermined as mestizos and Spaniards infiltrated the once all-indigenous political and physical territory of the city of Tlaxcala. Furthermore, the Crown and Church's demands for more money, goods, and labor put the cabildo—the local collectors of tribute and organizer of labor—in an increasingly antithetical position in relation to the indigenous commoners they purported to serve (Martínez Baracs 321–52). At various times throughout the seventeenth century, Tlaxcalan commoners questioned their loyalties to the cabildo, and even went as far as openly rebelling against the Tlaxcalan elites on several occasions (321–76).

It is during this time of instability and uncertainty that Zapata records his eyewitness accounts of Nahua elites evoking, in public performances, the discursive pillars of Tlaxcalan political authority and rights: 1) the assertion of a tradition of autonomy and noble rule that pre-dates and continues through Spanish colonization; and 2) the reminder of their role as loyal allies and faithful Christian subjects of the Spanish Empire. Whereas one might read the astute self-promotion of the Tlaxcalan elite class as self-serving, it is important to remember that the nobles understood themselves to be the embodiment of the altepetl. As such their well-being was inherently linked to that of their own indigenous subjects. Thus, the preservation of their social position was integral to the continued autonomy, dare I say existence, of the Tlaxcalan people.

Public spectacles such as religious fiestas, political oaths, and receptions for visiting dignitaries in seventeenth-century Mexico provided colonial subjects, including the Tlaxcalan elites, with the Geertzian "cultural frame" for "defining and advancing the claims of political authority" (Geertz 143; cf. Curcio-Nagy 3). Through the organization of and participation in such performances, native leaders conveyed—through an embodied, visual vocabulary—important information to their indigenous subjects regarding the altepetl's allegiance to the Church and Crown, and elite-class cabildo members' powerful position in the colonial social hierarchy (Ramos 185–86). In her discussion of Spanish/criollo public performances aimed at asserting Spanish authority in the colonial context, Linda Curcio-Nagy maintains that "large-scale spectacle became one tool in an arsenal of colonizing agents that included coercive force, discriminatory laws, religious institutions such as the Inquisition, and economic power" (3). Yet Spaniards were not alone in recognizing the efficacy of such public displays. Indigenous subjects, including the Tlaxcalan cabildo, also utilized public spaces for negotiating relationships and identities, and for shaping and responding to the context of the new colonial order.

In reading Zapata's descriptions of public spectacles, Diana Taylor's theorization of performance can be helpful in that she asks us to consider "how performed, embodied practices make the 'past' available as a political resource in the present by simultaneously enabling several complicated and multilayered processes" ("Performance" 68). Complicated and multilayered indeed, as visible in the following examples from Zapata's manuscript, Tlaxcalan performances of loyalty to the Spanish Crown and Catholic Church were regularly combined with references to the past, functioning as often-contradictory political resources with which Tlaxcalan elites asserted authority while simultaneously confirming subjugation.

The Record and Performance of Continuous Autonomy and Noble Lineage

Historia cronológica provides a year-by-year accounting of Tlaxcalan political successions from pre-Hispanic times through the late seventeenth century. This record gives proof of a noble Tlaxcalan control of the territory that is both continuous and accretive, having never succumbed to colonizers (Aztec or European). This narrative is a subtle, yet provocative, framing of Tlaxcala as always free and independent. It also serves to differentiate the Tlaxcalans from the Mexica, a conquered people. Thus this record not only asserts autonomy as natural for Tlaxcalans but also bolsters petitions for privileges or special status. This assertion of autonomy, however, should not to be read as rebellion against the Crown. The heirs of the pre-Hispanic *tlatoque* (altepetl rulers) understood that their special rights were confirmed and secured by embracing a subordinate social position as vassals to the Spanish Crown.

Layered among the yearly reports of noble rule of the altepetl, Zapata narrates how cabildo members publicly performed their pre-Hispanic histories in postconquest times. These performances served to alert Spaniards and indigenous alike of their noble lineage, establishing their high rank in New Spain's social hierarchy. Such assertions took place at a time when the Spanish Crown was intent upon restricting privileges of both conquistadors and indigenous noble privileges. Romero Galván points out that in this context we see two related phenomena: first, descendants of conquistadors developing a creole consciousness (we are from here, and therefore should rule here); and second, indigenous nobles re-articulating the fact that they have *always* been here, and therefore should rule here (352–53). Tlaxcala's justification of privileges and rights rested in written documents such as *cédulas* (royal decrees), jealously guarded in a locked chest in the cabildo hall. The unofficial histories such as this manuscript compiled by Zapata surely supported Tlaxcalan claims as well. But in addition to the written record, public performance—processions to honor the King or other ranking dignitaries, religious celebrations such as Corpus Christi, or a saint's day—provided a forum for establishing and securing these rights in front of all ranks of colonial society, illiterate and literate, commoners and elites, and Nahuas and Spaniards alike.

In colonial-period public processions, it was common practice for indigenous nobles—and Tlaxcala is no exception—to wear clothing and other signs/insignias of pre-Hispanic social and political power, visibly linking themselves to the ruling class of the past. On one hand, by dressing as preconquest rulers the Tlaxcalan elites of the colonial period affirmed subjugation to the Spanish Crown (my ancestors are now incorporated and subsumed into your political and religious ceremonies and rituals). On the other hand, these actions announced hereditary rights to power in this new context (Curcio-Nagy 50). Gibson saw processions in which New Spain's indigenous elites dressed as the "four 'kings' of conquest times" as demonstration of a nostalgic attitude toward the past (14). Likewise, in his analysis of similar processions in the Andean context, art historian Tom Cummins reads performances of pre-Hispanic Inka royalty as "resignation in the face of an irretrievable past" (222–23). Art historian Carolyn Dean, however, points to another possibility. She suggests that performances of royal Inka ancestry could have been deployed as a kind of "counterstrike" against threats to the political status of the descendants of the Inka noble lines (Dean 98). It is possible that Tlaxcalan performances of pre-

Hispanic royal ancestry in seventeenth-century processions—nostalgic or otherwise—provided a platform for affirming noble Tlaxcalan continuity, unity, and authority, smoothing over the jagged edges of conquest. The next section focuses in on one such procession narrated in Zapata's annals wherein the four pre-Hispanic/conquest-era indigenous rulers of Tlaxcala (Xicotencatl, Maxixcatzin, Tlehuexolotzin, and Citlalpopoca) are portrayed as ranking closest to, if not higher than, the King of Spain.

Aztaaxiluh (The Forked White Heron Feather)

On January 17, 1677, all of Tlaxcala marked Charles II's ascension to the throne with an elaborate procession of common-folk and dignitaries, carefully arranged in a pecking order according to rank, for their march through the streets of the altepetl. At the head of the procession on foot were the *macehualtin* (commoners), followed by Nahua political functionaries on horseback, and finally the Spanish and Nahua gobernadores. After these came a float carrying an indigenous man costumed as the young king of Spain, Charles II, flanked—on a yet higher level—by others portraying the four pre-Hispanic rulers, the tlatoque. Each wore indigenous regalia including the *aztaaxiluh*, the forked white heron feather headdress often associated with the pre-Hispanic ruling classes and their important warriors (Nicholson 73–75). Zapata writes, "nahui tlatoque quitlalique ymaztaaxiluh quitlamachcuique y huehuetque nahuitin tlacpac (551) (Above the king were the four rulers wearing the aztaaxiluh in imitation of the ancient ones).[11] What is striking about this performance is first and foremost the double bind of calling up the memory of pre-Hispanic Nahua rulers and inserting it into the present frame of a procession honoring the King. Whereas the explicit reason for the procession appears to be the public expression of loyalty to the Crown, the positioning of the tlatoque as not only closest to, but even higher than, the King warrants further consideration. Was this simply a nostalgic reminiscence of past glories, or were the Nahua elites attempting to project the image of equal (or greater) rank as that of the supreme ruler of the land?

The question becomes all the more interesting if one takes into consideration that at the time of this procession the collective political power of the heirs of the four tlatoque was tenuous at best. The polity was *not* intact: mestizos had married into noble houses and used Spanish support to enter the once all-indigenous governing body of Tlaxcala. At the time of this procession, in Zapata's annals we read how mestizos were disrupting the traditional rotational structure of the cabildo and, in his interpretation, were ruining of the integrity of the altepetl. In referring to one particular troublemaker, Nicolás Méndez de Luna, Zapata calls him the "gobernador mictlan mextiço" (510) (mestizo governor from hell). "Mochi iymac pouliuh." Because of him, Zapata writes, "everything was lost."

Is it possible that this performance was also a pointed barb at the mestizo infiltrators at the very time when, at least in Zapata's eyes, they were the cause of strife in the cabildo and the community? Was this simply a tactic to symbolically appear powerful and relevant, or was this a strategic reminder to both Europeans and mestizos that the true "higher" authorities were the *pipiltin* (noble indigenous class), those who were there before all others, wearing the aztaaxiluh?[12] But was this reminder minimized by the fact that the wearers of the aztaaxiluh, in this staging, signified power precisely because they rode closest to the foreign prince to whom they were subjugated? Considering the complex intercultural relationships of the time, it seems as if this performance satisfied the needs of many. In this single procession, the elites managed to embody all of the roles their intermediary position required while clearly announcing themselves as legitimate power brokers in New Spain's political hierarchy.

Loyal Military Allies

Another performative strategy for asserting Tlaxcalan elite political authority and rights—at a time when these were anything but certain—was the regular reminder of Tlaxcala's exceptional loyalty to the King (and his agents) by calling up the memory of their role as "first ally."

Similar to the mestizo Tlaxcalan chronicler Diego Muñoz Camargo in his version of the alliance with Hernán Cortés, Zapata makes no mention of the initial three-week battle between the Spaniards and the Tlaxcalans.[13] Nor does he record the actual first alliance with Cortés. Where one might expect details of the battles against the Mexica, perhaps heralding Tlaxcalan feats of bravery, the narrative here is terse and spare. In fact, "yn iquac poliuhque mexica" (132) (Then the Mexica were conquered) is the extent of the battle recorded in the entry for 1521. Instead, it is Zapata's eyewitness account (some one hundred and fifty years later) of a re-enactment of this "first" alliance with the Spaniards, staged to welcome the new viceroy, that takes up several pages of the manuscript. This episode stands out for its length and detail, but also as an example of Tlaxcala's strategic use of the past.

On February 15, 1670, Tlaxcalans gathered at the foot of the bridge into

Tlaxcalan territory at San Juan Atlancatepec (a congregation of Tepecticpac, on the outer ring of Tlaxcala on the road from Veracruz to Mexico City) for a scripted reception of the viceroy. From the elite cabildo members to the poor *macehualtin*, all arrived costumed in the pre-Hispanic rough cloth or sack-like dress of the commoner. As the viceroy's caravan approached, all of the "performers" beat together sticks for a "quahuitl quihuihuicaque" or "recepción de palíos" (Zapata y Mendoza 444–45). When the viceroy inquired as to the significance of the display, the Tlaxcalans responded, "Timitzmohuiquilizque y capa timohuica" (444) (We will follow you wherever you go). They continued, "hoticmatque y monetequipacholtzin ca yuhqui oquichiuque yn tachcoltzintzinhuan yn Marquez yunic oquitlanque yn izqui altepetl" (444) (We have known your concerns. This is what our great grandfathers did when, along with the Marqués [Cortés], they conquered all of the altepetl). The viceroy replied, according to Zapata, "yehuatzin ca huel oquimotlaçocamachitin yni tlatoli oquimitahuili ça neli amahuiztique tlaca yn atlaxcalteca yhuan yn amomahuiso yn amotemahuiztililiz anquinezcayotia ma totecuyo Dios amechmopili otlacauh yn amoyolutzin." (*Historia cronológica* 444) (you are truly impressive people. Of course, you are Tlaxcaltecans. And your respect and the respect that you give is clear. May our father God keep you. You are most worthy).

By re-enacting the military alliance with Cortés as a way to demonstrate loyalty to the viceroy, Tlaxcala offered a not-so-subtle reminder to the Spaniards of their indebtedness to their indigenous allies for their successes in New Spain. At the same time, with a shrewd reading of the audience's desire for the display of a mass of submissive subjects, here no tlatoque in sight, this performance persuaded the viceroy to voice mutual respect (as opposed to a hierarchical relationship), at least verbally confirming Tlaxcala's special status.

Christian Subjects of the Spanish Empire

> "When the wars were over and armed heroes were no longer required,
> native leaders marched in as champions of the new religion."
> (Osowski, *Indigenous Miracles* 3)

Assertions of continuous control of their territory, reminders of their noble lineage, and regular allusions to their role as ally to Spanish conquistadors would not be enough to maintain Tlaxcala's autonomy and special status. Perhaps the most important resource would be the regular public declarations of Tlaxcala's identity as faithful converts to the Catholic religion. Historian Edward Osowski has emphasized the crucial link between religious ritual and political negotiation in New Spain, reminding us that "only Christians had rights and protection under Iberian law: The Spanish world considered the possession of the 'true' faith the fundamental requirement for the political legitimacy of the indigenous leaders who were known to have descended from pre-conquest nonbelievers" ("Indigenous Centurions" 81). Here Osowski refers to the 1557 law that gave native leaders that had converted to Catholicism (or were descended from converts) swift access to the courts of law (*Recopilación de leyes,* II, Book 6.7, Law 1). Thus, following Osowski, it can be said that each public display or performance of Christian faith provided the means by which the indigenous elites could rightfully access the political sphere and confirm their integration and status in colonial New Spain (*Indigenous Miracles* 1–6).

For their part, the Tlaxcalan cabildo members regularly expressed their loyalty to the Crown (and confirmed their rights) through Catholic rituals performed in the public eye. The cabildo's sponsorship of religious celebrations such as the feast days of Tlaxcala's patron saint, Santa María de Asunción, and the elaborate Corpus Christi processions verified Tlaxcala's investment (both spiritual and financial) in the new order. Zapata's text notes the cabildo's contribution to what were considered "good works": he carefully records the expenses and labor provided by the Tlaxcalans in order to build, outfit, and maintain the chapels and to celebrate mass, high holy days, and other Catholic ceremonies. Throughout the most detailed portion of the text (covering the years 1662–1688), we read of religious statues adorned and paraded through the altepetl, the forging and installation of massive church bells, receptions for visiting Church officials, and elaborate funeral processions for the king (in absentia).

Beginning in 1651, the first year of Zapata's rotation as indigenous governor, the passages include more and more detail related to the religious duties organized and fulfilled by the cabildo, suggesting a community deeply embedded in the Catholic world. Events in the manuscript are regularly contextualized by the Saint's day they happen to fall on (or near), and the vast majority of the entries from 1651 and on center on religious ceremony and construction projects related to the Church. A pious man, in his first year as governor Zapata makes a point of the fact that he is responsible for the recovery of the mantle of Santa María de Asunción, hocked by the previous governor, Nacianceno, but now rightfully returned to the precious patroness of the altepetl: "yhuan hocçepa hocan yacuican nezqui yn imatotzin [. . .] catca mochi nicquixtin don Juan Buenaventura Çapata de Mendoza gobernador jues" (292) (and there, it appeared again her cloak [. . .]. It was I, don Juan Buenaventura Zapata y Mendoza, governor, who recovered it all).

In the years that follow, Zapata gives copious examples of the cabildo members' public performances aimed at consolidating their relationship with the Crown and the Church. In 1662, for example, he tells us of the dedication and blessing of Tlaxcala's temple of San Francisco in which the cabildo members accompany the effigy of Santa María de Asunción from the cabildo hall to the chapel, with a golden key resting in her hands. Tlaxcalan nobles carry their patron saint throughout the city, passing first by the temple of San José, where the Blessed Sacrament (the Host, representing the blood and body of Christ) joins the procession. From San José they proceed to the cabildo hall and on to the zócalo's portals, which have been strung with chains of flowers, *xochimatlatl*, for the occasion. Continuing on to the marketplace, the saints and their entourage join the Franciscans carrying their statue of Saint Francis. Together they march to the chapel, where the golden key is ceremoniously taken from the patroness's hands to open the locked doors (320–21). In this public procession, State and Church are linked together by physically walking from the cabildo hall (elite rulers), to the portales (constitutents), through the marketplace (economic center), and finally closing the circle at the church. Taylor has said that "embodied performances have always played a central role in conserving memory and consolidating identities in literate, semiliterate, and digital societies" (Taylor, *The Archive* xvii). Processions such as this one from Zapata's manuscript show how the physical occupation of space and these "embodied performances" reminded and confirmed the "who" and the "what" of the Tlaxcala altepetl for participants and observers alike. These public displays of the connections between Church, Crown, and native rulers highlight the fact that the Tlaxcalan elites were adept in negotiating their position in the social and political system. In other words, as Patricia Ybarra has stated, "the Tlaxcaltecans were experts at playing by the rules" (3). As faithful Christians, they were guaranteed, in theory, the full protection of the law. This would, in turn, include the ability to negotiate with the Crown and her agents on behalf of their constituents regarding labor and tribute obligations and territorial boundaries. The following example from Zapata's manuscript treats Tlaxcala's commitment to the role of Christian subjects of the Spanish Empire, manifest in the public events related to the death of King Philip IV and the subsequent succession of his son, Charles II.

Another one of the lengthier passages of the manuscript centers on the Tlaxcalan cabildo's sponsorship of the funeral procession for King Philip IV, and the public oath to his heir Charles II in 1666. Zapata took great pains in recording this elaborate performance of Tlaxcala's religious and political identity, which garnered much approval from the royal court in Spain and solidified, if only for a time, Tlaxcala's privileged place in the social order. In this passage his pride in the altepetl is evident. Yet he likely had an additional reason for such careful attention to the minute details of these events. He played a prominent, if not pivotal, role in the organization and execution of the processions as a respected elder statesman.

On May 29, 1666, news reached Tlaxcala of the death of King Philip IV. Zapata recalls the first procession to announce the passing of their beloved ruler. All of the colonial subjects dressed for mourning (in what he calls *molutotin*) to accompany the town crier as he announced the tragic news throughout the streets of Tlaxcala. Following his usual habit, Zapata carefully noted the processional order according to rank and commented that all of the tlatoque rode horseback with the Spanish dignitaries (362). Only high-ranking indigenous nobles and Spaniards had the legal right to ride horseback, and here Zapata rode among them, proudly representing Quiahuiztlan as a past governor.

One week after the announcement of the king's death and this melancholy procession through the streets, all of the *quauhxique* (carpenters) of Tlaxcala were called to build a catafalque in honor of King Philip IV. They were also charged with the construction of outdoor platform stages upon which the cabildo members, priests, and Spanish dignitaries would make public oaths to the new representative of the Hapsburg monarchy, Charles II. Zapata, representing Quiahuiztlan, and don Francisco Ruiz of Tepeticpac, were chosen by their noble peers to supervise the cabildo's material and labor contribution to the construction projects. In these passages he recalls the precise measurements of the structure, the vast quantities of supplies procured, and the richly painted canopies erected for the occasion (364–67). The catafalque, Zapata tells us, was placed inside *tocabillia* (our chapel), twenty-four *varas* long and fifteen wide (approximately sixty-six by forty-one feet), which he notes was taller than even the arches of the chapel, with three different levels (364–65). On the third level of the catafalque was an altar with a *çitial* or a small chair/throne upon which sat an image of Philip's son, the successor. Zapata describes the new monarch as "y piltzintl tohueytlatocatzin Carlos segodo yn ixiptlayotzin" (364) (his [Philip's] young son, our great *tlatoani* Charles the Second, his precious substitute). Zapata's use of the term *ixiptlayotl* is provocative in that it refers to an "image, likeness, or representation" (Karttunen 115) but can also suggest "standing in for someone" (Molina II.46v). The king may have died, but the monarchy was alive and well, albeit now embodied by a young boy.

The public pledge of fealty to then five-year-old Charles II, took place in Tlaxcala on August 15, 1666. On this auspicious day, the feast day of Santa María de Asunción, the pipiltin of Tlaxcala gathered first for a celebration of Christian mass, then commenced a procession through the streets with the royal standard guarded by two indigenous kings-at-arms and a veiled painting of the young heir to the throne. Tlaxcalan and Spanish dignitaries paraded from the cabildo hall, to the marketplace, toward Tecolostitlan and Quaquahxiuhtla, through the smaller market, and then back to the cabildo hall, proclaiming their allegiance to the Crown to the four directions of the altepetl. Again riding horseback, Zapata and his fellow comisario, don Ruiz, went before the people carrying the *bastón,* or ceremonial staff, which Ybarra notes is "generally associated with indigenous elders, who carry them as a sign of wisdom, authority, justice, and prudence" (8). Zapata proudly swore loyalty to the Christian king at each of the resting points of the procession, standing above the people on the stages that had been constructed under his guidance. Fireworks were launched, after which Zapata and Ruiz, each accompanied by a king-at-arms, threw coins to the crowds from silver platters. Later, at the doorway to the church of San José, the priests blessed the occasion with prayers and a public recitation of the hymn "Te Deum Laudamus." Through this public spectacle, the Tlaxcalan cabildo members not only informed the indigenous masses of their expected allegiance to the new Christian king, but also provided evidence of the elites' important position in the social-political order.

Several months after the oath ceremony, in October of 1666, King Philip IV was symbolically laid to rest by the Tlaxcalans in yet another public ceremony that coincided with the viceroy's visit. Again highlighting the Tlaxcalan elites' identity as faithful Christians, the cabildo members organized a funeral procession for the deceased ruler. Zapata describes the proceedings, which began in the cabildo hall. A golden crown wrapped in black cloth—standing for the body of the king—was placed on red cushion, protected with an embroidered canopy. A scepter and a rapier lay beside the crown, arranged in the form of the cross. Zapata was an integral participant in this solemn event, charged with carrying the imperial crown through the streets of Tlaxcala to the catafalque inside the chapel of San Francisco. He conveys a sense of awe upon entering the chapel and standing at the foot of the catafalque, resplendent in the light of the many candles: "Yn itech tobolu yuhqui ye comoniz y tecali mochi yztac çera" (372) (On top of the catafalque it seemed as if all of the flaming white candles would light the tomb on fire). Zapata and other chosen pipiltin placed the cushion, crown, scepter, and rapier in the catafalque, and finished the day's events with the funeral vigil and finally a sermon in *laticopa*, Latin. The following day, Zapata writes, there were substantially fewer people on hand for continued funeral events, but he states that "we" (here he seems to be referring to cabildo members) again celebrated mass and offered "Prayers for the Dead" at the sepulcher. Seven days later, the pipiltin again dressed in mourning to hear mass for King Philip IV at the church of San José (372).

Surely Zapata was pleased with his participation in these proceedings and considered himself a fine example of Tlaxcalan nobility. His gratification is undeniable when he later writes that the cabildo members received a letter from the Queen Regent herself (Mariana of Austria, mother of Charles II) lauding the Tlaxcalan's extravagant show of loyalty to her line:

> Axcan ypan ixhuitl tonali lunes a 20 de febrero yhuan ypan xihuitl de 1668 años yn ohuala yn iamatzin y cartatzin toçihuatecuiyotzin reyna yn opan mehuiltititica Castillan yn oquihualmotlacuilhuilili yn inican pipiltin toatoque tlaxcalteca hoquimomachtitin yca çe amatlauiluli yn queni nica oquimomahuizçotilique yn tohuey tlatocatzin ocatca torey ycan yn imahuizçotzin jura yhuan yn inetoquitzin horas ynic cotlayahualuloc yn omotlali quahutlapechtl yhuan tumulo acan iuhqui omochiuh ynic çenoya altepehuacan ynic çenoya auh yehuatzin ca huel oquimotlaçocamachiti y toçihuatecuiyotzin yn izqui tlamatl omochiuh oquimotili testimonio ynic oquihualmotitlanili yamatzin oquihualmomahuizçotili yn Tlaxcallan altepetl [...] huel mochoquilique ynic mochitin tlatoque yn iquac quicaque yn icartazin (sic). (394)

> (Today, the 20th of February in the year 1668, a letter arrived from our *cihuateuhctli* Queen in Castile. She wrote to the pipiltin and the tlatoque here in Tlaxcala. She had read in a written document how we had honored our great deceased tlatoani and our king with the admirable oath and the funeral honors, for which a procession was made and a stage and a catafalque constructed; nowhere else in all of the lands was this done as [we did]. And she, our great cihuateuhctli, gave great thanks for all that we had done. She read testimony of this, which was the reason she sent this letter in which she gave honor to the altepetl of Tlaxcala. [...] All of the tlatoque cried when they heard the words of the Queen's letter).

For a time, at least, Zapata and the Tlaxcalan cabildo members had summoned the royal gaze and, through their public performances of Catholic ritual in honor of their king, had again secured a favorable position in the evolving political scene of New Spain.

Yc mochi tlaqui (With This, Everything Ended)

One might read these examples gleaned from Zapata's manuscript and begin to believe that the colonial-period Tlaxcalan elites had simply become, for all intents and purposes, undiscerning servants of the European colonizers. Yet we must not be too quick to equate honor and respect for the King, or the proclamation of Christian faith, with relinquishing autonomy or power. Instead I have argued in favor of reading these seventeenth-century performances as examples of how Tlaxcalan elites deployed productive discourses in order to strategically and symbolically negotiate the social position of both the elite class and the altepetl at large. To be sure, Zapata's work is not to be taken as the "true" history of Tlaxcala; this is only one version, coming from a man who was watching the power and the glory of his line and his altepetl diminish and fade. His later entries to the manuscript, between 1678 and 1688, were likely a heartbreaking task for an aging man in that the noble rule of the cabildo was obviously falling apart. The old ways of the *pilli* rotating through the cabildo had ceased, and more mestizos joined the ranks of the municipal council. Zapata laments the election of the mestizo don Pascual Ramírez, representing his dear Quiahuiztlan, as governor of the cabildo: "Amo pili yn itech hoquizqui çan itlamozcalti totatzin frey Agostin de Artiaga" (566) (He wasn't a nobleman, he was just someone that our father Agustín de Arteaga had taken in). This same Ramírez would later be responsible for selling, without having first consulted with the pipiltin, important cabildo properties including the portales, the mesón, and the jail (634–37). What should have been a time to observe the splendid fruits of his life's labor was instead a sad ending for this Tlaxcalan patriot who, noting the sale of these properties, says succinctly, "yc mochi tlaqui" (636) (with this, everything ended). For Zapata, his beloved Tlaxcala had come to an end.

Zapata's story ends, but that of Tlaxcala, of course, does not. In the later colonial period, the elites would attempt, with somewhat limited success, to restore noble indigenous rule to the altepetl. But the pillars of authority and rights that for a time had served the noble class of Tlaxcala so well—performances of royal lineage, military alliances, and Christian conversion—began to falter during the eighteenth century with the transition from Hapsburg to Bourbon monarchs. The Bourbon Reforms frowned upon ostentatious public spectacles celebrating anything but the Crown, and their political policies were specifically aimed at unifying the state at the expense of local, independent political factions (Lockhart and Schwartz 347). But Tlaxcala would—and did—find new ways to assert autonomy at the crossroads of politics, religion, and the law. Neither annexation to Puebla at the end of the eighteenth century, nor the bitter divisions of the altepetl during the wars of Independence from Spain, would destroy what today is Mexico's smallest yet arguably most fiercely independent state, one that Zapata would surely recognize as home.

Notes

1. Ethnohistorians are responsible for previous scholarly work on this manuscript. Luis Reyes García and Andrea Martínez Baracs transcribed and translated the manuscript to Spanish in 1995. Their critical edition, which I cite (with my own translations, in consultation with Sabina de la Cruz [native-speaker of Nahuatl]), carefully describes content, anomalies, authors, and sources, as well as contextualizes the manuscript within both the field of Tlaxcalan historiography and the annals genre. James Lockhart has cited Zapata as the standout of the later years of the annals tradition, particularly for the quantity and quality of his treatment of Tlaxcala's past and for his treatment of seventeenth-century Tlaxcala politics (391). Camilla Townsend has carried out some of the more in-depth and thought-provoking analyses of Zapata's life and work and is presently completing the first detailed study of the annals genre, with further emphasis on Zapata's manuscript. These scholars have all pointed to the groundbreaking, yet unfortunately interrupted, dissertation work of Frances Krug on the Tlaxcalan-Puebla annals as being important for their research on Zapata and the annals genre in general.
2. Even though we may rightly call Zapata the primary editor and author of the manuscript, we also know that he did not have the final word. There are at least two additional hands involved in this manuscript, both of whom appear to have taken over after Zapata's death. The first seems to be his son, who very briefly picked up the narrative in 1691, after an approximately three-year gap. The second is that of don Manuel de los Santos y Salazar, a family friend (and indigenous Franciscan priest) who more than likely acquired Zapata's manuscript from the aforementioned son. Santos y Salazar added extensive marginalia and glosses, in Spanish and in Nahuatl, as well as cover pages to the document. Regarding don Manuel de Santos y Salazar, see Camilla Townsend's introduction to *Here in this Year* 21–40 and the introduction to the manuscript by Reyes García and Martínez Baracs 27–29. See also James Lockhart's assessment of Santos y Salazar's contribution to Zapata's text in *The Nahuas after the Conquest* 592–93, n. 53.
3. I take the phrase "negotiation within domination" from Ethelia Ruiz Medrano and Susan Kellogg's excellent volume *Negotiation within Domination: New Spain's Indian Pueblos Confront the Spanish State*.
4. See Travis Barton Kranz's expert analysis of the Tlaxcalan pictorial genre's framing of Tlaxcala as deserving of rights and privileges. His study focuses specifically on the *Lienzo de Tlaxcala* and images from Tlaxcalan chronicler Diego Muñoz Camargo's manuscript.

5. Manuscript in Paris: Méxicaine 212, collection E. Eug Goupil, Ancienne Collection J. M. A. Aubin. Reyes García and Martínez Baracs note that other copies of this manuscript in Mexico are in the following locations: one at the Biblioteca Nacional de Antropología e Historia (BNAH) Colección de Francisco del Paso y Troncoso Legajo 50; one in the holdings of CIESAS in Mexico City; and two in the city of Tlaxcala—one with recently deceased Tlaxcalan intellectual and muralist Desiderio H. Xochitiotzin (1922–2007) and the other with Tlaxcalan writer and teacher Isaías Bello.
6. It should be noted that after 1577 the compilation, editing, and authoring of postconquest annals was being carried out at a time when writing about the indigenous past or possessing such documents was prohibited by the Crown. That the annals genre thrived in an atmosphere of censure is not surprising, however, as we know that one of the hallmarks of colonial law in New Spain was that iteration was regularly met with noncompliance (Lockhart).
7. For versions of the alliance with Cortés and subsequent petitions for privileges based on service, see, for example, Gibson 26, 158–69; Lockhart, Berdan, and Anderson 2; Baber 24; Ybarra 14–15; and Sullivan.
8. Those familiar with Gibson's seminal work on the history of Tlaxcala might note a discrepancy in the timeline of Baber, who cites "first privileges" as being awarded in 1529. In Gibson's work, he states that the 1527 delegation did not appear to be successful and that the year 1535 marks "the first authenticated cases of royal privilege in the history of Tlaxcala" (164–65). Baber, however, notes that Gibson did not work in the Spanish archives for *Tlaxcala in the Sixteenth Century*, where she found evidence of earlier privileges.
9. See, for example, *Recopilación de leyes*, II, Book 6.1, Law 42, 1585: "Que los Gobernadores de Indios de Tlaxcala sean naturales."
10. Regarding modifications of Tlaxcalan privileges and the changing social structure, particularly the absolutist policies of Philip II, in colonial Mexico, see Gibson 107; Ybarra 17; Sullivan 11; Romero Galván 352.
11. Reyes García and Martínez Baracs translate *aztaaxiluh* to *aztaxilotl*, which they define as the braided red-and-white headdress with feathers worn by the nobles of Tlaxcala. However, it is more likely that *aztaaxiluh* refers to the *aztaxelli* (the forked white heron feather itself as opposed to the braided red-and-white headband). Many thanks to Justyna Olko, who pointed out that she has not seen attestations of *aztaxilotl* in extant documents, while references to *aztaxelli* are plentiful. Olko has written extensively the *aztaxelli* in her book *Turquoise Diadems and Staffs of Office* 139–43. Zapata does, however, use the term *aztaxilutl*, which he cites as being exchanged during the *xochiyaoyotl* or *guerras floridas* (ritualized wars aimed at capturing, enslaving, and finally sacrificing enemy combatants) with Huexotzinco Huitilhuacan (124–25). This term may be specific to Tlaxcalan Nahuatl.
12. Following Michel de Certeau, I use the terms *tactic* and *strategy* to suggests the

different ways that oppressed peoples negotiate (tactic) and the powerful dominate (strategy). See *The Practice of Everyday Life* 36–37.
13. Ybarra discusses the Tlaxcalan's intentional omission of the battles before alliance between the Spaniards and the Tlaxcalans (16). See Gibson's discussion of these events (15–27). Also, as a counterpoint to Tlaxcalan versions, Spanish soldier Bernal Díaz del Castillo devotes several pages in his chronicle to these battles; see chapters 62–65.

Works Cited

Baber, R. Jovita. "Empire, Indians, and the Negotiation for the Status of City in Tlaxcala, 1521–1550." *Negotiation within Domination: New Spain's Indian Pueblos Confront the Spanish State*. Ed. Ethelia Ruiz Medrano and Susan Kellogg. Boulder: University Press of Colorado, 2010. 19–44. Print.

Certeau, Michel de. *The Practice of Everyday Life*. Trans. Steven F. Rendall. Berkeley: University of California Press, 1984. Print.

Cummins, Tom. "We Are the Other: Peruvian Portraits of Colonial Kurakakuna." *Transatlantic Encounters: Europeans and Andeans in the Sixteenth Century*. Ed. Kenneth J. Andrien and Rolena Adorno. Berkeley: University of California Press, 1991. 203–31. Print.

Curcio-Nagy, Linda. *The Great Festivals of Colonial Mexico City: Performing Power and Identity*. Albuquerque: University of New Mexico Press, 2004. Print.

Dean, Carolyn. *Inka Bodies and the Body of Christ: Corpus Christi in Colonial Cuzco, Peru*. Durham: Duke University Press, 1999. Print.

Díaz del Castillo, Bernal. *Historia verdadera de la conquista de la Nueva España*. Madrid: Espasa-Calpe, 1968. Print.

Geertz, Clifford. *Local Knowledge: Further Essays in Interpretive Anthropology*. New York: Basic Books, 1983. Print.

Gibson, Charles. *Tlaxcala in the Sixteenth Century*. Stanford: Stanford University Press, 1952. Print.

Karttunen, Frances. *An Analytical Dictionary of Nahuatl*. Austin: University of Texas Press, 1983. Print.

Kranz, Travis Barton. "Visual Persuasion: Sixteenth-Century Tlaxcalan Pictorials in Response to the Conquest of Mexico." *The Conquest All Over Again: Nahuas and Zapotecs Thinking, Writing, and Painting Spanish Colonialism*. Ed. Susan Schroeder. Portland: Sussex Academic Press, 2010. 41–73. Print.

Krug, Frances. The Nahuatl Annals of the Tlaxcala-Puebla Region. Diss. University of California Los Angeles. n.d.

Krug, Frances, and Camilla Townsend. "The Tlaxcala-Puebla Family of Annals." 2007. Web. September 2011. April 1, 2012.

Lockhart, James. *The Nahuas after the Conquest: A Social and Cultural History of the Indians of Central Mexico, Sixteenth through Eighteenth Centuries.* Stanford: Stanford University Press, 1992. Print.

Lockhart, James, and Stuart B. Schwartz. *Early Latin America: A History of Colonial Spanish America and Brazil.* Cambridge: Cambridge University Press, 1983. Print.

Lockhart, James, Frances Berdan, and Arthur J.O. Anderson, eds. *The Tlaxcalan Actas: A Compendium of the Records of the Cabildo of Tlaxcala (1545–1627).* Salt Lake City: University of Utah Press, 1986. Print.

Martínez Baracs, Andrea. *Un gobierno de indios: Tlaxcala 1519–1750.* Mexico City: FCE, CIESAS, FCHT, 2008. Print.

Molina, Alonso de. *Vocabulario en lengua castellana y mexicana y mexicana y castellana.* 1571. Mexico City: Porrúa, 1970. Print.

Nicholson, H. B. "A 'Royal Headband' of the Tlaxcalteca." *Revista Mexicana de Estudios Antropológicos* 21 (1967): 71–106. Print.

Olko, Justyna. *Turquoise Diadems and Staffs of Office: Elite Costume and Insignia of Power in Aztec and Early Colonial Mexico.* Warsaw: PTSL, 2005. Print.

Osowski, Edward. *Indigenous Miracles: Nahua Authority in Colonial Mexico.* Tucson: University of Arizona Press, 2010. Print.

———. "Indigenous Centurions and Triumphal Arches: Negotiation in Eighteenth-Century Mexico." *Negotiation within Domination: New Spain's Indian Pueblos Confront the Spanish State.* Ed. Ethelia Ruiz Medrano and Susan Kellogg. Boulder: University Press of Colorado, 2010. 79–106. Print.

Ramos, Frances. "Succession and Death: Royal Ceremonies in Colonial Puebla." *The Americas* 60.2 (2003): 182–215. Print.

Recopilación de leyes de los reynos de las indias: Mandadas imprimir y publicar por la magestad católica del rey don Carlos II nuestro Señor. Madrid: Por la viuda de D. Joaquín Ibarra, 1791. Print.

Reyes García, Luis, and Andrea Martínez Baracs, eds. *Historia cronológica de la noble ciudad de Tlaxcala.* Tlaxcala: Universidad Autónoma de Tlaxcala, 1995. Print.

Romero Galván, José Rubén. "Fernando de Alva Ixtlilxóchitl." *Historiografía novohispana de tradición indígena.* Ed. José Rubén Romero Galván. Mexico City: UNAM, 2003. Print.

Ruiz Medrano, Ethelia, and Susan Kellogg, eds. *Negotiation within Domination: New Spain's Indian Pueblos Confront the Spanish State.* Boulder: University Press of Colorado, 2010. Print.

Sullivan, John J. *Sujeción colonial en el municipio tlaxcalteca del siglo XVI y la respuesta indígena.* Diss. University of California, San Diego, 1995. Print.

Taylor, Diana. *The Archive and the Repertoire: Performing Cultural Memory in the Americas.* Durham: Duke University Press, 2003. Print.

———. "Performance and/as History." *The Drama Review* (2006): 67–86. Print.

Townsend, Camilla. "Don Juan Buenaventura Zapata and the Notion of a Nahua Identity." *The Conquest All Over Again: Nahuas and Zapotecs Thinking, Writing, and Painting*

Spanish Colonialism. Ed. Susan Schroeder. Portland: Sussex Academic Press, 2010. 144–80. Print.

———. ed. *Here in This Year: Seventeenth-Century Nahuatl Annals of the Tlaxcala-Puebla Valley.* Stanford: Stanford University Press, 2010. Print.

Ybarra, Patricia A. *Performing Conquest: Five Centuries of Theater, History, and Identity in Tlaxcala, Mexico.* Ann Arbor: University of Michigan Press, 2009. Print.

Zapata y Mendoza, Don Juan Buenaventura. *Historia cronológica de la noble ciudad de Tlaxcala.* Ed. Luis Reyes García and Andrea Martínez Baracs. Tlaxcala: Universidad Autónoma de Tlaxcala, 1995. Print.

PART II
Religion

♦ 5

Translating the "Doctrine of Discovery": Spain, England, and Native American Religions

Ralph Bauer

When Chief Justice John Marshall ruled in the 1823 U.S. Supreme Court's landmark case *Johnson v. M'Intosh* that private citizens could not purchase land from Native Americans due to the federal government's "right of preemption," he invoked the so-called "Doctrine of Discovery" that, he assumed, had been established in the context of the Iberian conquests during the fifteenth and sixteenth centuries. He thereby perpetuated a long-standing British American intellectual tradition that sought to legitimate Protestant conquests in the New World by invoking the prerogatives claimed by Europe's Catholic powers, without engaging in a serious interrogation of the legitimacy of *any* European claims to the New World.

Apparently, Marshall was oblivious to (or chose to ignore) the considerable debate that this very fundamental question had created in early modern Spain.[1] There, in fact, the debate harked back to the medieval legal commentaries of Pope Innocent IV (1195–1254) on the question of the legitimacy of the crusades, which held that pagans had the same natural right as Christians to "dominion" (i.e., the right to self-government and property), although the pope had the prerogative to intervene in order to spread the gospel or to punish violations of "natural law."[2] When, some three hundred years later, Spain challenged Portugal's claims to the (is-)lands that the latter had "discovered" in Africa and the eastern Atlantic, Pope Nicholas V reaffirmed the Portuguese claims with the bull *Romanus Pontifex* (1442), taking up the arguments of the Portuguese Crown that its discoveries and conquests had been pursued "more indeed for the salvation of the souls of the pagans of the islands than for [the King's] personal gain."[3] Finally, in 1493, the year after Columbus's landfall, Pope Alexander VI issued the famous series of bulls collectively known as *Inter caetera* (later modified in the Treaty of Tordesillas of 1494). Although these bulls did not technically confer any titles of ownership over the newly discovered territories, they did grant a monopoly of access to Castile and Portugal for purpose of trade, travel, and missionary activities, thereby dividing up the spheres of influence between the two Iberian nations along a geographical line of demarcation that ran, pole to pole, 100 leagues west of the Azores.[4]

In the absence of any challenges to the explorers' and conquerors' common practice of taking possession of territories in the New World on behalf of the Iberian Crowns, it appears either that the papal bulls were initially considered to be sufficient legal grounds for a claim to ownership, or that there was no serious consideration of the legality of the Iberian occupations. Yet when, during the early decades of the sixteenth century, the papal bulls became increasingly the target of attacks by both Spanish scholastics and Northern European Protestants, the Iberian Crowns began to look for alternative legal foundations on which to ground their claims and seemed to be finding the solution in Roman law.[5] Thus, the Humanist Francisco de Vitoria, chair of theology at the University of Salamanca and appointed by King Ferdinand to inquire into the legal status of Spanish claims to territorial ownership in the New World, (correctly) opined that the papal bulls were not a sufficient basis for such territorial claims, since the pope had no jurisdiction over land but only over souls. Furthermore, even from the point of view of Roman law, Vitoria later reasoned in his 1539 *Relectio de Indis*, Castile had no claim to ownership of the New World because it was not a *terra nullius* (land without owners), since the American Indians, though they might be barbarians, held "natural legal rights as free and rational people." While Vitoria had thus cast serious doubts on the legal soundness of the Spanish conquest of the New World as it had hitherto been practiced, he also offered an alternative legal avenue in which conquest could (and would) be rationalized thereafter: he upheld the idea that a "just war" could in theory be waged by a Christian prince against pagans not merely on account of their paganism but rather if the latter engaged in violations of "natural law" (i.e., resisted proselytization, travel and trade).[6]

The reasons for this highly public inquiry into the legality of the early

Spanish conquests in the New World in early modern imperial Spain are complex and must be sought in part in the emerging inter-imperial rivalry among European powers and in part in the intra-imperial struggles over the Spanish Crown's attempts to centralize imperial authority over the newly gained territories.[7]

What is of interest for my purposes is the profound effect that this new legal situation had on the literary representations of Native American cultures and religions in the second half of the sixteenth and through the seventeenth centuries. As historians and literary critics have amply noted, the legal fiction that grounded Europeans' "rights of discovery" in the alleged Native American violations of "natural law" constitutes an important ideological context for much of the European ethnographic representation of Native American religious and cultural practices.[8] The notion, emerging since the middle of the sixteenth century, that Native American religions were a form of diabolism had an obvious role to play in legal considerations of the European territorial claims in the New World, as it appeared to violate the Thomist doctrine that man was, by the law of nature, endowed with a desire to know the true God by virtue of his reason. From this point of view, it is not surprising that in his recent comparative study, *Puritan Conquistadors: Iberianizing the Atlantic, 1550–1700*, Jorge Cañizares-Esguerra finds the devil lurking in every corner of the early modern textual archive about the New World, both Spanish and English. Indeed, he argues, it is this pervasive presence of the devil in a sort of "colonial discourse" shared by European writing about the New World across sectarian boundaries that makes Spanish and British American literature comparable: With regard to demonology, he writes, "the Puritans and Spaniards saw the world of colonization in remarkably similar terms," and "for all the confessional differences, the English and the Spaniards were ultimately cultural twins" (79, 76). But while Cañizares-Esguerra is certainly correct in arguing that, when it came to European perceptions of Native American religions, the Spanish American case must be seen as "normative" (215), rather than peripheral, in Atlantic historical developments, we must also keep in perspective some of the important differences between the Spanish and the English legal and theological contexts in the justification of dominion and the resulting divergences in attitudes toward and representations of Native American religions generally and in allegations of diabolism particularly.

This essay will explore the cultural transfer of Spanish ideas about the Europeans' alleged "rights of discovery" and the allegedly diabolical nature of Native American religions into the British American cultural context by focusing on the English transmissions of such important Counter-Reformation ethnographies as José de Acosta's *Historia natural y moral de las Indias* (1590). While English writers readily seized upon the doubts about the legality of the Spanish conquest that had been voiced by such influential Dominicans as Vitoria and (later) Bartolomé de Las Casas in early modern Spain, they typically based their own claims to possession on a notion of *vacuum domicilium* (empty or unused land) vis-à-vis *Spanish*, rather than Native American claims.[9] In other words, New World lands were typically considered to be "vacant" (or "virgin") by English writers if they were not yet possessed (or "raped") by the Spanish conquistadors. This ideology of all of non-Iberian America as an English "Virginia" (or "virgin land" rightfully owned by the "Virgin Queen" Elizabeth) forms the initial context of English representations of Native Americans and Native American cultures and religions (including their alleged "idolatry") that were significantly at variance with those evidenced in the Spanish American colonial archive from the beginning. Moreover, liberal English ideas, emerging in the context of the seventeenth century, of the New World as an alienable "wilderness"—with its peculiarly (proto-)Lockean notions about the integral role of agricultural labor in the state of nature[10]—militated against the development of an English proto-ethnographic literature of demonology as it was produced in the context of the Counter-Reformation missionaries' campaigns of "extirpation."[11] Instead (and with some notable exceptions), British American colonial writers generally applied a providentialist and typological, rather than proto-scientific, hermeneutics when writing about Native Americans and their cultural and religious practices that figured most prominently in the Anglo-American literature as a rhetoric not of *extirpation* but rather of *extermination*. Ultimately, a comparative perspective on law and religion in the Spanish and British colonial encounters will put into focus the reciprocal, rather than a priori, relationship between the history of demonology and the colonial encounter in the New World. In other words, if demonology was not yet a dominant and readily available topos in the early discourses of either the Spanish or the English discovery and appropriation, it increasingly became so in both realms, although it took different shapes in the various cultural contexts of colonial history.

Virtually all of the early English publications about the New World were translations of the writings of the Iberian explorers and conquerors (or Italian explorers sailing on behalf of an Iberian crown) or of such general cosmographies and Spanish imperial histories, translated by Richard Eden, as Sebastian Münster's *Cosmographia* and Peter Martyr's *Decades*. Therefore, early English perceptions of the New World, its inhabitants, and their religion were invariably shaped by the more utopian portrayals in early Humanist Spanish historiography of the New World (see Householder).¹² In these early English writings about the New World, as in the Spanish ones, there is little evidence that the English initially perceived Native American religions in terms of diabolism. This is remarkable because, as Keith Thomas has argued, the Protestant Reformation "did nothing to weaken" the belief in the devil: "indeed, it almost certainly strengthened it" in its conviction of human sin and sense of powerless in the fact of evil (470). Indeed, in sixteenth-century England, as on the continent, it was radical Calvinist reformers such as William Perkins who produced some of the most extensive and important treatises on demonology. Yet, to the extent that English writers about the New World encountered demonizations of Native American religions in their Spanish sources, they generally chose to ignore them, perhaps even suppress them. This can be partially explained in terms of the promotional character of much early English writing about the New World, which was intended to persuade adventurers to invest in the colonial enterprise.

When Richard Hakluyt, the most prolific Elizabethan collector of English travel literature, included in the 1598 edition of his *Principal Navigations*, his translation of parts of one of the most important texts in Spanish counter-Reformation demonology and ethnography, José de Acosta's *Historia natural y moral*, he did not select a single passage that linked Native American religions with diabolical perversions. Similarly, in Sir Walter Ralegh's *Discovery of the large, rich, and beautiful Empire of Guiana*, one of the most important and extensive Elizabethan New World ethnographies, the author makes no mention of the Devil. On the contrary, Ralegh reports showing a coin to the natives of Guiana that displayed an engraved image of Elizabeth. "[T]hey so admired and honoured [it]," he writes:

> as it had been easy to have brought them idolatrous thereof. The like and a more large discourse I made to the rest of the nations, both in my passing to *Guiana* and to those of the borders, so as in that part of the world her Majesty is very famous and admirable; whom they now call *Ezrabeta cassipuna aquerewana*, which is as much as "Elizabeth, the Great Princess, or Greatest Commander." (7)

Not unlike Christopher Columbus a hundred years before him, who asserted that the natives he encountered in the Caribbean had "no religion" and allegedly believed that the Spaniards were supernatural beings who had "come from heaven" and would therefore very easily be converted to Christianity (56), Ralegh here invoked an almost Lascasian notion of the Native impressionability. For Ralegh, it appears, "idolatry" was not a form of devil worship and a crime against God but rather, more positively (in almost a Machiavellian way), a useful tool in the affirmation of aristocratic power.

Similarly, in his *Briefe and true report of the new found land of Virginia*, first published in 1588 and one of the most important original Elizabethan ethnographic sources on Algonquian culture and religion in what today is North Carolina, Thomas Harriot provided a detailed description of Native religion, which, though flawed, had for him nothing to do with devil worship. "Some religion they haue alreadie," he wrote, "which although it be farre from the truth, yet beyng as it is, there is hope it may bee the easier and sooner reformed" (1588, E3 v). By using the word "reformed," he suggests that Native religion may provide the foundation for their eventual conversion to the Protestant religion. Algonquians are hereby not essentially different from European Christians before the advent of the Protestant (or Anglican) Reformation, when local saints were widely worshiped alongside God, except that the "Virginians" use different words. "They beleeue that there are many Gods which they call *Mantóac*," he wrote:

> but of different sortes and degrees; one onely chiefe and great God, which hath bene from all eternitie. Who as they affirme when hee purposed to make the worlde, made first other goddes of a principall order to bee as meanes and instruments to bee vsed in the creation and gouernment to follow; and after the Sunne, Moone, and Starres, as pettie goddes and the instruments of the other order more principall. (1588, E3 v–r)

Moreover, he continued, like Christians, the Virginians already believed in

> the immortalitie of the soule, that after this life as soone as the soule is departed from the bodie according to the workes it hath done, it is eyther carried to heauẽ the habitacle of gods, there to enioy perpetuall blisse and happiness, or els to a great pitte or hole, which they thinke to bee in the furthest partes of their part of the worlde towarde the sunne set, there to burne continually: the place they call *Popogusso*. (1588, E3 r)

He explained some of the apparent errors and uncertainties in Native accounts of the creation of the world by referring to their lack of "letters nor other such meanes as we to keepe recordes of the particularities of times past, but onelie tradition from father to sonne," thus echoing explanations made some fifty years earlier by Las Casas and other Dominicans that Native religions were evidence of man's innate tendency of knowing the true God, a knowledge that has suffered somewhat in the New World due to a lack of writing, just as it had in Catholic Europe due to the Church's corruption of the Latin canon. What was most important for Harriot, as it was for Ralegh, was the positive social effects of religion more generally. "What subtilty soeuer be in the *Wiroances* and *Priestes*," he wrote:

> this opinion worketh so much in manie of the common and simple sort of people that it maketh them haue great respect to their Gouernours, and also great care what they do, to auoid torment after death, and to enjoy blisse; although nothwithstanding there is punishment ordained for malefactours, as stealers, whoremoongers, and other sortes of wicked doers; some punished with death, some with forfeitures, some with beating, according to the greatnes of the factes. (1588, E4 v)

Thus, both Harriot's and Ralegh's ethnographies about the New World, written at the very end of the sixteenth century, still manifest a Thomist understanding of paganism in general and of Native American religions in particular.[13] Native religions, despite their apparent imperfections, are in no way seen as diabolical but as evidence of a memory (however faint) of their true creator, as evidence of man's universal strife to know the true God, and, thus, not as idolatry that must be extirpated but rather a solid foundation on which their reformation can be built.

In part, this apologetic view of Native American paganism must be seen in the context of the tenuous legal situation in which Elizabethan explorers operated in the New World. While English encroachments into North American territory (such as Harriot's "Virginia") were justified by Elizabethan lawyers by citing the first "discovery" of North America by John Cabot in 1496–1498 on behalf of the English crown, North America still fell within a part of the New World assigned to Spain's sphere of influence in Alexander's *Inter caetera* bulls—and England was, after all, still a Catholic country under Henry VII when these bulls had been issued.[14] The justification of English encroachments was on even more tenuous footing in the case of South America (such as Ralegh's "Guiana"), which not only fell (with the exception of Brazil) to the Spanish sphere of influence (according to *Inter caetera*) but had actually been first "discovered" by Christopher Columbus on behalf of the Spanish Crown during his third voyage in 1498. It was in this context that Elizabethan writers began to challenge the justness of the Spanish "rights of discovery" on a number of grounds. On the one hand, they claimed that the Spanish conquest had not been consistent with an apostolic mission but was, in fact, motivated by avarice and perpetrated through cruelty. On the other hand, they challenged the notion that "mere discovery" (i.e., without settlement) was sufficient ground for a claim to possession.¹⁵ With regard to the first argument, they found a ready ally within Spain herself—Bartolomé de Las Casas, whose *Brevíssima relación de la destrucción de las indias* was first translated into English in 1583 as *The Spanish colonie, or Briefe chronicle of the acts and gestes of the Spaniardes in the West Indies* and greatly came to promote the rise of the so-called "Black Legend" in the Protestant world, an anti-Spanish and anti-Catholic ideology that underwrote English and Dutch imperial expansionism in the New World.¹⁶ Elizabethan writers such as Ralegh, Hakluyt, and Harriot eagerly seized on Las Casas's rhetorical model and added their own examples with the intent of proving that the English were the "protectors" of Native American victims of Spanish illegal usurpations and cruelties. Thus, Ralegh even argued that the English Reformers would restore the "legitimate" rule of the Inca elite, who had wrongly been deprived of their dominion by Spanish usurpers, writing:

> [B]y my Indian interpreter, which I carried out of *England*, I made them understand that I was the servant of a queen who was the great cacique of the north, and a virgin, and had more *caciqui* under her than there were trees in that island; that she was an enemy to the *Castellani* in respect of their tyranny and oppression, and that she delivered all such nations about her, as were by them oppressed; and having freed all the coast of the northern world from their servitude, had sent me to free them also, and withal to defend the country of *Guiana* from their invasion and conquest. (7)

Despite the generally positive view that Marian and Elizabethan English writers took on Native American religions and cultures in the early years of English overseas exploration, in Protestant Europe, too, an alternative perspective began to emerge—one that, though apparently echoing the Counter-Reformation historians of the New World, was nevertheless distinctive in the meaning it attached to allegations of Native American satanism. In 1590, two years after its initial publication in England, Harriot's text was reissued by the Calvinist de Bry family at Frankfurt as the first volume for their *America* series, one of the most influential publications to articulate a distinctly Protestant ideological vision of America and its conquest by Europeans. Published simultaneously in English, Latin, German, and French, de Bry's edition of Harriot's text also included a new section with de Bry's copper engravings, most of them based on the watercolors by the English painter John White, who had produced them during his stay at the Roanoke colony in 1585. This new section also included a brief introduction by de Bry, the captions to the engravings, and some additional engravings (also based on watercolors by White) of the "ancient Picts" who had inhabited the British Isles in ancient times and who were supposed to illustrate the cultural similarities between modern Virginians and ancient Britons.[17]

As historians have widely noted, whereas White's watercolors and titles generally defamiliarize and decontextualize Native religious practices, emphasizing ethnic difference and exotic strangeness, de Bry recontextualizes and refamiliarizes ethnic elements by Europeanizing facial features and by including landscape settings. Of particular interest, then, is the representation of Native shamanism in the de Bry volume, as it stands in marked contrast to that in Harriot's earlier (unillustrated) English publication of 1588.

Thus, in an engraving of a Native shaman that was based on a John White watercolor entitled *The Flyer* (Fig. 1), the new caption reads, in the English edition "The Conjuror"; in the Latin edition, "Prestigiator" (meaning a trickster, one who practices deceit; juggler; impostor, cheat, deceiver); and in the German edition, "Der Schwarzkünster oder Zauberer" (Fig. 2) (meaning "one adept in the black arts or a magician"). Lest the reader fail to understand the

Fig. 1. John White, *The Flyer*.
Courtesy of The British Museum
(cataloged as *Indian Conjuror*).

new connotation of Native shamanism, de Bry's caption reads, "They haue comonlye coniurers or iuglers which vse strange gestures, and often cótrarie to nature in their enchantments: For they be verye familiar with deuils, of whome they enquier what their enemys doe, or other suche thinges" (1590, XI). Clearly, this interpretation of Native shamanism is in tension not only with Harriot's earlier portrayal of Native paganism but also with the connotation evoked by White's caption "The Flyer," which would have reminded the reader of the Greek god Hermes and European Classical paganism and possibly even of the Renaissance Hermetic tradition. Harriot's "The Conjuror" (Fig. 3), by contrast, strips the Native shaman of any connotation of a "learned" or "philosophical" Hermeticist in the tradition of such Italian Renaissance figures as

Fig. 2. Theodor de Bry, *Der Schwarzkünstler oder Zauberer*.
Courtesy of The Kraus Collection of Sir Francis Drake, Library of Congress.

Marsilio Ficino, Giovanni Pico de Mirandola, or Giordano Bruno or of the sort that still populated the Elizabethan court, such as John Dee, Walter Ralegh, and even Harriot himself.[18] The new edition of Harriot's text in 1590 instead evokes the European folk tradition of jugglers and witch doctors, perhaps foreshadowing the increasingly radical Protestant hermeneutics that would be applied in reading preternatural phenomena such as "flying" (or levitation) in both Protestant Europe and England.[19]

To be sure, this apparent change in attitude toward Native American paganism may in part be explained by the different places and contexts of publication—Elizabethan London in 1588 on the one hand and a Calvinist publishing house in the (predominantly Lutheran) free imperial city of Frankfurt in

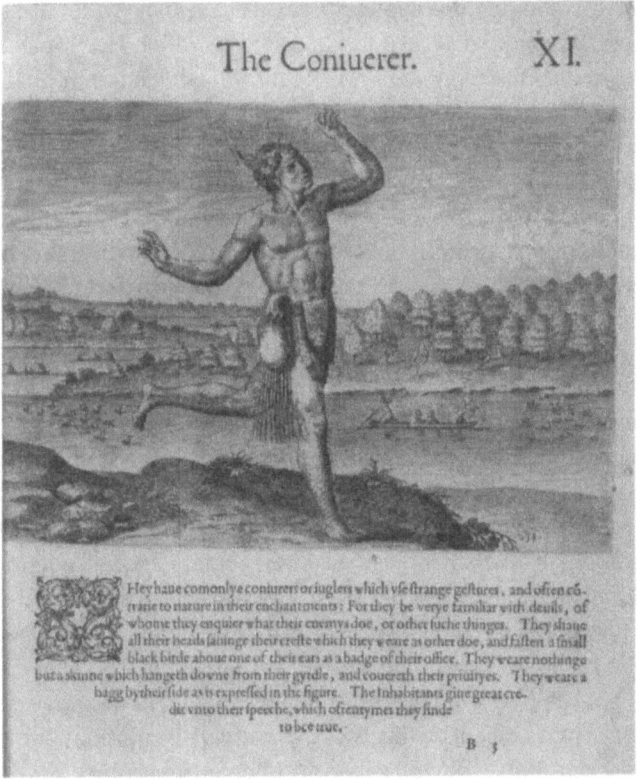

Fig. 3. Theodor de Bry, *The Coniverer*. Courtesy of The John Carter Brown Library, Providence, RI.

1590 on the other.[20] Yet the Frankfurt edition was the product not of de Brys alone but rather of a collaboration between the Frankfurt publishing house and Englishmen such as Richard Hakluyt, who had supplied Theodor de Bry with John White's watercolors during the former's stay in London and who had persuaded de Bry to use Harriot's text about English activities in the New World as the first of what had already been conceived as a multivolume work.[21] This fact suggests that attitudes in England toward Native Americans and their religions may also have been changing in the last decade or so of the sixteenth and the early decades of the seventeenth centuries, due in part, perhaps, to the first English experiences with their own colonial settlements, and in part to cultural changes at home. Thus, English theorists of the "rights of discovery," in defying the Iberian interpretation, insisted that only settlement, not "mere discovery," constituted a legal ground for claiming possession. The English therefore rushed to establish colonial settlements that they were still ill-prepared to maintain. The colonial expedition of 1585, in which Harriot and White had participated in the employment of Sir Walter Ralegh, had to be abandoned after the first year, when the colonists were unable to sustain themselves and were able to find little help from the natives (whom the English leader, Ralph Lane, had managed to antagonize by burning one of their leaders alive on account of a stolen silver cup). A second attempt was launched by Ralegh in 1587, this time under the leadership of the painter John White, but this colony fared worse than the one before. After a desperate White returned to England to seek help, he returned in 1590 only to find the colony abandoned, with no sign of the colonists save for the word "croatoan" carved into a wooden post. This second English venture came to be known as the "lost colony" of Roanoke and speculations ran high (then as now) as to the particulars of its fate.

But with the subsequent rise of the Stuart dynasty to the throne of England during the early seventeenth century and the radicalization of the conflict between sectarians and an increasingly calcified orthodox Laudian Church, interest in diabolism further intensified in England, especially among the elite in Church and State. Perhaps the most famous expression on this interest on the part of the political elite is the publication of James I's *Daemonologie* five years before his ascension to the throne of England in 1603. James's primary target was not malefic witchcraft but rather magic. He therefore attempted to delineate the lawful sciences (such as astronomy) from unlawful magic (such as divinatory astrology), as well as the art of conjuring spirits. Since God is all-powerful, there was nothing that the devil could do without God's permission. Instances of witchcraft were therefore to be interpreted as evidence of God's displeasure, which resulted in the withdrawal of his protection, thus allowing for malefic witchcraft. Witchcraft could therefore only be remedied by fasting and prayer, rather than, as in the Catholic context, through rituals of exorcism. It is for this reason that Protestant demonologists such as James deemed magic a crime worse than witchcraft itself, as the witch was an instrument of God's wrath, whereas the conjurer had "knowledge" but still attempted to resist or "trick" his way out of God's providence through his magic, which made his crime an offense against the Holy Spirit. The "first cause" in witchcraft is God, he wrote, "and the Devill as his instrument and second cause shootes at in all these actiones of the Deuil, (as Gods hang-man)" (n.p.). What had previously been primarily a *moral* question—an opposition between white magic and black magic (or malifice)—became in his text, as in many others in seventeenth-century Protestant England, primarily a question of "conscience," as Stuart Clark has put it (445): any sort of conjuring was increasingly seen as a crime against the sovereignty of God, Church, and State.

It was in this dual context—a new intellectual climate at home and in the wake of the first few disastrous confrontations with Native Americans on the ground abroad—that one of the greatest Counter-Reformation demonologies about the New World, José de Acosta's *Historia natural y moral,* saw its first complete translation into English in 1604 by Edward Grimstone.[22] The first Englishman who prominently picked up on Acosta's contention that Native American religions were diabolical in origin was the biblical scholar and millenarian Joseph Mede, who argued in his 1620s "A Conjecture Concerning Gog and Magogs in the Revelations" that "[T]he people of America are Colonies of the nation of Magog" (n.p.). Thus, Satan's army "shall come from those nations, which live in the Hemisphere opposite to us, whom the Best and most Great God in his secret judgement, for the most part shall not cherish with the light of his Gospel" (n.p.). Whereas the Old World (what he calls the "universal Hemisphere" of old), is the

> onely . . . partaker of the promised instauration, shall become the camp of the Saints, and the seat of this [God's] blessed kingdome . . . whatsoever nations are without this (in the places where the Ancients placed the seat of Hel) shall be reserved to the last triumph of Christ, to be destroyed by fire from heavn, by his just (though to us unknown) judgment. (n.p.)

In other words, the New World will be redeemed from the Devil only with the coming of the Apocalypse itself.[23]

In the literature about the first permanent English colony in America, Jamestown in Virginia, Acosta's and Mede's demonological interpretation of

Native American religion gained ground after the Powhatan confederacy's attack on the fledgling colony in 1622. Writing in 1625, and apparently remembering Acosta and Mede, the Anglican minister Samuel Purchas, Richard Hakluyt's successor as collector and historian of English overseas exploration and colonization, composed a short treatise entitled "Virginia's Verger," which offered an extended theoretical disquisition on what he called the "Law of Nature and Nations" and which was one of the most elaborate articulations yet in English of the justification of the English conquest. The English claim to the land had been established, he argued, by the rights of "first discovery, first actuall possession, prescription, gift, cession, and livery of seisin, sale for price natural Inheritance of the English their naturally borne, and the unnaturall outcries of many unnaturally murthered" (XIX: 225). To preempt conceivable objections that the acts of violence committed by the Indians had been in legitimate self-defense, Purchas emphasized their allegedly natural savagery and the diabolical nature of their religion:[24]

> [C]onsidering so good a Country, so bad people, having little of Humanitie but shape, ignorant of Civilitie, of Arts, or Religion; more brutish then the beasts they hunt, more wild and unmanly then that unmanned wild Countrey, which they range rather then inhabite; captivated also to Satans tyranny in foolish pieties, mad impieties, wicked idlenesse, busie and bloudy wickednesse: hence have wee fit objects of zeale and pitie, to deliver from the power of darknesse. (*Hakluytus* XIX: 231–32)

Similarly, John Smith, in his *General History of Virginia* (1624), published two years after the massacre, portrayed the Powhatans' religion as satanic spectacles on which he claimed to report with the authority of an eyewitness captive. In his *General History* he reproduced both de Bry's image from Harriot's account of "their idol Kiwasa" and de Bry/Harriot's designation of a Native shaman as a conjurer (Fig. 4). In Smith's account the conjuror (as well as the priest) appeared as a minion to an idol with clearly demonic characteristics. Thus, Smith reported that during his captivity among the Powhatans, "they entertained him with most strange and fearefull Coniurations" (48), and he concluded that the Powhatans' religion is essentially diabolical and entirely born of fear:

> All things that are able to doe them hurt beyond their prevention, they adore with their kinde of divine worship; as the fire, water, lightning, thunder, our Ordnance, peeces, horses, &c. But their chiefe God they worship is the Devill. Him they call Okee, and serue him more of feare then loue. They say they haue conference with him, and fashion themselues as neare to his shape as they can imagine. In their

Fig. 4. John Smith, "A description of the part of the adventures of Cap. Smith in Virginia," *The generall historie of Virginia, New England, and the Summer Isles.* (1624). Courtesy of The John Carter Brown Library, Providence, RI.

> Temples they haue his image euill favouredly carved, and then painted and adorned with chaines of copper, and beads, and covered with a skin, in such manner as the deformitie may well suit with such a God. (34)

This Okee, continued Smith, demands yearly sacrifices of fifteen children, which "they held to be so necessary, that if they should omit it, their Okee or Devill, and all their other . . . Gods, would let them haue no Deere, Turkies, Corne, nor fish, and yet besides, he would make a great slaughter amongst them." Although he also reported that the Indians held the English God as more powerful than theirs, given that he supplied them with weapons superior to their own, they appeared to be beyond salvation by human endeavors. "In this lamentable ignorance doe these poore soules sacrifice themselues to the Devill," Smith concluded, "not knowing their Creator; and we had not language sufficient, so plainly to express it as make them vnderstand it; which God grant they may" (38). This interpretation is a long way from Harriot's earlier portrayal of the "Virginians'" religion, as their alleged diabolism puts them beyond the possibility of salvation. For Smith, as for the majority of Protestant ethnographers in the seventeenth century, it was not man's business to extirpate or exorcise witchcraft. Thus, Smith, enduring the afflictions of Powhattan's satanic maleficence, commended himself to God, who miraculously sent him a young Indian maiden, Powhatan's daughter Pocohontas, and Smith and Jamestown were restored to God's good protection.

In New England, a similar transformation in the perception of Native religions took hold in the second part of the seventeenth century, especially after King Philip's War. However, unlike the representations of Native religions in late sixteenth- and early seventeenth-century Spanish accounts of conquest, the Puritan accounts of King Philip's War, such as William Hubbard's *A Narrative of the Troubles with the Indians,* Increase Mather's *A Relation of the Troubles with the Indians*, or Mary Rowlandson's *The Soveraignty and Goodness of God*, conceived of Native diabolism as something not to be extirpated but rather to be suffered. It was interpreted entirely within the Protestant understanding of witchcraft as a matter of "consciences," couched in the rhetorical structure of the Jeremiad, where Native Americans and their diabolical god prevailed only temporarily when God's protection of his "new Jerusalem" in New England was temporarily lifted as the colony's collective punishment for some of its internal backsliders and degenerates. In Mary Rowlandson's *The Soveraignty and Goodness of God* (1682), for example, the interior "wilderness" of the colonial soul was projected upon an exterior "Indian wilderness"—upon irredeemable "black creatures in the night," as Rowlandson wrote, "which made the place [of her captivity] a lively resemblance of hell" (393).

Similarly, in *Wonders of the Invisible World*, his account of the Salem witch trials, Cotton Mather, the most prolific New English writer of the seventeenth century, synthesized Mede's notion of the Hemisphere's Satanic past with the providentialist understanding of witchcraft as a case of conscience. One of the reasons, he argued, that New England was afflicted so severely by witchcraft in Salem and Andover in 1692 was that New England was located in America, which once was "the *Devils* Territories" before the arrival of the Europeans (xi). "When the Silver-Trumpets of the Lord Jesus were so sound in the other *Hemisphere* of our World," he wrote in his *Seasonable Discourses,* "the Devil got a forlorn Crue over hither into America, in hopes that the Gospel never would come at them here" (20). One of the weapons that the devil employed in his retaliation against the New English Christian vanguard was his art of mimesis, or imitation of the Christian church and rituals, such as an organization "after the manner of Congregational Churches," the celebration of a baptism, and a supper, as well as "Officers among them, abominably Resembling those of our Lord" (105). "Tis very Remarkable to see," he wrote, "what an Impious & Imputent *Imitation* of Divine Things, is Apishly affected by the Devil, in several of those matters, whereof the Confessions of our Witches . . . have informed us" (104). Clearly, Mather echoed here the demonology of José de Acosta almost a hundred years before, citing him in Grimstone's 1604 translation in one of the editions of *Wonders* printed by Benjamin Harris in 1693, which added to the previous editions of this work a number of natural and preternatural "curiosities" concerning the phenomenon of witchcraft, which Mather recorded in the empiricist spirit becoming of a member of the Royal Society of London (104). "[T]he Indians which came from far to settle about Mexico," Mather wrote, "were in their Progress to that Settlement, under a Conduct of the Devil, very strangely Emulating what the Blessed God gave to Israel in the Wilderness." Citing Acosta, Mather continued to relate the story of the Aztecs' migration to Mexico under the command of "the Devil" god Huitzilopochtli.

Thus, for Mather, the witches of Salem perpetuated a long tradition of diabolism already begun by the Aztecs in Mexico. However, if the American hemisphere is thus more dangerously exposed than its Old World counterpart to the machinations of a raging devil deprived of his last hideout, so well disguised by the Atlantic Ocean for millennia, it is only because of the sins of New Englanders that he was able to inflict any harm.

> The first Planters of these Colonies were a *Chosen Generation* of men, who were first so *Pure,* as to disrelish many things which they thought wanted *Reformation* else where; and yet withal so *Peaceable,* that they Embraced a Voluntary Exile in a Squalid, horrid, *American* Desert, rather than to Live in Contentions with their Brethren. . . . But alas, the Children, and Servants of those Old planters, must needs afford many, *Degenerate Plants,* and there is now Risen up a Number of people, otherwise Inclined than our *Joshua's* and the *Elders that outlived them.* . . . Hence tis, that the Happiness of *New-England,* has been, *but for a Time,* as it was foretold, and not for a *Long Time,* as ha's been desir'd for us. A Variety of Calamity ha's long follow'd this Plantation; and we have all the Reason imaginable to ascribe it unto the Rebuke of Heaven upon us for our manifold *Apostasies;* we make no Right use of our Disasters, if we do not, *Remember whence we are fallen, and Repent, and Do the first works.* But yet our Afflictions may come under a further Consideration with us: there is a further cause of our Afflictions, whose *Due* must be *Given* him. (x)

Both Spanish and English writers increasingly came to associate Native American religions not only with paganism but with Satanism in the course of their respective colonial encounters in ways that enabled them to justify violent conquest by the terms laid out in Medieval canon law, which denied the right to "dominion" to any pagan guilty of violations of "natural law." However, while the English writers appear to be following here on the rhetorical and ideological coattails of Spanish historians of the New World, the demonization of Native American religions took very distinct forms and served very different rhetorical purposes in the ethnographic literatures of each realm. In Spanish American Counter-Reformation ethnographies, such as Hernando Ruiz de Alarcón's *Tratado de las supersticiones y costumbres gentílicas que hoy viven entre los indios naturales de esta Nueva España*, Native religious rites were represented for the purpose of extirpation (or exorcism), as his entire text was written, the author explained (39–40), to serve as a guide to other missionaries in the detection of diabolism when they found themselves in its presence, though often without being able to tell the difference between Catholic sacraments and Native superstitions, whose forms had dangerously fused in the course of decades of missionary work.[25] In British America, by contrast, conquest was predicated on the legal notion of *terra nullius* and the fiction that America was a "virgin land" or "wilderness" that could be lawfully settled by Englishmen, not, as in the Spanish conquest, on the model of the *reconquista*— the subjugation and conversion of infidels, new American vassals whose labor could be exploited. This fundamental difference had profound consequences for the encounter between Europeans and Native Americans, for the colonial societies that developed in each realm, and also for the role that "diabolism" played there. Thus, whereas Englishmen did at times see themselves as victimized by the Devil and his New World minions, for Franciscans in New Spain (such as Motolonía or Jerónimo de Mendieta), the Devil's victims who must be redeemed were not primarily European settlers but rather the Native neophytes, who had to be liberated from his clutches through extirpation and exorcism. In predominantly Protestant British America, by contrast, diabolism continued to be interpreted as a "matter of conscience," as something that had to be suffered and endured as a sign of God's righteous displeasure, and therefore is most typically subsumed in the rhetorical structure of the American jeremiad. When considered comparatively, the histories of Spanish and British American perceptions of Native American religions suggest the important role that the colonial encounter itself played in shaping Western Christianity.

Notes

* I would like to thank James Muldoon for his helpful comments on drafts of this essay.

1. Marshall 2–3. For some recent discussions of the Marshall ruling and the early modern "rights of discovery" doctrine, see Newcomb; Muldoon, "John Marshall"; Miller; Lengel; and Weston. For more on this history of the Protestant tradition of legitimating conquests in the New World vis-à-vis the prerogatives claimed by Europe's Catholic powers, see Benton and Straumann.
2. On the origin of the concept of "dominion" in Roman law and its medieval adaptations by Thomas Aquinas, Pierre d'Ally, and Jean Gerson, see Burns 16–39; on "dominion" in the context of Spanish imperialism, see Marrero-Fente, *Bodies* 94–95; also Muldoon, *Popes* 105–10; and Williams 59–66.
3. Qtd. in Muldoon, *Expansion* 55–56. On the medieval origins of the Doctrine, see also Pagden, *Lords* 29–62; Williams 72; Miller; and Marrero-Fente, *Bodies* 93.
4. On *Inter caetera*, see Marrero-Fente, *Bodies* 94–95; also Benton and Straumann 19; on the notion of symbolic ownership, see Seed; also Pagden, *Lords* 63–102.
5. Benton and Straumann, 20.
6. On Vitoria and his legacy, see Benton and Straumann 20–29; also Pagden, *Lords* 46–61; also Pagden, *Fall* 57–108; also Williams 96–97.
7. The best account of this intra-imperial struggle is still David Brading's *The First America*; but see also John Elliott's *Empires of the Atlantic World*.
8. On "law as literature" and the role of legal "fictions" in the justification of the Spanish conquest, see Marrero-Fente, *La poética* 5 and 99–106; on the role of legal "ceremonies" in the conquest, see Seed; also Adorno; on British America, see Jennings; also Hulme.
9. For the role that the notion of *vacuum domicilium* played in the history of British imperialism from the seventeenth to the nineteenth centuries, see Armitage 97. Benton and Straumann (6) point out that both *vacuum domicilium* and *terra nullius* were only two among many notions employed by English imperialists in their attempt to rationalize possession. They also emphasize the importance of distinguishing between legal philosophers and colonial agents and promoters, the latter of whom frequently proved to be remarkably flexible and pragmatic in their attempts to find legal rationales for their colonial projects.
10. On the role that (proto-)Lockean ideas about the state of nature played in English colonial discourse, see Corcoran.
11. The literature on the Spanish campaigns of extirpation is vast; for only a couple of landmark studies, see Ricard; Mills; and Cervantes.
12. Sixteenth-century England also had its own more direct experiences with colonial enterprises in Ireland, and some of the early English ideas about Native Americans were therefore colored, as Nicholas Canny and others have shown, by English ideas about the "wild Irish" (17–44).

13. For a discussion of the tension between a Thomist (or "Realist") and a "Nominalist" understanding of paganism, see Cervantes 5–39.
14. For a discussion of the Elizabethan consideration of these legal issues, see Miller 15–19; also Pagden, *Lords* 90.
15. On the English challenges of Spanish claims to possession based on "mere discovery," see Miller 17–18.
16. On the formation of the "Black Legend," see Gibson; on the history of the term, see also Greer, Mignolo, and Quilligan, "Introduction."
17. On de Bry, see Bucher; Groessen; Gaudio; and Gravatt.
18. For a discussion see Yates, *Giordano* and *Occult*.
19. This "folk" tradition of witchcraft is also implied in de Bry's depictions of the smoke of Native campfires, as Michael Gaudio's study of de Bry's engravings has shown (45–86).
20. Indeed, Michiel van Groessen, in his excellent study of the de Bry voyages, has shown not only the tendency on the part of the de Bry family to emphasize the allegedly diabolical nature of paganism in the overseas world but also the differences between the Latin and the German texts in this regard—the German edition being more explicit on the topic than the Latin editions. See Groessen 219–48.
21. Hakluyt had persuaded de Bry to use Harriot's account of Virginia rather than, say, Rene Goulene Laudonniere's account of French activities in Florida that would become the second volume of the *America* series; Jean de Lery's or Hans Staden's accounts of Brazil, which would become the third; or Girolamo Benzoni's (very critical) account of the Spanish conquest, which would make up the fourth—all of which predated the activities of the English in the New World. See Groessen 57–63.
22. Not much is known about the translator, Edward Grimstone. He apparently translated various works from Spanish and French into English; see Hadfield 105–08.
23. For a discussion of Mede's place in the evolution of an imperialist ideology in Great Britain, see Armitage 94–97.
24. For a discussion of "Virginia's Verger" as a "cant of conquest," see Jennings.
25. For a discussion of Ruiz de Alarcón's treatise, see Andrews and Hassig.

Works Cited

Acosta, José. *The naturall and morall historie of the East and West Indies*. Trans. E. Grimstone. London: Printed by Val. Sims, 1604. Print.

Adorno, Rolena. *Polemics of Possession in Spanish American Narrative*. New Haven: Yale University Press, 2008. Print.

Andrews, J. Richard, and Ross Hassig. "Editors' Introduction: The Historical Context." *Treatise on the Heathen Superstitions That Today Live Among the Indians Native to This New Spain, 1629*. Hernando Ruiz de Alarcón. Ed. and trans. J. Richard Andrews and Ross Hassig. Norman: University of Oklahoma Press, 1984. 3–36. Print.

Armitage, David. *The Ideological Origins of the British Empire.* Cambridge: Cambridge University Press, 2000. Print.
Benton, Lauren, and Benjamin Straumann. "Acquiring Empire by Law: From Roman Doctrine to Early Modern European Practice." *Law and History Review* 28 (2010): 1–38. Print.
Brading, David. *The First America: The Spanish Monarchy, Creole Patriots, and the Liberal State, 1492–1867.* Cambridge: Cambridge University Press, 1991. Print.
Bucher, Bernadette. *La sauvage aux seins pendants.* Paris: Herman, 1977. Print.
Burns, J. H. *Lordship, Kingship, and Empire.* Oxford: Clarendon Press, 1992. Print.
Cañizares-Esguerra, Jorge. *Puritan Conquistadors: Iberianizing the Atlantic, 1550–1700.* Stanford: Stanford University Press, 2006. Print.
Canny, Nicholas. "The Permissive Frontier: Social Control in English Settlements in Ireland and Virginia, 1550–1650." *The Westward Enterprise.* Eds. Kenneth R. Andrews, Nicholas P. Canny, P. E. H. Hair, and David B. Quinn. Detroit: Wayne State University Press, 1979. 17–44. Print.
Canup, John. *Out of the Wilderness: The Emergence of an American Identity in Colonial New England.* Middletown: Wesleyan University Press, 1990. Print.
Cervantes, Fernando. *The Devil in the New World: The Impact of Diabolism in New Spain.* New Haven: Yale University Press, 1994. Print.
Clark, Stuart. *Thinking with Demons: The Idea of Witchcraft in Early Modern Europe.* Oxford: Clarendon Press; New York: Oxford University Press, 1997. Print.
Corcoran, Paul. "John Locke on the Possession of Land: Native Title vs. the 'Principle' of Vacuum Domicilium." Paper presented to the Australasian Political Studies Association, Monash University, 24–26 Sept 2007. Web. 5 Jan 2012.
Elliott, John. *Empires of the Atlantic World: Britain and Spain in America, 1492–1830.* New Haven: Yale University Press, 2006. Print.
Gaudio, Michael. *Engraving the Savage: The New World and Techniques of Civilization.* Minneapolis: University of Minnesota Press, 2008. Print.
Gibson, Charles. *The Black Legend: Anti-Spanish Attitudes in the Old World and the New.* New York: Knopf, 1971. Print.
Gravatt, Patricia. "Rereading Theodor de Bry's Black Legend." *Rereading the Black Legend: The Discourses of Religious and Racial Difference in the Renaissance Empires.* Ed. Margaret Greer, Walter Mignolo, and Maureen Quilligan. Chicago: University of Chicago Press, 2008. 225–43. Print.
Greer, Margaret, Walter Mignolo, and Maureen Quilligan. *Rereading the Black Legend: The Discourses of Religious and Racial Difference in the Renaissance Empires.* Chicago: University of Chicago Press, 2008. Print.
Groessen, Michiel van. *The Representation of the Overseas World in the De Bry Collection of Voyages (1590–1634).* Leiden: Brill, 2008. Print.
Hadfield, Andrew. *Literature, Travel, and Colonial Writing in the English Renaissance, 1545–1625.* Oxford, UK: The Clarendon Press, 1998. Print.
Hakluyt, Richard. *The principal nauigations, voyages, traffiques and discoueries of*

the English nation. London: By George Bishop, Ralph Newberie, and Robert Barker, 1599. Print.

Harriot, Thomas. *A briefe and true report of the new found land of Virginia of the commodities and of the nature and manners of the naturall inhabitants. Discouered by the English colon there seated by Sir Richard Greinuile Knight in the eere 1585.* London: By R. Robinson, 1588. Print.

———. *A briefe and true report of the new found land of Virginia of the commodities and of the nature and manners of the naturall inhabitants. Discouered by the English colon there seated by Sir Richard Greinuile Knight in the eere 1585.* Frankfurt: Theodor de Bry, 1590. Print.

Householder, Michael. *Inventing Americans in the Age of Discovery: Narratives of Encounter.* Aldershot: Ashgate, 2010. Print.

Hulme, Peter. *Colonial Encounters: Europe and the Native Caribbean.* New York: Methuen, 1986. Print.

James I, King of England. *Daemonologie in forme of a dialogue, diuided into three bookes.* Edinburgh: Printed by Robert Walde-graue printer to the Kings Majestie, 1597. Print.

Jennings, Francis. *The Invasion of America: Indians, Colonialism, and the Cant of Conquest.* Chapel Hill: University of North Carolina Press, 1975. Print.

Lengel, James. "The Role of International Law in the Development of Constitutional Jurisprudence in the Supreme Court: The Marshall Court and American Indians." *American Journal of Legal History* 43 (1999): 117–32. Print.

Marrero-Fente, Raúl. *Bodies, Texts and Ghosts: Writing on Literature and Law in Colonial Latin America.* Lanham: University Press of America, 2010. Print.

———. *La poética de la ley en las Capitulaciones de Sante Fe.* Madrid: Editorial Trotta, 2000.

Marshall, John. *The Life of George Washington.* 3 vols. Fredericksburg: The Citizens' Guild of Washington's Boyhood Home, 1926. Print.

Mather, Cotton. *Wonders of the Invisible World.* Ed. Reiner Smolinski. Lincoln: University of Nebraska Press, 2007. Print.

Mede, Joseph. "A Coniecture Concerning Gog and Magog in the Revelation" [1627]. *The Works of the Pious and Profoundly-Learned Joseph Mede, BD.* London: Printed by James Flesher for Richard Royston, 1664. Print.

Miller, Robert. "The Doctrine of Discovery in American Indian Law." *Idaho Law Review* 42 (2005–2006): 1–122. Print.

Mills, Kenneth. *Idolatry and Its Enemies: Colonial Andean Religion and Extirpation, 1640–1750.* Princeton, NJ: Princeton University Press, 1997. Print.

Muldoon, James. "John Marshall and the Rights of the Indians." *Latin America and the Atlantic World/El mundo atlántico y América Latina (1500–1850).* Ed. Renate Pieper and Peer Schmidt. Köln: Böhlau, 2005. 67–82. Print.

———. *The Expansion of Europe: The First Phase.* Philadelphia: University of Pennsylvania Press, 1977. Print.

———. *Popes, Lawyers, and Infidels: The Church and the Non-Christian World, 1250–1550*. Philadelphia: University of Pennsylvania Press, 1979. Print.

Newcomb, Steven. *Pagans in the Promised Land: Decoding the Doctrine of Christian Discovery*. Golden: Fulcrum Books, 2008. Print.

Pagden, Anthony. *The Fall of Natural Man: The American Indian and the Origins of Comparative Ethnology*. Cambridge: Cambridge University Press, 1982. Print.

———. *Lords of All the World: Ideologies of Empire in Spain, Britain, and France, 1500–1800*. New Haven: Yale University Press, 1995. Print.

Purchas, Samuel. *Hakluytus Posthumus, or Purchas his Pilgrimes* [London, 1625]. 20 vols. Glasgow: James MacLehose & Sons, 1905–1907. Print.

Ralegh, Walter. *The discouerie of the large, rich, and bevvtiful empire of Guiana with a relation of the great and golden citie of Manoa*. London: By Robert Robinson, 1596. Print.

Ricard, Robert. *The Spiritual Conquest of Mexico*. Berkeley: University of California Press, 1966. Print.

Rowlandson, Mary. *The sovereignty & goodness of God, together, with the faithfulness of his promises displayed; being a narrative of the captivity and restauration of Mrs. Mary Rowlandson*. Cambridge, MA: by Samuel Green, 1682. Print.

Ruiz de Alarcón, Hernando. *Treatise on the Heathen Superstitions That Today Live Among the Indians Native to This New Spain, 1629*. Ed. and trans. J. Richard Andrews and Ross Hassig. Norman: University of Oklahoma Press, 1984. Print.

Seed, Patricia. *Ceremonies of Possession in Europe's Conquest of the New World, 1492–1640*. Cambridge: Cambridge University Press, 1995. Print.

Smith, John. *The generall historie of Virginia, New-England, and the Summer Isles with the names of the adventurers, planters, and governours from their first beginning*. London: Printed by I.D. and I.H. for Michael Sparkes, 1624. Print.

Thomas, Keith. *Religion and the Decline of Magic* [1971]. Oxford: Oxford University Press, 1997. Print.

Tuveson, Ernest Lee. *Millennium and Utopia: A Study in the Background of the Idea of Progress*. Berkeley: University of California Press, 194 Lockhart, James 9. Print.

Weston, Blake. "John Marshall and Indian Land Rights: A Historic Rejoinder to the Claim of 'Universal Recognition' of the Doctrine of Discovery." *Seton Hall Law Review* 36 (2005–2006): 481–550. Print.

Williams, Robert. *The American Indian in Western Legal Thought: The Discourse of Conquest*. New York: Oxford University Press, 1990. Print.

Yates, Francis. *Giordano Bruno and the Hermetic Tradition*. London: Routledge, 1964.

———. *The Occult Philosophy in the Elizabethan Age*. London: Routledge, 1979.

6

Narrating Conversion: Idolatry, the Sacred, and the Ambivalences of Christian Evangelization in Colonial Peru

Laura León Llerena

The Huarochirí Manuscript (circa 1598–1608) is considered an exceptional colonial source. It is the only book-length indigenous text written almost entirely in Quechua by an anonymous Christianized native of the Andean region of Huarochirí (Peru). In this essay I argue that its exceptionality also resides in the complex and ambivalent discursive representation of conversion it conveys throughout its fifty folios. Written at a time when the methods used by evangelical missionaries to convert the native inhabitants of Huarochirí were undergoing a violent radicalization, the Huarochirí Manuscript can hardly be considered a text that conforms to the pastoral goals of the texts sponsored by the post-Tridentine Church in the Spanish American territories. I aim to emphasize this aspect of unconformity in the indigenous manuscript by analyzing the textual tension that exists when the HM narrative construction is considered in relation to two other sources that have not thus far received enough attention: the marginalia left in various folios of the Huarochirí Manuscript by Father Francisco de Ávila, a renowned extirpator of idolatries, and an unfinished treatise on native idolatries that he wrote in 1608 in Spanish, which includes information that can be found in the anonymous Quechua text.

As other studies have already shown, it is highly probable that the Indian or Indians who wrote the Huarochirí Manuscript were Father Ávila's assistants.[1] Ávila, a priest born in Cuzco and fluent in Quechua, was responsible for the Christian indoctrination of the inhabitants of one of the *reducciones* or Indian towns in the province of Huarochirí.[2] The Huarochirí Manuscript makes a number of references to Ávila and the violent campaign he started in Huarochirí and other neighboring provinces in 1608 to extirpate idolatries. The relationship between Ávila and the author(s) of the Quechua text has led some scholars to believe that the writing of the latter was a project that Ávila had entrusted to his native assistants. These were *indios ladinos* or Christianized Indians who, having learned Spanish and acquired to varying degrees European customs, acted as mediators between the indigenous society and the colonizers. Apart from the marginalia left by Ávila in the Huarochirí Manuscript, his relationship with the author(s) of the Huarochirí Manuscript seems also to be confirmed by the fact that the narrator of the indigenous text presents him- or herself in some passages as "we the Christians," employing the Quechua suffix *–nchik*, which indicates that the person being addressed—the reader—is included as part of "we."[3]

The Huarochirí Manuscript constructs the topography of the routes followed by both men and deities since time immemorial. It maps out the network of places, objects, and meanings that configured a world where human and sacred geographies were inseparable. Although the usefulness of this kind of information for the extirpator of idolatries is rather obvious, it cannot be assumed that the reasons for producing the text coincided with Ávila's intentions. This discrepancy, as I aim to demonstrate in the following pages, becomes discernible when attention is paid to Ávila's marginalia and to the ideological distance that lies between the priest's treatise and the Huarochirí Manuscript.

Sacred Genealogy in the Huarochirí Manuscript

> kaypim churani kay huc yayayuq guarocheri ñisqap machunkunap kawsasqanta *ima ffeeniyuqcha karqan*, imahinac kanankamapas kawsan, chay chaykunakta chayri sapa llaqtanpim quillqasqa kanqa imahina kawsasqanpas paqarisqanmanta. (*Ritos* 2, emphasis added)

> (I set forth here the lives of the ancestors of the Huaro Cheri people, who all descend from one forefather: *What faith they held*, how they live up until now, those things and more; village by village it will be written down: how they lived from their dawning age onward.) *Huarochirí Manuscript* 41–42, emphasis added.) [4]

The lines quoted above, which function as a kind of *incipit* of the Huarochirí Manuscript ("HM" from now on), seem to confirm the generally accepted hypothesis that the reason for writing the anonymous Quechua manuscript was to provide information that would aid the campaign to extirpate idolatries organized by Father Francisco de Ávila. Even though in the first few pages and chapters of the HM the narrator deals mainly with non-Christian beliefs and practices, the *incipit* incorporates the word *fe* (faith) in Spanish. There was no equivalent concept in Quechua to that of faith as understood by Christianity, even though in his *Vocabulario de la lengua general* (1608) the Jesuit Diego González Holguín included the Quechua word *yñicuy* as equivalent to "Fee por el acto del creer" (524) (faith by the act of believing).[5] The *Vocabulario*'s publication was contemporaneous to the probable time of writing of the HM, and it provides an insight not only into the studies that were being undertaken of the Quechua language but also into the transformation this native language was undergoing as it became a crucial tool in the indoctrination of the neophytes.

The narrator's decision to use the word *fe* in Spanish in the opening lines of the manuscript points to the HM's relationship with the evangelization ideology of those times. In a context of forced conversions, the use of the word *fe* to refer to indigenous rituals and beliefs establishes a relation of similarity between these beliefs and Christian ones. But because Indian practices could not be recognized as Christian, the similarity was interpreted as an imitation or diabolic inversion, making these practices reprehensible and punishable. This is clearly stated in the treaties on idolatrous beliefs and practices of the native inhabitants of New Spain and Peru written in the sixteenth and early seventeenth centuries.[6]

The manuscript implicitly conveys a sense of anxiety about the legitimacy of an indigenous religious and social structure that is in the process of being dislocated. Religious belief in the text is not constrained to the Christian sense of the sacred but refers rather to the social bonds established between men, ancestors, and gods: recognition and worship in return for protection. These bonds were crucial to the ordering of the economic, social, and political structure of the human world, hence the narrator's concern about how these relationships are being modified in the colonial context.[7]

The HM includes stories of deities, cultural heroes, and sacred entities that were linked to the origins and social structure of diverse kin groups inhabiting the Huarochirí region. The *huacas*, or deities, known as Paria Caca and Chaupi Ñamca appear in the text as the most important of the sacred beings, followed by Cuni Raya Vira Cocha, Pacha Camac, Tutay Quiri, Maca Uisa, Chuqui Suso, and Huallallo Caruincho, among others.[8] Although some of the

HM's chapters refer to "earlier times" while others are clearly set in the colonial context, all of them link the narrative to sacred indigenous beings and entities while scarcely mentioning the Christian God and the Virgin Mary.

Geography has a central role in the relationship conceived between the sacred and the human spheres. Deities and their mythical acts manifest themselves in the colonial present through local landscape features such as mountains, lakes, stones, and even weather-related phenomena such as rain, hail, thunder, and so on. Furthermore, each of these sacred entities is considered the "father" or "mother" of a particular kin group or community, meaning that the stories of "earlier times" in which *huacas* play a central role also serve to narrate how the social rights and duties of the huacas' "sons"—rights and duties that remained valid in the colonial present and beyond—were established. These rights and obligations were linked to different aspects of the social organization, such as the allocation of land to each community, the rotation of water usage for irrigation, and the hierarchy that had to be observed by participants in rituals honoring the regional *huacas*.

Although the narrator takes Paria Caca and Chaupi Ñamca as points of reference to establish a genealogy, neither of these is clearly positioned as a foundational figure that establishes a linear conception of time. It should be noted that missionaries had been preaching and teaching Indians the concept of providential history on a chronological basis for approximately seven decades. The results of this aspect of the evangelizing process are evident in the discursive temporal structure of two other contemporaneous texts to the HM written by native Andeans: *El primer nueva corónica y buen gobierno* (c. 1615–1616) by Felipe Guaman Poma de Ayala and the *Relación de antigüedades deste reyno del Pirú* (c. 1613) by Joan de Santa Cruz Yamqui Salcamaygua. In the texts by Poma and Pachacuti, indigenous history previous to the arrival of the Spaniards is incorporated into the Western Christian conception of time. These accounts identify the genesis of the world with a single god responsible for its creation, although in both texts there is also a moment where the narrators explain that at one point their ancestors lost their way and became idolaters.

If the HM's narrator had fully adopted the Christian idea of creation, it would have made sense for the first chapter to be entitled "del primero y mas antiguo Dios, o ydolo de esta gente y como estas provincias diçen que eran antiguamente tierra muy caliente, y como luego uuo otros ydolos tras del primero" (Ávila f. 116r) (of the First and Most Ancient God or Idol of This People and How They Say These Provinces Were Very Hot Lands in Old Times, and How Afterwards There Were Other Idols after the First One).[9] It would also have made sense for this chapter to start with the following sentence: "Es tradicion antiquissima que al principio y primero que otra cosa de que aya memoria, uvo unas Huacas o ydolos. . . ." (Ávila f. 116r) (It is a very ancient tradition that in the beginning, the first thing that there is memory of, there were two *huaca*s or idols). However, these citations have been taken not from the HM but rather from the *Tratado y relación* (1608) by Ávila. They are written in Spanish and draw upon some of the narratives contained in the HM. In contrast, the first chapter of the HM has not a title in Quechua but an ex post facto title in Spanish: "como fue antiguam(ente) los ydolos y como guerreo entre ellos y como auia en aquel tiempo los naturales" (*Ritos* 4, note 1) (How the Idols of Old Were, and How they Warred among Themselves, and How the Natives Existed at that Time) (*HM* 43). Unlike the text written by Ávila, the first chapter of the HM does not seem to transmit a sense of urgency to identify a creator god, originator of the world and humanity, similar to the Christian god. It is only by the end of this chapter, and in order to comply with an external demand made on the narrative, that the narrator abruptly states, "chaymantam kanan huk wakataq cuniraya sutiyuq karqan kaytam mana allichu yachanchik pariacacamantapas ichapas ñawpaqnin karqan o qipanpas" (*Ritos* 8) (Also, as we know, there was another *huaca* named Cuni Raya. Regarding him, we are not sure whether he existed before Paria Caca or maybe after him) (*HM* 44).

The external demand I refer to is made by Ávila, as can be verified by the fact that the quoted sentence is accompanied by a marginal comment in Spanish in Ávila's handwriting that says, "saber si dice que no se sabe si fue antes o después de Carhuincho o de Pariacaca" (*Ritos* 9, note 15) (Find out whether he says that it isn't known if he was before or after Caruincho or Paria Caca) (*HM* 44). The way the stories are organized and the form each takes give a clear idea of the narrative priorities of the HM. The main concern of its first chapter is not to present a linear genealogy of the native deities nor to pinpoint a moment of genesis for humankind, but rather to explain how in the past an immortal humanity faced problems of overpopulation and scarcity of food and how *huaca* Huallallo Caruincho intervened to control the population growth. The narrator states that "later" another *huaca* called Paria Caca "appeared" and defeated Huallallo who was cast out to another region (*HM* 44).

The pressure exerted by Ávila's marginal note quoted above did however generate two different answers in other chapters of the HM. In chapter fourteen, the opening lines written in Quechua state, "ñawpaqnin capitulopim ari unancharqanchik cunirayap kasqanta, pariacacamanta ñawpaqninchus o qipanchus karqan, chayta" (*Ritos* 196) (In the first chapter we made some remarks about whether Cuni Raya's existence came before or after Paria Caca's) (*HM* 88). In contrast to other chapters where the heading is clearly differentiated from the text, the opening lines of this chapter are not well spaced from the main text but written in large letters, seemingly acting as a title. The sentences that follow in chapter fourteen do not present a clear answer to the matter being discussed: "cuniraya viracocha ñisqanchikqa ancha ñawpamantataqsi karqan pariacacapas ima hayka wakakunapas paytaqa astawantaqsi yupaychaq karqan wakinninkunaqa "pariacacapas cunirayap churinsi" ñispam ñinku" (*Ritos* 196) (They say Cuni Raya Viracocha did exist from very ancient times. Paria Caca and all the other *huacas* used to revere him exceedingly. In fact, some people even say, "Paria Caca is Cuni Raya's son") (*HM* 88). The narrator makes a subtle reference to the existence of other versions of the genealogy of the native deities, complicating the possibility of establishing a parallel to the Christian god. The chapter is not concerned with discussing genesis in Christian terms; on the contrary, the narrative focuses on the relationship between Cuni Raya and Inca Huayna Capac and the former's announcement about the end of the Inca Empire. Furthermore, the following chapter seems to be justified only as a definitive answer to Ávila's demand for information about a linear genealogy of the sacred. Entitled "kaymantam iskaynin capitulo rimasqanchikta cunirayap caruinchumanta ñawpaq kasqantapas o qipan kasqantapas qillqasun" (*Ritos* 206) (Next We Shall Write about What Was Mentioned in the Second Chapter, Namely, Whether Cuni Raya Existed before or after Caruincho) (*HM* 91), this brief chapter—one of the shortest in the whole HM—adopts the discourse of a universalizing Christian theology from its opening lines:

> cuniraya viracochaqa ancha ñawpaqmantataqsi karqan manaraq pay kaptinqa manas kay pachapi imallapas karqanchu payraqsi urqukunaktapassachaktapas mayuktapas ima hayka animalkunaktapas kamarqan chakrakunaktapas runap kawsanqanpaq chayraykutaqmi chay cunirayakta "pariacacap yayansi" ñinku, "paytaqsi pariacacaktapas kamarqan" ñispa. (*Ritos* 206)

> (Cuni Raya Vira Cocha is said to have existed from very ancient times. Before he was, there was nothing at all in this world. It was he who first gave shape and force to the mountains, the forests, the rivers, and all sorts of animals, and to the fields for humankind's subsistence as well. It's for this reason that people in fact say of Cuni Raya, "He's called Paria Caca's father." "It was he who made and empowered Paria Caca.") (*HM* 91)

At the end of this chapter, the narrator states that in the following pages Cuni Raya's deeds will be recounted, but in fact there are no further stories told about this *huaca* as the protagonist, and he is only briefly mentioned again in chapters sixteen and thirty-one. Why was it so important for Francisco de Ávila to exert pressure on the HM's anonymous author(s) to determine a chronological genealogy of the indigenous deities? The concept of idolatry has to be carefully considered in trying to approach an answer, but due to the space constraints of this essay I will only highlight that this concept is intimately linked to a specific system of interpretation of Indian practices that aims to capture, make intelligible, and subjugate a culture that is considered "other." The marginal notes that correspond to Ávila's handwriting and his incomplete *Tratado y relación* shed light on the conceptual frames the priest deployed to access the meanings of what was considered sacred in the stories that make up the HM, as well as the limitations of these frames. The solution that Ávila tried to impose on the anonymous Quechua text—the same solution he resorted to in his own *Tratado y relación*—is the use of the narrative device of the simile, a common strategy deployed by many other authors of treaties dealing with idolatry in native America (Estenssoro 194–205). It was necessary for Ávila, just as it was for many others who tried to understand the religious system of the Incas, to identify a creator god and establish a linear narrative about humankind's genesis that could then be presented as a demonic imitation of the history of Christianity. Running out of patience after being unable to find answers to these questions in the HM, Ávila wrote in his own treatise:

> dexando ahora aquella tan dudosa question del origen cierto de estos yndios para otro tiempo (si Dios quisiere darlo) siendo tambien cierto que los progenitores de estos yndios despues del diluvio no pudieron referir las novelas y ynvenciones dichas a sus hijos: siguese que el Demonio que tan Señor ha sido de estos, lo conto y embusto. (f. 121v)

> (leaving aside for another time [if God so wishes] this very dubious question about the true origin of these Indians, and considering as well that it is also certain that after the deluge the forefathers of these Indians could not have told the mentioned lies and inventions to their sons then it follows that the Demon, who has been Master of all of them, told these stories and deceived them.)

As previously mentioned, in chapter fifteen the HM's narrator seems to finally yield to Ávila's pressure, identifying Cuni Raya Vira Cocha as a creator god similar to the Christian god. Although in previous chapters some stories deal with Cuni Raya as a regional *huaca*, it is in chapter fifteen that he appears assimilated into an Inca deity, Vira Cocha. It should be noted that the texts written about Peru that were in circulation by the end of the sixteenth century and the beginning of the seventeenth, including Garcilaso de la Vega's *Royal Commentaries of the Incas* (Lisbon, 1609), portrayed Vira Cocha as the creator god of the Incas. It appears from Ávila's own writings that his understanding of the religious system of the people of Huarochirí rested on the identification of Vira Cocha or Cuni Raya Viracocha as such.[10] Ávila may well have been influenced by Garcilaso's portrayal of Vira Cocha. Thanks to the collection of texts classified as ms. 3169 housed in the Biblioteca Nacional of Madrid, it is known that Francisco de Ávila read the *Royal Commentaries*. Folios 61 to 63v of ms. 3169 contain a series of notes made by Ávila about the origin and succession of the Incas that end with the following sentence: "All of this [information] has been taken out of the book of the Royal Commentaries by Garcilaso de la Vega, the first book, which is divided in nine books."[11]

The stories of the HM that refer to Cuni Raya as a local *huaca* characterize him as a trickster whose cunning and ploys become forces that are constantly modifying the world. This is suggested in the closing lines of the lengthy second chapter of the HM, in which the narrator states that Cuni Raya traveled around the area tricking other local *huacas* and people (*Ritos* 30). But the mention of his tricks is not meant to carry an implicit moral judgment, as would usually be the case in pastoral texts that focused on idolatry and the devil. Cuni Raya's tricks are witty ways out of complicated situations that are narrated in a comical tone. It is probably for this reason that the forced and ineffective parallel between the Christian god and Cuni Raya is restricted to a few passages.

But the tension between the anonymous author(s) of the HM and Francisco de Ávila goes well beyond the organization of the genealogy of the sacred in the indigenous world. In the following pages, I will highlight the discrepancies between the intentionalities of the indigenous narrator and of Francisco de Avila by comparing and analyzing the tensions that emerge between the HM's main narrative and the priest's marginal notes in Spanish, as well as his own incomplete treatise.

Textual Interventions

Some of the initial chapters of the HM (two, three, and four) seem to be explicitly linked to biblical stories in the Old and New Testaments that were used to educate the neophytes.[12] However, as I will show in the analysis of two of these chapters, the relationship between the HM and these biblical stories takes unexpected turns considering the historical context of conversion and extirpation of idolatries in which the Quechua manuscript was produced.

In chapter three, the narrator recounts how a llama warned its owner that in five days time the ocean would overflow bringing the world to an end. The llama goes on to explain that they could both be saved by climbing to the top of the mountain Villca Coto, which they do, thus managing to survive the flood. At this point in the story, the narrator intervenes to assert, "kay simiktam kanan christianokuna unanchanchik chay tiempo del [di]lobioktac paykunaqa hina villcacutukta qispisqanta unanchakun" (*Ritos* 36) (Regarding this story, we Christians believe it refers to the time of the Flood. But they believe it was Villca Coto mountain that saved them) (*HM* 52). In chapter four the narrator recounts a story "about the Death of the Sun" (*HM* 53) in which the sun disappears for five days leaving the world in darkness. During this time rocks banged against each other, and objects of daily use and domestic animals chased and ate people. The narrator puts an end to this story with the following sentence: "kaytam kanan ñuqanchik christi[a]nokuna unanchanchik jesu christo apunchikpaq wañusqanpi tutayasqantac kaykunaqa riman ñispa 'unanchanchik ichac ari chay'" (*Ritos* 38) (Here's what we Christians think about it: We think these stories tell of the darkness following the death of our Lord Jesus Christ. Maybe that's what it was) (*HM* 53).

One of the fundamental differences between the HM and the *Tratado y relación* by Ávila is that the former includes a point of view that is not Christian, or that at least has a nondogmatic understanding of Christianity, as can be seen from the stories above that refer to the origins and remote past of humankind. In these stories, the narrator does not usually make moral judgments about this non-Christian point of view. In his version of the HM's chapters that deal with the flood and the eclipse of the sun, Ávila states that the indigenous accounts were "un notable disparate" (notable nonsense) produced by "los autores de mentira de esta gente" (the authors of lies among this people) or by "engaños del demonio" (deceptions of the demon) (*Tratado y relación* f. 120v, f. 121r, f. 120r). However, although the HM's narrator allows for the coexistence and even the overlapping of differing points of view, it should be noted that this only happens in relation to stories that refer to "ancient times." None of the initial chapters of the HM establish any explicit connection with the colonial present in terms of the continuity of indigenous rituals or practices. Pointing out such a connection would have implied a denunciation of idolatrous practices that, as I will discuss in the following pages, does not seem to have been a purpose initially driving the HM narrative but may have been imposed on the text as its writing progressed.

It is also in "ancient times" that Pariacaca punished a woman by transforming her into stone, as narrated in chapter five. The narrator intervenes in the story to clarify: "chay rumis kanankamapas, imanam runap chankan, hina chankayuq rakayuq tiyan chaytas imanqanpaq ari kukakta chaysawa churapun kanankamapas" (*Ritos* 70) (This stone, just like a woman's legs with thighs and a vagina, stands there until today. Even now people put coca on top of it when they undertake something) (*HM* 59). Next to this sentence there is a marginal comment in Ávila's handwriting: "Nota y preguntar para que se pone esta coca" (*Ritos* 70) (Ask why they put this coca) (*HM* 59). This marginal note reveals the extent to which the culture that is being described in the main text remains alien to Ávila. The reason that coca was placed on top of the stone has already been explained in the story itself: it is an offering to honor the mythical figures that persist in the shape of rocks or stones as traces of the past acts of deities.[13] But Ávila was not interested in understanding the mechanisms through which meaning was produced in indigenous ritual practices. The priest was asking for more specific information so that he could denounce these practices and condemn them as idolatries. Many other marginal comments in Ávila's handwriting betray the same intention, as can be confirmed in the same chapter five, where he writes, "Preguntar como se dize este pucyo y en que parte esta" (*Ritos* 56, note 54) (Ask the name of this spring and where it is) (*HM* 57); in chapter eight, where he notes, "Este lugar donde esta sullca yllapa chuquehuampo esta abajo de Tumna entre sicicaya y sucya he de uerlo sauer como se llama" (*Ritos* 114, note 49) (This place where [crossed out: Sullca Yllapa] Chuqui Huampo is is below Tumna between Sisi Caya and Sucya. I have to see it and find out what it's called) (*HM* 69); and in chapter nine, when he writes, "saber este genero de canto y ponermelo en vn papel en lengua de chechhua todo lo que dizen" (*Ritos* 130, note 55) (Find out about this sort of song and write it down for me on paper in the Quechua language, from what they say) (*HM* 73). These and other marginalia by Ávila reveal the use he intended to make of the reading material.

Considering that both the campaign to extirpate idolatries and the constant gaze of Ávila over the text that was being written are crucial elements of the context in which the HM was produced, it is not surprising to find the word "idol" in the text. The word, however, is only used twice—once in the Spanish title of one of the chapters and then in a marginal note—and is absent from the main narrative in Quechua. It appears for the first time in the title of chapter one: "como fue antiguam(ente) los ydolos y como guerreo entre ellos y como auia en aquel tiempo los naturales" (*Ritos* 4, note 1) (How the Idols of Old Were, and How They Warred among Themselves, and How the Natives Existed at That Time) (*HM* 43). Like all the titles of the first six chapters, this one is written in Spanish in what appear to be ex post facto insertions to the Quechua text, as indicated by the quality of the ink and the tight space they occupy.

The use of the word "idols" in the title refers to the sacred entities that the narrator indentifies in the main Quechua text as *huacas*. In chronicles and ecclesiastical reports (*visitas*), the words *idol* and *huaca* usually appeared as synonyms. In his *Tratado y relación*, Ávila establishes this relationship of synonymy: "mando Cauillaca hacer junta de todos los *huacas* ydolos principales de la tierra" (f. 117r) (Caui Llaca summoned all the principal *huacas*, idols of these territories). However, the narrator of the HM does not establish this relationship, or at least not explicitly, in the main text of any of the thirty-one chapters and two supplements. The word "idol" appears again in chapter twenty-four when the narrative focuses on the rituals that take place during the Ñan Sapa festival. Referring to the local deities that were contacted by humans through the blowing of conch trumpets, the narrator employs the Quechua term *llaqtakuna*. The pre-Hispanic concept of *llacta* or *llaqta* referred to the identity established by the relationship between geographical territory and the ancestor or local *huaca*. The word *llaqtakuna* was encircled ex post facto and connected to a marginal comment in Spanish that reads "significa ydolo" (*Ritos* 326, note 81) (means "idol"). This comment in Ávila's handwriting appears to be an attempt to offer a translation that would help expand the typology of Andean idols.

It could be argued that the HM's narrative does not make an explicit link between *huaca* and *idol*: given that the narrator identifies itself as "we Christians," from a Christian point of view a *huaca* would implicitly be an idol. Although the HM is not shaped by an anti-idolatry rhetoric like that in Ávila's unfinished *Tratado y relación*, the use that the priest intended to make of the anonymous text can be perceived in the way the content and tone of the manuscript change from chapter seven onward: the narrator begins to give the names of seventeen different indigenous rituals, dances and festivities, including in some cases details about the time of year when these took place, which sometimes coincided with Christian celebrations, and the places where they were performed. However, this kind of detail only appears in ten of the thirty-three chapters that compose the HM.

Even when the details presented in some chapters seem to turn the tone of the narration into a denunciation, the way in which this information is presented, the mode of enunciation, the complexity of the structure of each story, the combination of different narrative genres, and above all the incorporation of anonymous voices with non-Christian points of view establish a distance between this manuscript and a denunciation or account of idolatries. When contrasting the HM and Ávila's *Tratado y relación*, what emerges is a clear struggle for the power to interpret a culture.

"Why Do You Do These Things?"

Returning to chapter seven of the HM, I consider this chapter to be very important because it marks the narrative moment when the heroic mythical past crystallizes into an idolatrous remainder in the Christian present. This chapter deals with rituals performed during the cleaning of irrigation canals, which, according to the story, exist thanks to *huaca* Chuqui Suso's deeds in ancient times. The narrator intervenes suddenly in the story to lament that "even now"—that is, when almost every native has been converted to Christianity—some people continue to perform these rituals, with nobody daring to stop them by asking "imaraykum chayhina ruranki" (*Ritos* 98) (Why do you do these things?) (*HM* 65). This is a crucial question that underlies why both the HM project and Ávila's own project were undertaken. In the Quechua manuscript, however, this question gives rise to a process of self-reflection on the part of the anonymous author(s). On the one hand, it proposes an outside gaze into native culture, marking a distance toward it. On the other, the formulation of the question reveals the uncomfortable place from which it is being enunciated: whoever asks the question is already inscribed in a colonial order that, through the use of writing and the Quechua language as an evangelizing tool, establishes a relationship of violence with indigenous culture. As far as Ávila's project was concerned, this question—in both its theological and its political dimensions—was a rhetorical one, since both the priest and Catholic Church had already formulated its answer before the question was asked. The supposed persistence of idolatry, the subject of Ávila's unfinished *Tratado y relación*, was what justified and sustained the colonial enterprise in its spiritual and material dimensions.

Indigenous beliefs about death and the rituals in honor of the deceased were a main source of concern for the treaties on idolatries in the New World. The HM touches on this subject in various chapters but in a particularly ambiguous way in chapter twenty-eight, entitled "imanam pariacacap mitanpi animakunakta qaraq karqan; chaymanta todos santospaqri imahinam ñawpa pacha unancharqan" (*Ritos* 364) (How People Used to Feed the Spirits of the Dead during Paria Caca's Festival and How They Thought about All Saints' Day in Former Times) (*HM* 130). Although the title seems to refer to the past, this chapter offers an explanation of why people in the colonial present carried on performing certain rituals related to the death of their loved ones.[14] Initially, the narrator seems interested in exposing a connection between the incomplete state of conversion to Christianity and the sustained ties with the indigenous past. However, the narrative opens up the possibility of understanding those continuities from a stance different to that of the discourse on idolatry:

ñam ari wakinnin capitulopi pariacacakta muchaypaq rispa, imanam runakuna wañuqninkunakta waqaq karqan qaraqpas karqan, chay chaykunakta rimarqanchik chay qarasqankunakta yuyarispam kanan runakuna manaraq alli xpistianoman tukuspa rimarqanku kay todos santo[s]paq: "hinataqmi viracochakunapas ayanta tullunta qaran mikuchin" ñispa "haku ygleciaman wañuqninchikkunakta qaramusun" ñispa ñawpa pachaqa ima hayka mikuykunaktapas alli chayasqakamata apaq karqan. (*Ritos* 364)

(In another chapter we have already told how, when people traveled to worship Paria Caca, they used to cry for their dead and feed them. Remembering those meals for the dead, people who hadn't yet sincerely converted to Christianity are known to have said, "The Spaniards also give food to their dead, to their bones, on All Saints' Day, they do feed them. So let's go to church. Let's feed our own dead.") (*HM* 131)

What seems to be a tone of denunciation regarding these rituals is accompanied by the use of the speculative mode with which the narrator attempts to explain that the continuity of these ceremonies could be linked to the perceived similarity between Christian ("The Spaniards also give food to their dead") and non-Christian indigenous practices.[15] Besides the evident distance that is established between the narrator, identified as "we Christians" in other passages of the HM, and those Indians who "hadn't yet sincerely converted," the use of the speculative mode opens a space to reflect on the effects of conversion from the native point of view. Thus, a question such as "Why do you do these things?" put forth in chapter seven should be understood not only as an admonishment of those who continued to perform certain rituals but also as a moment when the anxiety generated by the transition from the pre-Hispanic order to the colonial world view becomes explicit. This violent transition frames the narrator's concerns about the persistence of deities and rites from the pre-Hispanic past. The incursions of the past into the Christian present, as either the continuity or adaptation of beliefs and practices, destabilizes the category of "Christian Indian" and undermines the authority of the narrator. There is not one example in the HM of a clearly defined moment of rupture between the past and present. While for Ávila the stories about the indigenous pre-Hispanic past are "nonsense," "fables," and "superstitions," the HM makes it clear in several chapters that the claims made in colonial times by some *ayllus* regarding land ownership and water distribution rights were legitimized by their status as descendants of particular *huacas* and mythical heroes, something that the narrator does not condemn.[16]

Not even an event such as the arrival of the Spaniards in the Andean territory is considered in the HM to be a moment of rupture between past and present. The event is mentioned in eight different chapters (chapters 9, 10, 13, 14, 17, 18, 19, and 22) but as secondary contextual information to the story that each chapter is presenting. The narrator refers to the Spaniards' arrival as "appearing" (*rikurimurqan*), and nowhere is there a suggestion that the event was considered a watershed moment. However, the event is presented as having triggered a symbolic rupture. In various chapters of the HM, it is explained that after the Spanish appeared, the inhabitants of the region of Huarochirí began to modify the dates, the places, and even the form of their ritual practices as well as hiding objects they considered sacred.

Although the reference to people hiding sacred objects and secretly performing rituals seems to indicate an accusation of idolatry, the text also allows for the possibility of reading in it a denunciation of something other than the continuity of indigenous practices. In chapter seven, commenting on those people who continued to perform rituals related to the cleaning of irrigation canals in the present day, the narrator explains that "'rarqaktam pichamuni, padre; takikusaq upyakusaq' ñispam llullachin kaytaqa tukuy hinantin runakunam␣ruraytaqa ruran ichaqa wakinqa mana ñam␣ruranchu alli padreyuq kaspa wakinri pakallapiqa hinataq kanankamapas kawsanku" (*Ritos* 98) (And as for the Catholic priest, they fool him, saying, "Padre, I'm back from cleaning the canal, so I'm going to dance, I'm going to drink." As far as that goes, *all the people* do the same thing. True, *some don't do it* anymore because they have a *good padre*. But others go on living like this in secret up to the present) (*HM* 65, emphasis added).[17] Although the tone of a denunciation is evident, what is less clear is whether what is being denounced is the continuing of those rituals or the general inefficacy of evangelization, with few exceptions like those of the "good padre" mentioned in the quotation. It should also be noted that in the quoted passage the narrator refers to the division that existed in the native community between those who continued practicing rituals and those who did not practice them any longer. As discussed by Gerald Taylor, in the Quechua text the sentence that refers to the first group ("all the people") points to a description of the inhabitants of the whole Huarochirí region and not only of a particular community, while the second group ("some don't") is presented as a minority (*Ritos* 99, note 19). The distinction between the two groups also marks a contrast between the ancestral character of the native beliefs and practices, and the relative novelty of Catholic religion in that region. The description of the rituals performed in worship of Paria Caca—described in particular detail in chapter nine—becomes a vehicle for a reflection on religious conversion and the role of memory in that process. In ancient times, the narrator explains, the territories of the Yunca people, who had Huallallo Caruincho as their main *huaca*, were conquered by the "sons" of Paria Caca, who imposed the worship of this *huaca* amongst the vanquished: "chaymi kay yunkakunapas ñawpa *diosnintaqa* ña qunqaspa pariacacakta ña muchayta qallarirqan tukuy yunkakuna" (*Ritos* 120, emphasis added) (These Yunca groups, all the Yunca, once they forgot their former god, began to worship Paria Caca) (*HM* 71). The act of forgetting their former *dios* or god Huallallo Caruincho appears in the quoted sentence as a central element in the logic of conversion of the Yuncas to the cult of Paria Caca, only for it to be explained later that this cult took root as a result of an intense process of indoctrination: "chaymantam kay pariacaca ñisqanchikqa hanaq, maypim atirqan, chay pachallanpi tiyayta ña qallarirqan muchachikunqanpaqri unancharqan. . . . chaykunamantas sapanpi huqinta kamachirqan 'qammi watanpi ñuqap kawsasqayta qatispa pascuakunakta ruranki' ñispa" (*Ritos* 122) (Paria Caca then established his dwelling on the heights, on the same territory where he had conquered, and began to lay down the rules for his worship. . . . They say he gave a command to one particular person in each village: "Once every year you are to hold a paschal celebration reenacting my life") (*HM* 71).

Later in the same chapter, the narrator mentions the process of conversion to Christianity and the problems it faced:

> ichaqa kananqa ña qunqan kay pisi watallaraq kay doctor francisco de auila alli kunaqiyuq yachachiqiyuq kaspa chaypas manataqcha sunqukamaqa iñinmanchu ñataq huk padreyuq kaspaqa hinamantaqcha kutinman wakin runakunaqa christiano tukuspapas manchaspallam 'paqtac padrepas pipas yachawanman mana alli kasqayta' ñispallam christiano tukun rrosariokta resaspapas sumaq illantam apaykachan. (*Ritos* 138)

> (Nowadays, it's true, some have forgotten these practices. But since it's just a few years since they've had Doctor Francisco de Ávila, a good counselor and teacher, it may be that in their hearts they don't really believe. If they had another priest they might return to the old ways. Some people, although they've become Christians, have done so only out of fear. "I'm afraid the priest or somebody else might find out how bad I've been," they think. Although they say the Rosary, they still carry some *illa* amulet everywhere.) (*HM* 74)

According to the narrator, sincere conversion appears to depend on how effective the "counselor and teacher" of the new faith is, pointing to a subtle parallel between Francisco de Ávila and Paria Caca. Furthermore, the narrator calls attention to the fact that Ávila has not achieved a complete conversion of the Indians because they hold on to the memory of past beliefs through objects such as the *illas*, small sacred personal tokens that were believed to bring prosperity to their owners, which the new Christians still carried with them. In contrast, Paria Caca managed to make "all the Yunca" forget their former god and recognize him as their tutelary deity. Regardless of how precisely the narrator evaluates the conversion process, what it does reveal, albeit from a Christian Indian point of view, is how Indians perceived the process of conversion to Christianity and the place their beliefs and practices occupied in the new colonial order.

Conclusions

In this essay I have demonstrated how the complex, multilayered narrative of the Huarochirí Manuscript addresses in various ways the process of conversion to Christianity and the consequent changes in the concept of the sacred. The manuscript shows the mechanisms of negotiation and reconfiguration of native identity. Both operations are embedded in the rhetorical and conceptual dimensions of the text, which consequently imposes linguistic and semantic or cultural limits on Ávila and the colonial enterprise, limits that can be traced in almost unnoticeable elements such as marginalia. By underscoring the paradoxical centrality of marginalia and the importance of a parallel reading of the Huarochirí Manuscript alongside Ávila's *Tratado*, I have aimed to renew the discussion of the crucial question of the purpose of the Huarochirí Manuscript. And although there may not be a clear answer for that question, I believe there are enough elements—even if "marginal"—to reevaluate the historical and political relationship between Ávila and the author(s) of the Huarochirí Manuscript.

Notes

1. On the problem of authorship attribution of the HM, see Duviols's "Estudio biobibliográfico" and "Estudio y comentario etnohistórico," Taylor's "Introducción a la edición de 1987," and Durston's "Notes on the Authorship."
2. On Francisco de Ávila's biography, see Antonio Acosta's "Francisco de Ávila. Cusco 1573(?)–Lima 1647," and Pierre Duviols's "Estudio biobibliográfico."
3. In Quechua there are two forms of personal pronouns for the third person plural: *ñuqanchik* and *ñuqayku*. The first, as explained above in the use of the suffix *-nchik*,

is an inclusive form, while the second form, which would be indicated by the suffix *-yku*, excludes the person to whom the discourse is being addressed.
4. Throughout this essay, I quote Frank Salomon and Jorge Urioste's English translation of the Huarochirí Manuscript (*HM*) and Taylor's modernized paleography of the Quechua text (*Ritos*).
5. My translation. In the Quechua-Spanish section of the same *Vocabulario*, González Holguín points out that *yñiyninchik yñancanchic* means "Nuestra fe catolica" ("our Catholic faith"; 369). The verb to be taken into account is *yñiy*.
6. On the changes registered in the concept of idolatry in those centuries and specifically in the case of Peru, see Bernand and Gruzinski, *De la idolatría*; Duviols, *La destrucción*; Estenssoro, *Del paganismo*; and MacCormack, *Religion*.
7. On how those bonds legitimized native authority, see Ramírez 59–154; and on the colonial transformations of the relationships between ancestors and social organization, see Gose 139–55.
8. A *huaca* could be a person, an object (animals, plants, rocks, mummies, etc.), or a place.
9. All the references in English to Ávila's *Tratado y relación* correspond to my translation of the original manuscript in Spanish.
10. On the use of Christian religion's structure and the Western concept of paganism as interpretative frames for Inca culture, see MacCormack 205–48.
11. My translation.
12. Additionally, as noted by Salomon, chapter eight presents a story that at a certain point echoes, though subtly, Abraham's averted sacrifice of his son, Isaac (Introductory Essay 2).
13. For a differing interpretation of the physical traces left by past events, see Guaman Poma de Ayala 93–94.
14. Chapters one, nine, and twenty-seven of the HM also make reference to the rituals in honor of the deceased and resurrection.
15. The ritual offering of food to the dead was described and denounced in various writings that precede and follow the creation of the HM; see Arriaga.
16. *Ayllu* also alludes to a social, ritual, and territorial unit. The term is still widely used, and it usually appears as a synonym for social group or community.
17. Salomon and Urioste's translation of the HM to English includes the word *"padre"* (priest) in Spanish to indicate that it is also in Spanish in the Quechua manuscript.

Works Cited

Acosta, Antonio. "Francisco de Ávila. Cusco 1573(?)–Lima 1647." *Ritos y tradiciones de Huarochirí del siglo XVII*. 553–616. Print.
Arriaga, Pablo José de. *Extirpación de la idolatría del Piru*. 1621. *Crónicas peruanas de interés indígena*. Madrid: Atlas, Biblioteca de Autores Españoles CCIX, 1968. Print.
Ávila, Francisco de. *Tratado y relacion de los errores, falsos Dioses, y otras supersticiones, y ritos diabolicos en que vivian antiguamente los yndios de las Provincias de Huarocheri. Mama, y chaclla y oy tambien viuen engañados con gran perdicion de sus almas*. 1608. Manuscript 3169. Biblioteca Nacional de Madrid. f.115r–f.129r. Print.
Bernand, Carmen, and Serge Gruzinski. *De la idolatría. Una arqueología de las ciencias religiosas*. Mexico City: Fondo de Cultura Económica, 1992. Print.
Durston, Alan. "Notes on the Authorship of the Huarochirí Manuscript." *Colonial Latin American Review* 16.2 (2007): 227–41. Print.
Duviols, Pierre. "Estudio y comentario etnohistórico." *Relación de antigüedades deste Reyno del Piru*. c. 1613. Joan de Santacruz Pachacuti Yamqui Salcamaygua. Ed. Pierre Duviols and César Itier. Travaux de l'Institut Français d'Études Andines 74. Cusco: Institut Français d'Études Andines; Centro de Estudios Regionales Andinos "Bartolomé de Las Casas," 1993. 11–133.
———. *La destrucción de las religiones andinas. Conquista y colonia*. Mexico City: Universidad Nacional Autónoma de Mexico; Instituto de Investigaciones Históricas, 1977. Print.
———. "Estudio biobibliográfico de Francisco de Ávila." *Dioses y hombres de Huarochirí; Narración quechua recogida por Francisco de Ávila (¿1598?)*. Trans. José María Arguedas. Lima: Museo Nacional de Historia and Instituto de Estudios Peruanos, 1966. 218–40. Print.
Estenssoro Fuchs, Juan Carlos. *Del paganismo a la santidad: La incorporación de los indios del Perú al catolicismo, 1532–1750*. Lima: Instituto Francés de Estudios Andinos and Instituto Riva Agüero, 2003. Print.
González Holguín, Diego. *Vocabulario de la lengua general de todo el Peru llamada lengua qquichua o del Inca*. 1608. Lima: Universidad Nacional Mayor de San Marcos, 1989. Print.
Gose, Peter. *Invaders as Ancestors: On the Intercultural Making and Unmaking of Spanish Colonialism in the Andes*. Toronto: University of Toronto Press, 2008. Print.
Guaman Poma de Ayala, Felipe. *El primer nueva corónica y buen gobierno*. 1615. Ed. John V. Murra and Rolena Adorno. Trans. Jorge L. Urioste. 3 vols. Mexico City: Siglo XXI, 2006. Print.
The Huarochirí Manuscript: A Testament of Ancient and Colonial Andean Religion. Trans. Frank Salomon and George L. Urioste. Austin: University of Texas Press, 1991. Print.
MacCormack, Sabine. *Religion in the Andes: Vision and Imagination in Early Colonial Peru*. Princeton, NJ: Princeton University Press, 1991. Print.

Ramírez, Susan E. *To Feed and Be Fed: The Cosmological Bases of Authority and Identity in the Andes.* Stanford: Stanford University Press, 2005.
Ritos y tradiciones de Huarochirí: Manuscrito quechua de comienzos del siglo XVII. Ed. and trans. Gerald Taylor. Lima: Instituto de Estudios Peruanos and Instituto Francés de Estudios Andinos, 1999. Print.
Salomon, Frank. "Introductory Essay: The Huarochirí Manuscript." *The Huarochirí Manuscript: A Testament of Ancient and Colonial Andean Religion.* Trans. Frank Salomon and George L. Urioste. Austin: University of Texas Press, 1991. 1–38. Print.
Santa Cruz Pachacuti Yamqui Salcamaygua, Joan de. *Relación de antigüedades deste Reyno del Piru.* c. 1613. Travaux de l'Institut Français d'Études Andines 74. Ed. Pierre Duviols and César Itier. Cusco: Institut Français d'Études Andines; Centro de Estudios Regionales Andinos "Bartolomé de Las Casas," 1993. Print.
Taylor, Gerald. "Introducción a la edición de 1987." *Ritos y tradiciones de Huarochirí del siglo XVII.* Ed. and trans. Gerald Taylor. Lima: Instituto de Estudios Peruanos and Instituto Francés de Estudios Andinos, 1999. xiii–xxxiv. Print.

7

Old Enemies, New Contexts: Early Modern Spanish (Re)-Writing of Islam in the Philippines

Ana M. Rodríguez-Rodríguez

The textual representation of the Spanish colonial presence in the southern Philippines takes place in different types of texts, including historical treatises, political documents, *relaciones de sucesos*, and letters. Within this varied corpus, the *Historia de Mindanao y Joló*, written by the Jesuit Francisco de Combés (1620–1665) and published in Madrid in 1667, is remarkable for the completeness of its information and the nuances it introduces regarding Spanish contact with Islam in this period. The *Historia de Mindanao y Joló* exposes a writing process marked by complex mechanisms based on difference and processes of negotiation: negotiation with the expectations of Peninsular readers, with the knowledge acquired through direct contact with Islam, and with the transformations that this prolonged contact provokes in the writing subject. Missionary historians confronted the challenge of communicating the unique experience of a new reality while they negotiated identity, simultaneously dealing with the transformations of the self. Their texts reveal a physical and symbolic scenery in which "official" ideology, based on invalid stereotypes, does not always provide an appropriate mold to contain the process of comprehending both the Self and the Other in this new space.

The southern Pacific, where the colonial ambitions of the Spanish compete with those of the Portuguese and the Dutch, becomes the site of imperial rivalries and anxieties. These conflicts invite a questioning both of the definition of Spanish imperial identity and of the validity of Spanish perceptions of Islam, which were apparently well internalized due to the long and familiar history of confrontation. I will describe the context of those encounters during the Early Modern period in the Philippines and analyze the mechanisms in use there to represent the multifaceted contact with the Muslim Other, as well as including the impact that such writing may have on the self-definition and collective consciousness of those Spaniards engaged in imperial enterprise. The *Historia de Mindanao y Joló* shows numerous perceptions and representations that arise, on many occasions, from previous knowledge of the Muslim Other—knowledge that appears to make the unknown more familiar for author and readers but in reality prevents an authentic knowing, free from contaminating prejudices. The text's writing mechanisms reveal a profound intent to know, understand, and dominate an unknown reality that initially tries to move to familiar terrain by adapting to certain previously known parameters of confrontations with Islam. The anxiety that arises from applying old codes to new realities that are apparently similar in form but deeply different in essence is transferred to the writing process. This results in a decentered text that moves between the apparent confidence provoked by that which is previously known and the realization that existing knowledge actually contributes to confusion, chaos, and failure.

Islam and Spain in the Philippines in the Sixteenth and Seventeenth Centuries

When Magellan arrived in the Philippines in 1521, Islam already had a consolidated presence in the south of the islands and was starting to expand toward the Visayas and Luzon as part of the wider general growth of Islam in the Malayan peninsula and the Indonesian and Philippine archipelagos begun in the eighth century. The Spanish conquest did not start until 1565, and in only ten years they controlled the maritime provinces of the northern and central islands, including the Sultanate of Manila. This was perceived by the conquerors as providential, convinced as they were that their arrival at this particular moment had stopped the expansion and permanent establishment of Islam in the islands, as Antonio de Morga, among others, explains in his *Sucesos de las islas Filipinas* (1609).

Spanish colonial power in Islamic territory was problematic. Spaniards were at an peripheral point in the islands, far from the political, economic, religious, and cultural center from which emanated the authority that they wished to exercise in their confrontation with the Muslim Other, in a hostile space where there was a real and palpable danger of disintegration and literal and symbolic annihilation. Their authority in the Philippines was unstable, especially in the southern islands. Mindanao and Sulu, where Islam had established itself more strongly and had defied Spanish colonial power for three centuries. In the seventeenth century, in what constitutes one of the greatest resistances in the Spanish empire's entire colonial enterprise, Spanish confrontations with the Muslims of Mindanao and Sulu led to the abandonment of the Zamboanga fort, which meant the end of Spanish aspirations in Muslim-inhabited lands in the Philippines,.

Islam first arrived on the Sulu archipelago at the end of the thirteenth century and on Mindanao in the middle of the fifteenth century. Around 1600 the Islamic presence in Sulu was consolidated through political alliances with neighboring Muslim principalities in order to fight against the Western colonizing forces. At the beginning of the seventeenth century, especially during the kingdom of Sultan Qudarat (1619–1671), Spanish colonization and Christianization efforts in Mindanao also reinforced attitudes favoring the establishment of Islam by provoking a general awareness of belonging to the wider Islamic community.[1] Cesar Majul points out:

> Having adopted values that transcended their race and particular culture, they began to consider themselves as an historical people, yet assuming all the time that their history was not the result of their own making or efforts. Without their consciousness as well as all the benefits that Islam brought to the peoples of Sulu and Mindanao, they would have easily been swept away by Western colonialism and relegated to the limbo of conquered peoples. (78)

The arrival of the Spanish gave way to a series of political-military fights that determined life in the island for generations. Between 1599 and 1635, there were active rebellions against Spanish power, with the collaboration of Moluccan principalities and the Dutch. In 1635 the Zamboanga fort was established, clearly reflecting Spanish intentions: to conquer Muslim territories and convert the population. Muslim resistance grew, while Spaniards tried to implement their plan of depopulating Muslim areas and destroying their plantations. Threatened by a possible Dutch attack in Manila and exhausted by the ineffectiveness of their efforts, the Spaniards were forced to establish peace treaties with Muslim rulers. These treaties did not last long, however, due to Muslim refusal to accept Christian missionaries in their lands, mutual incursions into each other's areas, and constant accusations of peace violations. Finally, the Spaniards left Zamboanga and the other forts in the area in 1663, afraid of a Chinese attack in Manila led by the corsair Koxinga ("Coseng" in Spanish texts). There were no more significant attacks between the two sides for the next fifty years (Majul 165–66).

The difficulty of controlling such vast and dispersed territories and the scarcity of Spanish population meant that, even outside of these major conflict areas, Spaniards never had real control of the islands. Even areas that appeared to be secured, such as Manila, were isolated and dangerously vulnerable to possible attacks from nearby powers and to the rebellion of native and immigrant populations, immensely superior in numbers to the Spaniards. Henry Kamen explains that, as late as 1637, after some 80 years of colonization, only 150 houses in Manila were inhabited by Spaniards, even as the city grew through the continuous influx of Chinese immigrants, the growing *mestizo* population, and the arrival of black slaves that soon achieved freedom (208–9). Kamen correctly summarizes the real situation of the inhabitants of the island when he states that, in Spanish minds, "and even more surely in their maps, the Philippines featured as part of their 'empire.' Those who lived in the island knew better" (204). In Mindanao and Sulu, the consciousness of marginality was twofold: within the empire generally, and in the Philippines in particular. This marginality was determinant in the writing of *Historia de Mindanao y Joló*.

From the first years of the conquest, the central concern for the Spanish was the evangelization of the islands, an undertaking seen as the first step toward the Christianization of Asia (Kamen 233). The missionaries were often the only visible representatives of the metropolis, a privileged status that gave them enormous prestige and power, but that led Muslims(in whose territories the conquest and evangelization acquired a marked "Crusade spirit") to associate Spanish power with missionary activities. In 1565, the same year as Miguel López de Legazpi's arrival, the Augustinian order started its evangelization, followed by the Franciscans (1578), the Jesuits (1581), the Dominicans (1587), and the Augustinian Recollects (1606); very rapidly it was obvious to civil authorities that Spanish hegemony in the islands depended on the authority and prestige of these religious figures (Phelan 33). Religious power in the Philippines became immense, controlling a great amount of agricultural property and simply outnumbering the rest of the Spanish population (Mastura 104). The missionaries were also the ones to learn the native languages, giving them control in many of the communication channels between conquerors and indigenous peoples (Elizalde 57).[2]

The administration of Philip II saw the colonization of the Philippines as an opportunity to avoid repeating the bloody conquest in Mexico and Peru. It is clear that the conquest of the islands was strongly influenced by the indigenous defense movement led by Francisco de Vitoria and Bartolomé de Las Casas, who emphasized that the indigenous populations should retain their economic, political, and social rights according to natural law. The first archbishop of Manila, the Dominican Domingo de Salazar, attended classes taught by Vitoria in Salamanca and openly declared his admiration for Las Casas's doctrine. The Jesuit Alonso Sánchez wrote in a letter dated June 18, 1583, that Spaniards entered the new lands and damaged indigenous honor and lives, and that the natives therefore had the right to expel them as if they were pirates or tyrants, since the Spaniards, under the pretense of preaching, behaved like thieves (qtd. in Colín 1: 312). Unlike in the Americas, in the Philippines the Spanish encountered Muslims, a group the colonizers already knew well and often considered Spain's greatest enemy. This enmity greatly complicated the application of the legal protection that, in theory, the Spanish tried to apply to the other indigenous peoples. The American experience had already laid the foundations for methods of colonization, but they were not fully valid when dealing with the reencounter with the *"moro"* in the new colonial situation.[3] The presence of Islam freighted the confrontation with unavoidable cultural and religious aspects that were not present in the American model. It is important to point out that the conflict was not understood in racial terms, since there was no racial difference between the Philippine Muslim and non-Muslim populations at the moment of the Spanish arrival (Santos 34). The confrontation, then, was shaped from the very beginning by religious elements that cannot be separated from Spanish political ambitions in the region: "[F]or the Spaniards, the Sulus and Maguindanaos were a different case. They were simply Moros . . . their adamant foe with whom they had struggled since time immemorial, and over whom they won signal triumph with the fall of Granada in 1492. Thus the wars of Spain against the Muslim south took on the color of a crusade" (Demetrio 42).

These events were known in the center of the empire though oral and written testimonies produced by participants in the conquest and evangelization of the southern Philippines. Among them, the *Historia de Mindanao y Joló*, written by the Jesuit Francisco de Combés and published in Madrid in 1667, holds a prominent place. Combés arrived in the Philippines in 1643, as a result of Father Marcelo Mastrilli's petition in a letter to Phillip IV asking for forty Jesuit missionaries to evangelize Mindanao. After a stay in Manila, Combés was sent to Zamboanga in 1645 under the direct orders of Father Alejandro López. His time in the southern islands was very active, and, in addition to traveling extensively in the area, he performed diverse duties related to evangelizing and indigenous conversion, serving at times as ambassador and translator. After three years as rector in Dagami, he went back to Manila when Governor General Manrique de Lara received a threatening letter from the Chinese pirate Coseng demanding control of the Philippines. As a result of this crisis, the Spaniards abandoned the garrisons in the south of the archipelago, among them Zamboanga, a decision that Combés protested repeatedly, especially in the final book of his history.

Historia de Mindanao y Joló is a long treatise comprising eight books that exhaustively study the geography of the islands and the ethnic, social, political, and religious characteristics of their inhabitants. Additionally, it includes a presentation of the Spanish conquests in the area and of Spaniards' relationships and conflicts with the natives. Between the lines of the text, however, a failure is revealed, despite repeated attempts to highlight Spanish imperial representatives' ability to dominate the unstable political, religious, and cultural situation in the southern Philippines. The victories in Mindanao and Sulu that Combés celebrated in his *Historia* relieved the pressure of the constant Muslim attacks. Still, as Phelan reminds us, they were more spectacular than they were effective because they were not then consolidated with the occupation of extensive territories (138). In reality, the main goal—capturing Corralat in Mindanao and replacing him with a Spanish puppet—was unattainable (Majul 134). Corralat then declared a *jihad* against the Spanish and called on the sultans of Sulu, Ternate, and Makassar to expel all Spaniards from Muslim territories, igniting a very violent but inconclusive war.

From the first years of Spanish occupation, numerous participants in the conquest associated Filipino Muslims with the totality of Islam, as successors of the Turks, Tunisians, and Egyptians that Christianity had to confront in past and present times. Melchor de Ávalos, first *oidor* (judge) of the Manila *Audiencia*, describes them in 1585 as "desçendientes de los granatenses y otros enemigos . . . de las Españas" (Hanke 80) (descendants of Granadines and other enemies of Spain). Evangelization was understood as a pivotal part of the conquest process, and, as stated above, the religious orders carried great weight in the conquest and the cultural absorption it implied.

Francisco de Combés and His *Historia de Mindanao y Joló*

The *Historia de Mindanao y Joló* informs us of the elements that characterized Spanish-Muslim relations in this area of the world in the sixteenth and seventeenth centuries: instability, the urgent need to "create" the Philippines within the Spanish imagination, the difficulty of understanding the Other, and, above all, the reconsideration of Spaniards' relationship with Islam. As Barbara Fuchs reminds us, in Spain, "whether embraced or stigmatized, Moorishness becomes an essential component of national identity" (97). Through the different strategies employed in representing this contact and the mechanisms put to work to reflect, deform, complete, or annul the previously known and the novelty of the never-before-experienced, we can peer into the negotiation processes of conflictive identity in a marginal area of the empire, characterized by its status as an appendage, removed from the centers of colonial power.

We must remember that Combés, like the other Jesuits who worked in the islands, understood that abandoning Zamboanga and attempting to conquer the Philippine Muslim territories meant a failure that would undermine all the previous evangelization efforts with the indigenous population, both Muslim and non-Muslim. The *Historia de Mindanao y Joló* is part of a larger propagandistic network created by the Jesuits to discredit this decision by the civil authorities in an attempt to bring about reconsideration. It is this effort that is the main motivation of Combés's writing. Nonetheless, the text transcends this evident primary practical intention and offers the most complete view available of the history of Mindanao and Sulu since the Spanish arrival and representing at the same time the perception of and the process of understanding for the Muslim Other. Combés fluctuates continuously between two positions. He sometimes demonizes Islam, thus repeating the official discourse that promotes the absolute rejection of a religion perceived as an irreconcilable enemy of Christianity. On multiple occasions, however, he also separates himself from stereotypes and preconceived ideas and seems to build bridges that present a real possibility of communication between the two belief systems, and especially of the conversion of Muslims. It is clear that the *Historia*'s complex motivations, arguments, and opinions adapt themselves to the concrete ideological needs of each moment, on many occasions revealing the confrontation with Islam and its nuances to be merely an instrument to reach other goals.

Among these goals, eagerness to celebrate Jesuit glories and their prominent place in politics and evangelization of the islands stands out above all else. On numerous occasions the presentation of events clearly strives to show how it has been possible to leave "las espantosas tinieblas, y horribles obscuridades de la infidelidad" (77) (the hideous shadows, and the horrible darkness of infidelity) by means of the work of "los Ministros que se ocuparon en este tan santo, como trabajoso empleo ... todos merecedores de eternizarse en nuestra memoria" (115) (the Ministers who occupied themselves in this saintly and laborious job ... all worthy of perpetuating themselves in our memory). Combés takes care to emphasize repeatedly that Mindanao was the exclusive operations camp of the Jesuits, the great evangelical project of the order. He points out that in 1596 the island of Mindanao was adjudicated to the Jesuits by the ecclesiastic prelate of the Company with the confirmation of Governor Francisco Tello in 1597, and defended the Jesuit authority in the confrontations with Recollects and Augustinians for the spiritual possession of the island (157). Of course, he also defends Jesuit authority against the civil authority:

> En estos Pueblos no ay mas Alcalde, ni justicia, ni Gouierno, que el Padre; porque aunque reconocen al Gouernador de Samboangan, mas es en el miedo, que en el recurso, conseruandolos auersos a sombra de Españoles ... ; a los Padres los tienen por de otro linage de gentes. ... Cuydado, que oy los tiene pacificos, y mas justos, y en su proceder menos tiranos, pues ay quien entiende sus tratos, y puede deshazer sus engaños. (516–17)

> (In these villages there is no other Mayor, or justice, or Government, than the Father; because even though they recognize the Zamboanga Governor, it is more because of fear than of resource, keeping them averse to the shadow of Spaniards ... ; and they have the Fathers as another lineage of peoples. ... Care that has them today peaceful, and more just, and in their behavior less tyrannical, since there are those who understand their deals and can dismantle their deceptions.)

The real heroes represented in the *Historia* are not soldiers or governors but Jesuit priests each and every one of them idealized and surrounded by an almost superhuman aura of perfection. This labor of glorification is one of the text's main supporting pillars. The propaganda is reinforced with the narration of several miracles carried out by priests or inspired by their great reference point and spiritual model, Saint Francis Xavier. The text tries to relate the conquest of Mindanao with the supposedly supernatural events recognized as "miracles" caused by Jesuit intervention.

At the same time, the account of these events attempts to rescue from the periphery the evangelization labor in the southern Philippines, a marginal place compared to the rest of the territories managed by the Spanish monarchy, attempting to grant centrality to what is peripheral. Combés makes the isolation of the region explicit when he defines the Philippines as the "punto donde se cierra la Corona de España" (550) (point that closes the Spanish Crown) and "the region más desamparada, y remota de [las Indias]" (566) (most defenseless, and remote region in [the Indies]). We cannot forget that on several occasions Seville sent out proposals to abandon not just Mindanao and Sulu but the entire Philippine archipelago, fearing, as Spanish merchants did, that transatlantic commerce would be affected if Mexico and Peru received cheaper Chinese silks via the Philippines. While these merchants did not care much about the evangelical interests in the islands, things were quite different in the Court of Madrid, where representatives of the religious orders that worked in the Philippines constantly reminded the king of his commitment to convert Filipinos and avoid Dutch occupation of the islands. More than any other factor, it was the missionary and religious interest that made the Spaniards stay in such an unprofitable colony (Phelan 14). A book such as Combés's would have been fundamental as a Jesuit weapon of persuasion in Court for the preservation of the Philippines in general and of Mindanao and Sulu in particular, which were even more peripheral inside the empire and whose only possible supporting argument was without a doubt the defeat of the "Moor."

But for whom, then, is this text written? Combés is at all times conscious of who will be the final receptor of this text—primarily readers in Spain. He intends to present his own interpretation of the colonial reality in the southern Philippines for an audience that is in general completely ignorant of what happens in the islands, and for whom Combés's book would possibly be one of few opportunities to get inside this peculiar Spanish-Muslim encounter. From this point of view, the book is an attempt at collective and symbolic possession of a space in which there was no real control and that was not particularly attractive for the civil and military authorities, or even for commercial leaders. Combés tries to create the unreal image of evangelical success in the Muslim islands, which were never effectively Christianized, and to do so he elaborates a mythified reality, an idyllic vision of Mindanao. In his text he embarks enthusiastically on the project of transforming Mindanao and Sulu, which epitomize the failure of the confrontation with Islam and the empire's difficulties in the Philippines, into a space symbolic of the redeeming power of faith for natives and colonizers alike.

Combés, like many of the participants in the Spanish colonial endeavor in the sixteenth and seventeenth centuries, approaches his writing from a very particular state of mind, an almost unlimited faith in Spanish power and prestige and in their ability to achieve the spiritual unity of humankind, crushing Protestants and Turks and spreading the gospel in America and Asia (Phelan 4–5). The resistant Muslim population of Mindanao, Sulu, and the surrounding areas, which Combés positions in the center of his treatise, were standing in the way of this goal. In addition, the fact that this confrontation was against Islam jeopardized the fragile coexistence of the systems of conquest and conversion in the southern Philippines, which formed the basis of Spanish expansion. According to Dallmayr, "conquest entails the physical subjugation of alien populations and sometimes also their forced cultural assimilation; where the latter feature predominates, conquest gives way to conversion" (9). Both models share a fundamental characteristic, "the denial of meaningful human difference," although understood from different perspectives:

> In the case of conquest, difference is actually affirmed but in a radical-hierarchical way, which sacrifices mutuality in favor of the rigid schism of mind and matter, culture and nature, civilized people and savages. In the case of conversion, difference is denied through the insistence on a common or identical human nature—an identity that predestines native populations to be willing targets of proselytizing missions. (9–10)

In this way, "missionary efforts . . . were generally predicated on the assumption of a shared human nature and hence on the belief that native populations were basically predisposed to Christian faith and thus eager to accept the opportunity of salvation offered to them" (11–12). This model could not be applied to Mindanao and Sulu because Islam was not perceived as another indigenous belief. In fact, its Muslim inhabitants had created exactly the opposite image: obstinacy, inconsistency, and hatred for Catholicism. Combés's text expresses Spanish bewilderment at the realization that they had no policy with any guarantee of success to attract these "problematic" natives whose willingness to be converted was difficult to predict.

Combés's approach to this situation is characterized by certain disturbing contradictions: on the one hand he tries to gloss over the natives' more disorderly aspects, while on the other he cannot avoid pointing out the differences he perceives in them, oscillating continuously between a stereotypical condemnation of Islam and an attempt to avoid stereotypes and preconceived ideas. For this reason he sometimes minimizes the prevalence of Islamic practices in the archipelago, while at others he highlights the importance of converting this population at any cost. Sometimes he sets Muslims apart from the rest of indigenous peoples as representatives of malice, treason, inflexibility, and extreme violence, and sometimes he offers models of admirable behavior, real examples of idealized neo-converts. In this sense, chapters 12, 13, and 14 of Book I are especially significant. He tries to explain that the inhabitants of Mindanao and Sulu "ni son Moros, ni Gentiles, ni Christianos, sino . . . Ateistas" (46) (are not Moors, or Gentiles, or Christians, but . . . Atheists). Besides, they reject one of the signs of Muslim identity for the Spanish collective conscience, the feared "abominable sin," sodomy, removing them from the stereotypically condemnatory representation of Islam (56). Meanwhile, when describing how slavery works in these populations, he affirms "aunque esto era general en todas las Islas, en esta como tenida de la perfidia de Mahoma, es con excesso" (54) (although this was general in the Indies, in this one, gripped as it is by Mahomet's perfidy, it is with excess). The treatment of the imposing figure of Corralat, king of Mindanao, is illustrative: Combés's Corralat personifies the tyranny associated with Muslims, their obstinacy, natural stubbornness, inconsistency, and hatred of the Catholic faith, and epitomizes alterity through his Islamic faith (Combés, *Historia* 215).[4] Yet on other occasions Corralat is an exemplary leader who shows "vn ánimo verdaderamente noble, y generoso, y muy ageno de el natural de su Nacion" (305) (a truly noble spirit, generous and very alien to what is natural to his Nation). The Spanish-Muslim encounter in the southern islands takes place in this shifting space between attempted absorption and rejection, resulting in feelings of frustration and the permanent threat of failure that characterized this nonconquest.

Apart from Corralat, there are few other examples of individual characters who represent the Muslim population of the islands. This population is only an instrument, one that does not inspire interest or the desire to acquire familiarity but serves only to be manipulated through discourse. It is approached with abstraction, because specific anecdotes are not the goal of the representation. In any case, Combés doubts, is ambivalent, and does not know how to relate to the objects of his representation. When he needs to draw them closer to his readers, showing the possibility of bringing the islands to Catholicism, and thus the need to remain there, he presents magnified concrete examples of Muslim conversions to confirm the importance of the Jesuit work in Mindanao and Sulu:

> Costó mucho su reducion a la Fé, porfiando á los principios en defender obstinadamente su perfidia. . . . Diósele a entender, y quan enemiga es la luz de nuestra Santa Fé de las tinieblas de la Morisma . . . y festejóse el bautismo con las mayores demostraciones de regozijo, y aparato, que pudo hazer el gusto, que todos recibieron de tan ilustre triunfo. (469)

> (It was difficult to reduce him to the Faith, arguing stubbornly in the beginning to defend their perfidy . . . It was explained to him how much the light of our Holy Faith is enemy to the shadows of the Moors . . . and the baptism was celebrated with the largest demonstrations of happiness, and pomp, which could cause the pleasure that everyone received of this illustrious triumph.)

The higher the social standing of the converted, the more important the conversions are, as in the case of Libot, father-in-law of the feared corsair Dato Achen. Libot converts to Christianity, and he also rejects, before dying, the threats of the King of Burney, who has warned him "sino moria como honrado Principal en la ley de sus mayores, que le auia de quitar toda su hazienda, y castigar en su hija su necedad, haziendola esclaua, y al cabo dando su cuerpo por pasto de las fieras, echarle insepulto por essos campos" (519) (if he did not die as an honorable Chief in the Law of his elders, that he would take away all his property, and would punish his daughter for his foolishness, making her a slave, and at the end would give his body to the wild beasts, throwing his unburied body into the fields). Instead of leaving his new Christian faith, Libot "encargó a su hija le enterrasse como Chistiano, sin las ceremonias . . . de los Moros. . . . Assi lo executó la hija, aunque Mora" (519) (gave his daughter the job of burying him as a Christian, without the ceremonies . . . of the Moors. . . . This was executed by his daughter, although she was a Muslim). This daughter herself, some time later, is the object of a conversion campaign on the part of the Governor and the Jesuits, who try to convince her "con la verguença, que es tan poderosa con las mugeres de presuncion, y la amenaçaron con la afrentosa sepultura que auian de dar a su cuerpo, arrastrandole, y echandole en vn muladar," (521) (with embarrassment, which is so powerful with presumptuous women, and they threatened her with the insulting burial that they would give to her body, dragging it around, and throwing it in a dung heap). She responds that "Mora auia viuido, y Mora queria morir" (521) (Moor she ha[s] lived, and Moor she want[s] to die) because "la ley de los Moros es buena" (521–22) (the law of the Moors is good). Finally, "Dios N.S. dió esta vitoria, y triunfo Christiano a la mucha Fé del Maestro de Campo Don Pedro Cabiling . . . que como heredero de la Nobleza de aquellos Principales, es el reconocido Principe de toda la Christiandad Bisaya" (522) (God Our Lord gave this victory and Christian triumph to the great faith of the Maestro de Campo Don Pedro Cabiling . . . who, as heir to the nobility of those Heads, is the recognized Prince of all the Visayan Christianity), and the "Moor" Vley converts to Christianity and changes her name to Doña Catalina, a great victory for Spaniards that would be employed, as in Combés' text, with clear propagandistic aims. Even more striking was the conversion of Orancaya Vgbu, the general of Corralat's army and a distinguished member of his government, and that of Alonso Macombong, Sergeant of the Lutaos, who, after adopting his new religion, "mostró, hasta en el trage, quan aborrecida tenia su antigua secta, pidiendo luego sombrero, para hasta en el trage parecer mejor lo que era" (526) (showed, even in his clothes, how much he detested his old sect, asking rapidly for a hat, so that even his dress would show better who he was).

The narration of miracles by priests, or inspired by their spiritual model, Saint Francis Xavier, reinforces this same purpose.[5] The saint, whose protection is emphasized in the narration of war episodes, is given credit for the governor's and Father Mastrilli's health when, during a particularly difficult battle against Corralat's troops, the deadly bullets are deflected (250). Thanks to the presence and instruction of the priests, divine intervention is continuously presented or insinuated, especially in the victories against Muslims. The text tries to tie the conquest of Mindanao to Jesuit work in the islands, ennobling both by declaring them with manifestations of divine intervention.

For Combés, the evangelical enterprise itself justifies the Spanish presence in the islands, and its defense is one of the factors that necessitates the manipulation of the Moor figure in the text, adapting the model of the native predisposed to faith even as the author simultaneously doubts his own portrait of the feared and vilified Islam and of the likelihood of missionary success. Although some historians are surprised by the Spaniards' inability to interpret Filipino Muslims after centuries of contact with Islam (Majul 168), it was precisely this previous knowledge that obstructed the understanding of the reality of Mindanao and Sulu because it eliminated the option of approaching Muslim populations in the islands with equity and with the openness and questions that the very first visions of realities grant. With respect to Muslims, there are fewer questions, or their answers are known and difficult to rewrite, because the questions have been answered with notions inscribed in Spanish culture for centuries. Stereotypes were already fixed, and they inevitably invade the text. As Homi Bhabha explains, "The objective of colonial discourse is to construe the colonized as a population of degenerate types on the basis of racial origin, in order to justify conquest and to establish systems of administration and instruction" (70). Race, in medieval and early modern Spain, "was not color coded, however, but was defined as a descent group or lineage, or as a given religious identity" (Greer 9–11). It is precisely the Moorishness of these newly found populations that serves as a translating mechanism and, simultaneously and paradoxically, as a creator of essential Otherness based on religious difference. In the Philippines, the battles against Muslims started with a call to "Santiago" (Saint James, the Moor-slayer) (Combés, *Historia* 331; Barrantes 298) and thus immediately brought to mind the Reconquest.[6] The celebrations of victories against Philippine Muslims tie these events with battles against the Turks or liberations of captives in Northern Africa, a common occurrence during the sixteenth and seventeenth centuries in the Iberian Peninsula. A letter written by Father Juan López, narrating the welcome given in Manila to Hurtado de Corcuera after his victories in 1637, shows how these confrontations were interpreted. They were celebrated above all as victories against enemies of the Catholic faith, against "moros insolentes" (insolent Moors) that "maltrataban á Dios y á sus santos en sus santas imágenes, cortando á Cristo crucificado los brazos y diciendo que habian cautivado al Dios de los cristianos" (Barrantes 307) (mistreated God and his Saints in their holy images, cutting crucified Christ's arms and saying that they had captured the God of the Christians), and a minor episode is magnified in the texts, wherein the Moors ridicule a religious image and then destroy it. The anti-Moor religious message is omnipresent and is even included in the poems included in the decoration built to welcome the victorious governor, in the arches decorated with paintings and verses composed "al triunfo del señor gobernador" (to the triumph of the governor), who "espera en los Elísios blanda cuna / dando estandartes moros á los vientos" (Barrantes 314) (is awaited in the Elysian by a soft cradle / giving Moor banners to the winds).

A number of textual sources confirm the religious meaning that these confrontations had, understood and lived as one more episode in the ancient fight against Islam. A *relación de sucesos* (news pamphlet) published in Manila in 1638, narrating the victory against the king of Sulu that same year, highlights that in that "accion, y la pasada de Mindanao lo que mas se debe estimar al Gouernador, es en primer lugar el zelo grande de la honra de Dios, por rescatar los captivos Christianos vassallos del Rey N.S. y restaurar los vasos sagrados, imagenes, y ornamentos de las Iglesias, que estos enemigos han robado" (*Continvacion* 8v) (action, and the past one in Mindanao, what must be esteemed of the Governor is in the first place the great zeal for the honor of God, for rescuing the Christian captives, vassals of the King Our Lord, and restoring the sacred vessels, images and Church ornaments that these enemies had stolen). The religious aspects of the general conflict are emphasized, and the conflict is tainted with characteristics of a Crusade against Islam. It becomes something larger than a local fight, framing itself as part of the global and historical fight against Muslims, who are portrayed as the enemies of Christianity par excellence. The festivals that celebrated the victories in Manila emphasized these aspects and included processions with the rescued captives (307–08), imitating the ones that took place in the Iberian Peninsula after the rescue of prisoners from Algiers and other Ottoman enclaves in the Mediterranean, presided over by images of Christ and Saint Francis Xavier, "el primer apóstol de Mindanao" (the first apostle of Mindanao), who laid "los cimientos de nuestra Santa Fé en aquella isla, que hay quien juzgue ser una de las celebradas islas del Moro" (Barrantes 315) (the foundations of our Holy Faith on that island, which some judge to be one of the most celebrated islands of the Moor). The final celebration arrives with the presentation of a play about the conquest of Mindanao, written by the Jesuit Jerónimo Pérez: "no sin algunas tramoyas en que tuvieron su lugar el Zelo santo, la Fé y la Religion de la Compañía de Jesús, que encendieron el ánimo del Sr. D. Sebastian á vengar las injurias de Dios y atajar los daños que los cristianos de estas islas . . . padecían" (309) (not without some stage machinery where the Holy Zeal, the Faith and the Religion of the Company of Jesus had their place, which aroused the enthusiasm of Sir D. Sebastian to avenge the insults to God and put a stop to the damages that the Christians of these islands . . . suffered).

The writings of these years constantly return to this aspect of the confrontation with the inhabitants of Mindanao and Sulu. A letter published in Mexico in 1638, written by Father Marcelo Mastrilli, recounts the episode of the armless Christ, ill-treated by Muslims and inspiring to Spanish soldiers (Bobadilla 17v), who, under the protection of Saint Francis Xavier defeated Corralat after he boasted about having "al Dios de los Christianos debaxo de sus pies" (Bobadilla 29r) (the Christian God under his feet). As a response, Spaniards burnt Corralat's mosque (Bobadilla 32r).[7]

This is the textual and ideological universe in which Combés writes his text. With the information he receives and from his own observations as a witness of some of the narrated events, and under the weight of historically anti-Muslim official ideology and his religious order's anticolonial perspective, Combés approaches the Muslim Other both attracting it and repelling it, condemning it but always leaving open the possibility of integrating difference. The author moves among a variety of possible ways to codify the Other, those that repeat and confirm the fixed positions established by tradition as well as (and herein lies the originality and complexity of his writing) those that question preconceived ideas, after verifying that they do not meet the needs of the multifaceted reality of this newfound world. His narrative is a form of colonial identification, and it can be seen as a mode "of differentiation, realized as multiple, cross-cutting determinations, polymorphous and perverse, always demanding a specific calculation of their effects" (Bhabha 67). Combés's attempt to solve this conflict consists of elaborating (with the somewhat unrealistic enthusiasm that characterizes many texts written by Jesuit missionaries) a propagandistic weapon for his own evangelical activity, though one that is never completely free of contradictions. For the possibilities of converting Muslims, this propaganda displays a more conciliatory tone than that of the civil authorities—a fact which sometimes situates his writing in an uncomfortable intermediary position, where his only loyalty is to himself and to the glorification of the Jesuit order.

The differences are more polarized and the contradictions more evident than ever in the last Book of the *Historia*, in which, driven by the immediate need to convince civil authorities not to leave Zamboanga, Combés argues that Islam is a threat. He again tries to reaffirm Jesuit authority as an indispensable element in the conflict and the Jesuits' role as true defenders of Spanish interests in the islands. He is also aware of this issue's marginality in the broader task of colonial administration. He therefore magnifies a key element in his propagandistic effort to praise his order: the deaths of Fathers Alejandro López and Juan de Montiel at Corralat's court, presented as examples of martyrdom. The events that result in the two priests' deaths and the scenes describing their last moments are the culminating images of the book; in them, Combés employs all his expressive resources to describe the event in such a way as to reinforce the glorification of Jesuits.

Alejandro López had gone to Corralat's court as an ambassador of the Governor Manrique de Lara, and the reader can sense tragedy from the very start of the episode: "No dexaron de continuarse los presagios. . . . Despidiendose el Padre Iuan de Montiel de vn amigo intimo, . . . le asseguró por cierta su muerte. . . . Pero llegados al Pueblo del Rey, no vió mas demonstracion, que el silencio cuydadoso de los Moros" (543–44) (Premonitions did not stop happening. . . . As Father Juan de Montiel said goodbye to a close friend, . . . he assured him he would die. . . . But when they arrived in the King's village, he saw no other demonstration than the careful silence of the Moors). The tension grows with the interview between Alejandro López and Corralat until it reaches its climax when the priest boldly proposes that the king convert to Christianity. Finally, unable to reach an agreement, the two Jesuits are executed in a scene with strong visual impact, in which Combés emphasizes the violence of the Moors:

> le sobreuino vna lançada por las espaldas, que como auiso cierto de su fin, lo fue para que promptamente se dispusiesse para recibir la Corona, sacando vn Crucifixo que traía en el pecho, y arrodillandose con él en la mano, para recibir las vltimas heridas, hasta satisfacer con su sangre la insaciable sed de aquellas fieras. [. . .] el primer golpe el alfange, que le partió la cabeça, echandole en tierra el bonete que recogió, y se lo puso otra vez: segundó otro, [. . .] dos heridas le dexaron la cabeça en forma de Cruz hendida. (547–48)

(he received a spear wound in his back, that as certain notice of his ending, it was so that he promptly prepared himself to receive the Crown, drawing a crucifix he had in this breast, and kneeling with it in his hand, to receive the last wounds, till satisfying with his blood the insatiable thirst of those beasts. . . . [T]he first blow the cutlass, which opened his head, throwing to the ground his biretta, which he picked up and put back on. Another one followed . . . two wounds left his head in the shape of a cracked Cross.)

Combés, without reservations, proclaims the two Jesuits' status as martyrs (549), and rounds off this declaration by including their lives, which function as hagiographies, in his text.

But even in these last chapters there are ambivalent moments that reveal an inability to simplify the complexity of this encounter with Islam in a new world that forces the revision of preconceived ideas, since categories are dissolved and strict definitions must be loosened. In the middle of the riots provoked in Zamboanga by the announcement of the departure of the Spaniards, Ana Lampuyot, a fourteen-year-old Lutao girl, is the heroic figure who warns about a threat of treason, "como muy Española, y Christiana, porque prefirió la estimacion de su Fé a la que deuia su sangre" (623) (like a real Spaniard, and Christian, because she preferred the esteem of her faith to that she owed to her blood). Combés had introduced Lutaos in the first chapters of the book as especially conflictive natives, whose "trage Moro de turbante, marlota, armas, y secta, dizen claramente su descendencia" (40) (Moorish outfit with turban, gown, weapons, and sect clearly showed their lineage). Immediately below, he sees the other side of the coin, represented by Nicolás García, a Spanish second lieutenant "a quien vn amor desordenado le arrastró a vna traicion" (624) (who was dragged to treason by a disorderly love). Finally, he dies and we see the corpse of the treacherous Spaniard, who "auia ajustado barba, y trage al que vsan los Moros, para gratificarse mas con ellos, que el que es traydor al Rey de la tierra, a pocos passos lo será al de el Cielo" (625) (had let a beard grow, and wore a Moorish outfit, to gratify himself more with them, because one who betrays the King of the Earth will soon betray the King of Heaven).

Conclusions

In this text, the disorientation of the colonial subject in trying to interpret the Islamic Other is evident. Together with attacks that revive the humiliating rhetoric so common in anti-Islamic texts and that characterize Muslims as cruel, stubborn, traitors, and infidels, Combés tries to salvage the possibility of filling the void of cultural and religious difference through the hope of conversion, which would erase the disturbing complexity of the Other.

By emphasizing the conversions and the supposed miracles that accompany the Spanish presence in the islands, Combés indirectly suggests the possibility of the "great miracle" of the conquest of Mindanao and Sulu, taking a chance on the Jesuit policy that defended the conservation of the forts in the south of Mindanao in opposition to authorities who were more worried about not endangering trade in the Philippines. The *Historia de Mindanao y Joló* emerges above all else as a text that reveals an unusual view of the colonial and evangelical projects in the archipelago, rescuing the Jesuits' work from the margins of the empire and moving it to the center of contemporary discussions and concerns in the centers of power.

The text moves itself between attempts to highlight differences and an insistence on the possibility of domesticating the threat. This ambivalence provokes contradictions, since it tries to rhetorically unify contradictory discourses for representing the Muslim colonial subject. Beyond the immediate and apparent interests that shape the *Historia de Mindanao y Joló*, there is a more concealed but also more determinant engine in the complex representation of the *moro* in the text: the pressing need to dominate Muslim alterity and to regain control of the discursive structures that seize it. The Spanish-Muslim contact in the Philippines redefines the ability to interpret and assimilate difference, and in this way it also reconsiders a subject that in many ways had been constituted in opposition to the traditionally rejected Other. From this point of view, the periphery determines the center, destabilizing its foundations by opening the possibility of shattering categories that seemed to be firmly fixed but in reality are not. This is the biggest achievement of Combés's text, though likely not consciously pursued: the capacity to open the way for the exploration of unknown spaces for the colonial subject through a representation that is superficially anchored in stability but polyphonic and multifaceted at its core.

Notes

1. From now on, I will refer to this character as Corralat, since this is how seventeenth-century Spanish texts refer to him.
2. For years there have been polemic discussions regarding how the Jesuits acted as interlocutors with the natives, and they have even been accused of monopolizing this function by, for example, not teaching them Spanish to ensure their own role

as intermediaries with political authorities. This is Lodares's opinion, who declares, "Since that task kept them in a privileged position, they never bothered to evangelize or, much less, spread the use of Spanish. . . . In the Spanish Empire there was a place where Spanish was not only an invading language but was also guarded as a secret until the second half of the nineteenth century: that place was the Philippines" (29). Actually, the Jesuits spent the first months in the Philippines studying indigenous languages (Prieto Lucena 57).
3. The term "moros" was used by Spaniards to refer to Muslims in general in the Philippines. Until the middle of the twentieth century, this term had a pejorative charge, but in the last few decades there has been a revalorization of this name; nowadays it is understood as a mark of ethnic pride that reflects the singularity of Muslim Filipinos in the archipelago.
4. My quotations from Combés's book will always come from Retana's edition of 1897.
5. The beatification of Saint Francis Xavier took place in 1619, and three years later, on March 12, 1622, he was canonized along with Saint Ignatius of Loyola, the founder of the order. The Jesuits took advantage of these events to advertise their order and their evangelical and educational work, especially in Asia, where Saint Francisco worked profusely. The canonizations also brought public celebrations, which reinforced the will to disseminate the knowledge and faith of the saint. In *Relaciones de solemnidades y fiestas públicas de España*, Alenda includes several references to *relaciones de sucesos* about these celebrations.
6. In the appendix to his *Guerras piráticas*, Vicente Barrantes includes a letter written by Father Francisco López on September 15, 1637 (288–303), and another letter by Father Juan López entitled "Relación del recibimiento hecho en Manila al señor Hurtado de Corcuera, cuando volvia triunfador de Mindanao," which is not dated but which includes events from 1637, immediately after the victory against the Mindanaos (303–10).
7. This letter, which is precisely the one containing the petition for priests for the islands that brought Father Combés to the Philippines, is part of the *Relacion de las gloriosas victorias que en mar, y tierra an tenido las Armas de nuestro invictissimo Rey, y Monarca Felippe III. el Grande, en las Islas Filipinas, contra los Moros mahometanos de la gran Isla de Mindanao, y su Rey Cachil Corralat* . . . , attributed to Father Diego de Bobadilla.

Works Cited

Alenda y Mira, Jenaro. *Relaciones de solemnidades y fiestas públicas de España*. Madrid: Sucesores de Ribadeneyra, 1903. Print.
Barrantes, Vicente. *Guerras piráticas de Filipinas contra mindanaos y joloanos*. Madrid: M.G. Fernández, 1878. Print.
Bhabha, Homi. *The Location of Culture*. London: Routledge, 1994. Print.

Bobadilla, Diego de. *Relación de las gloriosas victorias que en mar, y tierra an tenido las Armas de nuestro invictissimo Rey, y Monarca Felippe IIII. el Grande, en las Islas Filipinas, contra los Moros mahometanos de la gran Isla de Mindanao, y su Rey Cachil Corralat, debaxo de la condvta de Don Sebastian Hurtado de Corcuera, Cauallero de la Orden de Alcantara, y del Consejo de Guerra de su Magestad, Gouernador y Capitan General de aquellas Islas.* Mexico City: Pedro de Quiñones, 1638. Print.

Colín, Francisco, S.J. *Labor evangélica, ministerios apostólicos de los obreros de la Compañía de Jesús, fundación, y progresos de su provincial en las islas Filipinas.* Ed. Pablo Pastells, S.J. Barcelona: Henrich, 1900. Print.

Combés, Francisco de. *Historia de las islas de Mindanao, Iolo, y sus Adyacentes. Progressos de la Religion, y Armas Catolicas.* Madrid: Herederos de Pablo del Val, 1667. Print.

———. *Historia de Mindanao y Joló.* Ed. W. E. Retana. Madrid: Viuda de M. Minuesa de los Ríos, 1897. Print.

Continvacion de los felices svccessos, qve N.S. a dado a las armas Españolas en estas Islas Filipinas, por los fines del año de 1637. y principios de el de 1638. Manila, 1638.

Dallmayr, Fred. *Beyond Orientalism: Essays on Cross-Cultural Encounter.* Albany: State University of New York, 1996. Print.

Demetrio, Francisco, S.J. "Religious Dimensions of the Moro Wars." *Mindanao Journal* 3.1 (1976): 35–64. Print.

Elizalde Pérez-Grueso, María Dolores, ed. *Repensar Filipinas. Política, identidad y religión en la construcción filipina.* Barcelona: Bellaterra, 2009. Print.

Fuchs, Barbara. "The Spanish Race." *Rereading the Black Legend: The Discourses of Religious and Racial Difference in the Renaissance Empires.* Ed. Margaret R. Greer, Walter D. Mignolo, and Maureen Quilligan. Chicago: University of Chicago Press, 2007. 88–98. Print.

Greer, Margaret R., Walter D. Mignolo, and Maureen Quilligan. "Introduction." *Rereading the Black Legend: The Discourses of Religious and Racial Difference in the Renaissance Empires.* Ed. Margaret R. Greer, Walter D. Mignolo, and Maureen Quilligan. Chicago: University of Chicago Press, 2007. 1–24. Print.

Hanke, Lewis, ed. *Cuerpo de documentos del siglo XVI sobre los derechos de España en las Indias y las Filipinas.* Mexico City: Fondo de Cultura Económica, 1943. Print.

de los Santos, Joel R., Jr. "Reflections on the Moro Wars and the New Filipino." *Mindanao Journal* 3.1 (1976): 22–34. Print.

Kamen, Henry. *Empire: How Spain Became a World Power. 1492–1763.* New York: Harper Collins, 2003. Print.

Lodares, Juan R. "Languages, Catholicism, and Power in the Hispanic Empire (1500–1770)." *Spanish and Empire.* Ed. Nelsy Echávez-Solano and Kenya C. Dworkin y Méndez. *Hispanic Issues*, vol. 34. Nashville, TN: Vanderbilt University Press, 2007. 3–31. Print.

Majul, Cesar Adib. *Muslims in the Philippines*. Quezon City: University of the Philippines Press, 1999. Print.

Mastura, Michael O. "Administrative Policies towards the Muslims in the Philippines: A Study in Historical Continuity and Trends." *Mindanao Journal* 3.1 (1976): 98–115. Print.

Morga, Antonio de. *Sucesos de las islas Filipinas*. Ed. Wenceslao Retana. Madrid: V. Suárez, 1909. Print.

Phelan, John Leddy. *The Hispanization of the Philippines: Spanish Aims and Filipino Responses. 1565–1700*. Madison: University of Wisconsin Press, 1959. Print.

Prieto Lucena, Ana María. *El contacto hispano-indígena en Filipinas según la historiografía de los siglos XVI y XVII*. Córdoba: Universidad de Córdoba, 1993. Print.

8

Art that Pushes and Pulls: Visualizing Religion and Law in the Early Colonial Province of Toluca

Delia A. Cosentino

The spacious Valley of Toluca, over the mountains to the west of Mexico City, enters into the Spanish imaginary with the publication of the travel accounts of a Franciscan general commissary, Fray Alonso Ponce, recorded by his secretary, Fray Antonio de Ciudad Real. In 1585, the men toured the principal settlement of Toluca City and a number of its surrounding towns, weaving a description of the landscape that reifies its inscription within Spain's colonial project. Through their mendicant eyes, the reader sees at once that this is an emergent Christian geography; their descriptions of the new and ongoing construction of religious architecture throughout the valley render native towns visible that had been largely absent from the broader imperial vision. Moreover, the account reminds the reader of the conting-encies of that evangelization effort; clearly sensitive to broader imperial interests, the authors note, for instance, that the valley is fertile with corn and houses the *estancias* that "críanse muchos puercos y hacense maravillosos perniles que tienen fama en toda la Nueva Espana" (Salinas 110). Indeed, widespread stock enterprises and haciendas could be found all over the Toluca Valley, controlled largely by provincial Spaniards; by the close of the sixteenth century, the principal city was a residential center where Indian families had been outnumbered by those of the more newly settled Europeans, mestizos, and mulattoes.

And yet the picture that emerges from sources outside of the friars' guided tour is a much more textured view of a largely native province with long-established patterns of cultural practice which complicate and enrich the understanding of a valley that was still considered an indigenous region, not a Spanish one. Called Nepintahihui, or "land of maize," by the Matlatzincas who maintained early cultural dominance in the area, the region was also home to scattered Otomi settlements (Romero Quiroz 9). With a Mexica invasion out of Tenochtitlan in the sixteenth century, Nahuas began to migrate into the valley and continued to do so even after the Spanish conquest. As elsewhere in colonial Central Mexico, Nahuatl served as the lingua franca of the sixteenth century. Perhaps most significantly in terms of native power structures left intact, town councils throughout the Toluca Valley, including in Toluca itself, were composed entirely of indigenous officials (Lockhart, *Nahuas and Spaniards* 202). The relative provincial nature of the entire valley, outshined by the neighboring Basin of Mexico to its east, permitted the impression of general stability in the early colonial period. However changes were clearly afoot, and local populations of the valley were engaged with and reacted to those changes in heterogeneous manners in accordance with their own relative positions of power.

Historians Ethelia Ruiz Medrano and James Lockhart, among others, have gleaned some information on the everyday experiences of regional native populations from court proceedings and notarial records during the later sixteenth century. But, especially given the relative scarcity of native-language documents and other records dealing specifically with the valley's indigenous people, the discipline of art history offers still more possibilities for making sense of the push and pull of the empire's hegemonic operations—particularly the church and the law—as they encroached upon life, and were themselves unsettled, in this particular corner of Central Mexico. A long history of art-making in native Central Mexico predates the use of written texts and reveals the sophisticated use of visual expression and the development of complex iconographies often serving overtly political ambitions. This was no less true in the colonial environment, as art forms of all sorts have been shown to have served as "points of contact and compatibility" between native and European populations, all of whom were busy exploiting the efficacies of visual expression for the negotiation of power positions (Boone and Cummins 11). Art historians working in this environment have sought to avoid suggestions of a harmonious hybridity and its visibility in formal terms, but instead attend to the processual nature of the artistic enterprise in a social environment characterized by the tensions of cultural heterogeneity (Dean and Leibsohn; Diel).

Two sets of artworks from the Toluca Valley during the second half of the sixteenth century form the basis of this discussion. Their tandem discussion is prompted in part by their shared temporal and geographic circumstances. These objects of visual culture originate in nearby towns in the valley of Toluca, in response to the centralized but dispersed forces of colonialism—the Spanish legal system and the institution of Catholicism—that were first to insinuate themselves in the area. In the town of Tlacotepec, south of Toluca, an extended struggle over land rights led to a court case ultimately heard by the Royal Audiencia in 1565; the resultant documentation includes two pictorial manuscript pages by native artists. One drawing each served as evidentiary material for the plaintiff and defendant, both indigenous. During the last two decades of the sixteenth century, in the town of Zinacantepec, west of Toluca, members of the local population produced a series of artworks for the recently built Franciscan church complex, including a number of murals covering the walls of the open chapel and a carved baptismal font. Plans for a *retablo* or altarpiece, perhaps never completed, also add texture to the developing view of a valley finding its visual place within the new colonial order. Strikingly, aforementioned artworks from both towns feature, among other iconographies, genealogical representations that, when juxtaposed, offer an opportunity to explore different cultural strategies for empowerment in a changing environment.

Aside from this particular content and their shared origins in the second half of the sixteenth century in towns outside Toluca, these sets of artworks would seem to have little in common. The Tlacotepec pictorials are mostly black ink drawings on European paper, with style and content drawn from ancient traditions in Central Mexican manuscript painting. Meanwhile, the Zinacantepec material is large, colorful, and overtly influenced by European representational ideas and Catholic interests. In the two towns, we see works that bespeak, at a formal level, vastly different conceptions of the world, perhaps corresponding to the vast divide between Spanish and native cultures. Yet the differences between the sets of artworks are only superficial.

Beyond the artifice of form, style, and pigment, much more profound complications of the colonial enterprise are revealed in each set of artworks; the devil is indeed both in the visual details and in the circumstances of their respective creations. All of these works were ultimately mediated by the very human hands of native agents living in the Toluca Valley. They demonstrate the recognition that colonial circumstances required strategic responses. Through different representational forms and processes, native artists and patrons negotiated their positions in the church and the eyes of the court, producing visual culture that simultaneously disquieted and reified the institutions of colonialism that most immediately challenged them. Ultimately, the very circumstances of art production and art use served to orient these provincial Tolucan towns ever more toward the metropolitan center, where the core of the colonial project resided. Art therefore became a force in this process of centralization.

Picturing Land Rights in Tlacotepec

The *Códice de Santiago Tlacotepec* is a body of textual and pictorial legal documents, now housed in the Bibliothèque Nationale in Paris and recently reprinted in facsimile form with analyses (Ruiz Medrano and Noguez).[1] The

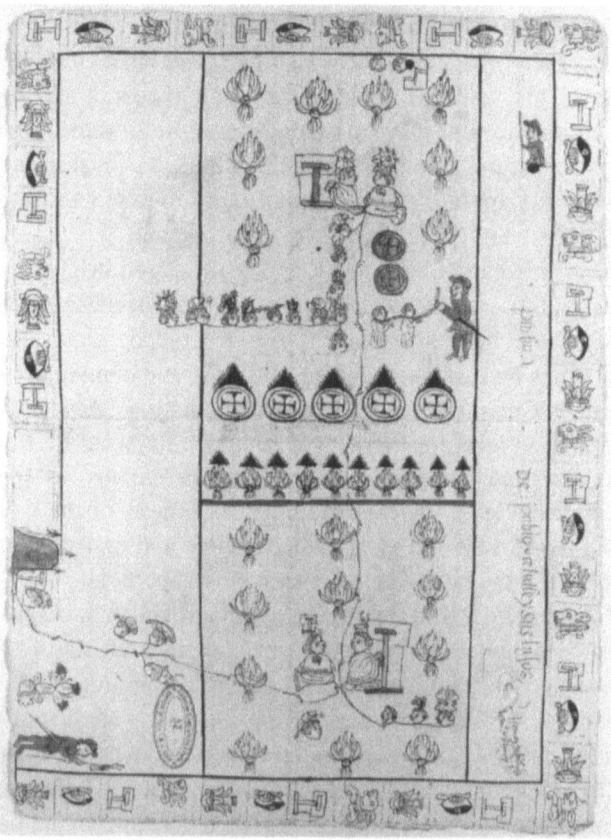

Fig. 1 *Genealogía de Ocelotl y sus hijos*, Tlacotepec, 1565. Courtesy of the Bibliothèque Nationale de France.

documents provide details of a land dispute in the traditionally Matlatzinca community for which the manuscript is named. The files record the details of a dispute between a Matlatzinca man and a Nahua latecomer to Tlacotepec, and the various attempts to settle the case closer to home before it ultimately arrives on the doorstep of the Royal Audiencia in Mexico City in 1565. The remaining documents date to that final round of adjudication and are of particular interest here because they include two ink drawings on European paper, 17 x 13 inches, attached to the transcripts of the same size and essentially serving as dueling visual claims to the land in question; one served as the argument of Pablo Ocelotl (Fig. 1), while the other sought to defend the claims of Alonso González (Fig. 2).

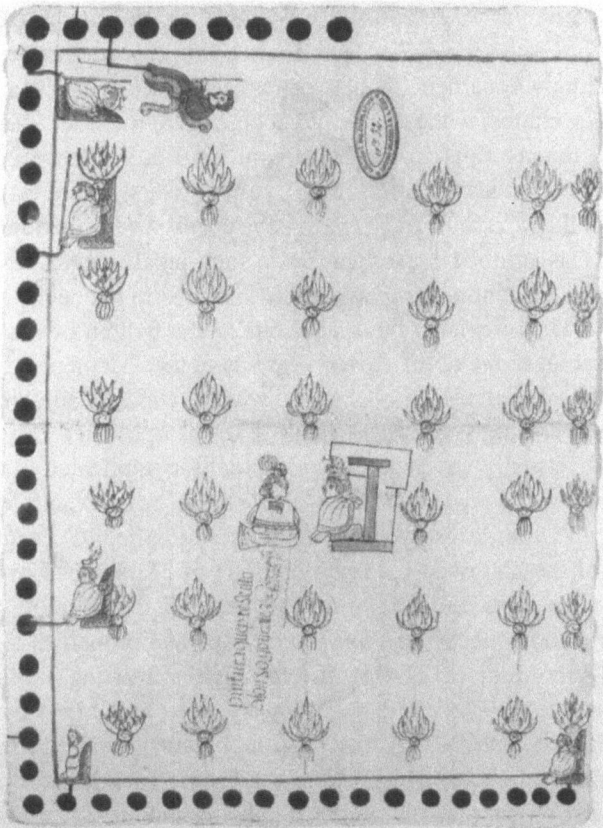

Fig. 2. Alonso González, Tlacotepec, 1565.
Courtesy of the Bibliothèque Nationale de France.

Both images were made by native artists from surrounding communities and are copies of earlier manuscripts, now unknown but presumably also locally produced. What we have, therefore, is the final iteration of the visual component of the case. We do not know whether they differ from their earlier models, although their similarities might suggest an internal dialogue that was consolidated as the case moved through the legal process over the years. The fact of their existence is revealing, as are—even more so—the differences between the partnered pictorials.

The Tlacotepec pictorials are part of a larger group of manuscripts from the first century of Spanish rule, which incorporate use of visual material in the legal context. Spaniards unaccustomed to such usage noted the continuance of an established native tradition during the colonial period, when *tlacuilos* (native artists) would work both in and out of the courtroom to produce images related to a particular dispute, usually between native litigants. According to the writings of Fray Alonso Zorita and other similar ethnohistorical sources, such images might document "in native characters" the details of a conflict, including parties, claims, witnesses, and outcome (128). In other cases, it appears that pictorial manuscripts would be incorporated as evidence in a dynamic courtroom where witnesses, often aided by interpreters, would essentially read the images in the course of their testimony, which would then be transcribed by notaries (Cosentino, *Landscapes* 224). Such legal images bespeak a profound native investment in the power of the visual form to convey some kind of spatial truth that transcended the limitations of the written or spoken word. It is likely that at least one of the earlier versions of the Tlacotepec drawings discussed here was an active part of the case when it was first adjudicated locally before reaching the high council of Spanish judges in Mexico City.

The more visually striking and conceptually complicated of the two images is the *Genealogy of Pablo Ocelotl and His Sons*. Made by Francisco Yquixitotol, an Otomi artist from the town of Xiquipilco, *Genealogy* presents the essence of the argument made by the man of Matlatzinca descent whose lineage had deep roots in the town of Tlacotepec. Pablo Ocelotl's intent with this image was to lay ancestral claims to the land and properties at the heart of the dispute (Ruiz Medrano 21–36). His rectangular drawing in black ink with minimal enhancements in a red wash largely reads as a bird's-eye view of a divided landscape. The two central quadrants feature stylized maguey plants from the top to the bottom, which create a patterned backdrop for other critical factors in the case, such as the financial value of the crops: two thousand pesos of *oro común* for the four thousand maguey plants—each symbol marked with the "tzontli" glyph, typical of the stylized forms that characterize Central Mexican manuscript painting (Noguez 50). Even more key to the pictorial and its message, however, is the genealogy that wends its way from the picture's margins, into the landscape, and up and down the central axis of the image. Lines link Pablo Ocelotl, shown among his siblings in the upper quadrant, to previous generations of his lineage in the lower quadrant and a primordial figure near a mountain glyph on the left-hand border of the page; these lines are enhanced with toe prints that imply both a passage of time and space between generations.

At a microcosmic level and following broader indigenous traditions in the representation of genealogy, this image stakes a primordial claim to the territory based on ancient biological connections. The pictorial demonstrates very clearly how Ocelotl's lineage has been interwoven with the territory over time, and it is precisely from this longevity that he derives his sense of legitimacy. Across Central Mexico, such genealogical authority is grounded spatially in native manuscripts. In what is perhaps the most expansive example, the ten maps of the Codex Xolotl become what Eduardo Douglas has recently described as a "narratives of place" for the historically critical region of Tetzcoco and especially for the claims of Xolotl and his royal bloodline (44). The painters of that extensive manuscript adopt the territory of the eastern shore of Lake Tetzcoco as the principal backdrop for the display of dynastic genealogy, carefully interweaving the narrative of descent with elaborate place signs to insist upon the cartographic location of authority. This manner of interweaving lineage with territory is a defining aspect of native genealogical traditions both in Central Mexico and in the well-known Mixtec Codices of Oaxaca (Cosentino, *Landscapes* 136–45).

Unlike the histories of Xolotl and the Mixtecs, which are largely oriented towards precontact history, Ocelotl's visual argument is literally framed by colonial reality. While Ocelotl's own identity is linked to that ancestral progenitor, in fact the calendar count that wraps around the edge of the page using the four Aztec year signs seems to mitigate the power of genealogical message. The calendar helps to emphasize a continuum between time and the space it frames, but because the count begins with the arrival of the tall, dark figure of Hernán Cortés in Tenochtitlan in 1519, Ocelotl's claim is immediately inscribed within the context of conquest. Indeed, the count continues until 1565, when the case arrives at the Audiencia; the start date as shown is particularly interesting given that the dispute over the lands will not begin until the 1530s. Although Xavier Noguez has pointed out that Ocelotl and other Matlatzincas were possibly released from Mexica imperialism with the European conquest (57), Ocelotl's pictorial demonstrates a new set of tensions that are ultimately inseparable from the processes of colonial change.

It could be that the mere presence of the Nahua on Ocelotl's land is seen as one symptom of the disorientation wrought by the presence of a new empire. Certainly, the pictorial contains other references to the ongoing dispute, with figures corresponding to the years 1544 and 1550 identified as indigenous judges adjudicating locally who brought no final resolution for Ocelotl (Noguez 51). Another small scene in the upper quadrant squares with recorded testimony that demonstrates just how personally vicious the fight got: witnesses report that Ocelotl and his wife were threatened with beatings, and even death, if they did not give up the fight for the land. We also learn that Ocelotl's Nahua challenger conspired with the town's fiscal, or church steward, to declare Ocelotl a "pagan" and have him arrested. One witness expresses uncertainty as to whether or not Ocelotl's own father has been baptized, thereby suggesting that there may be ongoing familial tension regarding new religious obligations within the colonial space of Tlacotepec (Noguez 50). What is clear is that for Ocelotl the land becomes a stage where these tensions play out; the Spanish-looking figure represented in hierarchical scale menaces two bound captives, and the pictorial records the multivalent forces that impede Ocelotl's sense of sovereignty.

Apparently much more savvy about the shifting tide in Central Mexico was the Nahua defendant in the case, Alonso González. It was in his defense that the other pictorial was made by an unnamed artist from the Tolucan town of Metepec. The transcripts of the case record González's story, dating back to 1538 or '39, when his father (pictured in the center, facing his mother) moved to Tlacotepec from another town and was given permission by the governor to take some of the lands and houses that Ocelotl had recently inherited from his father, until he could formally establish himself elsewhere in Tlacotepec. However he never moved, and instead, when González's father died in 1558 or '59, he left a will that stated the land now belonged to González (Ruiz Medrano 22–23). While Ocelotl took years to mobilize a challenge in front of a judge, González was busy securing his future: the pictorial that accompanied his case in front of the Audiencia reveals part of his strategy.

The familiar format presents a much simpler visual argument. A single clean rectangle constitutes the body of the manuscript, at the center of which are depicted two figures, likely his parents, including his father from whom he inherited the lands. These figures seem secondary, however, to the more captivating visual quality of the pictorial—the patterning of stylized maguey plants whose presence marks the space as mapped territory. Although Alonso González is surely motivated by the immense richness of the land, he does not make overt reference to the economic underpinnings of the case, with the representation of money, as Ocelotl's pictorial does. Instead, and especially in the absence of any deep family roots that he could have used to provide genealogical legitimacy to his claims, the maguey plants themselves become the rhythmic force behind this evidentiary pictorial. Indeed, one of Alonso González's main arguments about the legitimacy of his claims is precisely the implied economic and historic value of those magueys; the native cactus was widely cultivated for its *miel de maguey* and for *pulque*, which could be sold out of the house or at market, including in Mexico City. In this case, González's claim to the magueys is also his claim to the land itself; his testimony insists that his father personally cultivated the lands and planted the magueys (Ruiz Medrano 27), so that not only can he provide the will of his father that demonstrated his inheritance of the land, but his ownership has been consolidated by fruitful action—the successful cultivation of these extraordinarily valuable magueys, whose products no doubt ended up in the marketplaces of the Mexican basin.

González's actions follow the deeper pattern of history in the Toluca Valley, which both before and after the Spanish invasion served as a surplus corridor to the neighboring Valley of Mexico. Aztec Emperor Axayacatl first oversaw the subjugation of the largely Matlatzinca population of Tlacotepec and other regional towns in 1472, beginning Toluca's status as a province to the centralized power in the Basin of Mexico. With the refinement of Mexica rule, things began to change in the neighboring Toluca region: the empire builders quickly understood that the organization of certain communities in the Toluca Valley could satisfy their demand for particular commodities, including agricultural products and feathers. Thereafter, many of the region's economic resources and populations were dominated by the Mexicas' social and religious organization and its needs. The path of the Tolucan corridor was beaten and the groundwork for future conquest was laid by Mexica patterns of control in the region. The position of the Nahua González was surely boosted by such a proud history, which made his opponent Ocelotl a subaltern before González even arrived in Tlacotepec. In any case, his pictorial suggests that he was attuned to such colonial processes and, importantly, to their governing structures.

The focus in González's pictorial on the succession of local authority reflects this keen awareness of the Toluca Valley's changing dynamics and its trappings of power. The recognition of such governing dynamics begins in the lower right-hand corner, at the start of a simplified calendar count of black dots. Here, coordinate with the year 1519, almost certainly influenced by the count on Ocelotl's more complicated page (although interestingly, reversed to clockwise), is not Cortés but instead the figure of a Mexica-styled governor seated on the classic high-backed *icpalli* throne, identified by one of González witnesses as "don Juan" (Noguez 54). His active status as a *tlatoani* (one who speaks) is suggested by two speech scrolls that emerge from his mouth; some of his words are the ones that originally granted González's father squatting rights on Ocelotl's land. After Don Juan's death, a series of successive indigenous governors appears along the border, a couple of whom now hold a ruler's staff. One of these, identified as Diego Jacobo Motolinea, assumed power in 1556 and, significantly, is shown with the glyphic representation of water across his head—an allusion to his Catholic baptism (Noguez 55). The final figure included along the bordering count is a Spanish figure, seated in the European hip-joint chair; he is likely a judge that was brought into the case whose opinions, like those of the native governors, favored González.

It is the related but distinctive content of each of these pictorials that suggests a telling chronology. González's image is clearly derived from that of Ocelotl. One imagines that the latter in fact was part of the initial dispute as it was reviewed in Tlacotepec; with its content fleshed out following native traditions in manuscript painting, both in terms of content and usage, Ocelotl's pictorial would logically justify his demands. In contrast, González's image looks to the earlier genealogy for inspiration, but, lacking such content for itself, it demonstrates an investment in an ever-more-relevant notion of action as argument, here presented in visual form. Indeed, by the time his pictorial took its final shape, González had hired a Spanish lawyer who would carry his claims—and the image to support it—to Mexico City. In this way, the Nahua demonstrates not only his understanding of where his bread is most likely to get buttered but also, from a perspective relevant to art history, who exactly would be looking at the image.

Situating the Sacred in Zinacantepec

Even before the basis for Ocelotl's land rights case against the Nahua was being laid in Tlacotepec in the 1530s, larger territorial decisions were being made in the Toluca Valley that would have much broader implications for the overall population. Hernán Cortés turned the fertile valley into somewhat of a "personal enclave," awarding many of his closest allies choice *encomiendas* with clear financial potential (Lockhart, *Nahuas and Spaniards* 204–5). One of the largest was the town of Zinacantepec, assigned to Juan de Sámano, chief constable on Mexico City's council, who arrived in the early 1520s. Later, this *encomienda*—with substantial assets in tribute payments in maize—was passed down to his son and again to grandson, both of whom shared the Sámano name. Gradually enlarged under *congregacion* programs that led to its jurisdiction over smaller settlements in the area, Zinacantepec grew larger as a *cabecera*, or principal town. By the second half of the sixteenth century, the town had at least twelve *aldeas* (villages) or *estancias de visita* (outlying settlements). The population was around three thousand people, and despite its colonial consolidation under the Sámano *encomenderos*, it remained an essentially indigenous community—largely Otomi, with Nahuatl functioning at some level as a familiar tongue.

The Sámano family's interest in securing Zinacantepec's economic potential was undoubtedly the impetus at some level for its documented request for the permanent establishment of the Franciscan order in their town. Juan de Sámano, son and successor of the first *encomendero*, financed the project, which would naturally help to unify the settlements drawn into Zinacantepec through the congregation program. The *Codice franciscano*, dated to 1569, reveals tensions that led to the establishment of a monastery project in the town (18). Suggesting Franciscan resolution to the problem of a distant church overreaching its domain, the codex says that the project was precipitated by the request of Sámano and supported by Viceroy D. Martín Enríquez because of the negative local reception of clerics who had been installed by the archbishop of Mexico City over the course of five or six years, presumably during the 1550s or 60s. In this way, the Franciscans, who had previously only visited the town from their main regional base in Toluca City, together with Sámano, are cast as locals attending to indigenous concerns. Because the Franciscans mediate the larger colonial machine, their own interests are cloaked.

The Franciscan monastery of San Miguel was therefore begun in Zinacantepec in the late 1560s, with friars staying in Toluca until it could be completed. In 1585, when Ponce and Ciudad Real passed through, they declared it unfinished but well built, noting that two friars were residing there by that point (Salinas 110). A large walled atrium encloses a church and bell tower, with a monastery block housing an open chapel with a baptistery at its far end. A niche in the open chapel wall surely marked the apex of the Christian mass performed outdoors to accommodate groups of native neophytes gathered in the adjoining *atrio*; there, a restored *retablo* or altarpiece adorns the back wall of the niche. John McAndrew describes the architecture of Zinacantepec's monastery of San Miguel "as complete a picture of this whole sixteenth-century type [of open-air church] as Mexico can offer" (574–75). As with most Mexican architecture of the period, the local population was responsible for the monastery's construction; a document now in the national archives reveals that even into the 1590s, indigenous citizens of Zinacantepec doing church-related work were being compensated for their efforts with maize.[2]

Native architects and artists responsible for the Franciscan complex's structure and decorative program were clearly relying on European prototypes. In addition to the larger structural components matching others visible throughout Central Mexico and stemming from a centralized notion of ideal Christian architecture, more specific details, such as the classical columns supporting a five-arched portico fronting the monastery block and the traditionally shaped font housed in the baptistery, reflect the circulation of design models. The dependence on even more detailed European formal prototypes is in evidence in the monastery's ornamentation, particularly in a series of murals adorning the open chapel walls and in the carved surface of the stone baptismal font. The primary aim of the decorative program is unabashedly to promote Franciscan identity and its moral virtues, many of which are broader Christian ideals but here at Zinacantepec relate specifically to this particular mendicant brotherhood, which had the strongest religious foothold in the Toluca Valley (Cosentino, *Joyas* 26–29).

The mendicant friar and founder of the order, Saint Francis (d. 1226, canonized 1228), is naturally the dominant figure in the open chapel murals. Two scenes from his life flank the open chapel niche, drawn from the records of his official biographer, Saint Bonaventure. One is the Stigmatization of Saint Francis, the most pivotal event in the saint's life: atop the Italian Mount La Verna, dressed in his humble brown robe of poverty tied neatly at the waist with his iconic twisted cord, he beholds a vision of Christ as a winged seraph who bestows on him the bleeding wounds that mirror those endured by Christ during the crucifixion. The scene could be used to explain the five wounds, or stigmata, that would become Francis's defining attributes as *imitatio Cristi*, which were also popular design motifs on the facades of Franciscan establishments elsewhere in Mexico at the time. The other mural flanking the open chapel niche portrays the saint delivering his famous *Sermon to the Birds*, another legendary scene from his life that promotes a sense of Franciscan tenderness towards nature. In provincial Toluca, not unlike in the relatively rustic area of Assisi in Italy where the incident supposedly took place, this may have struck a particularly compelling note for locals.

Even more visually commanding, however, is the most interesting of the extant murals. Likely painted in the 1580s, the *Tree of Saint Francis* also ap-

Fig. 3. Tree of Saint Francis, Zinacantepec, circa 1585. Photograph by the author.

pears on the open chapel wall, above a door leading to the private monastery block (Fig. 3).

The primary figure assumes a reclining position on a small hill at the base of the painting, supporting his head with his right arm while grasping a large crucifix in his left hand; allusions to both La Verna and Francis's connection with Christ are surely implied by these elements. Most significantly, however, from his chest seems to grow a tree whose branches give way to flowers, leaves, and more than two dozen figures. In essence, the painting represents the spiritual family of the Franciscan order, including early members as well as colonial representatives. Twelve of the friars in Saint Francis's tree, for instance, clutch wooden crosses, paralleling in number the original band of Franciscans that entered Mexico (Cosentino, *Joyas* 62).

Further promotion of Christian virtues, especially as overseen by the Franciscans, continue through the details on the stone baptismal font, carved in 1581 (Fig. 4).

Four medallions, evenly spaced around the sides of the large basin (over one meter in diameter), feature pivotal scenes of Christian belief aimed at conveying some of the central tenets of the sacraments and their rewards. Logically given the function of an object intended to mark the neophyte's introduction into a Christian life, the Annunciation of Mary and the Baptism of Christ occupy two medallions, with another for the archangel Michael—shown

Fig. 4. Baptismal font, Zinacantepec, 1581. Photograph by the author.

battling the devil—for whom the monastery is named. The final scene further localizes Christianity within a specifically Franciscan and Mexican context. Here, the fourth-century San Martin of Tours is shown as a caballero atop his horse, dividing his cloak with a poor beggar; the Franciscans encouraged followers to see parallels between this event and one in the life of Saint Francis when he surrendered his own clothes for the needy; in the New World context, the narrative may suggest that the beneficiary of the divided cloak was an indigenous commoner (Montes Bardo 322). At Zinacantepec, the mural imagery reifies a sense of Franciscan goodness, generosity, and humility, the beneficiaries of which would naturally be the native populations of this town.

Between their content and naturalistic style, it is clear that the murals and font reflect the dominance of European source material, but these works also demonstrate how the imposed religious vision is localized in Zinacantepec. For instance, while the *Tree of Saint Francis* is clearly modeled loosely on the iconography of the Tree of Jesse, based on the book of *Isaiah*, in fact the mural is without exact precedent in European tradition (Cosentino, *Joyas* 55–65). The visual formula of a tree that emerges not from the groin (as in Jesse's branch) but from the heart has clear precedent only within the Mesoamerican tradition. Similarly, the baptismal font reflects a process of indigenous localization at two levels; its decorative motifs include volutes with dots like the water-filled symbols associated with the rain God Tlaloc or the song-scrolls accented with jade that mark the Augustinian murals at Malinalco (Reyes Valerio; Peterson 48–49), while an inscription carved in Nahuatl around the rim insists on both the creation and reception of the artwork by a native audience. Such imagery seems to leave little doubt that even as Sámano's *encomienda* was sanctioned by the Christian God in Zinacantepec, it was situated there by the town's native residents.

Push and Pull

In the previous sections, I have sought to show how a number of different artworks were created and took their distinctive visual forms in their respective towns during the second half of the sixteenth century in the Toluca Valley. In Tlacotepec, those artworks grew out of a local dispute, which, although it is now known in its final form mediated by the Royal Audiencia, was at least rooted initially in native traditions of both manuscript painting and legal practice. In contrast, the slightly later works from Zinacantepec, even with clear evidence of native production and reception, reflect the imposition of new forms of expression and new ways of seeing in that town. It is striking that the two most visually compelling images to come out of these two towns in the Toluca Valley rely on genealogical imagery as a strategy for expressing moral claims to power. The juxtaposition of those two images, which nicely demonstrate the cultural construction of genealogical legitimacy, here opens up the opportunity to highlight the push and pull of colonial realities in the Toluca Valley.

It is useful to be mindful that while genealogies purport to be about the past, in truth they are inevitably motivated by the present (Henige 97–102). In Tlacotepec, Ocelotl's multigenerational lineage is compelling for its insistence upon legitimacy based on long-standing genealogical ties to the landscape. An iconography that ties it firmly into native manuscript painting traditions also links it to broader tendencies to represent history through place; in this case, Ocelotl's personal identity is literally grounded in his family's association with his inherited plots of land in Tlacotepec, motivated ultimately by his natural desire to hold on to those lands in the second half of the sixteenth century. In contrast, the painting of St. Francis's tree in Zinacantepec is rooted in the life of a long-deceased saint, but it dwells especially on the imagined promise of rewards in the future; the family tree format embodies European ideas about a natural hierarchy of space, using branches that push upward with time to bring later generations ever closer to the glory of the Christian God (Klapisch-Zuber 120–23). In this way, the *Tree of Saint Francis* celebrates its presumed moral authority over indigenous tradition, including, conceptually, Ocelotl's historical claims to land, which could easily have been trumped by the *encomienda* system. In the simplest terms, the two genealogies can be understood to betray vastly different conceptions of the world that correspond to the push and pull of Spanish and indigenous interests in the sixteenth-century Toluca Valley.

In their respective contexts, however, these genealogies also highlight how colonialism sought to decouple native artistry from its local environment. Although also produced by a native artist, the counterpart to Ocelotl's pictorial may suggest a paradigmatic shift toward a type of visual form with new importance in the emergent Spanish court system. The legal pictorial submitted in defense of the Nahua González, while modeled on Ocelotl's, is comparatively dispassionate. The territory is effectively cleansed of narrative complications. Details have either been marginalized (the authorities who have confirmed his legitimacy are confined to the bordering calendar count) or subverted. Instead of witnessing his imperialistic act of planting and harvesting maguey products, the viewer can focus on the end result—row after row of the valuable commodity. It is with this pictorial that we might see the outlines of something akin to the imperial map, which, stripped of claims of historical legitimacy, helps to manufacture a sense of control through its very being—a *fait accompli*. It is impossible to say whence the idea for the new conceptual form of González's pictorial came, but it is easy to see how it fits within broadening imperial practices and an emergent map culture underpinned by scientific rationalism.

The relative absence of historical narrative from González's claims to land can be understood in conjunction with changing legal practices, ever more centralized and homogenized, in Central Mexico at large. Whereas native genealogies were once offered as evidence with some regularity at the local level, by the seventeenth century fewer pictorials were being incorporated into disputes (Cosentino, *Landscapes* 242–43). In these changing circumstances, extended ancestral ownership was no longer cited as the basis for property claims, suggesting an increasing disconnect with the past. Correspondingly, changing concepts of property and land, reinforced by Spanish policies, no doubt influenced the way native people related to their own territory. To begin with, by the seventeenth century, property and its measurements were identified with Spanish terminology (Lockhart, *Nahuas after the Conquest*, 166-70). Still more significantly, whereas land had formerly been regulated locally, increasingly properties were controlled through colonial law, which introduced new notions of territorial possession not related to ancestral claims (Kellogg 45–50). The adjudication of cases beyond the local level also precipitated the unhinging of disputes from local realities. While we cannot know how much his pictorial influenced the decision, the fact that the distant commission of the Royal Audiencia awarded the newcomer González what had long been Ocelotl's land suggests multiple ways that Tlacotepec was becoming woven into the imperial fabric.

Meanwhile, in nearby Zinacantepec, the context for the upward-rising St. Francis Tree suggests a similar process decoupling the local. Despite its clear proclamation of Franciscan authority and Christian redemption, the mural was inherently localized through the circumstances of its local creation and as part of the ancient mural tradition in Central Mexico. In the early colonial context, the genre of wall paintings in fact became one of the more harmonious sites of Spanish and native "contact and compatibility." By century's end, however, new artistic avenues were presenting themselves in Zinacantepec, as documented by an extant contract found among notarial records in Toluca.[3] The contract discusses details of a *retablo*, or altarpiece, a genre of visual culture that increasingly replaced the use of murals in monasteries throughout Central Mexico during the first century of colonial rule. Although we have no physical evidence of the completed *retablo* as described in the contract, the document reveals a fascinating view of the arc of Zinacantepec's own art history. We learn that in 1594 the community commissioned a Spanish sculptor by the name of Juan Montaño to make an elaborate gilded altarpiece for the church; it is likely this was the same sculptor who collaborated on the carved wooden choir in Mexico City's metropolitan cathedral on the Zócalo. Fittingly, given his reputation and the level of detail outlined in the contract, the total cost was enormous: 2,350 pesos, to be paid by all the citizens of Zinacantepec, rich and poor alike (Lockhart, *Nahuas and Spaniards* 227–28, 286 n.36; Cosentino, *Joyas* 83–90). The commissioning of a metropolitan master at great expense to the community was a clear shift from the earlier vogue of a tradition born closer to home, which relied on native creators and limited payment with homegrown products such as maize.

In the cases of Tlacotepec and Zinacantepec, then, we can see that one defining characteristic of the valley of Toluca in the sixteenth century was its intensifying relationship with the capital city of Mexico, where new artistic genres of a distinctly colonial nature were increasingly asserting their influence. In the realm of Spanish law, maps were clearly seen as legitimate visual expression and became ever more pervasive in the archival records through time, whereas native manuscripts of varying genres, such as the ones from Tlacotepec, were first tolerated and then virtually abandoned. In the Catholic Church, the altarpiece, especially one crafted by European artists, became the visually and conceptually dominant form: it was grand, it was costly, and it was hierarchical in its structure and iconography. It is curious that Zinacantepec's *retablo* commissioned from the big-city Spanish artist is not known today, and indeed no further record remains. Was it never completed because of prohibitive costs and other realities that might have pushed back on the plan and cause Zinacantepec to remain a provincial town even today? It is hard to say, of course, but this analysis of various artworks from the region and the related processual nature of visual practice is intended to show how the provincial valley of Toluca in the late sixteenth century was woven—through the work of its own native artists and patrons navigating colonial religion and law—into the Spanish imperial fabric.

Notes

1. *TLACOTEPEC: Pièce du Procès de Pablo Ocelotl et ses Fils, contre Alonzo Gonzáles.* Part of the ex-Aubin collection, it is found today at France's Bibliothèque Nationale in Paris (BNF 32).
2. Archivo General de la Nación, Ramo de Indios, vol. 5, exp. 92b, f.93v. See Colín 476.
3. Notaria no. 1: legajo 3, exp. 91, ff. 177–78, Juan de Morales, 1591–1599.

Works Cited

Boone, Elizabeth, and Thomas B. F. Cummins. "Colonial Foundations: Points of Contact and Compatibility." *The Arts in Latin America, 1492–1820.* Ed. Joseph J. Richel and Suzanne Stratton-Pruitt. Philadelphia: Philadelphia Museum of Art, 2006. 11–21. Print.
Códice franciscano, siglo XVI. Informe de la Provincia del Santo Evangelio al visitador licenciado, Juan de Ovando. Mexico City: Salvador Chávez Hayhoe, 1941. Print.
Colín, Mario. *Índice de documentos relativos a los pueblos del Estado de México, ramo de Indios del Archivo General de la Nación.* Mexico City: Biblioteca Enciclopédica del Estado de Mexico, 1968. Print.
Cosentino, Delia. *Landscapes of Lineage: Nahua Pictorial Genealogies of Early Colonial Tlaxcala, Mexico.* Diss. University of California, Los Angeles, 2002. Print.
———. *Las joyas de Zinacantepec: Arte colonial en el Monasterio de San Miguel.* Zinacantepec-Toluca: Colegio Mexiquense de Cultura, 2003. Print.
Dean, Carolyn, and Dana Leibsohn. "Hybridity and its Discontents: Considering Visual Culture in Colonial Spanish America." *Colonial Latin American Review* 12.1 (2003): 5–35. Print.
Diel, Lori Boornazian. *The Tira de Tepechpan: Negotiating Place under Aztec and Spanish Rule.* Austin: University of Texas Press, 2008. Print.
Douglas, Eduardo de Jesús. *In the Palace of Nezahualcoyotl: Painting Manuscripts, Writing the Pre-Hispanic Past in Early Colonial Period Texcoco, Mexico.* Austin: University of Texas Press, 2010. Print.
Henige, David. *Oral Historiography.* London: Longman, 1982.
Kellogg, Susan. *Law and the Transformation of Aztec Culture, 1500–1700.* Norman: University of Oklahoma Press, 1995. Print.

Klapisch-Zuber, Christiane. "The Genesis of the Family Tree." *I Tatti Studies* 4.1 (1991): 105–29. Print.
Lockhart, James. *Nahuas and Spaniards: Postconquest Central Mexican History and Philology*. Stanford: Stanford University Press, 1991. Print.
———. *The Nahuas after the Conquest: A Social and Cultural History of the Indians of Central Mexico, Sixteenth through Eighteenth Centuries*. Stanford: Stanford University Press, 1992. Print.
McAndrew, John. *The Open-Air Churches of Sixteenth-Century Mexico: Atrios, Posas, Open Chapels and other Studies*. Cambridge: Harvard University Press, 1965. Print.
Montes Bardo, Joaquín. *Arte y espiritualidad franciscana en la Nueva España. Siglo XVI*. Jaén: Universidad de Jaén, 1998. Print.
Noguez, Xavier. "Estudio iconográfico." *Códice de Santiago Tlacotepec*. Ed. Ethelia Ruiz Medrano and Xavier Noguez. Zinacantepec-Toluca: Colegio Mexiquense/Instituto Mexiquense de Cultura, 2004. 47–58. Print.
Peterson, Jeanette Favrot. *The Paradise Garden Murals of Malinalco: Utopia and Empire in Sixteenth-Century Mexico*. Austin: University of Texas Press, 1993. Print.
Reyes Valerio, Constantino. "La pila bautismal de Zinacantepec, Estado de México." *Boletín del Instituto Nacional de Antropología e Historia* 31 (1968): 24–28. Print.
Romero Quiroz, Javier. *Zinacantepetl: Zinacantepec*. Zinacantepec: Ayuntamiento de Zinacantepec, 1989. Print.
Ruiz Medrano, Ethelia. "Contenidos y contextos." *Códice de Santiago Tlacotepec (Municipio de Toluca, Estado de México)*. Ed. Ethelia Ruiz Medrano and Xavier Noguez. Zinacantepec-Toluca: Colegio Mexiquense/Instituto Mexiquense de Cultura, 2004. 14–36. Print.
Ruiz Medrano, Ethelia, and Xavier Noguez, eds. *Códice de Santiago Tlacotepec (Municipio de Toluca, Estado de México)*. Zinacantepec-Toluca: Colegio Mexiquense/Instituto Mexiquense de Cultura, 2004. Print.
Salinas, Miguel, ed. *Datos para Toluca*. Toluca: Gobierno del Estado de México, 1927. Print.
Zorita, Fray Alonso. *Life and Labor in Ancient Mexico: The Brief and Summary Relation of the Lords of New Spain*. Ed. and trans. Benjamin Keen. Norman: University of Oklahoma Press, 1994. Print.

PART III
Law

9

The Rhetoric of War and Justice in the Conquest of the Americas: Ethnography, Law, and Humanism in Juan Ginés de Sepúlveda and Bartolomé de Las Casas

David M. Solodkow

> LEOPOLDO: Así es como dices Demócrates; yo, no obstante, creo que las causas que justifican las guerras, o no existen o por lo menos son rarísimas.
> DEMÓCRATES: Yo, al contrario, creo que son muchas y frecuentes . . . el príncipe bueno y humano no debe obrar jamás con temeridad o codicia. Debe agotar todas las soluciones pacíficas . . . si, después de haberlo intentado todo, nada consiguiera y viera que su equidad y moderación son desbordadas por la soberbia y maldad de hombres injustos, no ha de tener reparo en tomar las armas ni en parecer que hace una guerra temeraria o injusta. —Juan Ginés de Sepúlveda, *Democrates secundus, sive de iustis belli causis apud Indios* (c. 1547)[1]

> (LEOPOLDO: That is what you say, Democritus; I, on the other hand, believe that the causes that justify wars either do not exist or are at least extremely rare. DEMOCRITUS: I, on the contrary, believe that they are many and that they are frequent. . . . The good and humane prince should never act recklessly or with greed. He should exhaust all possible peaceful solutions [but] if, after he has tried everything, he is unable to achieve anything and he sees that all his equanimity and moderation are swamped by the arrogance and evil of unjust men, he should not hesitate to take up arms, nor to appear to wage a rash or unjust war.)

The fictional Renaissance dialogue between Leopoldo and Democritus on the banks of the River Pisuerga was never published in Spain because of fierce opposition to the publication of anything written by its author, the theologian Juan Ginés de Sepúlveda.[2] *Democrates segundo, o de las justas causas de la guerra contra los indios* consists of two books; it employs a literary form of the dialogue, which was much in use during the Renaissance. Although it reproduces, according to the author himself, the classical dialectical approach of the exchanges between Socrates and his interlocutors, we can nevertheless argue that it is a hybrid text. Rooted in canon law, it takes inspiration from biblical and patristic sources, and uses intercalated texts from Greek and Roman philosophers. The method of exposition employs both syllogism and theological *disputatio*, a technique drawn from classical rhetoric that includes repetition and digression. The *disputatio* helps to ground the propositions and arguments in citations from classical authors, all in order to convince the interlocutor and, understandably, the reader.

At a time when Sepulveda was not as controversial, he had the same two characters, Democritus and Leopoldo, engage in dialogue in the tranquil surroundings of the Vatican gardens, in a publication entitled *Demócrates primero* (1535), dedicated to the Duke of Alba.[3] However, in 1547, the conditions that greeted the return of Leopoldo, "un alemán con resabios luteranos" (Brufau Prats xvi) (a German with Lutheran tendencies), and Democritus, a Greek sage who justified war when it corresponded to what he considered "just causes," were profoundly different, coinciding with the uprising of the *encomenderos* in the Spanish possessions in the wake of the 1542 New Laws prohibiting the perpetual enslavement of the indigenous population.[4] As Brufau Prats suggests, the dialogue responded perfectly to the needs of the colonizers who sought to invalidate the New Laws of 1542. For him, it fulfilled a major objective of persuasively defending the manner in which the conquest had been carried out and the benefits the Spanish nation had enjoyed from it (xxi–xxii).

The theologians and jurists of the Court understood at an early stage that it was not going to be a simple matter to "satisfy" the conscience of the Crown or to prove the "morality" of its actions. The problem, from the start, was how to justify the invasion of the Americas and how to benefit from indigenous labor without contravening either canon or natural law. According to Silvio Zavala, two theoretical approaches were employed to justify the invasion. The first, legal and political, was based on the possession of a *fair title*, which could be used to justify colonial penetration (*Instituciones* 15).[5] The second, anthropological in nature, is more relevant here and was based on diminishing the legal status of the Native American because of their barbarity, sinfulness, depravation, and infidelity (15). These two linked, complementary interpretative approaches have deep roots in European political, legal, and religious traditions and institutions and in continual attempts to justify the invasion. Regardless of overlaps in doctrinal change, regardless of the authors' passion for attacking the Other or defending the Other's "innocence," one thing is clear: prevailing ideas about the indigenous population—its anthropological, theological, and legal status within the Catholic world view—determined and shaped the European expansion in the Americas (Zavala, *Instituciones* 53). Of central importance are the different ethnographical perspectives on the conquest that derive from this insight.[6]

It should be remembered that the Catholic Church had only recently managed to synthesize and make official its theological and anthropological position on the indigenous populations of the Americas in the bull *Sublimis Deus*, approved on June 9, 1537, during the third year of the papacy of Pope Paul III (Alessandro Farnese, 1468–1549). The text of the bull defends the freedom and capacity of indigenous populations to embrace Christianity. However, as Rolena Adorno points out, "*Sublimis Deus* has also suffered confused interpretations. Decreed in order to establish the freedom of the Indians, the bull came to be interpreted, erroneously, as a (needed) declaration of their humanity" (*Polemics* 107).

In Alexander VI's first bull, *Inter caetera* (3 May 1493),[7] the Kingdom of Castile was granted, in gift, perpetual dominion over "islands and mainlands remote and unknown and not hitherto discovered by others, to the end that you might bring to the worship of our Redeemer and the profession of the Catholic faith." The basis of the donation was found not only in the antecedents that have already been mentioned but also in the body of Roman law known as the *Ius gentium*. In ancient Rome the status of conquered peoples was determined and regulated by the *Ius gentium*, which in the Ciceronian period was associated with the so-called natural law: whereas Roman citizens lived under the *Ius civile*, the other peoples who were won to the Empire as a result of colonial expansion were subjected to natural law. Indeed, Alexander's bull applied the concept of "gentium"—the term usually applied to people who were not citizens of the Empire—to Amerindians. The bull alluded to these "peoples," referring to them as "barbarous nations," and recommended to the Catholic kings that they should be "overthrown" (*deprimantur*) and "brought" (*reducantur*) "to the Christian Faith."[8] This context is explained by Sepúlveda when he notes:

> Aquellas regiones pasaron al domino de los españoles ocupantes por el Derecho de gentes, no porque no fueran de nadie, sino porque aquellos mortales que las ocupaban estaban faltos por completo del gobierno de los cristianos y de pueblos civilizados. . . . [P]or muchas razones, pues, y con el más legítimo Derecho divino y natural, pueden ser sometidos esos indios con las armas a dominio de los españoles si rehúsan su poder. (101)

(Those regions passed into the control of the occupying Spaniards under the Law of Nations, not because they belonged to nobody but because the mortals who occupied them entirely lacked Christian and civilized government.... For many reasons, then, and according to the most legitimate and divine law, these Indians may be subjected to the control of the Spanish by force if they reject their dominion.)[9]

While theologians and jurists may have produced documents such as the *Siete proposiciones* (Seven Propositions) and the *Ordenanzas de Burgos* of 1512–1513 (The Laws of Burgos), which sought to salve the conscience and moral doubts of the Crown, for its part the *Demócrates segundo* justified the actions of the *encomenderos*, supported state terrorism, provided a theoretical justification for the modification of the New Laws and, employing Aristotle, sought to prove the anthropological inferiority (natural slavery) of the indigenous population by citing acts *contra naturam* (cannibalism and human sacrifice) and idolatrous practices. Democritus observes:

¿Qué diré ahora de la impía religión y nefandos sacrificios de tales gentes, que al venerar como Dios al demonio no creían aplacarse con mejores sacrificios que ofreciéndoles corazones humanos? . . . [P]ensaban que debían sacrificar víctimas humanas y abriendo los pechos humanos arrancaban los corazones, los ofrecían en las nefandas aras y creían haber hecho así un sacrificio ritual con el que habían aplacado a sus dioses.... Así pues, ¿dudaremos en afirmar que estas gentes tan incultas, tan bárbaras, contaminadas con tan nefandos sacrificios e impías religiones, han sido conquistada por rey tan excelente, piadoso y justo. (68–71)

(What should I say now of the impious religion and abominable sacrifices of those people who, in worshipping the Devil as if he were God could think of no better way to placate him than by offering up human hearts? . . . They believed they should make human sacrifices and, opening up human breasts, ripped out their hearts and offered them up on their abominable altars, believing that in this way they had made a ritual sacrifice with which they had placated their gods.... So why should it surprise us that these ignorant peoples, so barbarous, contaminated by such abominable sacrifices and impious religions, should have been conquered by such an excellent king, so pious and so fair.)

Adorno asserts that for Sepúlveda the indigenous population of the Americas was not devoid of rationality and that therefore indigenous barbarism should not be seen as an innate feature but as a cultural trait ("Los debates" 53). This view explains the importance that Sepúlveda gave to anthropological classification with which he inferred indigenous barbarism: without it, Democritus would have been left without arguments.

In the dialogue, Leopoldo is enlightened by the "wise" words of Democritus, a clear alter ego of Sepúlveda himself. Nevertheless, Leopoldo, in addition to functioning as an *aide memoire* to Democritus and serving as the pretext to ask questions that already had an answer, may also be thought of as the representation, or allegory, of the conscience and moral doubts of the Spanish Crown. Democritus, for his part, fulfills the role of the sage, the theologian and jurist who conjures away the Catholic guilt of the Crown and its moral dilemmas, providing enlightenment through scholastic syllogisms and Aristotelian doctrine. Perhaps the celebrated Valladolid Debates in 1550–1551 represented nothing other than the highest practical fulfillment of the moral obligation accorded to the prince by Democritus.[10]

One of the first doubts Leopoldo insists on resolving—in addition to the question of whether there were just reasons to declare war—is whether the actions of the Spanish Crown overseas corresponded to notions of Christian piety and justice. At the very beginning of the dialogue, Leopoldo declares to Democritus that, while wandering the grounds of Prince Philip's palace with his friends, he has seen Hernán Cortés passing by and that, after he reflected for a moment with his comrades on the "heroic deeds" of the Emperor Charles's knights, certain thoughts have begun to prey on his mind. Democritus does not answer Leopoldo directly but launches into an extensive digression, showing off his great learning in patristic texts and the Gospels, citing Saints Augustine, Paul, and Gratian. He begins by modifying Christ's instruction that, if attacked, we should "turn the other cheek." He reminds Leopoldo that Christ's phrase does not contradict the Natural Law principle according to which "a todo hombre le está permitido repeler la fuerza con la fuerza dentro de los límites de la justa defensa" (44) (every man is permitted to defend himself by opposing force with force with force within the limits of the just defense). From this argument emerges the first and, according to Democritus, most important and natural justification of the war—namely, that *it is lawful to fight force with force*. This trope was to become an essential part of the doctrinal justification of colonial penetration every time the indigenous population resisted colonial occupation. Its underlying principle is apparent in the *Requerimiento* [Requirement] and in the legislation that made it possible to enslave and sell supposed cannibals (1503), and which was in turn based, precisely, on the alleged cannibal's violence and their resistance to the invaders.[11] Several years later, in 1555, the Franciscan Toribio Benavente (Motolinia) sent a letter to Charles V excoriating Las Casas for obstructing the task of evangelization. In it, he took up Sepúlveda's argument and justified the use of force against the indigenous population of Mexico with the argument that the practice protected the innocent and banished idolatrous practices. Las Casas, on the other hand, was always arguing against the use of violence; according to George Mariscal, the Dominican "[r]easserts the absolute contradiction between Christian values and the application of preemptive military force" (272).

At the same time, Democritus explains the basics of natural law to Leopoldo: that in all parts it "tiene la misma fuerza, sin depender de apreciaciones circunstanciales ... es la participación de la ley eterna en la criatura dotada de razón ... de esta ley eterna es partícipe el hombre por la recta razón e inclinación al deber y a la virtud" (47) (has the same authority, independent of any circumstantial considerations. ... It is the presence of eternal law in all creatures invested with reason. ... Man is a part of this eternal law as a result of his noble reason and his inclination to duty and virtue). Like Las Casas, though for different reasons, Sepúlveda was establishing the basis of *humanist universalism* according to a alternative viewpoint that posited the existence of different degrees of humanity.[12] Democritus argues that further justification of the colonial enterprise is found in the protection it offers to the innocent victims of human sacrifice, missionary preachers and natives who wished to hear the message of the Gospel, but who were unable to do so, or were attacked, as a result of indigenous resistance.

Democritus organizes his interpretation of natural law around the principle of reason, which, in marked contrast to his use of humanist universalism, is conceptualized in purely Eurocentric (particularist) terms. According to Sepúlveda, reason is defined entirely in relation to European and Christian parameters. The problem of who possesses reason, understood in terms of intellectual faculties and the power of discernment, was an important one, since the degree of inferiority assigned to the subject depended on the recognition of these attributes. It should be emphasized that Sepúlveda repeats on many occasions that the legal consequences of the victor's triumph were to be applied according to the nature of the Indians. As Democritus says:

> Si es lícito y justo que los mejores y quienes más sobresalen por naturaleza, costumbres y leyes imperen sobre sus inferiores, bien puedes comprender, Leopoldo, si es que conoces la naturaleza y moral de ambos pueblos, que con el perfecto derecho los españoles ejercen su dominio sobre esos indios del Nuevo Mundo e islas adyacentes, los cuales en prudencia, ingenio y todo género de virtudes y humanos sentimientos son tan inferiores a los españoles como los niños a los adultos, las mujeres a los varones, los crueles e inhumanos a los extremadamente mansos, los exageradamente intemperantes a los continentes y moderados. (*Demócrates* 64)

(And well will you be able to comprehend, Leopoldo, if you understand the nature and morality of both peoples, that it is lawful and just that the best—those who are prominent because of their nature, customs and law—should rule over their inferiors; it follows that it is perfectly lawful for the Spanish to exercise dominion over these Indians of the Americas and the neighboring islands who, in prudence, wit, and all manner of virtues and human feeling are as inferior to the Spanish as children are to adults, women to men, the cruel and inhuman to the extremely gentle the exaggeratedly intemperate to the continent and moderate.)

Arising from the assertion that it was acceptable to respond to aggression with aggression was a second justification, consisting of "the recovery of spoils unjustly seized" (51). In this case, Democritus based his argument on the Old Testament example of Abraham against the Elamite king, concluding that it was lawful to make war not only to recover property but also that of friends—the "good" indigenous—that had been unjustly seized (52). This interpretation was much rehearsed, too, during the military advance of the conquest and was a constitutive aspect of the *defensa del inocente* [the defense of the innocent], which Jáuregui discusses in his *Canibalia* (121–39). On a number of occasions, the invaders used the pretext that Atahualpa or Moctezuma had subdued other peoples, or that the cannibals would plunder the Caribbean islands and make off with Taino women as spoils of war. This second cause, then, buttressed the argument that the Spaniards were acting to help people who had supposedly been subjugated either by the cannibals or by some "tyrannical" chief. A third justification derived from the second was based on the imposition of punishment on those responsible for the offense (52). Confronted with this new argument, Leopoldo, somewhat shocked, asks, "¿Aseguras que la venganza de las injurias está permitida a los buenos y virtuosos varones? Según eso ¿qué fuerza tienen para ti aquellas divinas palabras del Deuteronomio: 'para mí la venganza y yo daré la retribución'? ¿Acaso no indican que este derecho es privativo exclusivamente de Dios?" (5) (You maintain that vengeance for these injuries is permitted to good and virtuous gentlemen? If this is the case, what force do the divine words of Deuteronomy have for you? "Vengeance is mine, and retribution." Do these words not mean that this right is exclusive to God alone?). Democritus's answer is simple: he states that God frequently exercised his vengeance through his ministers, princes, and judges—that is, through Spaniards.

To these principal justifications, Democritus says, should be added others that, though they are considered secondary (53), nevertheless defined the invasion at the profoundest level and were of fundamental importance within the colonial context and in the theological and legal discussions of the time. He is referring to the anthropological identity of the indigenous population: "aquéllos cuya condición natural es tal que deban obedecer a otros, si rehúsan su gobierno y no queda otro recurso, sean dominados por las armas; pues tal guerra es justa según opinión de los más eminentes filósofos" (53) (those whose natural condition is such that they should obey others and who, if they reject this government, leave no alternative but to defeat them by force of arms, because the most eminent philosophers believe such a war to be just). Leopoldo considers this to be a "strange doctrine," "far from the usual opinion of men" (53), while Democritus replies that it is strange only for the unschooled but that it is well-established knowledge for philosophers. Naturally, the philosopher he alludes to is Aristotle, who argued in Book I of his *Politics* that slavery was intrinsic to the inferiority of certain peoples (barbarians) and even of women and children.

The question follows: how to determine the inferiority of these barbarian-slaves? In response, Democritus differentiates between jurists and philosophers. The former supported the case for the inferiority of the barbarians in the *ius gentium*, whereas the philosophers identified both their inferiority and their consequent servile nature with their "torpeza ingénita" (congenital stupidity) and their "costumbres inhumanas y bárbaras" (54) (inhuman and barbaric customs). This implied a double aspect to their alleged inferiority, linked on the one hand to "congenital stupidity" and on the other to specific "practices" (cannibalism, sodomy, idolatry, human sacrifice) that, in the working out of their mechanisms and procedures, transformed the indigenous population into a barbarous and inhuman Other. As Anthony Pagden has shown, the methods commonly used in the fifteenth century to classify Otherness refer to an indeterminate number of human "attributes" concerning not only the psychological characteristics of the Other but also geographical location, originating in Columbus's orientalist discourse (Hulme). Nevertheless, Pagden concludes that the most common method employed to classify and characterize Otherness was the analysis of "conduct"—that is, of the actions of these Others (13).

The double anthropological distinction ("congenital stupidity" and "practices") made by Democritus is important because of its generalizing consequences. There was no way that the indigenous population could avoid being labeled inferior; either because they were so by nature or because they demonstrated their status by the way they lived day by day. For Democritus, then, the principle of inferiority was based on the belief that if some men were more intelligent and were guided by "true reason," there was no impediment to their ruling and protecting those considered inferior. That is, (European) "perfection" rules (American) "imperfection," force (the military power of the Empire) imposes itself over the "weakness" of indigenous resistance, and, finally, the "virtue" of the *conquistadores* overcomes the "barbarian vices" of the indigenous population. Democritus continues: "tan conforme a la naturaleza es esto, que en todas las cosas que constan de otras muchas, ya continuas, ya separadas, observamos que una de ellas, a saber, la más importante, tiene el dominio sobre las demás" (54) (so true to nature is this that in all cases where things are made up of many other things, be they connected or separate, we observe that one of them, which is the most important, has dominion over the others). Las Casas, who was Sepúlveda's principal opponent and responsible for countering, point by point, each accusation concerning the alleged savage nature of the indigenous population, constructed a system to interpret the concept of "barbarism" specifically to contest of Sepúlveda; the scheme was subsequently included at the end of his *Apologética historia sumaria*. Las Casas picked apart the notion of barbarism, breaking down its ideological, unidirectional, and generalizing certainties, and suggested that it should be understood in terms of manners, kinds, and degree—in other words, he proposed a relativist vision of the concept.

For Las Casas, there were several barbarian identities, and not all forms were essentially sinful, nor incapable of modification. His aim was to correct mistakes that derived from the misuse of the concept. The first kind of barbarism for him corresponds, in general terms, to any nation that has lost the use of reason as a result of internal dissent. At this individual level, barbarism was associated with particular patterns of conduct (psychological barbarism) caused by the loss of reason or its momentary alteration, whether as a result of emotional violence or of confusion caused by a particular event:

> por cualquiera extrañez, ferocidad, desorden, exorbitancia, degeneración de razón, de justicia y de buenas costumbres y de humana benignidad, o también por alguna opinión confusa o acelerada, furiosa, tumultuosa o fuera de razón. Así como algunos hombres, dejadas y olvidadas las reglas y orden de la razón y la blandura y mansedumbre que deben tener por su naturaleza los hombres, ciegos de pasión, se convierten en alguna manera o son feroces, duros, ásperos, crueles, y se precipitan a cometer obras tan inhumanas que no las harían peores las bestias fieras y bravas del monte, que parecen haberse desnudado de toda naturaleza de hombres. (*Apologética historia* 8: 1576)

> (because of any strangeness, ferocity, disorder, exorbitance, degeneration of reason, justice, good habits, and human benignity, or for any other confused or irrational, furious, tumultuous, or insane opinion. Thus, just as some men, having abandoned

and forgotten the rules and order of reason and the gentleness and meekness that should mark the natures of men, blinded by passion, become in some way, or are, ferocious, hard, coarse or cruel, and throw themselves into committing such inhuman acts that not even the wild and angry beasts of the forests would commit them, and appear stripped of all human nature.)

Las Casas considered the second kind of barbarism to be the product of a specific absence, or lack, of a quality. He described it as a relative barbarism, or *secundum quid*, that existed in relation to something else. Among this category, Las Casas included all those who lacked a literary expression, discipline, and training in letters (8: 1577). Here, Las Casas followed the traditional Greek notion of barbarism—that is, people who were considered barbarian because they did not speak Greek. Nevertheless, Las Casas's opinion was based on a linguistic relativism: the fact that a people X does not understand a people Y does not mean that Y has no language. It therefore followed that people Y had as much right to consider X barbarian if they could not understand their language: "así, estas gentes destas Indias como nosotros las estimamos por bárbaras, ellas también, por no entendernos, nos tenían por bárbaros, conviene a saber, por extraños" (8: 1577) (thus, as we consider these people from these Indies to be barbarian, they, too, because they cannot understand us, considered us to be barbarians—that is, to be different). In this way, Las Casas stood Sepúlveda's logic of unidirectional, Eurocentric barbarism on its head. The third category of barbarism developed by Las Casas was used to "explain" didactically the differences between varieties of barbarians already laid out in Aristotle. Las Casas did not deny the Aristotelian concept of natural slavery used by Sepúlveda to justify the war against the indigenous population, because he considered it to be fundamentally correct. Instead, he explained in great detail the kinds of barbarism Aristotle had in mind when he thought of natural slavery. The natural slave barbarians were those known as *simpliciter*, who:

> por sus extrañas y ásperas y malas costumbres o por su mala y perversa inclinación salen crueles y feroces y extraños de los otros hombres y no se rigen por razón, antes son como estólidos o fantochazos, ni tienen ni curan de ley ni derecho, ni de pueblo ni amistad ni conversación de otros hombres, por lo cual no tienen lugares ni ayuntamientos ni ciudades porque no viven socialmente, y así no tienen ni sufren señores ni leyes ni fueros ni político regimiento, ni comunican en usar de la comunicaciones a la vida humana necesarias, como son comprar y vender y trocar, alquilar y conducir, hacer compañía unos vecinos con otros. (8: 1580)

(because of their strange, crude, and evil habits or their evil and perverse inclination, are more cruel, ferocious, and apart from all other men and are not governed by reason but are, rather, ignorant or grotesque, and incapable of cure whether by law, society, friendship, or conversation. Therefore, these kind do not live in fixed places, settlements, or societies, because they do not live in society and therefore they do not tolerate masters, nor laws, nor rights, nor political organization, nor do they communicate using the forms of communication that are necessary to human life.)

According to this conceptualization, it was clear that the indigenous population of the Americas could not be made to fit the third category because—as Las Casas's ethnographic findings showed—they had political organization, trade, cities, lords, laws, government, religion, and the like. According to Las Casas there were two reasons such barbarians might exist: the first associated with the place where they had been born—that is, the determinist hypothesis—and the second explained by custom. Las Casas had spent the first 20 chapters of the *Apologética historia* arguing that the climate in the Americas was benevolent and demonstrating that, as a result, the indigenous population was naturally predisposed to healthy and moderate customs and was therefore ready to receive the Word of God. Furthermore, Las Casas came to the conclusion that not all barbarians lack reason, are slaves by nature or can be subjugated by force. For him, they were sovereign and free (8: 1582). With this argument he shattered the *tabula rasa* that Sepúlveda sought to create using his personal interpretation of Aristotle's position on slavery. It is true that the interpretive efforts of Las Casas were intended to undermine indigenous barbarism as a justification for their extermination or designation as natural slaves, but despite these theoretical efforts, the indigenous population of the Americas was nevertheless barbarian according to his scheme. Indeed, the logic went further: the barbarism of the indigenous inhabitants of the Americas fulfilled more than one of the four categories he had created:

Síguese luego que todas estas gentes [los indios] son bárbaras *largo modo* según alguna cualidad, y ésta es, la primera, en cuanto son infieles, y esto sólo por carecer de nuestra sancta fe, que se dice infidelidad *pure negativa* (o según pura negación), que no es pecado como queda declarado, y así se contienen cuanto a esto dentro de la especie cuarta. Compréndase también dentro de la segunda por tres cualidades: la una, en cuanto carecían de letras o de literal locución, como los ingleses; la segunda, porque son gentes humílimas, que obedecían en extraña y admirable manera a sus reyes; la tercera, por no hablar bien nuestro lenguaje ni nos entender; pero en ésta tan bárbaros como ellas son, somos nosotros a ellas. (8: 1591)

> (It follows, then, that all these [Indians] are barbarians *largo modo* as a result of some quality they possess—because they are infidels, in that they lack our Holy Faith; we describe this as infidelity *pure negativa* (resulting from pure negation). This is not, as has been declared, a sin, and therefore this kind of infidel falls under the fourth category. They fall within the second "category," too, for three qualities they possess: first, because they were unlettered or lacked literary expression, like the English; second, because they are a most humble people that obeyed their kings to a rare and admirable degree; third, because they did not speak our language well nor understand us, but in this, as they are barbarian to us so we are to them.)

Clearly, the fourth kind of barbarism that Las Casas attributed to the indigenous population, in contrast to the form of barbarism declared by Democritus, did not support the waging of just war. According to Las Casas, indigenous barbarism was a result of their infidel nature:

> todos aquellos que carecen de verdadera religión y fe cristiana, conviene a saber, todos los infieles, por muy sabios y prudentes philósofos y políticos que sean ... no hay alguna nación—sacada la de los christianos—que no tengan y padezcan munchos y muy grandes defectos y barbaricen en sus leyes, costumbres, vivienda y policías; las cuales no se enmiendan ni apuran y reforman en su vivir e manera de regimniento, sino entrando en la Iglesia, rescibiendo nuestra sancta y católica fe, porque sola ella es la ley sin mancilla, que convierte las ánimas, limpia las heces de toda mala costumbre, desterrando la idolatría y ritos supersticiosos, de donde todas las otras suciedades, vicios e máculas privada y públicamente proceden. (8: 1583)

> (all who lack the true Christian religion and Faith, it should be understood, are infidels, however wise and learned they may be as philosophers or politicians.... There is no nation—apart from the Christian nations—that do not suffer from many, and very large, defects expressed in their laws, customs, manners and ways of life; and these are not altered or purged or reformed by discipline, but by their entering the Church, receiving our Holy Catholic Faith, because this is the only unstained law, that converts souls, cleanses the filth of bad customs, exiles idolatry and superstitious rites, from which all other forms of filth, vice, and stains, whether private or public, derive.)

Employing the same procedures of grading and classifying the concept of *barbarism*, Las Casas again applied relativism to the state of infidelity, differentiating among its various causes. The worst kinds of infidels were those, such as the Turks and the Moors, who, having knowledge of True Doctrine, rejected it, and, furthermore, fought against it. In the case of these voluntary or militant infidels, Las Casas argued that there was a case for just war to be waged. Simultaneously he created a kind of faith in which infidels did not reject doctrine voluntarily but because they were ignorant of the divine word. This category encompassed the indigenous Americans, and as a consequence, their relative, softened barbarism meant it was impossible to apply the military criteria urged by Sepúlveda. Las Casas made a clear distinction between natural and canon law. The latter should neither overpower nor undermine the former. This implied that it was wrong to argue that the *infidelity* of the indigenous populations constituted necessary or *just cause* to dispossess them of their natural rights (the right to government, to social order and organization, and to private property). On this, Las Casas coincided with Francisco de Vitoria, who argued the same considering natural and human law.

Vitoria argued that in contrast to the Moors and the Jews—the other ethnic groups against whom "just" war was waged—the indigenous of the New World neither knew nor rejected the doctrine of Christ; nor had they invaded Christian lands. Therefore, military principles—and the legal consequences derived from them that were applied to the Jews and Moors—could not be applied to the indigenous population. Several years before Vitoria wrote *De indis*, Matías de Paz (c.1468–1519), another Dominican friar from Salamanca and one of the principal ideologues of the Burgos Laws, wrote in his *Del dominio de los reyes de España sobre los indios* (1512) (*On the Authority of Spanish Kings over the Indians*) that the indigenous population could only be accused of "passive infidelity," a sin of omission, and not of its "positive" form, infidelity by commission, as was the case with the Saracens, Turks, Jews, and other heretics in general.

For a thinker like Las Casas, the justification of the European occupation of the New World, and of the Papal Donation, had a purely and exclusively religious foundation, based on the "potentiality" of the indigenous population to understand and accept Christian doctrine. Nevertheless, while it is true that he recognized the natural right of the natives, Las Casas maintained that any system based on natural law was imperfect if not subject to the spiritual law of God, as demonstrated in the proof of the second conclusion of his *Tratado comprobatorio* (127). Las Casas respected the natives and believed they had rights, but he could not accept that there could be any religious or philosophical "truth" other than the Christian one. As Luis Villoro has indicated, this illustrates the limits of Las Casas's thought when it came to recognizing the irreducibly Other: "Las Casas cannot accept the possibility of multiple truths. . . . It will be unthinkable for Las Casas that the Indian could convince him of the validity, however limited; of his own vision of the world . . . [T]he life of the other can have no more sense or destiny than conversion to our own world" (6).

In his *Demócrates segundo*, Sepúlveda also considered faith to be a determining factor when it came to applying force and justifying war. Thus, he proposed a fourth justification or cause derived from the previous ones: the conversion of the indigenous population to the "true" faith: "De esta religión privadamente *se origina una cuarta* causa que justifica sobremanera la iniciación de la guerra contra los indígenas, pues atañe al cumplimiento de un precepto evangélico de Cristo y se dirige a atraer por el camino más próximo y corto a la *luz de la verdad* a una infinita multitud de *hombres errantes entre perniciosas tinieblas*" (87; my emphasis) (From this religion in particular, *a fourth cause originates*, which amply justifies the initiation of war against the natives, since it concerns the fulfillment of a precept of Christ consisting in attracting, by means of the closest and most direct route, an *infinite multitude of men who wander in pernicious darkness* toward the *light of Truth*). These causes, which justified the colonial occupation, the war against the natives, and the plunder of America by the empire, had theoretical consequences that, according to Democritus, were "beneficial" for the conquered Other:

> A éstos [los indios] les es beneficioso y más conforme al derecho natural el que estén sometidos al gobierno de naciones o príncipes más humanos y virtuosos, para que con el ejemplo de su virtud y prudencia y cumplimiento de sus leyes abandonen la barbarie y abracen una vida más humana, una conducta morigerada y practiquen la virtud. Y si rechazan su gobierno, pueden ser obligados por las armas, y esta guerra los filósofos enseñan que es justa por naturaleza . . . [E]n suma, [los filósofos] nos enseñan que es justo naturalmente y beneficioso para ambas partes, el que los hombres buenos, excelentes por su virtud, inteligencia y prudencia, imperen sobre sus inferiores. (55–56)

> (It is beneficial to these [Indians], and truer to natural law, that they be subjected to government by nations or princes who are more human and virtuous than they, so that, because of the virtue of the latter, their prudence and compliance with the law, [the Indians] abandon their barbarism and embrace a more human life, conduct themselves more nobly, and practice virtue. And if they reject this government, they may be obliged by force of arms, and the philosophers teach us that this war is naturally just. . . . In sum, [the philosophers] teach us that it is naturally just and beneficial for both parties that good men, excellent because of their virtue, intelligence, and prudence, should rule the inferiors).

Sepúlveda was responsible for the emergence of a new ideological current, characteristic of colonial discourse. Enrique Dussel has called this current "emancipatory"; that is, modernity signifies a "benefit" that the "civilized" offer to the "barbarians" in order to wrest them from *savagery* and relocate them in European time (*1492*, 99–107). The "emancipatory" effect of Europe on its periphery was to be highly productive and long-lasting, and it resulted in a collection of pedagogical practices that were employed in the conversion, education, and cultural transformation of the Other. As Dussel argues in his critique of Sepúlveda:

> El que las otras culturas "salgan" de su propia barbarie o subdesarrollo por el proceso civilizador constituye, como conclusión, un progreso, un desarrollo, un bien para ellas mismas. En esto estriba la "falacia del desarrollo" [desarrollismo] ... [L]a dominación que Europa ejerce sobre otras culturas es una acción pedagógica o una violencia necesaria (guerra justa), y queda justificada por ser una obra civilizadora o modernizadora. (104–5)

> (That those other cultures should "leave" their own barbarism, or underdevelopment, as a result of the civilizing process, constitutes for them, in the end, progress, development, and benefit. ... It is here that the "fallacy of development" [developmentalism] lies; ... The domination exercised by Europe over other cultures is a pedagogical action, or a necessary violence (a just war), and is justified as a civilizing and modernizing act.)

The benefit for the natives, at least for those who did not die as a consequence of the invasion, will consist of more than merely passing from a state of "imperfection" to another that is "perfect": from "barbarism" to "civilization," from "vice" to "virtue." Democritus even argues that the natives owe a debt to the king, because the amount taken in booty for the Crown is, in terms of its utility, infinitely less than what the Crown has given them (98).

Toward the end of the first book, Leopoldo says that, having paid close attention to the words of Democritus, he has been released from all the doubts and scruples that were plaguing him (101). He prepares a summary of the topics or causes that justified the war against the indigenous population. From a careful reading of Leopoldo's summary, it is possible to divide the alleged causes into four distinct categories, principal among which is the degraded human state of the natives: 1) *the anthropological cause* (being by nature slaves, barbarians, uneducated, and inhuman); 2) *the repressive and corrective cause* (the punishment of cannibalism and the expulsion of idolatry); 3) *the tutelary cause* (defense of the innocent): "librar de graves injurias a muchísimos inocentes mortales a quienes los indígenas todos los años inmolaban" (102) (to free vast numbers of innocent mortals from the gravest outrages, whom the natives used to sacrifice every year); and 4) *Christian evangelization* (by force if necessary). The anthropological conceptualization contained in *Demócrates segundo* illustrates Dussel's description of the ideological and political procedures that lie at the root of modernity. For him, modernity "can be read as the justification of an irrational praxis of violence" that is bolstered by casting the modern civilization as superior and developed; a civilization that will oppose and educate the "barbaric, coarse and primitive people" (472). In this major contribution to the understanding of modernity, Sepúlveda's doctrine is clearly described.

A focus on the violent consequences of the conquest shows that it is not entirely risky to assert the material triumph of Sepúlveda's hypothesis. This material triumph was openly opposed to the thought—and to the symbolic or bureaucratic triumph—of the Salamanca School personified by Francisco de Vitoria and by the political, philosophical, and historiographical treatises of Las Casas. It should not be forgotten that the "prohibition" against waging war on the indigenous population came very late, 188 years after the arrival of Columbus.[13]

This essay has emphasized the instrumental role of ethnographic discourse in relation to the legal apparatus of the Spanish Crown and its constant modifications, setbacks, cancelations, contradictions, and material consequences and effects. One of the most important conclusions to be drawn from the historical reading presented here concerns the incompatibility between the legal norms and the concrete realities of their implementation.[14] Accordingly, it is of little consequence to remark that in contrast to other colonial powers, Spain developed an extensive legal system for its colonies; it is more important to demonstrate the final consequences of the process of violent appropriation of the lives and possessions of Others.[15] On the other hand, a critical examination of legal discourses illustrates the dialectical interrelations between anthropological conceptions of the Other and the formulations of the colonial judicial system. During the century that saw the establishment of the legal bases for what subsequently evolved into "human rights" (Las Casas) and international law (Vitoria), one of history's greatest genocides occurred, a genocide which was to have extremely far-reaching political, economic, religious, and cultural consequences for the future history of humanity.

Notes

1. *A Second Democritus: On the Just Causes of the War with the Indians*. Unless otherwise indicated, all translations are mine. I would like to thank James Lupton for his wise and careful revision of the essay.
2. Sepúlveda encountered resistance to the publication of his *Demócrates segundo* not only as a result of his tireless opposition of Las Casas but also because the book did not garner support in Salamanca, where a pseudo-Lascasian position had been adopted that inspired the drafting of the New Laws in 1542. In response, Sepúlveda decided to analyze the criticisms of the detractors and wrote his *Apologia pro libro De Justis Belli Causis*, which was authorized for publication by Rome. This text repeated the same doctrine as his *Demócrates segundo* without employing the literary form of the dialogue. The manuscript was finally published in 1892, thanks to the efforts of Marcelino Menéndez Pelayo.
3. According to Jáuregui, Francisco de Vitoria was unconvinced of the legal and moral justifications of the conquest of the Indies (122–23).
4. Brufau Prats suggests that the immediate dissatisfaction of the *encomenderos* was just another stage in the process initiated years before by Montesinos. The fear of open and violent opposition was used to apply pressure on the Crown (xv).
5. Raúl Marrero-Fente points out that there was a prior legal framework for occupying newly discovered empty lands, but that framework did not accounted for inhabited lands (*La poética* 93).
6. Regarding this point, Felipe Castañeda asserts that classifying indigenous people as cowardly, ferocious, or brave also indicates to what extent they are seen as displaying adequate development as human beings (106).
7. The content of the first papal bull was modified to "correct" and "extend" the donation and establish the Spanish territorial limits in the face of complaints and petitions from the Portuguese Crown. The first bull, *Inter caetera* (3 May 1493), should, strictly speaking, be known as a *donation*. It was followed by *Eximie devotionis* (also dated 3 May 1493), which was followed by the second *Inter caetera* (published 4 May 1493, a day after its predecessors). Although this bull also reproduced the first section of the original donation, it introduced some variations regarding the demarcation of the territory. The fourth bull, *Dudum siquidem* (26 September 1493), was intended to correct the second *Inter caetera*, which, while it referred to a demarcation line, had imprecise wording. To resolve problems with the kings of Portugal, it guaranteed that lands could be occupied as long as they were not possessed by another Christian prince (Castañeda Delgado 322). There was a fifth bull, *Piis Fidelium* (25 June 1493), which granted spiritual authority to Friar Bernardo Boyl, the priest who sailed on Columbus's second voyage and was responsible for evangelization efforts (322).
8. The Latin version of the bull may be consulted in *Colección documental del descubrimiento* (1470–1506), vol. 1.
9. Marrero-Fente says of the Laws of Burgos that "the most outstanding part of this legal

fiction is an introduction of legal instruments as laws in times of peace, which replaced the brutal practices of the military conquest." Physical violence and psychological torture are hidden behind these laws (*Bodies* 96).
10. Las Casas also shared this position and fervently believed that the meetings, and the information he and other theologians provided, really could heal, or at least stop, the mistreatment of the indigenous population.
11. On the *Requerimiento*, see Patricia Seed.
12. Ramón Grosfoguel points out, "Beyond political-economy paradigms what all fundamentalisms share (including the Eurocentric one) is the premise that there is only one sole epistemic tradition from which to achieve Truth and Universality. . . . It is this 'god-eye view' that always hides its local and particular perspective under an abstract universalism" (212–14).
13. Zavala asserts that Law 9, Title 4, Book III from the *Recopilación de las Leyes de Indias* (1680), based on previous legislation, expressed in a stronger language the order not to wage war against Indians because of religion or social control (*La filosofía* 37–38).
14. According to Marrero-Fente, Spanish legislation needs to be considered as a set of "organized social practices of violence that prescribed what to do, what to seek, and how to exercise control over newly found people and their territories" ("Human Rights" 248).
15. Marrero-Fente points out that the most important contradiction of the colonial legal apparatus is that the proliferation of laws only succeeded in causing the indigenous population to be "deprived of their rights and oppressed by the *encomenderos*" (*Bodies* 96).

Works Cited

Adorno, Rolena. "Los debates sobre la naturaleza del indio en el siglo XVI: Textos y contextos." *Revista de Estudios Hispánicos* (PR) 19 (1992): 47–66. Print.

———. *The Polemics of Possession in Spanish American Narrative*. New Haven: Yale University Press, 2007. Print.

Aristotle. *Politics*. Ed. R. F. Stalley. Trans. Ernest Barker. Oxford: Oxford University Press, 1995. Print.

Brufau Prats, Jaime. "Estudio histórico." *Demócrates segundo. Obras completas de Francisco Vitoria*. 3 vols. Salamanca: Excelentísimo Ayuntamiento de Pozoblanco, 1997. Print.

Casas, Bartolomé de Las. *Apologética historia sumaria. Obras completas*. Vols. 6–8. 14 vols. Madrid: Alianza, 1992. Print.

———. *Tratado comprobatorio sobre las Indias*. Tenerife: Universidad de la Laguna, 1996. Print.

Castañeda Delgado, Paulino. *La teocracia pontifical en las controversias sobre el Nuevo Mundo*. Mexico City: UNAM, Instituto de Investigaciones Jurídicas, 1996. Print.

Castañeda, Felipe. *El indio: Entre el bárbaro y el cristiano. Ensayos sobre filosofía de la conquista en Las Casas, Sepúlveda y Acosta*. Bogota: Alfaomega Colombiana and Universidad de los Andes, 2002. Print.

Dussel, Enrique. *1492: El encubrimiento del otro (el origen del mito de la modernidad)*. Bogota: Anthropos, 1992. Print.

Grosfoguel, Ramón. "The Epistemic Decolonial Turn: Beyond Political Economy Paradigms." *Cultural Studies* 21.2–3 (2007): 211–23. Print.

Hulme, Peter. *Colonial Encounters*. London: Methuen, 1986. Print.

Jáuregui, Carlos. *Canibalia: Canibalismo, calibanismo, antropofagia cultural y consumo en América Latina*. Córdoba: Casa de las Américas, 2005. Print.

Mariscal, George. "Bartolomé de Las Casas on Imperial Ethics and the Use of Force." *Reason and Its Others. Italy, Spain and the New World*. Ed. David R. Castillo and Massimo Lollini. Hispanic Issues vol. 32. Nashville: Vanderbilt University Press, 2006. 259–78. Print.

Marrero-Fente, Raúl. *Bodies, Texts and Ghosts: Writing Literature and Law in Colonial Latin America*. Lanham: University Press of America, 2010. Print.

———. "Human Rights and Academic Discourse: Teaching the Las Casas-Sepúlveda Debate at the Time of the Iraq War." *Hispanic Issues On Line* 4.1 (2009): 247–59. Web.

———. *La poética de la ley en las Capitulaciones de Santa Fe*. Madrid: Trotta, 2000. Print.

Pagden, Anthony. *The Fall of Natural Man: The American Indians and the Origins of Comparative Ethnology*. Cambridge: Cambridge University Press, 1982. Print.

Paz, Fray Matías de. *Del dominio de los reyes de España sobre los indios*. Intro. Silvio Zavala. Mexico City: FCE, 1954. Print.

Sepúlveda, Juan Ginés de. *Demócrates segundo. Obras completas*. Vol 3. Ed. and trans. J. Brufau Prats. Intro. A. Coroleu Lletget. Pozoblanco: Artes Gráficas, 1997. Print.

Seed, Patricia. *Ceremonies of Possession in Europe's Conquest of the New World, 1492–1640*. Cambridge: Cambridge University Press, 1995. Print.

"The Bull *Inter Caetera* (Alexander VI), May 4, 1493." Resources for Indigenous Cultures around the World. Native Web. N.p. Web. 19 March 2012.

Villoro, Luis. "Sahagún, or the Limits of the Discovery of the Other." *1992 Lecture Series: Working Papers No. 2*. College Park: Dept. of Spanish and Portuguese, University of Maryland at College Park, 1989. Print.

Vitoria, Francisco de. *Relectio de Indis o libertad de los indios*. Ed. L. Pereña and J. M. Pérez Prendes. Madrid: Consejo Superior de Investigaciones Científicas, 1967. Print.

Zavala, Silvio. *La filosofía política en la conquista de América*. Mexico City: FCE, 1977. Print.

———. *Las instituciones jurídicas de la conquista de América*. Mexico City: Porrúa, 1988. Print.

◆ **10**

Human Sacrifice, Conquest, and the Law: Cultural Interpretation and Colonial Sovereignty in New Spain

Cristian Roa

Human sacrifice has long been treated as a pivotal *topos* for understanding Mesoamerican culture and spirituality. In addition to its role as a vital source of energy to support life according to indigenous beliefs, it has also been recognized as a ritual activity that shaped the religious, economic, and political life of Central Mexico.[1] These views have a strong hold in the research within the fields of anthropology and religious studies, but they were equally well formulated early on by Spanish explorers, conquistadors, and missionaries. Human sacrifice is of deep interest not just as an object of knowledge but also in terms of colonizers' discursive appropriation of the ritual killing and consumption of humans. Reports of human sacrifice in accounts of exploration and conquest conveyed Europeans' strong emotional responses toward an alien practice along with their uneasy fascination with this particular form of cultural difference. It seems fair to say that human sacrifice captured the imagination of colonizers in ways that no other Mesoamerican cultural achievement did. European representations of the practice tended to aestheticize indigenous forms of sacrificial violence as a means of unveiling an ontological transgression. By exposing procedures and ritual uses of human remains that redrew the cultural boundaries of the human body, these representations chiefly sought to elicit an emotional response from the reader. At the same time, these reports textualized a desire for sacrifice through their figurative treatment of observation, inquiry, recording, cultural crossing, imagined situations, and embodied experience.

European discourses on human sacrifice generated new ways of approaching cultural difference and the colonial relationship by contrast to Caribbean referents. The conquistadors' closest point of reference for people thought to engage in the killing and consumption of humans was the ethnic category of "Carib," applied by colonizers to any people reported to practice cannibalism in the Antilles and northern South America. Though they considered human sacrifice to be inhumane, their response marked a clear departure from the policies that claims of cannibalism had brought about in the Caribbean. The Cannibal Law of 1503 authorized colonizers to capture and enslave local inhabitants in areas deemed to be populated by Caribs (Palencia-Roth 21–63). As a category of ethnic identification, the word "Carib" combined claims about the consumption of humans in Antillean island and coastal populations with colonizers' perceptions of hostility against Spanish presence (Hulme 70–73). However, this form of human categorization did not carry over into the conquest of Mexico. Quite the contrary, even as the first reports of human sacrifice in the Gulf of Mexico and Yucatan noted that the practice involved feasting on parts of the human body, this information did not translate into a legal response based on the Caribbean precedent. While sacrifice may have come to define the people from a European point of view, it did not become the basis for an ethnic label such as "Carib" or inform colonial policy as claims of cannibalism had informed the Cannibal Law of 1503.

In terms of the colonial relationship, the subject of sacrifice brings to our attention to the ambivalence characteristic of the cathexis of colonial desire in conquest accounts. The topic was relevant for interpreting Amerindian cultural difference and defining a colonizing mission, but it only indirectly related to the legality of conquest itself. Reports about human sacrifice quite expressly conjure up feelings of dread and repulsion and thus introduce the reader into a space that is as much affective as it is referential. In these cases, the conquistadors' psychical reality is the focus of discourse and their libidinal responses become crucial when it comes to making sense of sacrifice itself. Stories about the Europeans' encounter with sacrifice and descriptions of sacrificial sites tend to efface the distinction between affect and event. The conquistadors' imagination becomes a constitutive component in the reality of sacrifice, proleptically anticipating the introduction of Christianity as the new law of the land. In conquest narratives, the experience of coming into contact with sacrifice becomes a powerful platform not only for articulating cultural difference, but also for envisioning a meaningful colonial relationship. This act of transfer from human sacrifice to Christian law, however, can only work because, as in the Freudian uncanny, the "symbol takes over the full functions of the thing it symbolizes" (Freud 244). I argue that within the supplementary relationship that cultural interpretation has with the enunciation of the law, representations of human sacrifice were instrumental in the creation of a new idiom of colonization in which cognitive and affective ambivalence functioned as a condition of possibility of colonial affirmation.

The Forensic Scenario

Members of Juan de Grijalva's expedition to Yucatan and the Gulf Coast in 1518 spread the earliest news of human sacrifice on the coast of Mexico based on finding human remains atop a pyramid in Isla de Sacrificios. Juan Díaz, the army's chaplain, wrote a report of this episode that would be widely published in Europe and became the main source for Peter Martyr d'Anghiera and Gonzalo Fernández de Oviedo, who later also reported the incident.[2] After observing a basin with blood, four decomposing bodies, and other human remains such as heads and bones when inspecting the pyramid, Grijalva stays at the site and tries to establish what has happened. The setting, with its peculiar architectural characteristics and the lifeless bodies, provokes the forensic question of what happened and sets an inquiry into motion. In this reported chain of events, the significance of the findings resides in the position of the observer, who desires to find out whether they were the remains of people who have been sacrificed. Grijalva orders that a native from the area be brought from the ships to question him. Díaz remarks that the informant fainted on the way, thinking the Spaniards were bringing him to be sacrificed, but he does explain to them how they offered the hearts and blood to their gods, took flesh from the legs and arms to eat, and did this to their enemies in war. Díaz does not make much of the incident or the information obtained about human sacrifice, but Oviedo and Martyr later rework this information to treat sacrifice as a salient manifestation of indigenous cultural difference in the region.

The fact that human sacrifice quickly became crucial in shaping Spanish views of the human groups they encountered in Mexico has an immediate religious and political explanation. Human sacrifice is sternly condemned in biblical and patristic sources as a form of pollution and an activity that in principle could not be tolerated within colonial rule. In addition, it appears in numerous accounts as a discovery or revelation with implications beyond the simple declaration of what was seen or done. Feelings such as repulsion and fear are a centerpiece of the information contained in descriptive and narrative discourse. Though Díaz's matter-of-fact account only mentions with some amusement the informant's frightened reaction when brought to the pyramid for questioning, it is the emotional response of Spaniards confronted for the first time with this information that becomes prominent in subsequent narratives about the discovery of human sacrifice. Grijalva's stumbling across the sacrificial scene atop the pyramid of Isla de Sacrificios will later appear as a step toward the revelation of an uncanny truth. The sacrificial scene provides a forensic scenario—that is, a paradigmatic setup in which traces of the killing of humans create a demand for an explanation of what took place there.[3] This demand may be conveyed by the narrative of an inquiry or rhetorically performed by a narrator who incites the reader to feel outrage about the practice. What matters in these accounts is the affective significance of sacrifice, which resides quite precisely in facilitating the superimposition of the psychical reality of a European mind over the human and geographical reality that is the object of these descriptions. In these cases, affective responses are the key condition enabling cultural interpretation. This particular forensic scenario also provides a script for the elicitation of an affective response in the reader, whether through the reported experience of an observer, a rhetorical address to a reader, or a combination of both.

Reports of sacrifice excite affective responses by creating scripts in which a repertoire of these responses becomes discursively meaningful. A few years after Grijalva's expedition, Peter Martyr described this sacrificial scene in his *De Orbe Novo Decades*. He introduces it with a rhetorical address to Pope Leo X decrying the activity and the people who practice it: "Proh crudele facinus, Pater Sancte, Proh truculentas hominum mentes, stomacho claudat portas Beatitudo tua ne perturbetur" (149) (What cruel crime, Holy Father! What fierce human souls! Hold the doors to your stomach so that Your Beatitude is not discomfited). His report of the site integrates an account of sacrificial procedures and practices with the description of the remains, paraphernalia, and architectural features that the explorers observed. He portrays sacrifice as a form of victimization of those who are killed, made all the more horrible by the way it is carried out. Instead of beheading the victim, the sacrificers extract the hearts from live victims, smear their idols' lips with hot blood, burn the hearts and entrails in the open air, and eat the flesh from arms and legs. He also notes that the Europeans saw a gutter filled with coagulated blood in the manner of a slaughterhouse, thus conveying the sense of humans treated like animals. By anticipating his reader's consternation and rhetorically inducing it, Peter Martyr sets a tone that will justify his characterization of sacrifice as *facinus* (a heinous crime). It is possible that he considered sacrificial violence toward another human to be against natural law and concluded that it was therefore a criminal practice. His description, however, highlights the procedures, ritual uses of body parts, and number of sacrifices rather than pronouncing an abstract judgment about the practice itself.

Martyr's European readers had most likely witnessed the carnage of war or were at least familiar with descriptions of rotting corpses in battlefields. They also knew about various gruesome forms of capital punishment involving hanging, decapitation, quartering, or impaling. That describing a sacrificial site should draw out such a strong affective response is indicative of the emotional resonances excited by the revelation of new forms of killing. He is rhetorically reenacting the experience of the forensic scenario, which functions performatively as a location to decry the horror and inhumanity of sacrifice. The knowledge he has unveiled, however, is not so much that of the practice itself as it is that of the horror and revulsion Díaz himself had not provided in his original account. More importantly, perhaps, these feelings solidify a bond among observer, historian, and audience. Inducing a shared emotional response to sacrifice also establishes a psychical position from which to validate the system of truth, virtue, and understanding underlying Martyr's interpretation.

Many years after the conquest of Mexico, Gonzalo Fernández de Oviedo elicits similar feelings to those elicited by Martyr in recounts the incident in his *Historia general* (2:135).[4] He describes in vivid detail the sacrificial paraphernalia, decaying bodies, and skeletal remains and explains that the Spaniards were filled with consternation (*quedaron espantados*) when observing the site because they suspected what had taken place there. In the interrogation, the local informant explains to them through gestures the sacrificial technique, the consumption of human flesh, and the use of war captives in sacrifice. Four elements come into play in this particular script: 1) the observation of a ritual site, 2) an affective or emotional response on the part of an observer based on a suspicion, 3) the interrogation of an informant by means of gestures, and 4) a corroboration of the original fear. In Oviedo's version of the episode, it is the feelings of consternation among the observers that are later validated by the responses of the informant or, more accurately, by the observers' interpretation of the informant's signs. However, the quality of communication between the informant and the Spaniards or the constraints of his interrogation remain beside the point, because Oviedo's constative statements rely primarily on the observers' affective response. The structure of feelings first evoked by the unanticipated encounter with the sacrificial scene functions as the primary evidence.

Human Sacrifice as Law

Accounts of the conquest of Mexico readily exploit the rhetorical potential of human sacrifice, capitalizing on the affective content to provide a convincing rationale for action. The *cabildo* (municipal council) of Vera Cruz in July 10, 1519, signed an account of Hernán Cortés's exploration of Yucatan and the coast of the Gulf of Mexico, claiming to present the first eyewitness account of human sacrifice in Mexico. This document, also known as Cortés's First Letter, purported to improve on the quality of information produced by the two previous expeditions of Francisco Hernández de Córdoba in 1517 and Juan de Grijalva the following year, both conducted under the authority of Diego de Velázquez, the Governor of Cuba. Cortés had himself sailed under Velázquez's instructions, but overstepped them when founding the town of Vera Cruz. As José Rabasa shows, the letter's emphasis on the "systematic collection of information for conquest" played a critical role in justifying the establishment of a government independent from Velázquez's authority in order to pursue a new policy of settlement (98–99). In fact, after narrating the events leading to Cortés's appointment as captain, the account provides a full account of the land and its people. The letter's account of human sacrifice is the most crucial piece of new evidence that the *cabildo* purports to offer in support of its settlement policy.

This letter presents human sacrifice as a pivotal argument for the creation of a new colony because of the way it links conquest to religious change. The letter does not add anything new to what was known to members of Grijalva's expedition. It nonetheless brings into play the affective significance of encountering anew the fact of human sacrifice and highlights the experience of those Spaniards who have witnessed the practice:

> Y tienen otra cosa horrible y abominable y dina de ser punida que hasta hoy [no se ha] visto en ninguna parte, y es todas las veces que alguna cosa quieren pedir a sus ídolos, para que más aceptasen su petición toman muchas niñas y niños y aun hombres y mujeres de mayor edad, y en presencia de aquellos ídolos los abren vivos por los pechos y les sacan el corazón y las entrañas y queman las dichas entrañas y

corazones delante de los ídolos ofresciéndoles en sacrificio humano. Esto habemos visto algunos de nosotros, y los que lo han visto dicen que es la más cruda y más espantosa cosa de ver que jamás han visto. (143)

(They have a most horrid and abominable custom which truly ought to be punished and which until now we have seen in no other part, and that is that, whenever they wish to ask something of the idols, in order that their plea may find more acceptance, they take many girls and boys and even adults, and in the presence of the idols they open their chests while they are still alive and take out their hearts and entrails and burn them before the idols, offering the smoke as sacrifice. Some of us have seen this, and they say it is the most terrible and frightful thing they have ever witnessed. [Pagden 35])

At the same time that the text excites horror and abomination in the reader, it turns toward its opposite by concluding that "es cierto que si con tanta fee y fervor y diligencia a Dios serviesen ellos harían muchos milagros" (144) ("it is certain that if they were to worship the true God with such fervor, faith, and diligence, they would perform many miracles" [Pagden 36]). Moreover, the letter argues that the local inhabitants' degree of civility and rationality is optimal and that teaching and persuasion would therefore readily deliver them from their error. The witnesses' fright establishes the initial psychical positioning of the conquistadors, but the letter hampers the uncanny effects by foreseeing the possibility of change through the Christian message when interpreting sacrifice as an expression of "fervor, faith, and diligence" and envisioning "many miracles" in potentiality. The text thus effects a transference from feelings of abomination to the opposite—fondness and inspiration. Therefore, within the letter's argument, human sacrifice plays a key role in the deliberative rhetoric of conquest, and although it does not contribute to establishing the legality of conquest per se, it does help to define an end (conversion through persuasion) and the notion of a good to be attained.[5]

The letter's ambivalence is not simply a product of the simultaneous repugnancy to and fascination for a Christian reader of the affective content linked to human sacrifice. Rather, that ambivalence is implied in the tension between observation and cultural interpretation as two distinct moments in the text. Abomination is tied to witnessing, and fondness is tied to the metonymical substitution of aberration for devotion. This displacement is the condition that makes Cortés's narrative of religious change possible as a goal of the conquest. The claim that some Spaniards have witnessed the action underscores the validity of the contradictory emotions the letter attempts to provoke. As both an abomination and a sign of devotion, sacrifice provides a sense of what settlement and conquest can help accomplish. This form of ambivalence facilitates the introduction of a redemptive conquest narrative in which the proleptic substitution of evil for virtue transforms repudiation as a function of seeing into an evangelizing impulse. Only conquest and persuasion stand between error and virtue to settle the matter. In that regard, the letter's movement from witnessing to interpreting functions primarily as a means of cathecting colonial desire.

This process of metonymic substitution is a condition of possibility for the enunciation of colonial law within the letter's conquest narrative. The town council presented the letter as a new account of the land and its people, including "la manera de su vevir y el rito y cerimonias, seta o ley que tienen, y el fruto que en ella Vuestras Reales Altezas podrán hacer" (106) ("the way in which they live, their rites and ceremonies, religions and customs, and what profit Your Highnesses may gain from it" [Pagden 3–4]). A more literal translation would render "seta o ley" in this passage as "sect or law," two key meanings in discussions of human sacrifice. The first notion of law as equivalent to religion is particularly relevant with regard to the New Testament interpretation of Christ as the end of the law.[6] However, the word "law" does not cover the exact same semantic field as "religion," and it is more accurate to think of their relationship as a metonymic one.[7] In a second sense, law is a code of justice exemplified by texts such as Alfonso el Sabio's *Siete Partidas* or Justinian's *Corpus Iuris Civilis*. Peter Goodrich has argued that "the Judeo-Christian tradition of law depended heavily upon the image of a divine legislator" and noted that Justinian's *Corpus* was studied as a sacred text during the Renaissance (5358–59). The conquest narrative thus focuses on the introduction of a new law that displaces human sacrifice in terms of both a rhetorical (through persuasion) and a political (through legitimate rule) transfer of sovereignty.

The implications of human sacrifice for legitimate rule rely precisely on the chain of metonymic substitution: sacrifice for law, evil law for virtuous law. This meaning would be fully articulated twenty years later by Francisco de Vitoria, whose fifth just title to wage war against Amerindians includes "leges iniquas et tiranicas, puta, quia sacrificant homines innocentes" (99) (iniquitous and tyrannical laws, for example, because they sacrifice innocent human beings). Vitoria's homonymous use of *lex* makes perfect sense in relation to Western legal tradition, but it also amounts to a metaphysical subsumption.[8] Sacrifice as a legal mandate significantly reduces the semantic range covering way of life, devotion, and propitiatory ritual by centering its meaning within the scope of legal categories such as "iniquity" and "tyranny." It literalizes its meaning to codify it as a just title for conquest, but it eliminates the ambivalence that makes it symbolically effective.

Sacrifice and Colonial Ambivalence

The representation of fear as the psychical reality of human sacrifice in conquest accounts introduces some of the effects described by Sigmund Freud in his influential account of the uncanny in Western aesthetics. At first sight, sacrifice appears to be unfamiliar in the sense that it is a culturally different way of killing; it evokes an alien ontology and involves a treatment of the body that is not commensurable with the conquistadors' understanding of violence. For sacrifice to be frightening, however, the mind must recognize a known experience and, in that sense, let fear function as a form of understanding. In the Freudian uncanny, it is the inclusion of the familiar with the unfamiliar that creates the ambivalence characteristic of the frightening experience in literary texts and in patients. The unfamiliar in these cases is something that was supposed to remain secret but came to light. The frightening effect of sacrificial scenes is linked to the recognition of a colonial situation that remains unaccounted for by Spanish discourses on sovereignty and the legitimacy of conquest. The legal fiction of conquest and its ontology surface in terms of the cognitive ambivalence Freud sees as causing the sense of the uncanny.

This blurring of boundaries between the real and the imaginary, unsettling as it may be, turns out to be an effective way of articulating colonial desire. Encountering the horror of sacrifice for the first time does not simply provide a memorable narrative moment. It also informs the position the conquistadors occupy in relation to the people they meet and territorializes a geographical area. When Francisco López de Gómara narrates Jerónimo de Aguilar's rescue from Yucatan during Cortés's expedition, he relates that Aguilar's report of sacrifice and human consumption aroused fear and wonder among the Spaniards. He also explains how Aguilar's mother lost her mind upon hearing that her son had been a captive among people who ate human flesh, screaming every time she saw roasted or broiled meat, "desventurada de mi este es mi hijo, y mi bien" (f. 9r) ("Woe is me! That is my son and my own!" [Schroeder, Cruz, Roa, and Tavárez 77]). Even as López de Gómara ridicules Aguilar's mother's inability to distinguish imagination from reality, it is also clear in the account that her accentuated psychical reality brings forth her own personal fear of consuming her son. Peter Martyr, for his part, was setting a similar mechanism into motion when he told the pope to hold his stomach and compared the sacrificial site to a slaughterhouse. What made him sane was that he was speaking as a cultural geographer. The question, therefore, is how the feelings of consternation that the sacrificial scene brings to the surface are validated and rhetorically regulated for the purpose of producing particular knowledge effects.

The problem with Aguilar's mother is her disconnect from the sacrificial scene the narrator would deem appropriate to excite her fear and, therefore, legitimize her performance. In that sense, rhetorical control over the recreation of the sacrificial site plays an essential role in managing and regulating the accepted affective significance of the experience. This is also true when feelings need to be occluded. During his campaign to regain control of Tenochtitlan, Hernán Cortés sends Gonzalo de Sandoval to Calpulalpan, one of Tetzcoco's dependent towns known to the Spaniards as Pueblo Morisco, in a punitive expedition for the killing of more than forty Spaniards. Bernal Díaz del Castillo explains that Sandoval found the blood of sacrificed Spaniards splattered on the walls; two pieces of skin flayed from conquistadors' faces, with beards still attached; horsehides hanging in front of the gods; and an alphabetic inscription in a house stating that Juan Yuste and others in his company had been imprisoned there (328–29). López de Gómara explains that one of the reasons for Sandoval's determination to raze the town was that he had seen the remains of the sacrificed Spaniards (ff. 72v–73r). But he does not raze the town and instead pardons the people out of compassion, leaving Cortés's command to avenge the death of the Spaniards unfulfilled.

Both Díaz del Castillo and López de Gómara explain Sandoval's decision as an act of compassion at the sight of wailing mothers and children captured by Spaniards in their pursuit of the townspeople. While the description of the conquistadors' skins evokes the horror that the sacrificed Spaniards had endured, both historians remain indifferent to Sandoval's decision to turn the page on the sacrifice of Yuste and his companions. In this case, containing the punishment was a politically wise decision on Sandoval's part because Cortés needed to make allies among communities surrounding Lake Texcoco in order to turn the tide of war against Tenochtitlan within the basin of Mexico. In their representation of the sacrificial scene at Calpulalpan, Díaz del Castillo and López de Gómara significantly muffle the conquistadors' feelings for their sacrificed comrades. If Sandoval averted a massacre out of compassion for the people he came to punish, then one must assume that he experienced a complete emotional reversal. In stating that pain for the plight of the conquered explained Sandoval's decision, these historians were rhetorically shifting their focus to the reality of war and political alliances.

Díaz del Castillo's description of Huitzilopochtli's altar at Templo Mayor and his account of the sacrifice of Spaniards in Tlatelolco's temple during the siege of Tenochtitlan best exemplify this rhetorical manipulation of affect. At Templo Mayor, he records having observed various images: flayed indigenous faces hanging from Huitzilopochtli's image, blood splattered all over the altars, basins containing hearts, incense burners, and a plethora of decorative elements. He concludes, "tenían tantas cosas muy diabólicas de ver. . . . y, como hedía a carneçería, no víamos la ora de quitarnos de tan mal hedor y peor vista" (193) (they had so many all-too-diabolical things to see. . . . As it smelled of slaughter, we could not wait to get away from such a foul odor and worse sight). When writing these episodes more than thirty years later, he still evokes his disgust, his sense of occupying a diabolical space, and his eagerness to leave. In Díaz del Castillo's narrative, it is human sacrifice that constitutes the major focus of the indigenous resistance to conquest and colonization. In that context, the author's representation of Huitzilopochtli's altar at Templo Mayor as a dreadful place in the midst of an awe-inspiring urban landscape forcefully plays out the tensions and ambivalences articulating colonial desire.

The conjunction of attraction and fear is embedded in the narrative of the temple visit itself, which begins with his description of the panoramic view of the city amid the lake in all its vastness. Although Tenochtitlan was the city that dazzled Díaz del Castillo and its inhabitants were desirable vassals for the king, it also was a menacing place. According to the *Historia verdadera*, it is Nahua gods who ordain both war and sacrifices, limiting the conquistadors' ability to negotiate peace and political submission. Sacrifice has a presence in the unfolding of the events in the narrative, presenting an unpredictable threat to the lives of Spaniards and to the success of their enterprise. In terms of representing cultural difference, sacrifice limits dialogue, communicability, translatability, and, therefore, cultural authority. Spaniards were utterly unequipped to engage in negotiations with Huitzilopochtli, regardless of whether Cortés could manage to present himself as Quetzalcoatl's envoy or not.

Writing about human sacrifice, Díaz del Castillo quite deliberately presents his reader with the impossibility of generalizing a truth or creating a common ground for negotiation because of the incommensurable differences between conquistadors and Mexicas with regard to war, worship, and divinity. When narrating the short-lived Mexica victory over the Spaniards in late June 1521, he provides a vivid description of the sacrifice of Spaniards on top of Tlatelolco's main temple crafted to put the reader in the position of envisioning the crossing into a different cultural form of truth:

> y tornó a sonar el atanbor *muy doloroso* del Vichilobos, y otros *muchos* caracoles y cornetas . . . y todo el sonido dellas espantable, y . . . vimos que llebavan por fuerça las gradas arriba a nuestros conpañeros. . . . vimos que a muchos dellos les ponían plumajes en las cabeças y con unos como abantadores les hazían bailar delante del Huichilobos. . . . luego les ponían despaldas ençima de unas piedras . . . y con unos

navajones de pedernal los aserravan por los pechos y les sacavan los coraçones bullendo y se los ofreçían a *los* ídolos . . . y los cuerpos dávanles con los pies por las gradas abajo; y estavan aguardando *avaxo* otros indios carniçeros, que les cortavan braços y pies, y las caras desollaban, y las *adovaron* después como cuerpo de guantes, y con sus barbas las guardavan para hacer fiestas con ellas quando hazían borracheras, y se comían las carnes con chilmole. . . . Pues desque aquellas crueldades vimos todos los de nuestro real y Pedro de Alvarado y Gonçalo de Sandoval y todos los demás capitanes; miren los curiosos letores questo oyeren qué lástima terníamos dellos, y dezíamos entre nosotros: —¡Oh, gracias a Dios que no me llebaron a mí oy a sacrificar! (*La historia verdadera* 391)

(again there was sounded the dismal drum of Huichilobos and many other shells and horns . . . and the sound of them all was terrifying, and we all . . . saw that our comrades . . . were being carried by force up the steps. . . . we saw them place plumes on the heads of many of them and with things like fans in their hands they forced them to dance before Huichilobos, and after they danced they immediately placed them on their backs on some rather narrow stones . . . and with stone knives they sawed open their chests and drew out their palpitating hearts and offered them to the idols . . . and they kicked the bodies down the steps, and Indian butchers who were waiting below cut off the arms and feet and flayed the skin of their faces, and prepared it afterwards like glove leather with the beards on, and kept those for the festivals when they celebrated drunken orgies, and the flesh they ate in *chilmole*. . . . When we saw those cruelties all of us in our camp said the one to the other: "Thank God that they are not carrying me off today to be sacrificed" [*The History* 287–88].)

Bernal Díaz del Castillo mastered a technique for representing human sacrifice that combined, from an eyewitness perspective, the aesthetic force of sacrificial performance with its most frightful and horrific effects. David Boruchoff argues that Díaz del Castillo "repeatedly violates the Aristotelian principle of *mimesis* in conjoining attributes drawn from contradictory moral or ethical dimensions" (353). This is a salient characteristic of the sacrificial scene quoted above where we see the reader thrust "into an ongoing historical process beyond the comprehension that derives from prior experience" (Boruchoff 356). As Boruchoff compellingly demonstrates, Díaz del Castillo's dissonant representation of sacrifice violates the conceptual and aesthetic paradigms of his time, but it also goes a step further by drawing attention to his own performative experience. When we read the sacrificial performance as setting into motion a Mexica ontology, Díaz del Castillo tells us he is observing Spaniards forced to dance before Huitzilopochtli and then having their beating hearts extracted from their chests, their faces turned into masks, and their flesh butchered for feasting. His concluding remark portrays himself and other soldiers picturing themselves being carried off to sacrifice. Seeing the sacrifice of others as his own establishes the central focus of the sacrificial story; it is a script about the crossing of cultural boundaries both perceptually and imaginatively.

A comparison of these reports of human sacrifice reveals that responses are presented within various possible scripts that modify the affective resonance that observations acquire within discourse. Truth is performed very differently in these accounts according to whether the focus is on the scene of sacrifice itself or on the context surrounding the emergence of the sacrificial scene. These forensic scenarios are not so much about horrifying sightings of human remains as about managing ways to symbolically assimilate sacrifice into the colonial discourse by employing varied affective content. It is the psychical reality of the colonizer that prevails in these representations of sacrificial sites, thus privileging a subject position in which cultural uncertainty fades under the affect; doubt is resolved by suspicion, revulsion, disgust, and an unsaid truth already known but never truly unraveled. Homi Bhabha reads the unfamiliar (*unheimlich*) in colonial discourse in relation to its possibility of reversal—that is, when the performance of truth occupies an "undecidable enunciatory space where culture's authority is undone in colonial space" (136). However, while Spanish colonial sources may convey a sense of fear regarding their own cultural authority when reporting on human sacrifice in New Spain, they also script and rhetorically manage its affective significance as a way to effectively cathect colonial desire. The fear of sacrifice and other manifestations of colonial anxiety are informed in these representations by a dynamic process of figuration in which aesthetic release (the surfacing of a hidden affect) and an accentuated psychical reality (thoughts, images, and symbols carrying affective content) facilitate the subsumation of cultural difference within discourse. Human sacrifice is not incommensurable because of the actions it involves; its incommensurability is only one mode of articulating its affective significance for the colonizing subject.

Sacrifice as Supplement

Human sacrifice provided an incredible rhetorical malleability in terms of the figurative effectiveness of its placement within substitution chains. In the *cabildo*'s letter, the reference to human sacrifice only indirectly relates to its attempt at self-legitimating. The reference to Spaniards witnessing human sacrifice is in this case no more than a supplement to the legal discourse legitimating conquest. It is inessential in the sense that the conquistadors themselves do not employ it as a cause for just war on the Amerindian population that practices it, but it significantly strengthens the *cabildo*'s ability to legitimate its rebellion against Velázquez. The evangelization project to eradicate sacrifice establishes a moral ground enabling the conquistadors to denounce Velázquez's greed and claim they are pursuing a selfless goal. The end of sacrifice, however, implies the introduction of a *new law*. When Cortés urges the people of Cozumel "que no veviesen más en la secta gentílica que tenían, pidieron que les diese ley en que viviesen de allí en adelante" (*Cartas de relación* 125) ("to renounce their heathen religion . . . they asked him to give them instead a precept by which they might henceforth live" [*Letters from Mexico* 18]). The notion of *ley* here implies both the sense of religion and that of law. In fact, Cortés responds to the chieftains' request by preaching the Catholic faith and leaves a cross and images of the Virgin Mary in their temples. Peter Martyr's Latin rendition of Cortés's account has "Lege[m] petu[n]t Barbari, qua[m] sequant[ur]" (152) (The barbarians request a law to follow), which reiterates the *cabildo*'s metonymic chain linking sacrifice and law within the conversion narrative.

The displacement from law as religion to law as code of justice becomes explicit later in Cortés's Second Letter, when he recounts how he preached to Moctezuma and his nobles the doctrine of one universal god, eternal, who created all things. He claims they readily helped him topple the gods of the Great Temple, clean the altars, and place Christian images. Then he issued the prohibition against sacrifice, claiming that "de ahí adelante se apartaron de ello, y en todo tiempo que yo estuve en la dicha cibdad nunca se vio matar ni sacrificar alguna criatura" (239) ("from then on they ceased to do it, and in all the time I stayed in that city I did not see a living creature killed or sacrificed" [Pagden 107]). Based on the alleged transfer of sovereignty from Moctezuma to the Spanish king, Cortés invokes first the Christian god's position regarding sacrifice and later the king's laws to stop sacrifice. It befits Cortés's conquest narrative that the two notions of law remain distinct, because his successful substitution of religious symbols and laws is equivalent to the assertion of Spanish sovereignty. This pattern of substitution moreover correlates to the implementation of colonial rule as reflected in the 1523 royal decree ordering authorities "to destroy idols and temples and punish natives engaging in idolatry, ritual sacrifice, and cannibalism" (Tavárez 32).

As the law of the other, however, sacrifice easily stands to be subsumed within conquest practices. Cortés, for instance, talks about his inability to prevent allied troops from killing forty thousand people in one day during the siege of Tenochtitlan (Pagden 262; 422). He expresses shock in his Third Letter when he states that "la cual crueldad nunca en generación tan recia se vio ni tan fuera de toda orden de naturaleza" (422) ("no race, however savage, has ever practiced such fierce and unnatural cruelty" [Pagden 262]). Inga Clendinnen believes Cortés perceived the killings to be an expression of "an unnatural indifference to death: a terrifying, terminal demonstration of 'otherness,' and of its practical and cognitive unmanageability" (94). I would argue, however, that he is conveying instead the uncanny truth of conquest. Massacres were a common staple of conquest, and Cortés himself had ordered and led the massacre of unarmed people in both Tlaxcala and Cholula. Moreover, his horror toward his allies' cruelty becomes clear when he explains that the following day "y también dije a todos los capitanes de nuestros amigos que en ninguna manera consintiesen matar a los que se salían. Y no se pudo estorbar, como eran tantos, que aquel día no mataron y sacrificaron más de quince mil ánimas" (425–26) ("I also told the captains of our allies that on no account should any of those people be slain; but they were so many that we could not prevent more than fifteen thousand being killed and sacrificed that day" [Pagden 264]). The forty thousand killed the day before were most likely sacrificed as well. Cortés was aware throughout his campaign that his allies continued to practice human sacrifice, but he had to tolerate it because he needed their military assistance. Fierce and unnatural cruelty establishes Cortés's metonymic distancing from sacrificial violence as a component of conquest by suggesting its inessential supplementary function.

According to Díaz del Castillo, Cortés did attempt to convince the Tlaxcalans to end human sacrifice when they surrendered to the Spaniards (147–48). However, they fearlessly replied that they would not abandon their gods and would continue sacrificing people. The conquistador finally decided to disregard the matter, following the advice of a priest and other soldiers accompanying him. Díaz del Castillo further claims that when Cortés preached to Moctezuma in the Great Temple, the Lord rebuked him and the conquistador ceded and apologized (193–94). Certainly, he was in no position to take action or to enforce his prohibition in Tlaxcala or Tenochtitlan. Díaz del Castillo attempts to emphasize the conquistadors' vulnerability before a formidable enemy in order to counter attacks against the legitimacy of the conquest.[9] The issue of legitimacy also explains why at the same time that he denies Cortés's success in stopping sacrifice, he also omits any reference to the sacrifices performed by indigenous allies in the siege of Tenochtitlan. These mutually contradictory mentions and omissions of sacrifice serve these authors well within the rhetorical use their texts make of the practice. In all cases sacrifice provides clues with regard to the need for military conquest and the conditions under which Spanish conquistadors were able to exercise their claims of sovereignty over indigenous subjects.

Although human sacrifice is to remain safely at the margins of the text of conquest so that Spanish sovereignty may be asserted, it also works as an enabling condition of conquest and colonization. As an object of desire and a means of cathecting colonial desire, it stood for the Europeans' cultural limit. Fray Bartolomé de Las Casas reports that during the conquest of Guatemala, Pedro de Alvarado was accompanied by between ten thousand and twenty thousand indigenous troops. The friar explains that Alvarado "consentíales que comiesen a los indios, que tomaban. Y así había en su real solemnísima carnicería de carne humana, donde en su presencia se mataban los niños y se asaban, y mataban el hombre por solas las manos y pies, que tenían por mejores bocados" (Brevísima 56) ("he gave them leave to eat the prisoners they took, thus setting the royal seal of approval on the establishment, in his camp, of a human abattoir where he himself would preside over the slaughter and grilling of children and where grown men were butchered for the sake of their hands and feet which were generally held to be the best cuts" [*A Short Account* 63]). A new element in the chain of metonymic substitutions, sacrifice for food implies a literal displacement of sacrificial practice.[10] Insofar as Las Casas explains it in terms of Alvarado's greed, it stands as a supplement to Alvarado's conquest, but the sheer number of allied troops feeding on enemy captives under Alvarado's watch in this case suggests that the figure of the transfer also accepts a reading of transculturation. If that is true, Alvarado has crossed the cultural divide Díaz del Castillo feared when observing his comrades being sacrificed in the temple during the siege of Tenochtitlan and revealed sacrifice to be a tool of conquest.

It is as a figure of culture crossing that human sacrifice most effectively cathects colonial desire. Representations of ritual killing and human consumption open the path to the psychical reality of the colonizer to territorialize the human and geographical reality to be conquered. These images provide conquerors and historians a means of transit between cultures to translate the cultural heteronomy of the moment into a figurative repertoire for envisioning the conquest enterprise. In its most threatening aspects, sacrifice suggests the irreversibility of crossing cultural boundaries and the entrance into an ontology that remains in the body as food after death. Both an imaginative and literal trespassing, the conquistadors' experience of human sacrifice is textualized through mechanisms of linguistic substitution to reestablish order, symbolic autonomy, and thus cultural meaning. In that sense, it conveys a desire for language. As an idiom of colonization, representations of human sacrifice effect the imposition of culture through language, similar to the way Derrida that argues the power of naming is equivalent to establishing sovereignty, a law originating elsewhere (39). In that regard, representing human sacrifice can be nothing other than the constitutive moment of colonial power.

Notes

1. Many scholars highlight the significance of human sacrifice. Laurette Séjourné asserts that it was intimately linked to everyday life among the Aztecs (17); Alfredo López Austin characterizes it as part of the most conspicuous stereotypes about pre-Hispanic societies (1:432); Yolotl González Torres states that no other people gave so much ritual importance to human sacrifice as the Mexica (302); Davíd Carrasco talks about sacrifice as "a way of life for the Aztecs" (3); Kay Read ascribes to it enormous explanatory power when she looks at "sacrifice as a coherent religious system" (129); and Eric Wolf considers it "central to Aztec political and ritual life" (133). The centrality of human sacrifice has various explanations. Christian Duverger's and Yolotl González Torres's in-depth studies of human sacrifice highlight the need to liberate energy in order to support human life as its essential function. Eduardo Matos Moctezuma interprets human sacrifice at Templo Mayor as a reenactment of myth that was instrumental to agricultural production and the establishment of Mexica power (*Muerte* 115; "Templo," 135, 162). López Austin distinguishes between the energetic use of sacrifice based on the Nahua worldview and its practical political function of maintaining a balance between tribute extraction and military control of subjugated populations (1:432–38). From a wider regional perspective and going back to the classical period, Enrique Florescano has traced the roots of sacrifice to agricultural cults focusing on the gods of the netherworld, particularly the cultivation of corn as a basic mythical theme in Mesoamerica (72–75, 193).
2. Jorge Gurría Lacroix shows that Peter Martyr and Gonzalo Fernández de Oviedo had access to other written and oral sources (10). However, their accounts of Grijalva's exploration of Isla de Sacrificios do not go beyond the information provided by Díaz.
3. I use the word "scenario" in the sense of "meaning-making paradigms that structure social environments, behaviors, and potential outcomes" (Taylor 26).
4. It appeared in the 1535 edition.
5. On Cortés's rhetorical conquest, see Carman (61–71).
6. "finis enim legis Christus ad iustitiam omni credenti" (Rm 10,4) (Christ truly is the end of the law so that there may be justice for everyone who believes.)
7. References to Christ's law in the New Testament—for instance, 1 Cor. 9, 21—are clearly metaphorical. When referring to the new covenant, the word of choice in the New Testament is "novum testamentum" (Lc 22, 20).

8. According to Jonathan Barnes, homonymy was one of the key problems Aristotle needed to solve in order to argue for the possibility of metaphysics. Insofar as a signifier can allude to entities in more than one sense, it becomes difficult to argue that there is a primary way in which things exist.
9. Adorno explains his criticism of Francisco López de Gómara and Fray Bartolomé de Las Casas, noting his claim that they were "sacrificers of innocent people" (154–169). Also, Sara Beckjord analyzes Díaz del Castillo's word choices that allude to sacrifice when describing the hammocks the Cholultecas brought to receive the Spaniards, showing how he used the threat of sacrifice as a rhetorical device to legitimize the subsequent massacre ordered by Cortés (154).
10. While most scholars focus on the religious and political meanings in the ritual use of the body in human sacrifice, Burr Brundage (217) provides evidence of battlefield sacrifices among the Otomí in which sacrificed bodies were sliced up to be sold in chunks at the marketplace.

Works Cited

Adorno, Rolena. *The Polemics of Possession in Spanish American Narrative*. New Haven: Yale University Press, 2007. Print.

Barnes, Jonathan. "Metaphysics." *The Cambridge Companion to Aristotle*. Ed. Jonathan Barnes. Cambridge: Cambridge University Press, 1995. 66–108. Print.

Beckjord, Sara. "'Con sal ají y tomates': Las redes textuales de Bernal Díaz en el caso de Cholula." *Revista Iberoamericana* 61.170–71 (1995): 147–60. Print.

Bhabha, Homi K. *The Location of Culture*. London: Routledge, 1994. Print.

Boruchoff, David A. "Beyond Utopia and Paradise: Cortés, Bernal Díaz and the Rhetoric of Consecration." *MLN* 106 (1991): 330–39. Print.

Brundage, Burr Cartwright. *The Fifth Sun: Aztec Gods, Aztec World*. Austin: University of Texas Press, 1979. Print.

Carman, Glen. *Rhetorical Conquests: Cortés, Gómara, and Renaissance Imperialism*. West Lafayette, IN: Purdue University Press, 2006. Print.

Carrasco, Davíd. *City of Sacrifice: The Aztec Empire and the Role of Violence in Civilization*. Boston: Beacon Press, 1999. Print.

Clendinnen, Inga. "'Fierce and Unnatural Cruelty': Cortés and the Conquest of Mexico." *Representations* 33 (1991): 65–100. Print.

Cortés, Hernán. *Cartas de relación*. Ed. Ángel Delgado Gómez. Madrid: Castalia, 1993. Print.

———. *Letters from Mexico*. Trans. Anthony Pagden. New Haven: Yale University Press, 1986. Print.

Derrida, Jacques. *Monolingualism of the Other; or, The Prosthesis of Origin*. Trans. Patrick Mensah. Stanford: Stanford University Press, 1998. Print.

Díaz, Juan. *Itinerario de la armada del Rey Católico a la isla de Yucatán en la India.* Trans. Joaquín García Icazbalceta. Mexico City: Editorial Juan Pablos, 1972. Print.

Díaz del Castillo, Bernal. *Historia verdadera de la conquista de la Nueva España.* Ed. Carmelo Sáenz de Santa María. Madrid: Consejo Superior de Investigaciones Científicas, 1982. Print.

———. *The History of the Conquest of New Spain.* Ed. and trans. Davíd Carrasco. Albuquerque: University of New Mexico Press, 2008. Print.

Duverger, Christian. "The *Meaning of Sacrifice." Fragments for a History of the Human Body.* Ed. Michel Feher. Vol. 3. New York: Zone, 1989. 366–85. Print.

Fernández de Oviedo y Valdés, Gonzalo. *Historia general y natural de las Indias.* Ed. J. Pérez de Tudela y Bueso. 4 vols. Biblioteca de autores españoles, vols. 117–21. Madrid: Ediciones Atlas, 1992. Print.

Florescano, Enrique. *The Myth of Quetzalcoatl.* Trans. Lysa Hochroth. Baltimore: John Hopkins University Press, 1999. Print.

Freud, Sigmund. "The 'Uncanny.'" (1919). *The Standard Edition of the Complete Psychological Works of Sigmund Freud.* Ed. James Strachey and Ana Freud. Trans. James Strachey. Vol. 17. London: The Hogarth Press, 1959. 218–56. Print.

González Torres, Yolotl. *El sacrificio humano entre los mexicas.* Mexico City: Fondo de Cultura Económica, 1985. Print.

Goodrich, Peter. "Law and Religion: Law, Religion, and Critical Theory." *Encyclopedia of Religion.* Ed. Lindsay Jones. Detroit: Thomson Gale, 2005. 5358–61. Print.

Gurría Lacroix, Jorge. "Historiografía del descubrimiento de México." Foreword. *Itinerario de la armada del Rey Católico a la isla de Yucatán en la India.* By Juan Díaz. Trans. Joaquín García Icazbalceta. Mexico City: Editorial Juan Pablos, 1972. 7–24. Print.

Hulme, Peter. *Colonial Encounters: Europe and the Native Caribbean, 1492–1797.* Methuen: London, 1986. Print.

Las Casas, Bartolomé de. *Tratados de 1552. Obras Completas.* Ed. Ramón Hernández, O.P., and Lorenzo Galmés, O.P. Vol. 10. Madrid: Alianza, 1992. Print.

———. *A Short Account of the Destruction of the Indies.* Trans. Nigel Griffin. London: Penguin, 1992. Print.

López Austin, Alfredo. *Cuerpo humano e ideología. Las concepciones de los antiguos nahuas.* 2 vols. Mexico City: UNAM, 1980. Print.

López de Gómara, Francisco. *La [h]istoria de las Indias, y conquista de Mexico.* Zaragoza: Agustín Millán, 1552. Print.

Martyr, Peter. *Opera: Legatio Babylonica. De Orbe Novo Decades Octo. Opus Epistolarum.* Graz: Akademische Druck-u. Verlagsanstalt, 1966. Print.

Matos Moctezuma, Eduardo. *Muerte a filo de obsidiana. Los nahuas frente a la muerte.* Mexico City: Secretaría de Educación Pública, 1975. Print.

———. "The Templo Mayor of Tenochtitlan: Economics and Ideology." *Ritual Human Sacrifice in Mesoamerica.* Ed. Elizabeth H. Boone. Washington: Dumbarton Oaks Research Library and Collection, 1984. 133–64. Print.

Palencia-Roth, Michael. "The Cannibal Law of 1503." *Early Images of the Americas.* Ed.

Jerry M. Williams and Robert E. Lewis. Tucson: University of Arizona Press, 1993. 21–63. Print.

Rabasa, José. *Inventing America. Spanish Historiography and the Formation of Eurocentrism.* Norman: University of Oklahoma Press, 1993. Print.

Read, Kay Almere. *Time and Sacrifice in the Aztec Cosmos.* Bloomington: Indiana University Press, 1998. Print.

Schroeder, Susan, Anne J. Cruz, Cristian Roa, and David E. Tavárez, eds. *Chimalpahin's Conquest: A Nahua Historian's Rewriting of Francisco López de Gómara's* La Conquista de México. Stanford: Stanford University Press, 2010. Print.

Séjourné, Laurette. *Pensamiento y religión en el México antiguo.* Mexico City: Fondo de Cultura Económica, 1957. Print.

Tavárez, David. *The Invisible War: Indigenous Devotions, Discipline, and Dissent in Colonial Mexico.* Stanford: Stanford University Press, 2011. Print.

Taylor, Diana. *The Archive and the Repertoire: Performing Cultural Memory in the Americas.* Durham: Duke University Press, 2003. Print.

Wolf, Eric R. *Envisioning Power: Ideologies of Dominance and Crisis.* Berkeley: University of California Press, 1999. Print.

Vitoria, Francisco de. *Doctrina sobre los indios.* Ed. and trans. Ramón Hernández Martín. Salamanca: Editorial San Esteban, 1992. Print.

Vulgate. *Biblia sacra: Iuxta Vulgatam versionem.* Ed. Bonifatius Fischer and Robert Weber. Stuttgart: Deutsche Bibelgelsellschaft, 1994. Print.

◆ **11**

Legal Pluralism and the "India Pura" in New Spain: The School of Guadalupe and the Convent of the Company of Mary

Mónica Díaz

On February 26, 1806, a group of twenty-six indigenous women in New Spain signed a petition to transform the school for Indian women of Our Lady of Guadalupe in Mexico City into a convent, the first one that would allow indigenous women to profess as nuns without class restrictions. The *colegialas* (teachers) stated that it was their wish to see their school transformed into a convent: "Queremos y consentimos, y aún suplicamos a nuestro Director el Señor Marqués de Castañiza que procure y promueva en todos los modos posibles y conforme a las Leyes de estos reynos, la erección de este colegio en convento de religiosas de la Compañía de María Santísima llamada de la Enseñanza para Indias doncellas de toda la América " (AGN, Colegios, vol. 8, exp.4, f. 41) (We agree with and even beg our director Sir Marquis of Castañiza that he procure and promote in all possible ways, and according to the laws of these kingdoms, the establishment [transformation] of this school into a convent of religious women of the Company of Mary called of the Enseñanza for Indian girls of all the Americas).

Although the transformation of the school took place on the eve of the Mexican independence, the religious praxis and the discourse supporting it correspond more to the legal pluralism of the colonial period, fostered by the creation of two distinct republics, each with a different set of right and obligations, as well as to the ongoing initiatives of the Bourbon reforms. In the midst of contradictory moves that sought to de-Indianize parish life and weaken church power, the exclusively indigenous school became another cloister that required indigenous women to be *puras* and *limpias* (pure/clean), promoting ethnic exclusivity and therefore an implicit strengthening of indigenous self-identification.[1]

The rhetorical construction of the petition is built on two key elements: the reference to the laws of the territories under Spanish colonial rule and the appeal to the paternalistic relationship of the colonial state toward indigenous peoples. These elements reveal the fundamental role of a "colonial rhetoric" in the constitution of a discourse of socio-ethnic identification (39).[2] Corporate indigenous communities learned to maneuver within the new colonial system and used the language of the legal and religious apparatus in surprisingly effective ways.[3] Both the indigenous women from the school and creole clerics adhered to legal categories of difference in their written documentation. Yet the petition composed and signed by the indigenous *colegialas* of Guadalupe constitutes only a piece in a larger puzzle of Indian political culture during the late colonial period; although this case is unique because of the agency shown by the women, the majority of the documentation involving the transformation of the school into a convent was written by male religious authorities.

With the support of the indigenous women in the school, the institution's director and confessor, the creole Juan Francisco de Castañiza y Larrea, believed that the exclusively Indian precinct would be viewed more positively by the population as a convent than as a school, and that more parents would trust the education of their daughters to consecrated women than to *colegialas* (AGN, Templos y conventos, vol. 24, exp. 12, fol. 366). Regardless of whether this idea was in fact true, it is worth noting the social prestige that convents still had in the nineteenth century, as well as the clear identification of the group of women as "Indian," even without belonging to the noblility.[4] Convents were founded soon after the first settlers arrived into New Spain, granting spiritual and social distinction to the town where a cloister was established (Lavrin 43). Yet by the eighteenth century the establishment of new convents slowed, and great emphasis was given to the reformation of the existing ones.[5]

This essay examines the colonial politics involved in the transformation of the school of Guadalupe for indigenous women founded by the Jesuits in 1753 in Mexico City into the Convent of the Company of María Santísima de Guadalupe y Nueva Enseñanza. The documentation produced as part of the transformation of the school into a convent reflects the manner in which certain indigenous communities maintained a cohesive identity based on early constructions of ethnic difference. Moreover, it examines a historical instance in which the category of "Indian" was championed by creole religious authorities (referred to as "creole patriots") in a multifaceted attempt to carry out certain aspects of the Bourbon reforms and at the same time to maintain a tradition of paternalistic care and control toward the peoples in the republic of Indians.[6] Ultimately, I show the colonial legacies of social discrimination that survived into the Republican period in this particular instance of local religious expression. My main focus is on language and the rhetorical mechanisms used to negotiate a space of difference. The reimagined space of the school-convent for indigenous women on the eve of the independence took the form of a social and discursive practice that relied on an intricate web of social networks (Arias 32). Before delving into the documentation, a few words are in order regarding the notion of identity employed in this essay, and the legal and religious dimension of the term "Indian" (indio).

Group Identification

In recent years, the usage of "identity" as a category of analysis has come under close scrutiny, especially by social scientists. Rogers Brubaker and Frederick Cooper, among the most critical voices, point out the problematic nature of the term, which is usually torn between "hard" meanings and therefore essentialist visions of identity, and "soft" meanings that propose a malleable and fluid construction of the term, leaving us "with a term so infinitely elastic as to be incapable of performing serious analytical work" (11). It has been proven time and again that the nature of the colonial enterprise in the Americas fostered a transculturated set of experiences that allowed for hybrid modes of representation and identification. Recent scholarship in colonial studies, aware of this social hybridity, has favored a more nuanced understanding of colonial practice and identity formation (Fisher and O'Hara 15). In this context, malleable and fluid constructions of identity should still be privileged, yet a few considerations proposed by Brubaker and Cooper might refine our analysis of social constructions.

Brubaker and Cooper propose to think about *identification* rather than identity, to view it as a process, an active term derived from a verb; in this way, it calls for reflection about the agents doing the identifying (14). We can differentiate between the manner in which people—either as individuals or in groups—identify themselves because they share an attribute, such as ethnic background, and the external identification established by an authoritative institution. Richard Jenkins elaborates by adding that identity is never unilateral and that all identities are constituted as a dialectical process between internal and external concepts of identification (18–19). This process is implicated in Pierre Bourdieu's concept of the "habitus"; although largely ambiguous, the habitus refers to a set of dispositions which generate structured social practices and representations (72). The highly structured context of the religious institution in the colony upheld the representation and self-constructions of communal identifications, reinforcing the structures upon which groups established their identifications. Identity formation is a flexible social construct, but also an active and continuously pragmatic one. In this way, identity is a category of practice rather than a category of analysis (Braubaker and Cooper 5). In the context of the transformation of the school for indigenous women into a convent, localized religious practices and aspirations enabled the continuity of a cohesive indigenous identity largely based on early colonial concepts of difference.

A useful way to understand the particular conundrum of "Indian" identity is given by José Rabasa in the introduction of *Without History*, in which he asserts that "nothing remains the same after the invasion, and yet modes of communalism and their corresponding life forms have survived to the present" (2). The notion of indigenous communalism does not necessarily require an across-the-board definition of a particular group; indigenous life forms survived in different ways and for various reasons.[7] As Rabasa proposes, it is in the studying of the forms in which order was created and disorder contained, such as the regulation of an exclusively indigenous school-convent, that we can deconstruct ethnic identification and representation exercised in discursive practices (17). The identities created through language are largely products of negotiation and rhetorical exercises of power.

The central region of Mexico was organized into ethnic states or *altepetl*, upon which Spanish socioeconomic organizations, such as municipalities, jurisdictions, and Indian parishes (or *doctrinas*), were built (Gutiérrez 35). Although there was no consensus about the way to deal with the indigenous population in the first years of colonization, the idea of two different separated spaces prevailed. Around the 1530s, two independent republics were instituted, the *república de indios* and the *república de españoles*. At first, the label *indio* was an empty category used as part of the confusion of the alleged arrival to the Indies by the explorers, and to differentiate Indians from non-Indians. It was due to Bartolomé de Las Casas that the colonizers began to apply the "millennial doctrine of the obligation of prince and Church," through which special protection had to be given to widows, orphans, and the wretched of the earth (Borah 80).

According to the judicial condition of *miserabiles*, the Indians were to have special legal assistance, and their cases and complaints were taken under special royal and church protection. Woodrow Borah asserts that Francisco de Vitoria proposed in one of his lectures at Salamanca in 1539 that the Indians might be regarded as in need of special legal assistance since they were not able to govern themselves. In 1545, with the support of other bishops, Bartolomé de Las Casas reiterated the proposition of declaring Indians "miserables" in the full judicial sense of the term, in a letter addressed to the *audiencia* (high court) (81). Although the term was used by many "defenders" of the Indians, it was more often a rhetorical construct than one with real judicial meaning during the sixteenth century. It is important to acknowledge the rhetorical dimension of legal writing. As Raúl Marrero-Fente has pointed out, the representation of the law contains hidden strategies of discursive domination (22).

The discourse of the Indian as miserable, together with the promulgation of the New Laws in 1542, which stipulated the rights to freedom and to communal existence for Amerindians who had embraced Christianity, provided indigenous peoples with a common ground to defend their rights and to create a cohesive ethnic identity (Martínez 97).[8] The rhetoric of purity of blood and lineage fostered by the establishment of two republics allowed the survival of native communities with their own hierarchies and an official recognition of Indian purity. Ultimately, it was recognized that the original inhabitants of the Americas "were unsullied by Judaism and Islam and had willingly accepted Christianity," putting a fundamental semantic weight on the concept of purity of blood (Martínez 5). As Rolena Adorno has illustrated, there were native and mestizo authors who took up the pen to recast their genealogical histories in order to claim lands, rights, and power; their writing centered on two elements: the interpretation of the wars of conquest and claims about their society's acceptance of the Christian gospel (*Polemics* 139).

Spanish reconfiguration of pre-Hispanic organization did not always respect ethnic differences or *altepetl* dynasties, yet corporate indigenous communities learned to utilize the universalizing labeling of *indio* instead of their individual ethnicities without necessarily losing their ethnic memory. Once relocated geographically through *reducciones* and the initial *encomienda* system, indigenous peoples established bonds of solidarity with other *indios* and worked at developing an identity that would allow them to present their claims to the crown and the church more effectively. Still, not all indigenous communities had the same experiences; just as colonial power was not monolithic, neither were the responses of indigenous peoples. It has become clear that corporate indigenous communities under religious tutelage tended to acquire an identity defined in Christian terms and usually understood in search of a particular goal as the founding of a confraternity or in search of leadership in the local parish.

The persistence of a common sense of belonging to a community that identifies itself as indigenous, precisely because it knows too well the limitations and advantages that the category conveys in its religious and legal dimensions, does not involve the stagnation of the definition of what it means to be Indian. There were important shifts in the constitution of an Indian identity throughout the colonial period, since identities are flexible constructs that respond to the needs of those who use them. Robert Jackson contends that racial identities, which were created for the most part on paper, did not necessarily reflect social or cultural realities (5). This kind of disconnect is mostly true for the cases in which these categories were imposed on the subject rather than negotiated and self-acquired. In the documentation of the transformation of the school into convent, there was little direct engagement of indigenous agents that could provide evidence of such a situation, yet in other instances, such as earlier foundings of convents for indigenous women or negotiations for seminaries for indigenous men, we know that community leaders were active in negotiating these spaces with colonial officials. In a process of transculturation, the category of "Indian" that was hammered out in the sixteenth century survived well into the eighteenth and nineteenth centuries.[9] We can attest to the Indians' ability to align with the colonial state's limiting laws and paternalistic view in processes of negotiation, and the manner in which laws are put into action by creole clerics to champion the cause of the convent at a key moment in time.

Bourbon Reforms and Mexican Independence

The numerous written testimonies that accompany the petition to transform the school, the constitutions of the new convent, and the legal procedures to approve the transformation of the school can be described as contradictory within a context deeply affected by Bourbon reforms and on the eve of independence. The documents regarding the transformation of the school of Guadalupe disclose, as Ruth Hill describes it, a fissure between history, or material reality, and discourse (2). Two teleological narratives surrounded the transformation of the school into convent: the Bourbon reforms and independence from Spain. Although neither political initiative prioritized indigenous matters, both affected the indigenous populations deeply. However, it is important to highlight how, at a religious and cultural level, indigenous communities understood political change and used it to their advantage.[10] One of the purposes of the Bourbon policies was the integration of Indians into colonial society through education reforms, and the Convent of Guadalupe had a clear didactic purpose: the indigenous women were supposed to serve their own people by educating them. Yet the constitution of the new convent stated that the girls admitted to the school's convent had to be pure Indian; it could not accept women from any other *casta*. Although "integration" was the ultimate purpose of the convent-school in the context of the reforms, the long-standing division between the two republics fostered a clear ethnic consciousness among the indigenous women and their families and among the creole clerics who pushed for the founding; this consciousness in turn facilitated the racialized division of society.

Another of the Bourbon initiatives had to do with the eradication of indigenous languages and the promotion of education among the native populations. The convent's documentation directly engages these proposals, yet the contradiction resides in the mere existence of a space of difference where purity of Indian blood was required to enter. As Santa Arias has argued, particularly for this period, "these spatialities of power formed core elements of governmentality and identity construction" (32). By looking at the convent as a spatial representation of power relations, we can appreciate the significance of the discursive production surrounding the convent and the negotiation of categories of identification. The republic of Indians, the Indian parishes, and the general Indian court were all spaces opened by the colonists to control the natives; in turn, these became places that fostered a communal identity. The convents exclusively for indigenous women that materialized in the eighteenth century also functioned as a space of negotiation and reinforcement of a well-articulated ethnic identity.[11]

After Mexico's separation from Spain, the legal category of *indio* was suppressed in civil law, yet we can attest to its continued usage in all documentation pertaining to the convent in the aftermath of independence. The categories of difference, and particularly the definition of *indio*, were entrenched in religious practice. In the early nineteenth century, parish priests and parishioners alike continued to rely on sixteenth-century canon law and colonial pastoral manuals; according to Matthew O'Hara, it was a combination of legal, social, and cultural forces that allowed for the survival of the category of *indio* while it was being suppressed by civil law (*"Miserables"* 15). Even when legal discourse eliminated the category of *indio*, it was evident that indigenous people were not going to disappear, and the imagined integration that began with the aims of the Bourbon policies and was renewed by liberal policies was far from materializing. The cultural and political autonomy that the colonial system had granted to the *pueblos de indios* was restrictive and discriminatory but at the same time offered certain benefits to corporate indigenous communities; most significantly, it facilitated the shaping of a cohesive ethnic identity. Karen Caplan has gone further, arguing that indigenous identity persisted in Mexico, not only culturally but also and more importantly politically, and that the new system of governance that developed after independence reflected "significant continuities from the colonial era" (226–28).[12] In short, indigenous communities in many parts of Mexico became Mexicans but continued to be indigenous, and in their documented affairs they continued to recall two of the most effective rhetorical strategies of colonial times: their status as *miserables* (miserable) and their purity of Indian blood.

More than just a continuation in the usage of colonial language and rhetoric, indigenous communities from central Mexico and the parish priests assigned to them found in early constructions of difference the means to acquire benefits, such as a convent and a school for their daughters and flock. The imperial plans to promote economic growth and material well-being (Scardaville 509), and later the idea of creating equal citizens, failed to acknowledge local culture, particularly in the religious realm. As Matthew O'Hara notes, the corporate identities and practices of colonial subjects were not easy to manipulate, and often parish reorganizations by colonial officials led to organized local responses (*Flock* 91). The documentation showcases creole patriots championing an indigenous matter, yet the active participation of indigenous women and their families in requesting another cloister for their "nation" is equally important.

A New Convent for Indigenous Women

Conventual life in the Americas was restricted to Spanish and *criolla* women until the eighteenth century. Only a few *mestizas* were accepted as nuns in the first years of the colony; indigenous, black, and all other *casta* women were only allowed to enter convents as servants. In the eighteenth century, the viceroy and clerical authorities established three convents exclusively for indigenous nobility. The first, the Convent of Corpus Christi in Mexico City, opened its doors in 1724; the Convent of Nuestra Señora de la Purísima Concepción de Cosamaloapan opened in Valladolid, present-day Morelia, in 1737; and in 1782 the Convent of Nuestra Señora de los Ángeles was founded in Antequera, present-day Oaxaca.

The school for indigenous women of Our Lady of Guadalupe was founded by the Jesuit Antonio de Herdoñana on the feast day of Guadalupe, December 12, 1753. The school was located within the indigenous pueblo of San Sebastián, or Atzacualco, and it received twenty women who served as teachers of more than seventy indigenous girls. The teachers in the school did not have to take religious vows, but they had to follow a religious rule that was written based on the Summary of the Company of Jesus (Foz y Foz 419). Financial constraints and the expulsion of the Jesuits made the school's situation unsustainable. The marquis of Castañiza had been appointed confessor of the teachers in 1781 and director of the school in 1791. He undertook the transformation of the school into what would become the first convent to allow any Indian woman to join, regardless of her noble status.

Juan Francisco de Castañiza y Larrea (1756–1825) was a respected ecclesiastical figure in New Spain. His family traveled from Spain in the first half of the eighteenth century to settle in the Americas; the noble title was granted to his father by Charles III in 1772 (Foz y Foz 422). Castañiza y Larrea had been professor and director of the Colegio of San Ildefonso in Mexico City before being chosen as confessor and soon thereafter as director of the school of Our Lady of Guadalupe. Later in his life, Castañiza was appointed bishop of Durango (1815) until the time of his death. When the Marquis documented his reasons to transform the school of Our Lady of Guadalupe into the convent of the Company of Mary, he divided his argument into two categories: reasons of benefit and reasons of necessity. The necessity, Castañiza stated, lay in the fact that the only three convents for indigenous women were Capuchin convents that accepted only nobles, or *cacicas*. For that reason, he stated, many of the Indians who aspired to enter religion but lacked the strength to follow such a strict rule could not achieve their goal; and even if they were *limpias* (pure), they did not possess the *calidad* (quality) of the caciques and therefore could not attain religious life (AGN, Templos y conventos, vol. 24 exp. 12 fol. 365).[13]

As illustrated earlier, the creation of two distinct republics produced two different sets of rights and obligations for the inhabitants of each, a legal pluralism; the republic of Indians mirrored the republic of Spaniards in its concern with "purity," producing a discourse based on *calidad* and not on race. *Calidad* as a concept was loosely based on social status and genealogy but disconnected from any biological meaning. The label of *indio puro* was determined through a combination of genealogical, cultural, and physical characteristics. The concept of *indio* was a Spanish invention, yet indigenous communities understood the established system and its language and adopted it, granting equal importance to lineage and purity of blood as their counterparts in the republic of Spaniards. The individual and collective discourse of possessing *calidad* and purity granted indigenous people access to public office in native government and allowed them to occupy posts in religious organizations such as confraternities and brotherhoods. And in the case of convents, it symbolically placed native women at the same level as Spanish nuns.

The notion of *calidad* is found in numerous documents from the eighteenth century; it referred to skin color but also conveyed other social markers such as occupation, honor, integrity, and place of origin (Carrera 6). Historians have pointed out the inconsistencies and imprecision of assigning socio-ethnic labels to individuals during the Colony, since it often had to do with a process of self-identification in bureaucratic or religious procedures, such as censuses and baptismal records.[14] Although categories of difference were fluid and malleable, particularly for the urban poor who were labeled using the *casta* system, it is important to recognize the existence of communities that maintained a collective identity in ethnic terms, which was usually employed with a particular goal in mind, as in the cases in which native leaders from a particular community initiated a petition or negotiated a space for "their people."[15]

As part of the legal procedure that had to be followed to get the approval for the convent, several religious authorities gave their opinion on the matter of the school's transformation. The provincial of the Augustinian order, Fray Manuel Melero, supported the idea, noting again that there were many Indian women who desired to follow religious life but could not join the Capuchin convents of the caciques since they did not possess the *calidad*, even though they were pure from birth. The discourse on *calidad*, as explained by Ruth Hill, referred to estates, and to conditions such as nobility, rather than to ethnic markers (215). As illustrated by Juan Arce de Otálora's treatise on nobility and its privileges, a person who could legally prove legitimate descent from indigenous nobles acquired *calidad*, according to Spanish laws (Hill 217).

In the documentation of the Convent of the Company of Mary, we find *calidad* paired with the status of being noble, or *cacica*, yet *cacicazgo* (chieftainship) was not equivalent to possessing material goods and richness; it had to do with a special status that nobles negotiated with the crown in the early years after the conquest. Caciques were exempt from paying tribute, and they were not supposed to hold certain occupations deemed lowly. *Cacicazgos* did not remain static for the duration of the colonial period; many disappeared due to lack of successors or their inability to prove lineage. In the areas where *cacicazgos* survived, their success was due to an awareness of their genealogy and a clear effort to maintain a pure Indian lineage that would allow them to claim their special status, as well as their ability to negotiate with colonial officials to have their titles recognized by the crown. Yet by the eighteenth century, the majority of caciques retained only their titles and the respect from people in their communities. The social difference between a *macehual* (commoner) and a cacique was no longer noticeable, if it ever had been. The genealogical imagination of clean, pure Indian lineage was constructed on the basis of a pre-Hispanic notion of ethnic pride, but it was reworked with the tools bestowed by coloniality.

The constitutions of the convent stipulated that the women admitted as students into the convent school should be *indias puras* (pure Indian). The document proceeds to explain that for a candidate to be pure Indian, her parents must be regarded as Indians in their towns and hold a profession suitable to Indians in their republic, or must have paid tribute as was required of all indigenous people (AGN, Colegios, vol. 8, exp. 6, fol. 143) The constitutions clarify that the children of *meztindios* and *indias* can be admitted because they are regarded as legitimate Indians, yet under no circumstance can any Spaniard, mestiza, or mulatta be accepted. It becomes evident that the discourse of *limpieza* does not have to coincide with that of *calidad*; in this way, all indigenous peoples were able to maintain their "clean" lineage in order to contend their purity and have access to a space of difference.

Returning to Fray Manuel Melero's testimony from the province of the Augustinians, we can attest to the manner in which he links the petition of the convent to the rhetoric of colonial paternalism toward indigenous people. Fray Melero evokes the customary piety of a king who has always made a distinction between this "class" of people and the rest of his vassals in procuring with particular determination anything that would lead to the well-being of the indigenous people (AGN, Templos y conventos, vol. 24, exp. 12, fol. 371). Fray Melero uses the word *"clase"* to differentiate indigenous peoples from others, a word choice that illuminates our understanding of the value system of the hierarchical arrangement of society. The semantic load of the word "class" is clearly dissociated from ownership of material goods; instead, it reflects the way society had been built upon criteria from centuries earlier, and it survived to keep the *pueblos de indios* in a lower place in the social ladder. In the same vein, a group of priests from Valladolid signed a document in 1807 supporting the cause of the convent–school by referring to the women as "inditas" (little Indians) (fol. 432). The use of the diminutive reflects the paternalistic relationship of the colonial church with its indigenous subjects; moreover, it reinforced the legal and theological meanings that the category of *indio* conveyed, under which the Indians were regarded as minors in need of protection.

Fray Manuel Melero refers to the women who wish to become nuns as "pobre indias" (poor Indians) who cry because they do not have the amount of convents that Spanish women have (fol. 371). The image of the poor Indian can be linked to that of the *miserable* used by Fray Joaquín Ramírez de Arellano. He rationalizes the fact that Indian women are not received in the numerous convents for Spaniards and *criollas* in the city by saying that they would be despised by the nuns who reside there; hence the need for the new foundation. He elaborates: "Tendrán pues las miserables indias un convent de instituto suave, cual es el de la Enseñanza" (fol. 376) (They will have, the wretched Indians, a convent with a gentle rule, that of the Enseñanza). The wretched, poor *inditas* were recurrent constructions of indigenous women in religious and legal documentation from the earliest depictions up to the nineteenth century. It is significant that although these were colonial constructs imposed on a subaltern group, they were adopted by indigenous peoples to negotiate benefits for their pueblos and to maintain, as much as possible, ethnic autonomy.

In addition to the stereotypical depictions of colonial subjects, which echo the rhetorical constructions of the law and theological justifications for the differentiated treatment of natives, creole clerics emphasized in their defense the role that education played in this new foundation. The teaching mission of the convent of the Company of Mary for indigenous women was fundamental, for it would ensure that the convent was well received by public opinion. Historian Pilar Foz y Foz explains that this particular religious order distinguished itself from other orders by combining contemplative and active modes of religious life; its origins are French, and it was not founded until the seventeenth century. The constitutions of the order were largely based on the Summary of the Jesuits, and the vow of total enclosure was not as strict as it was for other orders since teaching was the core of their apostolic mission (7).

The teaching mission of the Company of Mary aligned itself with Bourbon reforms that sought to educate Indians. Therefore, in the numerous documents arguing for the need for the convent–school of the Company of Mary of Guadalupe, the greatest emphasis was given to the kind of education the indigenous women would receive from other indigenous women who had been consecrated to religion, and the effect that it would have in their communities. As one of the defenders of the transformation argued, indigenous women were ideal to educate other indigenous women, since they would be capable of speaking to them in their native language and gradually switch into Spanish. The other benefit repeatedly referred to in the documents was the role that women who were educated would later fulfill as mothers, and how the education that they received would be communicated to their own children. Fray Joaquín Ramírez elaborated on this point, stating that the women would learn what was needed according to their *calidad*, returning thereafter to their pueblos and becoming mothers who by nursing their children would inculcate the first ideas of religion (AGN, Templos y conventos, vol. 24, exp. 12, fol. 376). Fray Joaquín Ramírez stressed ethnic difference as he reflected on the most basic principle of the conventual foundation. It was Ramírez's opinion that indigenous women were going to be educated according to their *calidad* and not following a universal belief of what women in general should be taught. *Calidad* in this sense referred both to their lack of noble blood and to their status of Indians.

In addition, the Marquis of Castañiza stated that the most important benefit of transforming the school into a convent was the manner in which the education of the indigenous women would improve, given that the teachers were going to be consecrated religious women and would have to abide by their vows and follow the religious rule and constitutions. He argued that the school of Guadalupe was in a state of total relaxation and that under those circumstances—that is, without taking formal vows—the rule could not be followed (AGN, Templos y conventos, vol. 24, exp. 12, fol. 366). Similarly, Fray Antonio García from the Convent of Santo Domingo stated that it would be greatly beneficial for the indigenous teachers to have taken religious vows so they would be detached from all materials things and would therefore be in a better position to teach with greater care, charity, and demureness to the indigenous *colegialas*. He added that once the indigenous women returned from being educated in the convent school, they would benefit their communities more through their example and behavior [than] from the priests' teachings (fol. 367).

Fray José de San Martín also supported the transformation of the school into a convent. He considered the convent very useful because it would allow indigenous women who felt the call to religious life to pursue it without restrictions. He mentioned the great satisfaction that parents would receive by entrusting the education of their daughters to religious, rather than secular, women. Fray José de San Martín elaborated on the kind of education the girls would receive and the benefits that would be brought to them. He concluded that the establishment of the convent–school would be greatly beneficial to improving the education of the Indians, who through their association with enlightened people and their dealings with them would become polished and get rid of the backwardness apparent in them (fol. 375). This last comment on the part of Fray José de San Martín is one of the ambivalent discursive defenses of Indian women; while he considered indigenous commoners apt for religious life, he explicitly placed them within a mass of uneducated and coarse people in need of instruction.

Against All Odds

A crowned portrait of an indigenous nun from the Convent of the Company of María Santísima de Guadalupe y Nueva Enseñanza has survived (Fig. 1). From the inscription on the portrait, we know that Manuela Meza professed in 1827, when María Luisa del Corral was prioress of the cloister. Like the other three convents for indigenous women in New Spain, the founders at the Convent of Guadalupe were all creole women, and colonial officials tried to keep the convent under a creole government for as long as possible. Castañiza made sure that the first two prioresses were creole, and it was not until the second one died in 1827 that María Luisa del Corral became the first indigenous nun to be elected prioress, becoming responsible for directing the convent for indigenous women (Foz y Foz 437). It is significant that the portrait of an Indian woman as a crowned nun was produced under an indigenous government.

In a way, the portrait can be considered a reaffirmation of the indigenous character of the convent, which strengthened the ethnic exclusivity and identity of the women residing in it. As Fernando Coronil states, "From historical and anthropological studies we know that the body is everywhere a source of symbolic production and that social groups use bodily imagery to challenge, confirm, or play with the existing social hierarchies" (95). The exclusively indigenous school opened by the nuns of the Convent of the Company of Mary of Enseñanza Nueva might not have been devoted to the elites, but the symbolism of their particular rule and the teaching nature of the cloister permitted a distinctive agency. Manuela Meza from the pueblo of Capuluac is portrayed following in part the conventions of the genre of the crowned nun, which would usually represent a passive nun wearing the insignia of her religious order and that of her symbolic marriage to Christ. In contrast, Manuela Meza is embodying the active and apostolic mission of the order; she is depicted with an open book in her hands in the active role of reading. Moreover, the inscription on the portrait proudly identifies her and her family as members of an indigenous community. This portrait conveys the image of an educated indigenous woman who most likely was also a teacher of other Indians and who had proudly reached this level of social prestige by means of her ethnic difference.

Fig. 1. Portrait of Manuela Mesa, anonymous, 1827. Josefina Muriel Collection. Courtesy of Arqueología Mexicana.

It is worth noting that the Bourbon change in policy toward the Catholic Church during the eighteenth century was not an attack on the spiritual power of the church; rather, it was concerned with the property owned by ecclesiastical institutions.[16] This fact helps to explain why the convent was still viewed positively, at least in the first decades of the nineteenth century: society for the most part kept "colonial" values alive while embracing certain "enlightened" ideologies for different purposes.

Creole clerics, particularly the ones engaged in defending the transformation of the school of Guadalupe into a convent-school, were involved in the construction of a patriotic epistemology, "creat[ing] and validat[ing] knowledge in the colonies along lines that mimicked and reinforced wider public principles of socio-racial estates and corporate privileges" (Cañizares-Esguerra 206). In their "defense" of the convent, they recalled early indigenous acceptance of Christianity. One of the lengthy arguments for the convent evoked the disposition found in the *nación de indios* to save their souls after Hernán Cortés spoke about religion to Moctezuma, placed the images of Jesus and the Virgin Mary on top of their idols, and solemnly sang the *Te Deum laudamus* (AGN, Templos y conventos, fol. 387). The new convent would cater both to indigenous women who were not nobles but wished to follow religious life and to indigenous families who wanted to give their daughters an education. In what seemed like a recognition of and a conscious effort to support and acknowledge the piety of indigenous women and their families' eagerness for a formal, religious education, creole clerics produced documentation that contained highly ambivalent representations of indigenous peoples. In these documents, Indians were still depicted as *miserables* and used the earliest images of rapid conversion.

The discursive representations of the indigenous women of Guadalupe and the communities that would benefit from the convent portrayed indigenous women as pious and eagerly awaiting the founding of another convent for their "race." On the other hand, they were presented as being in significant need of education to eradicate their supposed natural coarseness. Moreover, clerics were supportive of the improvement of the *pueblos de indios* through a more generalized education, yet this alleged improvement had no practical application in society because the separation of what they continued to call Indians and Spaniards was still promoted and did not seem to have a reachable end, even when the legal category of *Indian* had been suppressed. Ultimately, the indigenous people and certainly the women in the school who signed the petition to transform it into a convent were members of a corporate indigenous community with a clear sense of identity based on the ongoing separation of ethnic groups. By taking part in conventual life as a local religious expression, indigenous women and their students became part of the larger body of the Roman Catholic Church and at the same time reaffirmed their ethnicity. The indigenous women from the religious community of Guadalupe did not argue for integration, nor did their cleric counterparts; both of them saw in the religious institution another outlet for power and authority.

Although in practical terms the transformation was the addition of a convent to the already existent school, for the *pueblos de indios* and for the women who belonged to the school, this change meant being symbolically elevated to the same level as consecrated Spanish and creole women, in a parallel space that mirrored the institutions of the elites but maintained socio-ethnic difference. The rhetoric of the law in its figurative use of the word *miserable*, the official acknowledgment of their continued pure Indian lineage, and the paternalistic relationship that portrayed them as *inditas* granted colonial subjects the tools to achieve recognition of their aptitude and desire to have the same opportunities in the religious arena as the rest of colonial society. Although integration was the discursive motive for the support of the convent-school, in practical terms the convent became another instance of affirming ethnic difference and another way to legitimate their identification as an indigenous community within colonial society.

Notes

1. I have chosen to use ethnicity rather than race to refer to the kind of identity sought from the indigenous perspective. Although an imperfect tool of analysis, I believe it describes more closely the colonial ideology of difference.
2. According to Yolanda Martínez-San Miguel, a reading of "colonial rhetoric" would be "an attempt to identify and deconstruct the discursive and narrative strategies used to construct an American or 'mestizo' perspective that negotiates its place within and/or against metropolitan and imperial projects, in epistemological, political, or philosophical terms" (39).
3. An excellent example would be the case of Felipe Guaman Poma de Ayala in Peru, who, as Rolena Adorno has argued, utilized ecclesiastical rhetoric to cross cultural barriers successfully (*Guaman Poma* 57).
4. Indigenous nobles were interested in preserving their lineage in order to maintain their territorial rights and their power in the *pueblos de indios*.
5. The reformation of the convents concentrated on the adoption of the "common life," supported by the archbishop of Mexico, Francisco Antonio de Lorenzana (1766–72), and put into practice by his friend Francisco Fabián y Fuero, bishop of Puebla (1765–73) (*The First America*, Brading 495). This initiative produced a great deal of opposition from elite nuns and their families. For a detailed discussion on the "common life," see Margaret Chowning.
6. As an example of a "creole patriot," Brading refers to the case of Antonio Joaquín Rivadeneira y Barrientos, an eighteenth-century creole judge of the high court, who attacked ardently the bishop of Puebla, Fabián y Fuero's edict which forbade the use of indigenous languages when dealing with Indians (*The First America*, 497). For a detailed examination of creole patriotism and its origins, see Brading, *The Origins of Mexican Nationalism*.
7. Brubaker and Cooper refer to a similar phenomenon, calling it *commonality, connectedness*, or *groupness* (20).
8. María Elena Martínez notes that the special judicial-theological status of native

people would have not been problematic had it not been for the steady increase of a mixed-ancestry group of people that tried to benefit from the special status of Indians. Martínez explains that "native people who committed moral offenses were at times accused by their enemies of having Spanish-Indian parentage in order to have them tried by inquisitors" (104).

9. By this I mean that there were cases where indigenous peoples adopted certain cultural traits from European culture such as language and on occasion dress, but maintained an indigenous ethnic identity.
10. This is illustrated for the cases of Oaxaca and Yucatán by Karen Caplan, who states that after Mexico's separation from Spain, indigenous peoples in these states exercised the rights of their "new" universal citizenship but at the same time participated in indigenous councils as they were identified and self-identifies as *indígenas* (231). Peter Guardino analyzes political culture in the state of Guerrero, noting how colonial or "traditional" elements were assimilated into the new "modern" political culture, in a continuous negotiation of praxis and communal identity (10–11).
11. I have examined this point at length in my book *Writings from the Convent: Negotiating Ethnic Identity in Colonial Mexico*.
12. The liberal discourse of the Indian as a free citizen and of universal equality concealed the continuation of the way that indigenous peoples were actually considered and affected their later role in the making of the "Mexican nation." It was also key in the stagnation of certain stereotypes constructed in colonial discourse about indigenous peoples. Charles Hale illustrates this point with José Luis Mora's picture of indigenous communities: "[I]n their present state and until they have undergone considerable changes, [the Indians] can never reach the degree of enlightenment, civilization, and culture of Europeans nor maintain themselves as equals in a society formed by both" (223). Numerous historical studies examine how indigenous communities challenged this discourse by resisting and negotiating hegemonic structures of power.
13. The Capuchin order, also known as *discalced*, or barefoot, was committed to a more austere life of poverty and prayer (Socolow 93).
14. See, for example, Robert Jackson.
15. For more on the *castas* and the urban poor, see Cope.
16. Josefina Muriel notes that in 1807 the convent owned six houses that produced 2,000 pesos, and another six houses that produced between 216 and 120 pesos each year. There were other sources of income, such as donations that had been invested and produced a significant amount of money (498–99).

Works Cited

Adorno, Rolena. *Guaman Poma: Writing and Resistance in Colonial Peru*. Austin: University of Texas Press, 1986. Print.

———. *The Polemics of Possession in Spanish American Narrative*. New Haven: Yale University Press, 2007. Print.

Archivo General de la Nación, México (AGN), Collections: Colegios and Templos y Conventos.

Arias, Santa. "Rethinking Space: An Outsider's View of the Spatial Turn." *GeoJournal* 75 (2010): 29–41. Print.

Borah, Woodrow. *Justice by Insurance: The General Indian Court of Colonial Mexico and the Legal Aides of the Half-Real*. Berkeley: University of California Press, 1983. Print.

Bourdieu, Pierre. *Outline of a Theory of Practice*. Trans. Richard Nice. 1977. Cambridge: Cambridge University Press, 2004. Print.

Brading, David. *Church and State in Bourbon Mexico: The Diocese of Michoacán, 1749–1810*. Cambridge: Cambridge University Press, 1994. Print.

———. *The First America: The Spanish Monarchy, Creole Patriots, and the Liberal State, 1492–1867*. Cambridge: Cambridge University Press, 1991. Print.

———. *The Origins of Mexican Nationalism*. Cambridge: University of Cambridge, 1985. Print.

Brubaker, Rogers, and Frederick Cooper. "Beyond 'Identity.'" *Theory and Society* 29 (2000): 1–47. Print.

Cañizares-Esguerra, Jorge. *How to Write the History of the New World: Histories, Epistemologies, and Identities in the Eighteenth-Century Atlantic World*. Stanford: Stanford University Press, 2001. Print.

Caplan, Karen. "Indigenous Citizenship: Liberalism, Political Participation, and Ethnic Identity in Post-Independence Oaxaca and Yucatán." *Imperial Subjects: Race and Identity in Colonial Latin America*. Ed. Andrew Fisher and Matthew O'Hara. Durham: Duke University Press, 2009. 225–47. Print.

Carrera, Magali. *Imagining Identity in New Spain: Race, Lineage, and the Colonial Body in Portraiture and Casta Paintings*. Austin: University of Texas Press, 2003. Print.

Chowning, Margaret. *Rebellious Nuns: The Troubled History of a Mexican Convent, 1752–1863*. New York: Oxford UP, 2006. Print.

Cope, R. Douglas. *The Limits of Racial Domination: Plebeian Society in Colonial Mexico City, 1660–1720*. Madison: University of Wisconsin Press, 1994. Print.

Coronil, Fernando. "Can Postcoloniality be Decolonized? Imperial Banality and Postcolonial Power." *Public Culture* 5.1 (1992): 89–108. Print.

Díaz, Mónica. *Indigenous Writings from the Convent: Negotiating Ethnic Autonomy in Colonial Mexico*. Tucson: University of Arizona Press, 2010. Print.

Fisher, Andrew, and Matthew O'Hara. Introduction. *Imperial Subjects: Race and Identity in Colonial Latin America*. Ed. Andrew Fisher and Matthew O'Hara. Durham: Duke University Press, 2009. Print.

Foz y Foz, Pilar. *La revolución pedagógica en Nueva España (1754–1820)*. Vol. 1. Madrid: Instituto Gonzalo Fernández de Oviedo, 1981. Print.

Guardino, Peter. *Peasants, Politics, and the Formation of Mexico's National State: Guerrero, 1800–1857*. Stanford: Stanford University Press, 1996. Print.

Gutiérrez, Natividad. *Nationalist Myths and Ethnic Identities: Indigenous Intellectuals and the Mexican State*. Lincoln: University of Nebraska Press, 1999. Print.

Hale, Charles. *Mexican Liberalism in the Age of Mora, 1821–1853*. New Haven: Yale University Press, 1968. Print.

Hill, Ruth. *Hierarchy, Commerce, and Fraud in Bourbon Spanish America: A Postal Inspector's Exposé*. Nashville: Vanderbilt University Press, 2005. Print.

Jackson, Robert H. *Race, Caste, and Status: Indians in Colonial Spanish America*. Albuquerque: University of New Mexico Press, 1999. Print.

Jenkins, Richard. *Social Identity*. London: Routledge, 2004. Print.

Lavrin, Asunción. "Women and Religion in Spanish America." *Women and Religion in America: The Colonial and Revolutionary Periods*. Vol. 2. Ed. Rosemary R. Ruether and Rosemary S. Keller. San Francisco: Harper and Row, 1981. 42–78. Print.

Marrero-Fente, Raúl. *La poética de la ley en las Capitulaciones de Santa Fe*. Madrid: Trotta, 2000. Print.

Martínez, María Elena. *Genealogical Fictions: Limpieza de Sangre, Religion, and Gender in Colonial Mexico*. Stanford: Stanford University Press, 2008. Print.

Martínez-San Miguel, Yolanda. *From Lack to Excess: "Minor" Readings of Latin American Colonial Discourse*. Lewisburg: Bucknell University Press, 2008. Print.

Muriel, Josefina. *Conventos de monjas en la Nueva España*. 1946. Mexico City: Jus, 1995. Print.

O'Hara, Matthew. *A Flock Divided: Race, Religion, and Politics in Mexico*. Durham: Duke University Press, 2010. Print.

———. "*Miserables* and Citizens: Indians, Legal Pluralism, and Religious Practice in Early Republican Mexico." *Religious Culture in Modern Mexico*. Ed. Martin Austin Nesvig. Lanham, MD: Rowan and Littlefield, 2007. 14–34. Print.

Rabasa, José. *Without History: Subaltern Studies, the Zapatista Insurgency, and the Specter of History*. Pittsburgh: University of Pittsburgh Press, 2010. Print.

Scardaville, Michael. "(Hapsburg) Law and (Bourbon) Order: State Authority, Popular Unrest, and the Criminal Justice System in Bourbon Mexico City." *The Americas* 50.4 (1994): 501–25. Print.

Socolow, Susan Migden. *The Women of Colonial Latin America*. Cambridge: Cambridge University Press, 2000. Print.

◆ 12

Our Lady of Anarchy: Iconography as Law on the Frontiers of the Spanish Empire

John D. (Jody) Blanco

> The Governor-general is [all the way] in Manila, the king is in Spain, and God is in Heaven.
> —Colonial Philippine proverb

At the center of virtually every Philippine Christian town or city stands an image of Jesus Christ, the Virgin Mary, or a saint. This image—usually a small sculpture called a *santo*—also marks a crossroads between pagan idolatry and Christian iconolatry, animistic spirits and Christ's Incarnation, superstition and miracle, native and Spanish traditions—all of which popular belief (Spanish as well as indigenous) and the spiritual ministry itself have never ceased to conflate and confuse. In the foundation narratives of popular devotions to the Santo Niño de Cebu in Cebu City (1521; rediscovered in 1565), Nuestra Señora de la Paz y Buen Viaje (Our Lady of Peace and Safe Passage, commonly known as the Virgin of Antipolo) in Antipolo City (1626); La Virgen del Rosario (the Virgin of the Rosary in Manila, also known as "La Naval") (1646); and Our Lady of Caysasay in Lipa, Batangas (1688), it is said that the *santo* or holy image would leave the church or shrine that housed it and go walking at night.[1] Conversely, the paintings of Nuestra Señora de Candelaria (Our Lady of the Candles) in Jaro, Iloilo (1587) and Nuestra Señora de los Dolores de Turumba (the Virgin of Turumba for short) in Pakil, Laguna (1788), manifested a different kind of marvel upon their discovery. In Jaro, the image would express a divine will by becoming suddenly heavy, thus making it difficult for its discoverers to move. In the case of the Virgin of Turumba, her painted image was found in the Laguna de Bay in 1788, but instead of proceeding to the nearest port, the sailors who found the image were directed by a freak storm to disembark on the farther shore of Pakil. Miraculously, the image emerged from the waters and winds of the lake unblemished.

Now, it is said that God works in mysterious ways. Yet one must conclude from these miraculous foundation narratives that these ways are neither infinite nor very original: we find the same stories of images of the Virgin and Christ littered across the landscape of Spain in the fifteenth century and of the Americas in the sixteenth and seventeenth centuries (Christian, *Local Religion* 70—93). Colonial administrators and subjects alike would seek out these channels of divine intercession for the healing of the sick and afflicted, protection from the dangers of war and poverty, and the release of the devil's power over those who either refused to be baptized or who had apostatized from an earlier baptism. Were these not the very same reasons for seeking out the shrines in Spain (Christian, *Local Religion* 93–105)?

If we suspend our belief in the miracle as it stands, we confront a paradox that characterizes the spread of Christianity on the frontiers of Asia. That is, the origin stories and legends belonging to most devotional cults in the Philippines were to a varying degree transmitted by the Spanish religious orders themselves, at the same time that these very orders were engaged in expunging the idolatrous beliefs and "superstitions" of the natives they hoped to convert. In fact, the efflorescence of these cults in the archipelago coincided with the Inquisition's persecution of local devotions and agrarian cults associated with sacred images in Europe (Tavárez and Chuchiak 51–77). What role did the translation of these traditions serve in the evangelizing effort, and what were the implications of these traditions for the efficacy or inefficacy of Spanish law?

The argument that I outline in this essay is twofold. The first concerns the role of icons and devotional cults in the Philippines, which did not and do not merely supplement or complement the rule of law but in fact substitute for and (in certain cases) even *supplant* it. The relegation of this phenomenon to the prehistory of international law neglects the way the exceptional logic that governs these cults and icons provided both the basis for and the antidote to Spain's colonial sovereignty both in the Philippine archipelago and in the Americas. The second concerns the way the iconography of law—iconography *as* law or in the place of law—allows for and even promotes the survival and fortification of native customs and traditions against the direct intrusion of the colonial state and its institutions into the life of the colonized. This raises the paradox of Christianity and Christianization in the colonial setting: while it ideologically buttresses the *spirit* and general goals of Spanish sovereignty, it undermines the *letter* of colonial laws and policies. At the root of both arguments lies the religious concept of economy [*oikonomia*] and its paradoxical relationship to the law, which it paradoxically claims to fulfill by overturning.

Between Empire and Theocracy

The use of Christian imagery and icons in the conquest of the New World is well known. Men such as Christopher Columbus and Spanish conquistador of New Spain (Mexico) Hernán Cortés were devout Christians, and their religious piety thoroughly informed their understanding of the discovery and conquest (Watts 73–102; Gruzinski, *Images* 31–49). We may recall that, according to Cortés's soldier and chronicler Bernal Díaz del Castillo, during the Spanish expedition that led to the siege of Tenochtitlan, almost every encounter between Cortés's band and native society concludes with the conquistador's injunction for the leaders' "idols" to be smashed and for an image of the Virgin Mary to be erected in their place (see Díaz del Castillo 1:61–63, 83, 94, 122–23). For Gruzinski, the replacement of objects interpreted to be "idols" by images of the Virgin and Christ was inseparable from all other acts of war during the Spanish conquest. Spiritual and temporal conquest, in the eyes of Columbus and Cortés, were one and the same thing.

It would be natural to conclude from these examples that Christianity and evangelization, with its props and names, served as a ready pretext for imperial conquest; and that its value for the conquerors was to provide a fully-formed ideology for the kinds of depredation and exploitation that were to transpire in the Americas and the Philippines over the next three centuries. Despite the writings of Bartolomé de las Casas protesting the destruction of the Indies, or the Salamancan jurist Francisco de Vitoria's arguments outlining the conditions under which Spain's overseas conquest might be considered lawful, the role that religion played in ensuring the continuity of Spain's empire overseas seems beyond question. Yet the common sense and facility that allow us to associate the rhetoric of God's approaching kingdom with the preservation of an imaginary colonial status quo can both obscure and illuminate the contesting notions of authority, law, and order between the temporal and spiritual powers throughout the colonial period. It leads to a tendency to reduce the fashioning of imperial hegemony to a question of promoting colonial ideologies and to regard the Church as a "superstructural" appendage whose primary task was to provide a discourse and cultural practice that merely reproduced and expanded the *telos* of imperial conquest and the aggrandizement of land and people.[2]

At the root of this tendency is the assumption that the division of spiritual and temporal powers offers an imperfect, primitive version of the division between church and state, where the church provides a mystical and metaphysical narrative that justifies and promotes Spanish sovereignty. John N. Figgis's studies of medieval law, however, remind us that the division between imperial and papal authority belonged to an entirely different understanding of law and institution that revolved around the presumed unity of Christendom:

> In the Middle Ages Church and State in the sense of two competing societies did not exist; you have instead the two official hierarchies, the two departments if you will: the Court and the Curia, the kings' officials and the popes'. But in these controversies you have practically no conception of the Church, as consisting of the whole body of the baptized set over against the State, consisting of the same people, only viewed from a different standpoint and organized for a different end. It is a quarrel between two different sets of people—the lay officials and the clerics the bishops and the justices, the pope and the kings; it is not thought of under that highly complex difficult form of a quarrel between two societies, each of which was composed of precisely the same persons, only one is called the State, for it deals with temporal ends, and the other Church, as the Christian community. Such a notion would only be possible if the sense of corporate personality in Church and State had been fully developed. This was not the case. (Figgis, *Churches* 71)[3]

This pre-Westphalian Eurocentric unity rendered the division between pope and emperor fluid and grounded in the unity of a historic mission. As Catholic jurist Carl Schmitt would write in his controversial work *Nomos of the Earth*: "the antitheses of emperor and pope were not absolute, but rather *diversi ordines* (diverse orders), in which the order of the *respublica Christiana* resided."[4]

What concerns us here is the original concordance and coordination of the temporal and spiritual powers in the articulation of *legal* title to overseas possessions. "The papal missionary mandate," Schmitt continues, "was the legal foundation of the conquista. *This was not only the pope's position, but also that of the Catholic rulers of Spain, who recognized the missionary mandate to be legally binding*" (111, emphasis added). To put it another way, it would be anachronistic to consider theology as an ancillary justification for the conquest of the Americas and the Philippines, with the right of discovery and occupation (which Salamancan jurist and founder of international law Francisco de Vitoria rejected) serving as the primary one (see Anghie, 321–36). As Schmitt contends, the primary justification of legal title (and hence the origins of international law) arises from the sixteenth-century assumption shared by Crown and Pope alike. Royal and Church patronage were at bottom two faces of the same historic mission of world dominion; and that their divergence had more to do with their respective forms of administration rather than some notion of their divergent and autonomous spheres of authority, as was the case in the post-Westphalian (1648) division between Church and State in Europe.

The underlying unity between spiritual and temporal powers—and by extension, theology and law—in the historic mission of world salvation, is what prompts Schmitt, in a later reflection, to remark that the conquest of the Americas (and by extension, the Philippines) was achieved not by *ideological* means but by *iconographic* ones (Schmitt, "La tensión" 5–6). In a largely forgotten essay on the "planetary tension between East and West," Schmitt discusses the coincidence and correspondence between the discovery and occupation of the Americas and the outbreak of religious wars on the European continent as follows:

> One commonly explains the great world political struggle that exploded in the period of the discovery and conquest of the New World, the first global controversy in universal history, as a dispute among confessional dogmas . . . . [But] the issue concerning religious images leads us to more profound historical visions . . . . It is not difficult to comprehend that the Reconquest of Spain was a conquest on behalf of the cult of images of the Virgin. But my observation, that the conquest of the New World's discoverers and conquistadors brought along the sacred Image of [the Spaniards'] historical deeds in the form of the Immaculate Virgin and Mother of God Mary, has not (in my mind) been fully understood. ("La tensión" 5–6)

The stake in Schmitt's emphasis on the icon refers to the indissoluble unity of spiritual and temporal powers in the historic mission of the *respublica Christiana*: the sacred or messianic character of historical deeds from which *both* law *and* religion derive. Does God bear witness to, and bless, the profane acts of human fallibility? For Schmitt, this is the essential message of Christianity's contribution to international law. As he says elsewhere, "Christianity, quintessentially speaking, is neither morality, doctrine, sermon about penitence, nor is it a religion in the sense of something to be studied comparatively alongside other religions; rather, it is a historical event in its infinite uniqueness. It is the incarnation in [the form of] the Virgin" ("La tensión" 5–6). Beginning with the Incarnation, Christendom made international law possible insofar as the law would subsume all peoples under a universal history. It becomes possible to believe that a divine spirit manifests itself in the flesh of human history, endowing it with a principle and end that at once provide for the basis of international law and also endow it with a final end. As Paul's second letter to the Corinthians famously states, "The letter kills, the Spirit gives life" (2 Corinthians 3:6 [NIV]). Between this belief and any other (including nonbelief), there is no room for compromise.

Why would such a historic mission depend on icons to convey its universality? If we follow Schmitt's line of thinking here, the image of the Virgin Mary (likewise, for that matter, those of Jesus Christ and the saints) does not exist for the sake of allowing heathens and converts to imagine what she may have looked like; its function is only secondarily pedagogical. On a primary level, the image attests to the legitimacy of a Christian tradition that enjoys the authority of law or dogma, even (or especially) when that tradition contradicts *written* laws—the prototype of such laws being the Mosaic Law banning the production of idols. Mindful of this proscription and its deployment in the iconoclastic controversies of the Byzantine Empire and in the Lutheran and Calvinist reform movement against the Church, the Counter-Reformation Council of Trent (1545–1563) defended the Church's policy on the production of religious images as follows:

> The holy Synod enjoins on all bishops, and others who sustain the office and charge of teaching, that, agreeably to the usage of the Catholic and Apostolic Church, received from the primitive times of the Christian religion, and agreeably to the consent of the holy Fathers, and to the decrees of sacred Councils, they especially instruct the faithful diligently concerning the intercession and invocation of saints; the honor (paid) to relics; and the legitimate use of images: teaching them, that the saints, who reign together with Christ, offer up their own prayers to God for men; that it is good and useful suppliantly to invoke them, and to have recourse to their prayers, aid, (and) help for obtaining benefits from God, through His Son, Jesus Christ our Lord, who is our alone Redeemer and Saviour . . . . Moreover, that the images of Christ, of the Virgin Mother of God, and of the other saints, are to be had and retained particularly in temples, and that due honor and veneration are to be given them; *not that any divinity, or virtue, is believed to be in them, on account of which they are to be worshipped; or that anything is to be asked of them; or, that trust is to be reposed in images, as was of old done by the Gentiles who placed their hope in idols; but because the honor which is shown them is referred to the prototypes which those images represent.* (Council of Trent, 234–35, emphasis added)

This rather extensive passage means to highlight two aspects of Christian doctrine that exist in tension with one another, both directly pertaining to the spiritual conquest or evangelization of the Americas and the Philippines in the sixteenth and seventeenth centuries and its relation to the law. The first is that the holy doctrine of the intercession and invocation of saints through images comes not from the authority of Scripture but rather from "the usage of the Catholic and Apostolic Church, received from the primitive times of the Christian religion, and agreeably to the consent of the holy Fathers, and to the decrees of sacred Councils." To put it in a drastically schematic fashion, the authority of this doctrine arises from Church tradition, following the practices of the early Christians who interpreted the Gospel in this way, instead of deriving directly from the New Testament. Tradition, not scripture; the "spirit" of the letter and not the letter itself.

At the Second Council of Nicea in the eighth century, Patriarch Nikephorus of Constantinople defended the use of religious images against the iconoclast charge of idolatry when he cited the authority of images as part of Church tradition:

> In effect, in everything, custom has full power, and deeds prevail over words. To tell the truth, what is a law, if not a custom consigned to writing. *Conversely, custom is an unwritten law.* In effect, even amongst the grammarians, if by chance they happen to note in a text a discrepancy between a word and the prevailing rule, and seeing that custom is of a different opinion to that which is written down, they cite the tradition, arguing that it is the rule of the rule. (qtd. in Mondzain 130–31)

The formulation of tradition as "the rule of the rule" was, not surprisingly, pronounced by Nikephorus in order to defend the doctrine of religious images as icons. It is on this doctrine that the Council of Trent's iconophilic doctrine of images is based.

The second feature of the passage from the Council of Trent on the invocation of saints and the use of images, one with which we are of course more familiar, is that the veneration of images must in no way be confused with their worship; nor should their intercessory power be interpreted as a direct expression of God's will or of the will of the image that is invoked. The point in this qualification is to prevent what we might today call the "fetishization" of images, which would ascribe to them a will or power that is inherently connected to their appearance or substance. In a larger sense, however, it also betrays the Church's wish to limit the ambiguity unleashed by the idea of tradition—Church tradition, but also "tradition" more broadly—with respect to the law. If tradition had a say in determining or challenging the law, as the doctrine of the orthodoxy of images clearly shows, what were the limits of such recourse to expediency? To what degree was the Church, in fact, abetting new forms of paganism?

The term used by Nikephorus and other Church fathers for accepting tradition as the rule of the rule, the spirit of the letter, the life of the law, was *oikonomia*, economy. Marie-José Mondzain's extrapolation of this limit-concept within Church doctrine reads as follows: "The sacralization of custom is assimilated to the sacralization of the daily, profane world by he who accepted its bondage. Laws cannot be inflexibly applied, so great is human diversity, so fragile is the obedience of humans. In order for the law to be visible, it must be subjugated to its own conditions of application; it must, like Christ, humanize itself" (132). Let us remark on the following coincidence: just as the European powers were beginning to bring the labor and commodities of the Americas and Asia under a standard of value that would enable the emergence of a world economy, religious missionaries were transplanting the sacralization of custom, *oikonomia*, to Spain's new possessions. As we will see, this peculiar understanding of the law in its historical manifestation (as opposed to its formal or logical coherence or rationality), gives rise to divergent ways of reading imperial rule on the frontiers of Christendom.

Translating Traditions

How does the economy of Christian grace, its ability to "humanize" the law while simultaneously upholding and promoting it, translate into the early workings of the Spanish empire's historic mission overseas? We need look no further than the spread of religious images and the rise of devotional cults around them to trace the vicissitudes of the *respublica Christiana*, as the Spanish empire's historic mission ceased to possess legitimacy before the emergent powers that were redefining the basis of international law in the seventeenth century. In 1571 the soldiers of conquistador López de Legazpi find an image of the Virgin Mary on the banks of Manila Bay (present-day Ermita), elevated atop the trunk of a tree and surrounded by pandan leaves. Recognizing that the image had become an object of worship among the natives, they enshrined it as Our Lady of Guidance, with the understanding that the Virgin would intercede in assisting Spanish galleons to find their way into the bay. In naming the image after a popular devotion in Spain, Legazpi and the conquistadors immediately relate it to confraternities and churches of the same name (in Burgos, Pontevedra, Sevilla, and even the Canary Islands) prior to the discovery of Mary's image on the shores of Manila Bay. The spontaneous linkage via the name does not stop there: after López de Legazpi's successors built a chapel to shelter the image, subsequent administrators named the fort facing the chapel "Nuestra Señora de Guía"; later, a galleon was also named after this designation of the Virgin. Other early images of the Virgin follow a similar trajectory: the Virgin of the Rosary, instrumental in the defeat of the invading Dutch by the Spaniards, was reproduced as an insignia worn by all crew members of the Spanish fleet; Our Lady of Peace and Safe Passage, or the Virgin of Antipolo, traveled on board the galleons sailing the Pacific between Acapulco and Manila, protecting an otherwise largely incompetent enterprise marked by rampant corruption. This power of the icon is clearly at work in ambulatory and fluvial processions where the image is ceremoniously transferred [*traslación*] from the original site of its discovery to the nearby church.[5] By contact and contiguity, by the rhizomatic extension of the name to imagine, intend, project, or anticipate an underlying order, the Christian economy brings coherence and continuity to uncharted space and heterogeneous social relations, homogenizing them and disposing them to spiritual guidance and administration. In the absence of real networks of control and communication that would achieve such an objective, the Spanish empire depended upon what Serge Gruzinski calls a "baroque *imaginaire*" that simultaneously conjured the unknown recesses of the imagination and delivered them to an ideal order (see *Images at War* 96–160).

Here, the specificity of the Virgin as a limit-figure at once within and outside Christian theology, cannot be overlooked: above all other figures, she is the testament to the incarnation of the Word into flesh and theology into history. In the folds and arabesques of her mantle, all historical contingencies and flights of human freedom resolve themselves into a grand design (see fig. 1). Only this can explain the fervor with which the early conquistadors, up to and including Legazpi, devoted themselves to the cult of the Virgin Mary. By exposing the icon to the precarious conditions of their own existence—let us recall that Nuestra Señora de Guía was found perched atop a tree trunk, surrounded by a pile of pandan leaves placed there by heathens—the conquistadors bore witness to the sanctification of the life and activity of *all who encounter it*, elevating their day-to-day existence to a higher sphere of meaning.

"The institution of the icon," Marie-José Mondzain writes, "which it is not possible to frame or pin down, is the small-scale model of an ecclesiastic institution: it permits the production of rules for an open and profane space, which the church can traverse in all senses and appropriate for itself . . . . For

Fig. 1. Philippine image or *santo* María Santísima de la
Esperanza Macarena, Santa Maria, Bulacan (Philippines).
Courtesy of Francis Jason Díaz Pérez III.

the iconophile [. . .] everything that the icon invades becomes sacred and therefore the property of the ecclesiastical power" (162).

As a representation of the Church, the Virgin is thus the image *par excellence* of the Christian economy. By simultaneously emblematizing and relaying the Word into humanity, icons of the Virgin and saints engendered the fertile conditions for the Christian sacralization of all aspects of life. The icon endlessly converts its surroundings, transforming the relations of contingency, contact, and contiguity into those of continuity and coherence with the unfolding of a divine plan. On an institutional level, the icon designates a precinct around which a town or village may be reduced. On a cultural level, the icon claims for itself a feast day on the calendar, creates confraternities of devotion and worship, leads ambulatory and fluvial processions that sanctify the town space, and in some notable instances acquires fame as a shrine and destination of pilgrimages. By contact or invocation, the icon facilitates or dispenses divine intercession in the form of miracles. In the eyes of the Virgin, profane space becomes converted into *virgin territory*—a space traversed by a matrix of *imaginary* or *imaginable* relations wherein profane space may be redeemed.[6]

From an understanding of the icon's role in the organization of ecclesiastical space, we can see the double-sided nature of the economy/*oikonomia* and its unfolding in the project of evangelization. On the one hand, the economy and invention of tradition outlined the terms and conditions under which a particular community would become part of the Christian *respublica* and thereby predisposed to live under the administration of the Spanish Crown. On the other hand, as foundational narratives show, the economy and invention of tradition also stressed the necessity that the Christian *respublica* maintain faith in and with the life of the people who fall under the shadow of imperial law—up to the threshold of any possible systematic contradiction with Christian dogma. Conversely, the incorporation of the life, language, and customs of the colonized presented at once a prospect and a calculated risk to the Spanish Crown, if not to the Church itself. As a prospect, the legitimation of tradition facilitated the natives' submission to the sovereign and their acculturation to Spanish ways ("Hispanization"). As a risk, the limits to complete control of the imagination often led to "breaks in the system," wayward manifestations of religiosity. Colonial history is full of such examples—men and women claiming to be the Virgin Mary or Jesus Christ, holy images that play tricks on the populace and make blasphemous promises, native healers who cure ailments by divine intercession, etc.

When confronted with these and other claims, missionaries were placed in a difficult position: they were accountable to the *imaginaire* that they had unleashed on the native populace, yet they had to work with the circumstances in which such an imaginary order developed in the life of the colonial subject. Indeed, this ambivalence is inscribed in the foundational narratives of many cults of Christ, the Virgin Mary, and the saints in Spain, the Americas, and the Philippines.[7] As we have seen earlier, many such narratives feature a back-and-forth negotiation between the community of believers and the parish priest in which the image of the Virgin "wanders" outside her shrine to the site of her initial discovery, or where the image "resists" being taken to a parish or town out of seeming preference for another.[8] The errant character of these images reminds both priest and parishioners that they are each guests in the other's house and that, beyond the empty letters of laws that had no hope of being fulfilled, the economy of salvation provided a safety valve in the maintenance of a lasting, if unstable, relationship.

Virgin, icon, church tradition. Many scholars set out to examine the popular devotion to the Virgin Mary around the world by applying theological categories already supplied by the Church or by applying the social scientific criteria of a disenchanted, "modern" rationality.[9] Regarding these approaches, our discussion of the concepts of economy and tradition has sought to avoid focusing on either side of the theological-secular divide at the expense or subordination of the other. It seems to me that the unique role of the Virgin Mary is rather to demonstrate their underlying continuity and coherence. As both a historical personage and an allegorical figure of *history itself*, Mary's unique capacity to demonstrate the complementary nature of divine grace and human agency/free will is inseparable from the Church's capacity to ceaselessly calibrate the law of scripture and empire with the unwritten law of custom and tradition: submitting *akribeia* (respect for the rigorous application of the law) and *parabasis* (the law's transgression) to an intermediate and provisional sphere of judgment, also known as the economy or *oikonomia* of grace and redemption. That this sphere of judgment can be indissolubly linked at once to the individual experience of carnal intimacy and the universal pretensions of the world's largest institution: only this explains how it was possible for Virgin Mary to serve as a frame of reference both for the Christian marauders who decimated the New World with genocide, smallpox epidemics, and slavery and for the colonial subjects who, across geographical and linguistic divisions, came to identify themselves as members of one and the same community.[10] Finally, through the image as icon, the relationship between Mary and the Church moves beyond that of analogy. As a limit phenomenon, miracles dissolve the threshold between sacred and profane history: hollowing out a space where divine dispensation, the ramifications of institutional authority, and the "practice of everyday life" renegotiate the terms of their cohabitation.

The Sacred and the Obscene in the Practice of Philippine Folk Christianity

On the outskirts of the town of Dolores, Quezon province, approximately 200 kilometers outside Manila, lies the foot of Mt. Banahaw, a mountain that has been the site of religious pilgrimages since colonial times. Unlike most religious pilgrimages in the Philippines, however, these have never received official sanction or promotion by the Church. Missionaries identified it as a site of controversy, as the density of the forests and inaccessibility of the uneven terrain around the mountain made it a suitable place for unconverted and recently converted Christians to escape their forced settlement in Christianized communities. From almost the beginning of the colonial period to the nineteenth century, these pueblos were administered by a skeleton crew of Spanish officials and residents, which usually consisted of a priest or missionary, the major landowner (*encomendero*) by Crown grant, a government-appointed mayor (*alcalde-mayor*), and perhaps a native militia led by a Spanish petty officer (*alférez*). Until the nineteenth century, Spanish pioneers, traders, and adventurers were prohibited from settling outside Manila. As for the escaped refugees of forced Hispanic acculturation across the archipelago, called *remontados*, these sub-populations often created and maintained settlements just beyond the reach of Spanish officialdom; or picked up and moved to other towns, a mobile and transient labor force (see Scott; and Ileto).

The local residents of the towns around Mt. Banahaw refer to the many holy sites visited by religious pilgrims and tourists by using the Spanish word *puesto* (transliterated in Tagalog as *puwesto*); and the act of conducting a visit to these holy sites is *pamumuwesto*. These sites display natural wonders and miraculous signs that validate the legend of Mt. Banahaw as the New Jerusalem. Popular legend relates how God, angry with the Jews for turning away from the law and crucifying His only Son, sent four angels to transport Jerusalem by its four corners to the other side of the world. As fortune would have it, the angels accidentally "dropped" the city as they were placing it in Quezon province, where the city fell to the earth in inverted form. And all that was to be revealed on the outside became buried within, in the heart of the mountain, accessible only through the caves.[11] As Agripino Lontok, the hermit and mystic of the mountain around the turn of the twentieth century, knew, the Holy City only reveals itself in the traces left by Christ, Mary, Joseph, and the saints—a footprint of Christ at the bottom of a natural spring (Bakas), a cave that swallows unrepentant sinners alive (Husgado), the curative properties of certain waterfalls and springs. In a versified, anonymous first-person narrative of Agripino Lontok's religious experience, the narrator returns from his descent into a mountain cave with the following stanza:

At ito ang dala sa aking pagbalik
sa mundong ibabaw na di matahimik:
apoy sa puso at hangin ng langit,
handang ipamahagi ang nakamtang dikit
sa Kuweba ng Lahi, Bundok ng Ninuno,
Banahaw ang ngalan—ako'y kanyang sugo.

(A heart aflame, the wind of the heavens:
These are what I carry with me in my return
To the unquiet world above
 I, emissary (of New Jerusalem)
Prepared to share the grandeur I now carry within
From the cave of our Race, the mountain of our Ancestors
Banahaw its name.) (Mayuga)

Fig. 2. Makeshift shrine inside the *puwesto* Ina ng Awa (Mother of Mercy) cave (photo courtesy of author)

Fig. 3. Makeshift shrine to the Virgin Mary before the *puwesto* Husgado (Place of Judgment) cave (photo courtesy of author)

Fig. 4. Makeshift shrine atop outcropping boulders at the foot of the *puwesto* Sta. Lucia Falls (photo courtesy of author)

In addition to these miraculous signs, however, residents and travelers alike have established makeshift shrines throughout the area, which vary greatly in terms of the attention they attract and dedication to their upkeep (fig. 2–4). Some mimic the shrines that Philippine families regularly build in or around our houses, with an image of Christ or the Virgin Mary placed in a niche surrounded by cemented rocks. In others, these same images are placed like sentinels guarding entrances to a cave, or in elevated areas around the Sta. Lucia falls, where they gaze out and down at the surrounding riverbed from boulders streaked with candle wax and surrounded by withered garlands.

Gazing at the open display of these images and signs scattered across the mountain, behind waterfalls or perched atop promontories and exposed to the elements, one gets a sense of how natives must have reacted to the discovery of similar images throughout the archipelago during the colonial period: discoveries that most often serve as the foundation narratives of Christian communities and the erection of stone churches and shrines on the outskirts of the nearby pueblo (see Mojares 138–71). The open display of these religious images against the surrounding environment is striking, almost scandalous. Here they stand, randomly grouped together, exposed to the elements, not to mention the fingers and lips of devout pilgrims and the black soot from candles made of animal fat.

The sky is their ceiling; some of the images are even broken or chipped. But perhaps as scandalous as their exposure to the elements is the exposure of *nature* to the naked sovereignty of their gaze and the divine power that it implies. If Mt. Banahaw contains the mystic city of Jerusalem in its depths— a city that can only be glimpsed by signs that leak out to the "world above" in the form of a scene or display—the icon as a visible image also gestures toward the invisible archetype that is the divinity and commemorates its incarnation in human history. The Church never took this power lightly, which is why the doctrine of images has been in part responsible for both the East-West Schism in 1054 and the European wars of religion involving Catholic and Protestant sects in the sixteenth century.

The irruption and saturation of divine presence throughout the mountain through these makeshift shrines and their images convey an unruly, *obscene* display of spiritual authority. By using the word "obscene," my intention is not to evaluate this authority in a moralistic or ethical sense, but rather to emphasize the etymological prefix *ob-* (against, opposed to), to highlight a central technique of this authority—the abolition of distance and perspective.[12] This abolition of distance certainly accounts for the intensity of religious experience among the settled populations around the mountain, as evidenced by the proliferation of religious cults over the course of the past century (estimated to number around 60 in 1999; see Bernardo). Of greater importance, however, this characteristic of spiritual authority conveyed in the religious image captures the peculiar dynamic established between law and the Christian evangelizing effort on the frontiers of the Spanish empire in the seventeenth century. While one may view native conversion as ultimately facilitating the rationalization and coherence of a legal order, the Philippine case also demonstrates the formalization of that order's *incoherence, in and for the sake of law itself*. The implications of this argument point to a divergent way of understanding the intersection of law and religion in the context of frontier Christianity (i.e., in the Americas as well as Asia), which is often studied under the ideas of "juxtaposition," syncretism, hybridity, and transculturation but rarely in the context of Christian pastoral economy and theocracy. While ideas of hybridity and syncretism direct our attention to the transformation of native, Creole, and mixed-blood (*mestizo/a*) cultures in the Americas and the Philippines, they say nothing about how the law itself begins to anticipate and make provisions for its failure or breakdown on the colonial frontier, which allows the law to interact with native societies in surprising and original ways.

The sacralization of colonial space and the homogenization of the populace for the purposes of imperial rule should thus not lead us to misjudge the essentially anarchic character of this spiritual economy on the Spanish frontiers. In the Philippines, the cult of saints and the veneration of images involved the same operations devised by the religious missionaries of the sixteenth and seventeenth centuries. As I hope to have demonstrated, the suturing of native and Church traditions and the work of cultural homogenization through the imprecise character of religious orthodoxy centered on images and icons. At the same time, however, this focus contributed to the increasing autonomy of the spiritual power in relation to the temporal, and to the emergence of what Filomeno Aguilar calls a fragmented and feudalistic "friar power" throughout the archipelago. In promoting the cult of *santos*, missionary orders succeeded in erecting a bulwark against the reach of monarchical authority throughout the colonial period, by means of deploying a variety of strategies that I have studied elsewhere—the policy of *cúmplase* / " obedezco pero no cumplo" the preservation of ecclesiastical privilege, friar immunity against civil jurisdiction, and so forth (Blanco 64–94). In the middle of the eighteenth century, royal treasurer Gregorio de Viana summed up this authority as follows:

> [E]l despotismo de los Ministros Doctrineros es tan absoluto, como que casi son los únicos que mandan en estas Yslas, y que gobiernan a su arbitrio los Pueblos y

Provincias, y sin reconocer de V.M., ni obedecer mas leyes y reales ordenes, que las que convienen a sus intereses, y máximas, siendo constante y notorio, que en todo lo demás no obedecen sino a su voluntad, como lo justifica el que no hay ley, ni Cedula, ni ordenanza, que se observe por Los Doctrineros, en los puntos del Real Patronato; en la administración de los Sacramentos a los enfermos; en las Tanorías, y demás cosas en que se interesa la conveniencia; y sobre todo en las escuelas, para la enseñanza del idioma español. (40)

[T]he despotism of the ministers of the parishes has reached absolute extremes: it is as if they are almost the only ones who command in these islands; and they govern the villages and provinces according to their own rules, without recognizing your Majesty or obeying any laws or royal decrees beyond those which suit their own interests and rules, these being constant and outrageous, and obey no others except when they so desire it, as if justified by the fact that there is no law, affidavit, or Ordinance that these Preachers observe, particularly with regard to the rights of royal patronage, or the administration of Sacraments to the sick, or in the matter of enforced domestic service or any other matter pertaining to their convenience; and above all the question of schools, for the teaching of the Spanish language. (Blair and Robertson 50:118–36)

As I hope the Philippine case has shown, spiritual economy may facilitate the task of empire while simultaneously undermining it. This is because, at bottom, the messianic act of "humanizing" the law not only completes the law but also abolishes it.

Notes

1. A point of departure for understanding the importance of holy images, called *santos* in the Philippines, is Joaquin, *Culture and History* 61–69; and Joaquin, *Nick Joaquin* 15–35. For Our Lady of Caysasay, see Cruz. On the history of the cult of the Virgin in Antipolo, see *Breves noticias acerca de la Virgen de Antipolo* (anonymous); and Reed, in Forshee 151–206. For an account of urbanization in the nineteenth century, see Bernáldez Pizarro, folio 14 ("De las grandes poblaciones de Yndios"). An abbreviated version of this chapter appears in Blair and Robertson (eds.), v. 51, 181–262.
2. For a critique of this methodology regarding "base" and "superstructure," see Williams 75–82.
3. In a later work, Figgis adds, "[In the medieval period] the whole spirit of both is to identify Church and State. The Pagan State was also a Church, and the medieval Church was also a State; *the* Church and *the* State in theory. Each governs the whole of life and the problem is not whether you take power from one society and give it to

the other, but where you tilt the balance of authority—on to the side of the lay officials or to that of the clerics" (Figgis, *Political* 78).
4. Schmitt, "La tensión planetaria" 61–62 and 112–13.
5. For an example of this procession, see Gorospe, S.J., and Javellana, S.J.
6. My discussion on the sacralization of space takes inspiration from Deleuze and Guattari's distinction between "striated" and "smooth" spaces (474–500).
7. For Spain, see William Christian, *Local Religion*; and Gruzinski, *Images* 96–160. On baroque culture as mass culture, see Maravall 57–145.
8. For the Santo Niño de Cebu, see Joaquin, *Culture and History* 60–69.
9. With regard to the former, one may cite the remarkably small amount of attention she is given in the New Testament and end with the popular movement to have the Church canonize Mary's role as Co-Redemptrix, Mediatrix, and Advocatrix of the divine plan. With regard to the latter, anthropological and sociological studies such as those of William Christian Jr., Marina Warner, Sandro Sticca, and Victor Turner and Edith Turner have highlighted various factors that render the devotion, if not worship, of the Holy Virgin entirely "reasonable," or at least explicable in human terms: see Christian, *Apparitions*; and Reed, in Forshee, 151–206. In this respect, the cults of the Virgin Mary and the saints merely draw upon an authority that empires and institutions have already bestowed upon the Catholic Church.
10. On the Virgin of the Rosary (Virgen del Rosario) and the Virgin of Guadalupe (Virgen de Guadalupe), see Hall 178.
11. For a popular retelling of this story by a German tourist, see www.malapascua.de/Volcanoe-Map/Mount_Banahaw/hauptteil_mount_banahaw.html. Last accessed 1 March 2011.
12. This reading is inspired in part by Jean Baudrillard's use of the term in "On the Ecstasy of Communication," in Foster 126–33.

Works Cited

Aguilar, Filomeno. *Clash of Spirits: The History of Power and Sugar Planter Hegemony on a Visayan Island*. Honolulu: University of Hawaii Press, 1998. Print.

Anghie, Antony. "Francisco de Vitoria and the Colonial Origins of International Law." *Social & Legal Studies* 5 (1996): 321–36. Print.

Baudrillard, Jean. "On the Ecstasy of Communication." *The Anti-Aesthetic: Essays in Postmodern Culture*. Ed. Hal Foster. New York: The New Press, 2002. 126–33. Print.

Bernáldez Pizarro, Manuel. *Dictamen sobre las causas que se oponen a la seguridad y fomento de las Yslas Filipinas y providencias que exigen para remedio*. Manuscript, 1827. Print.

Bernardo, Troy. "The Altar of Mt. Banahaw." *Filipino Spirituality*, 5 Oct. 2001. Web. 1 April 2011.

Blair, Emma, and James Robertson, eds. *The Philippine Islands, 1493–1898: Explorations by early navigators, descriptions of the islands and their peoples, their history and records of the Catholic Missions, as related in contemporaneous books and manuscripts, showing the political, economic, commercial and religious conditions of those islands from their earliest relations with European nations to the beginning of the nineteenth century.* 53 vols. Cleveland: A. H. Clark, 1962. Print.

Blanco, John. *Frontier Constitutions: Christianity and Colonial Empire in the Nineteenth-Century Philippines.* Berkeley: University of California Press, 2009. Print.

Breves noticias acerca de la Virgen de Antipolo (anonymous). Manila: E. D. McCullough and Co., 1904. Print.

Büchner, Andere. "Banahaw, Holy Mountain of the Philippines." *Mt. Banahaw, Luzon, Philippines.* Manila Times. 28 March 2004. Web. 1 April 2011.

Christian, William A. *Local Religion in Sixteenth-Century Spain.* Princeton: Princeton University Press, 1981. Print.

———. *Apparitions in Late Medieval and Renaissance Spain.* Princeton: Princeton University Press, 1989. Print.

Cruz, Dierdre de la. *All His Instruments: Mary, Miracles, and the Media in the Catholic Philippines.* Diss. Columbia University, 2006. Ann Arbor: ProQuest, UMI Dissertations Publishing. Print.

Deleuze, Gilles, and Felix Guattari. *A Thousand Plateaus: Capitalism and Schizophrenia.* Trans. Brian Massumi. Minneapolis: University of Minnesota Press, 1988. Print.

Díaz del Castillo, Bernal. *The Memoirs of the Conquistador Bernal Díaz del Castillo; Written By Himself; Containing a True and Full Account of the Discovery and Conquest of Mexico and New Spain.* vol. 1. Trans. John Ingram Lockhart. London: J. Hatchard and Son, Piccadilly, 1844. Print.

Figgis, John N. *Churches and the Modern State.* London, New York: Longmans, Green, and Co. 1913. Print.

———. *The Political Aspects of Saint Augustine's* City of God. London: Longmans, 1921.

Forshee, Jill, Christina Fink, and Sandra Cate, eds. *Converging Interests: Traders, Travelers, and Tourists in Southeast Asia.* Berkeley: International and Area Studies, University of California at Berkeley, 1999. Print.

Gorospe, Vitalino, S.J., and René Javellana, S.J. *The Virgin of Peñafrancia: Mother of Bicol.* Manila: Bookmark, 1995. Print.

Gruzinski, Serge. *Images at War: Mexico from Columbus to* Blade Runner *(1492–2019).* Durham, NC: Duke University Press, 2001. Print.

Hall, Linda. *Mary, Mother and Warrior: the Virgin in Spain and the Americas.* Austin: University of Texas Press, 2004. Print.

Ileto, Reynaldo. "Reflections from Microhistory" (n.d., typescript). Print.

Joaquin, Nick. *Culture and History: Occasional Notes on the Process of Philippine Becoming.* Manila: Solar Pub. Corp., 1988. Print.

———. *Nick Joaquin Revisited: La Naval de Manila and Other Essays.* Ed. Alberto S. Florentino. Manila: De la Salle University Press, 1998. Print.

Maravall, José Antonio. *Culture of the Baroque: Analysis of a Historical Structure.* Trans. Terry Cochran. Minneapolis: University of Minnesota Press, 1986. Print.
Mayuga, Sylvia. "On Holy Week Pilgrimage." *Inquirer.net.* 3 April 2007. Web. 1 April 2011.
Mojares, Resil. "Stalking the Virgin: The Genealogy of the Cebuano Virgin of Guadalupe." *Philippine Quarterly of Culture and Society* 30 (2002): 138–71. Print.
Mondzain, Marie-José. *Image, Icon, Economy: The Byzantine Origins of Modern Art.* Trans. Rico Franses. Stanford: Stanford University Press, 2005. Print.
Reed, Robert. "The Cult of the Virgin of Antipolo." *Converging Interests: Traders, Travelers, and Tourists in Southeast Asia.* Ed. Jill Forshee, Christina Fink, and Sandra Cate. Berkeley: International and Area Studies, University of California at Berkeley, 1999. 151–206. Print.
Schmitt, Carl. *Nomos of the Earth in the International Law of* Jus Publicum Europaeum. Trans. G. L. Ulmen. New York: Telos Press, 2003. Print.
———. "La tensión planetaria entre Oriente y Occidente y la oposición entre Tierra y Mar," *Revista de Estudios Políticos* 81 (1955): 3–28. Print.
Scott, William Henry. *Barangay.* Quezon City, Philippines: Ateneo de Manila University Press, 1994.
Sticca, Sandro. "The Montecasino Passion and the Origin of the Latin Passion Play." *Italica* 44: 2 (June, 1967): 209–19.
———. The *Planctus Mariae in the Dramatic Tradition of the Middle Ages.* Athens: University of Georgia Press, 1988.
Tavárez, David, and John F. Chuchiak. "Conversion and The Spiritual Conquest of the New World." *Religion and Society in Latin America: Interpretive Essays from the Conquest to the Twenty-first Century.* Eds. Lee Penyak and Walter J. Petry. Maryknoll, NY: Orbis Books, 2008. 51–77. Print.
Turner, Victor, and Edith Turner. *Image and Pilgrimage in Christian Culture.* New York: Columbia University Press, 1995. Print.
Viana, Don Francisco Leandro de, Fiscal de la Audiencia de Manila. *Libro de cartas, y consultas, dirigidas á su Majestad y Señores Ministros en el año de 1767.* Bound handwritten manuscript: 1767. Manuscript.
Warner, Marina. *Alone of All Her Sex: The Myth and the Cult of the Virgin Mary.* New York: Vintage, 1983. Print.
Watts, Pauline Moffitt. "Prophecy and Discovery: On the Spiritual Origins of Christopher Columbus's 'Enterprise of the Indies.'" *American Historical Review* 90.1 (1985): 73–102. Print.
Williams, Raymond. *Marxism and Literature.* Oxford: Oxford University Press, 1978. Print.

◆ Afterword:
Teleiopoesis at the Crossroads
of the Colonial/Postcolonial Divide

José Rabasa

> *Teleiopoiós* qualifies, in a great number of contexts and semantic orders, that which *renders* absolute, perfect, completed, accomplished, finished, that which brings to an end. But permit us to play too with the other *tele*, the one that speaks to distance and the far removed, for what is indeed in question here is a poetics of distance at one remove, and of an absolute acceleration in the spanning of space by the very structure of the sentence (it begins at the end, it is initiated with the signature of the other).
>
> Jacques Derrida, *The Politics of Friendship* 32

The essays included in this volume participate in the dual definition of *tele* that Derrida succinctly lays out in this passage from his essay "Loving in Friendship: Perhaps," the second chapter of *The Politics of Friendship*. The assumption of the existence of design and purpose in nature and history—that is, of development toward an end—corresponds to the first meaning of the term *tele*. The second meaning of *tele*, which suggests an opening, is more obscure and calls for a reminder of a sentence by Nietzsche that underlies Derrida's comment: "Alas! If only you knew how soon, how very soon, things will be—different" (qtd. in Derrida, *Politics* 31). The final word, "different," invokes a future philosophy stated in the conditional: "if only you knew." The "perhaps" in the title, "Loving in Friendship: Perhaps," a recurrent punctuation device throughout the essay, questions but also inaugurates the possibility of forming a community. In our case, the community would be defined at the interstices of the colonial/postcolonial divide. Whereas the colonial defines the distant place from which writers, painters, speakers, dreamers, and rebellious souls speak to us, the postcolonial belongs to that place in which we would remain vigilant of all forms of colonialism. In the instead of the *tele* that institutionalizes an end, Derrida invokes the end that defines the possibility of a beginning of *difference*. Whereas many of the essays rightfully remind us that modern forms of imperialism were first implemented in the early colonization of the Americas, we must also remember (and learn to listen to) those colonial subjects writing, painting, singing, and what not (i.e., cooking, dancing, praying, loving) for future audiences at the crossroads of the colonial/postcolonial divide.

Let us keep in mind that postcoloniality consists of a broad range of situations and definitions, from the postcolonial state that achieved independence in the aftermath of World War II to a theoretical vigilance on the ways scholarship and politics reproduce colonial forms of domination. Postcoloniality, understood as a period following a history of colonialism, is not exempt from internal colonialisms, as witnessed in the states formed following the wars of independence in Latin America and, for that matter, in postcolonial states in Africa and Asia. I would argue, though some of my friends in colonial/postcolonial studies may strongly disagree, that the state is by definition a colonial institution—namely, the decolonization of the state is an oxymoron. It is on the basis of the postcolonial as systematic vigilance of the recurrent forms of colonialism that scholars, writers, and filmmakers have come to recognize voices in the distant past that sought future souls to resonate with. It is all about listening to the voices from the past but also listening to each other in our differences. For the postcolonial imagination dreams of worlds comprised of singularities. Not a multicultural world that is all too easily appropriated but a world in which we systematically interrogate the grounds of friendship. We ought to welcome Michel de Montaigne's turn of the phrase that he attributes to Aristotle: "O my friends, there is no friend." Montaigne's apostrophe asserts the absence of a secure ground of agreement. The task may consist of a will to disagree and debate—indeed, to cultivate the dangers of remaining in solitude.

While writing, inevitably from a postcolonial condition (defined minimally from the fact that, even if under the influx of new forms of empire, Latin America is no longer subject to a colonial regime—Puerto Rico being the exception), the essays in this volume draw lessons from a wide array of colonial-era pictorial and written texts for learning to circumvent and resist the violence that characterizes our time. For while there was a genocide in the times of Bartolomé de las Casas, Juan Ginés de Sepúlveda, José de Acosta, Bernardo de Vargas Machuca, Juan Buenaventura Zapata y Mendoza, and the anonymous painters of saints in the Philippines, to name just a few references—I cannot even try to exhaust the corpus constituted in the essays—ours too is an age of genocide, perhaps even more insidious. The moralizations of violence in the past pale in comparison to our own moral high ground. Lest we forget this, our hubris will betray insensitivity toward those who preceded us in fault while anticipating our own shortcomings. For although the essays document how the modernity that first emerged in the early colonial period continues to haunt our present, they also remind us of the imaginings in colonial texts that call on us to recognize possible articulations of postcoloniality. Shuttling back and forth over the colonial/postcolonial divide is inherent to imperial enterprises.

All the essays in the volume share the notion that the discovery and conquest of the New World, beginning in 1492, marked the beginnings of modernity. As in the case of all periodization, we have come to agree—and perhaps, hopefully also to disagree—on the beginnings that postulate a point zero, a moment when it all started. The grounds of disagreement would, obviously, also include those scholars who question the notion that there was ever a colonial regime in Latin America at all, favoring instead the concept of the *virreinato*. It remains to be thought whether the *virreinato* was in fact a modern institution resulting from the 1492 watershed. At any rate, in this periodization of modernity, the thought of such radically different thinkers, such as the Peruvian sociologist Aníbal Quijano and the German political theorist Carl Schmitt, shares a common ground. Personally, I have strong reservations on the totalizing effort of world system theories (Quijano) and universalizing principles of imperialist dominion (Schmitt), that constitute a singular modernity that ultimately privileges (even if to condemn it) European expansionism as comprising all forms of life. For while European modernity can be defined, perhaps, in unambiguous terms, I would argue that at least in the case of the experience of Amerindians, the condition or exigency of being part of modernity—minimally in the demand to interact with institutions that were imported into the Americas—does not, should not exclude the possibility of also dwelling in worlds that cannot be subsumed under modernity or capitalism. These are able subjects of colonial regimes who were forced to deal with European institutions often from spaces that we may define as non-capitalist and non-modern. I prefer the suffix *non-* to *pre-* because of the built-in teleology of the latter, an instance of the *teleiopoetic* that, in Derrida's diagnosis, "*renders* absolute, perfect, completed, accomplished, finished, that which brings to an end."

Under Quijano's or Schmitt's periodization, all participants in the colonial world would be by definition part of modernity. Las Casas and Sepúlveda, Vargas Machuca, or the historian of Tlaxcala, Buenaventura Zapata, to mention just a few of the authors discussed in the volume, all participate in modernity. One might say that, under this formulation, there was no space outside of modernity. Arguably, this position has become habitual in our reflections on modernity, whether in the mode of dominant or of alternative conceptualizations.

There is little room for what may be considered as merely non-modern, as radically distinct from a *tele*, that privileges a *not yet* modern. The colonial pictorial and written texts examined in the essays seem, at least to me, to suggest the recognition of plural-world forms of dwelling. As several of the authors argue, we find texts (European and indigenous) that interrogate developmental inevitability.

In the remainder of this afterword, I will invoke two instances of *teleiopoesis* in colonial texts that open possible thought in the future; one is by a European, the other by a Nahua. I will privilege the work of Bartolomé de las Casas for the radical invention of future thinkers who might make a difference. Instances of such a reception can be found in diverse forms of expression ranging from the Centro Bartolomé de las Casas in San Cristóbal de las Casas, Chiapas (an organization that continues the long struggle initiated by the Dominican friar in the sixteenth century), to Icíar Bollaín's *También la lluvia*. (In this 2010 film, a character playing Las Casas runs through the gamut of possible objections to the semblance of a counter-imperial Las Casas—note that this film juxtaposes the peripeteia endured by a film crew intent on making a film about the Spanish conquest when they find themselves immersed in and documenting the 2000 *guerra del agua* in Cochabamba, Bolivia). As a supplement to Derrida's definition of the *teleiopoetic*, I will appeal to an influential theoretician of postcolonial and subaltern studies—namely, Gayatri Chakravorty Spivak.

From a European perspective, we find an instance of *teleiopoesis* in Las Casas's dismantling of the concept of development—whose meaning is bound to a *tele* defined by the passage from latency to fulfillment or by the progress from an earlier to a later stage—in his dissolution of the civilization/barbarism binary. The long tradition of authoritative readings of Las Casas that emphasize his contribution to the recognition that "all men are born equal" (hence, that all men can be educated) needs to be countered by learning to read the strategies Las Casas deployed for neutralizing developmental tropes. The utopian figure of the noble savage counters the transparency of the civilization vs. barbarism binary. Spivak offers an entry for reading figuration when she writes, "the meaning of the figure is undecidable . . . we must attempt to dis-figure it, read the logic of the metaphor" (*Death* 71). For Spivak, dis-figuring would resist the "clamor for the rational destruction of the figure, the demand for not clarity but immediate comprehensibility by ideological average" (71). *Teleiopoesis* is very much in Spivak's mind in this passage, in the book as a whole, and we may trace the options laid out by Derrida in the epigraph cited at the start of this essay: Spivak juxtaposes "rational destruction for immediate comprehensibility" with what she refers to as the "force of literature as cultural good," which in my reading points to de-figuring as manifesting its logic to further the undecidable.

By emphasizing the fact that Las Casas's critique of the civilization/barbarism binary anticipates the United Nation's 1948 Universal Declaration of Human Rights, we offer a clear instance of "that which *renders* absolute, perfect, completed, accomplished, finished, that which brings to an end." Another option is to consider the violence implied in the recognition that all people can be educated, developed, brought into the fold of civilization—indeed, that all people are equal. But let's examine the *teleiopoetic* in Las Casas in greater detail and suspend the rush to reduce his thought to "immediate comprehensibility by ideological average."

One take on Las Casas's interrogation of the binary rests on a reading of the last section of the *Apologetica historia sumaria*, which relativizes the term "barbarism" by analyzing its possible referents. A question that recurs in scholarship on Las Casas is whether the Dominican friar in this book (or others such as the *Tratado comprobatorio . . . sobre las Indias. Año 1552*) reintroduces a version of the binary by creating a hierarchy of truth that posits the superiority of Christianity. This gesture inevitably assumes the superiority of our own understandings of and openness to cultural differences. As such we are finally able to *render absolute* the thought that remained imperfect in Las Casas. Although Las Casas throughout his life remained a Christian, more specifically a Catholic—indeed, an adherent to universalism—we ought to keep in mind that not all Catholics thought alike and that, perhaps, his ultimate point was to unleash an infinite polemic on what it meant to claim Christianity. Las Casas was also throughout his life a subject of the Spanish empire, a condition that did not keep him from denouncing the whole enterprise of the Americas, indeed, from calling for the dismantling of the colonial project. Could Las Casas be otherwise than a Catholic? Yes, he could have fled Spain to join the communities of *marranos* or Protestants in, say, Amsterdam. But that would have made him ineffectual in Spain's internal politics. Then again, we must also ask ourselves whether we, today, can sidestep debates on the meaning of democracy.

Las Casas's *teleiopoesis* can be illuminated through the utopian figure of the *buen salvaje*, or noble savage, who in Las Casas can be read as laying out the semantic field underlying the civilization vs. barbarism binary. Let's pursue the figure of the noble savage as an undecidable one and attempt to read the logic of the metaphor. Consider the following prototypical instance of the *buen salvaje*, one that can be found in many places in Las Casas's work:

> Las gentes de las islas de los Lucayos, que el almirante descubrió las primeras ... Todas a una mano, hombres, y mujeres, eran de aspectos angélico ... y es necesario que así sea dispusición todas por la mayor parte de estas Indias, porque, como habemos dicho, es aspecto y figura del cielo y la virtud de las estrellas ... esta graciosa y hermosa dispusición destas gentes favorecen.
>
> (The people from the island of the Lucayos, the first discovered by the admiral ... All of them, men and women, had angelical features. ... And it is necessary that it should be so over the most part of this Indies, because, as we have said it, the semblance and figure of the sky and the virtue of the stars ... Favor the gracious and beautiful disposition of these peoples. [*Apologética historia sumaria*, I:178–79])

This passage could be taken as an instance of Las Casas's blindness toward the different Amerindian peoples. It could also be taken as an indication of Las Casas's definition of Amerindians as weak, feeble subjects, incapable of resisting the Spanish conquest. The argument would insist that this version of the noble savage distorts the real Indian, as if Las Casas were making empirical factual statements rather than constructing a utopian figure. As we remain vigilant of the *tele* that might lead to its deadening in a transparent concept, we need to learn to disfigure the noble savage in order to understand the force of its metaphoricity. Allow me to cite an essay I wrote years ago that builds on Johannes Fabian's *Time and the Other*:

> Fabian here calls into question all the supposed attributes that enable the West to claim superiority over the "rest" of the world, and projects a utopian scenario where the Time of the Other invades the West; one recognizes these topics in Las Casas's rebuttals of the political and economic lack of self-sufficiency attributed to Amerindian cultures. By juxtaposing Fabian and Las Casas we may define a historical narrative where from the start of European expansionism in the sixteenth century there was an eminent collapse of the myth that placed universal priority in the West's historico-temporal patterns. (Rabasa, "Utopian" 270)

It is precisely in the space that anticipates that the "Time of the Other Invades the West" where the non-modern emerges as a rem(a)inder outside the absorption of all life by capital. As such, the noble savage figure conveys a logic that renders oxymoronic all calls for development or education. In the end, who is to say that God has not chosen to reveal truth directly to the Amerindians without need of an apostle? Who has the temerity to define the terms and meaning of revealed truth, of what it means to be Christian?

I have cited Spivak's *Death of a Discipline*, which offers a call for a new comparative literature, a call that implies a critique of the models defined under the auspices of world literature. This critique has been reiterated in her more recent *An Aesthetic Education in the Era of Globalization*. My reading of Las Casas's utopian figure of the noble savage aims to differentiate the *world* and the *global* from the *planetary*, to borrow Spivak's term in her discussion of the undesirability of the concept of world literature as the basis for a new comparative literature (see chapter 3 of *Death of a Discipline*). I and (to my mind) Las Casas would agree with Spivak's concluding comments on the future of the planet: "The planetarity of which I have been speaking in these pages is perhaps best imagined from the precapitalist cultures of the planet" (*Death* 101). Although the gist of this volume is comparative—Spanish, creole, mestizo, imperialist, anti-imperialist, Nahuatl, Quechua, and Filipino texts coexist and converse with each other—full-blown comparisons tend to be suspended in favor of montage, juxtaposing the texts and certainly suspending any notion that they form part of world literature. As this turn was not articulated in the volume, I remain subject to correction. But that is the point, my friends—remember, there is no friend. Indeed, these non-modern and non-capitalist forms of life might be understood both as communities to come and as the remains of development's claims on the globalization of the whole planet. Even though I would suspend the assumption of a shared set of values regarding comparative models of world literature, I would hope for a future in which these essays will be read against the grain of homogenizing models that disregard the need to read in the original languages, more emphatically indigenous languages such as Nahuatl and Quechua explored in three of the essays in the collection.

Let me conclude by citing an instance of *teleiopoesis* in the work of Domingo de San Antón Muñón Chimalpahin Quahtlehuanitzin, the great historian of Chalco:

> Ayc polihuiz ayc ylcahuiz, mochipa pialoz, ticpiazque yn titepilhuan in titeixhuihuan in titeyccahuan in titemintonhuan in titepiptonhuan in titechichicahuan, in tetentzonhuan in titeyxquamolhuan in titeteyztihuan, in titetlapallohuan in titehezçohuan, intitlayllotlacatepilhuan, in ipan otiyolque otitlacatque in icce tlaxillacalyacatl moteneuhua Tlayllotlacan Tecpan, y huel oncan catca y huel oncan omotlahtocatillico yn izquintin in tlaçohuehuetque in tlaçotlahtoque chichimeca, in tlayllotlacatlahtoque in tlayllotlacateteuhctin, ynic mitohua inin tlahtolli "Tlayllotlacan Tecpan pielli." (Chimalpáhin, *Las ocho relaciones*, II: 272–73)

> (Never will it be lost or forgotten. It will always be kept, because we will keep it. We who are the younger brothers, the children, the grandchildren, the great-grand-

children, the great-great-grandchildren, the very elders. We who are their beard, their eyebrow, their color and blood. We who are the descendants of the Tlailotlaca, who have been born and live in the first *tlaxillacalyacatl*, called Tlailotlacan Tecpan, where the rulers, the beloved ancients and beloved *tlatoque* Chichimeca, the *tlatoque* and *teuctin tlailotlaca*. Hence it is called "Tlailotlacan Tecpan archive." [my translation])

This closing passage from Chimalpahin anticipates future readers of "we who are their beard, their eyebrow, their color and blood." Perhaps in the future Chimalpahin will speak to us of ways to write history, or simply to write, that complicate our narrative structures, our desires for clarity and absolute certainty, our privileging of authors, our tendency to shut down debates by deploying allegedly definitive truths. I am glad to say that the essays in this volume lay out the beginnings for a reassessment of the historiography of the colonial/postcolonial divide that should inspire future generations of readers.

Works Cited

Bollaín, Icíar. *También la lluvia*. Morena Films, 2010. Film.
Casas, Bartolomé de Las. *Apologética historia sumaria*. Ed. Edmundo O'Gorman. 2 vols. Mexico City: Universidad Nacional Autónoma de México, 1967. Print.
———. *Tratado comprobatorio sobre las Indias. Año 1552*. Facsimile. Intro. Eduardo Aznar Vallejo and Trans. Gloria Díaz Padilla. Tenerife, Spain: Universidad de la Laguna, 1996. Print.
Chimalpáhin, Domingo. *Las ocho relaciones y el memorial de Colhuacan*. Paleography and translation by Rafael Tena. 2 vols. Mexico City: Consejo Nacional para la Cultura y las Artes, 1998. Print.
Derrida, Jacques. "Loving in Friendship: Perhaps." *The Politics of Friendship*. Trans. George Collins. London: Verso, 2000. 26–48. Print.
Quijano, Aníbal. "Coloniality of Power and Eurocentrism in Latin America." *International Sociology* 15.2 (2000): 215–32. Print.
Rabasa, José. "Utopian Ethnology in Las Casas's *Apologética*." *1492–1992: Re/Discovering Colonial Writing*. Hispanic Issues 4. Ed. René Jara and Nicholas Spadaccini. Minneapolis: The Prisma Institute, 1989. 263–89. Print.
Schmitt, Carl. *The Nomos of the Earth in the International Law of Jus Publicum Europaeum*. Trans. G. L. Ulmen. New York: Telos Press, 2003. Print.
Spivak, Gayatri Chakravorty. *An Aesthetic Education in the Era of Globalization*. Cambridge, MA: Harvard University Press, 2012. Print.
———. *Death of a Discipline*. New York: Columbia University Press, 2003. Print.

◆ Contributors

Santa Arias is an associate professor of Spanish at the University of Kansas. Besides numerous articles, she has authored the monograph *Retórica, historia y polémica: Bartolomé de las Casas y la tradición intelectual renacentista* (2001) and coedited three volumes: *Mapping Colonial Spanish America: Places and Commonplaces of Identity, Culture and Experience* (2002); *Approaches to Teaching the Writings of Bartolomé de las Casas* (2008); and *The Spatial Turn: Interdisciplinary Perspectives* (2008). Her new book project concerns the politics of geographical discourse in late eighteenth-century narratives about the Americas.

Ralph Bauer is an associate professor of English and Comparative Literature at the University of Maryland, College Park. His publications include *The Cultural Geography of Colonial American Literatures: Empire, Travel, Modernity* (2003/2006); *An Inca Account of the Conquest of Peru* (2005); and (coedited with José Antonio Mazzotti) *Creole Subjects in the Colonial Americas: Empires, Texts, Identities* (2009).

John D. (Jody) Blanco teaches Filipino, Latin American, and Asian/American literatures and cultural studies at the University of California, San Diego. He is the author of *Frontier Constitutions: Christianity and Colonial Empire in the Nineteenth-Century Philippines* (2009/2010). He has also translated Julio Ramos's *Divergent Modernities in Latin America* (2001). His current research examines the rise of early trans-Pacific forms of cultural globalization during the sixteenth and seventeenth centuries.

Delia Cosentino is an associate professor in the History of Art and Architecture Department at DePaul University in Chicago. She is author of *Las Joyas de Zinacantepec: Arte Colonial en el Monastery de San Miguel* (2007). She curated the exhibition *Reverence Renewed: Colonial Andean Art from the Thoma Collection* (2009) and has published essays on Nahua pictorial genealogies.

Mónica Díaz is an assistant professor at Georgia State University, where she teaches colonial Latin American literature and culture. She is the author of numerous articles and the book *Indigenous Writings from the Convent: Negotiating Ethnic Autonomy in Colonial Mexico* (2010).

Kris Lane holds the France V. Scholes Chair in Colonial Latin American History at Tulane University. He is the author of *Colour of Paradise: The Emerald in the Age of Gunpowder Empires* (2010), *Quito 1599: City and Colony in Transition* (2002), and *Pillaging the Empire: Piracy in the Americas, 1500–1750* (1998). He has also annotated and edited the writings of Bernardo de Vargas Machuca (2010). His current project traces the history of slavery and penal servitude in the Potosí mint.

Laura León Llerena is an assistant professor of Latin American literature at Northwestern University. Her research focuses mainly on sixteenth- and seventeenth-century colonial Latin America, exploring themes of translation and colonization of indigenous languages, and narratives of definition and redefinition of social and cultural identities in early colonial contexts.

Raúl Marrero-Fente is professor of Spanish and law at the University of Minnesota. He is the author of *Trayectorias globales: estudios coloniales en el mundo hispánico* (2013); *Bodies, Texts, and Ghosts: Writing on Literature and Law in Colonial Latin America* (2010); *Epic, Empire and Community in the Atlantic World: Silvestre de Balboa's* Espejo de Paciencia (2008); *Playas del árbol: Una visión trasatlántica de las literaturas hispánicas* (2002); *La poé-*

tica de la ley en las Capitulaciones de Santa Fe (2000); and *Al margen de la tradición: Relaciones entre la literatura colonial y peninsular de los siglos XV, XVI, y XVII* (1999). He is currently working on a book project entitled *A Global History of Imperialism and Colonialism in the Hispanic and Lusophone Worlds, 1400–1600.*

Kelly McDonough is an assistant professor of colonial literatures and cultures at the University of Texas at Austin. Her research focuses primarily on Mexican and indigenous studies, with an emphasis on postconquest Nahua intellectualism, indigenous cultural and linguistic revitalization projects, and decolonizing methodologies. Her first book, *Reading and Writing Nahuas: Mexican Indigenous Intellectuals from the Colonial Period through Today*, will be published in 2013 by the University of Arizona Press as part of the First Peoples: New Directions in Indigenous Studies initiative.

José Rabasa teaches in the Department of Romance Languages and Literatures at Harvard University. He is the author of *Tell Me the Story of How I Conquered You: Elsewhere and Ethnosuicide in the Colonial Mesoamerican World* (2011); *Without History: Subaltern Studies, the Zapatista Insurgency, and the Specter of History* (2010); *Writing Violence on the Northern Frontier: The Historiography of Sixteenth-Century New Mexico and Florida and the Legacy of Conquest* (2000); and *Inventing America: Spanish Historiography and the Formation of Eurocentrism* (1993). He is the co-editor of The *Oxford History of Historical Writing*, vol. 3, 1400-1800 (2012).

Cristian Roa is an associate professor of Latin American and Latino studies at the University of Illinois at Chicago. He is the author of *Histories of Infamy: Francisco López de Gómara and the Ethics of Spanish Imperialism* (2005) and coeditor of *Chimalpahin's Conquest: A Nahua Historian's Rewriting of Francisco López de Gómara's* La conquista de México (2010). He has published in journals such as *Hispanic Review, Confluencia, Revista Chilena de Literatura,* and *Colonial Latin American Review.*

Ana M. Rodríguez-Rodríguez is an assistant professor of early modern Spanish literature at the University of Iowa. Her work focuses on Christian-Muslim relations in the Mediterranean during the sixteenth and seventeenth centuries. Currently she is writing a book exploring Spanish textual representations of the phenomenon of captivity during this period and preparing a critical edition of the *Libro de cassos impensados*, by Alonso de Salamanca. She also works on the Spanish presence in the Philippines during the first centuries of colonial rule. She completed a PhD at the University of Wisconsin-Madison in 2007 and is currently finishing a second PhD at the Universidad Complutense de Madrid.

David M. Solodkow is an associate professor at the Universidad de los Andes (Bogotá, Colombia). His areas of expertise are colonial studies with an emphasis on racial and ethnic classification and ethnographic writing. He has published two co-edited books: *Poéticas de lo criollo. La transformación del concepto 'criollo' en las letras hispanoamericanas (siglos XVI al XIX)* (2009), in collaboration with Juan Vitulli, and *Perspectivas sobre el Renacimiento y el Barroco* (2011). He completed the PhD at Vanderbilt University in 2009.

Ezekiel Stear is a PhD candidate in the Department of Spanish and Portuguese at the University of Kansas. His doctoral research focuses on Nahua intellectuals' responses to Christianization and Spanish policies during the sixteenth and seventeenth centuries.

Ivonne del Valle is an assistant professor at the University of California, Berkeley and is interested in the interface of Christianity, technology, colonialism, and globalization. She is currently working on two projects: one on the drainage of the lakes of Mexico City in which she studies the way the Mexicas and the Spanish empire handled the region they inhabited, and another on the role of colonization in the creation of epistemologies and political theories that transformed the way Europe understood and fashioned itself. She is the author of the book *Escribiendo desde los márgenes. Colonialismo y jesuitas en el siglo XVIII* (2009).

◆ Index

Compiled by Santa Arias and Raúl Marrero-Fente

Acosta, José de, xvi–xvii, xviii, 3–23, 24n–25n, 46, 96–97, 105, 106, 109, 132n, 264
Adorno, Rolena, xiii, 22, 37–38, 111n, 183–84, 218n, 225, 237n
Aguilar, Filomeno, 257
Aguilar, Jerónimo de, 209–10
Alenda y Mira, Jenaro, 155n
Alexander VI, x–xi, 94, 99, 183
Alvarado, Pedro de, 212, 216
Alvarado Tezozomoc, Hernando de, 72
Anales de Juan Bautista, xvi, xvii, 51–68
Anales de Cuauhtitlan, 54
Anales de Tlatelolco, 54
Arias, Santa, xxin, 56–57, 59, 223, 227
Aristotle, 6, 7, 21, 184, 188, 190–91, 218n, 264
Ávila, Francisco de, xviii, 117–32, 132n

Barnes, Jonathan, 218n
Barrantes, Vicente, 149, 150–51, 155n
Baudrillard, Jean, 259n
Beckjord, Sara, 218n
Benton, Lauren, 111n
Berdan, Frances, 74, 87n
Beuchot, Mauricio, xxin
Bhabha, Homi, 53, 64, 149, 151, 213
Black Legend, 100, 112n
Borah, Woodrow, 225
Boruchoff, David, 212
Bourdieu, Pierre, 224
Brading, David, 111n, 237n
Brubaker, Rogers, 223, 237n
Brufau Prats, Jaime, 182, 197n

Brundage, Burr Cartwright, 218n
Bulls of Donation, x, xii

Cano, Melchor, xiii, xxi,
Canny, Nicholas, 111n
Cañizares-Esguerra, Jorge, 95, 236
Caplan, Karen, 228, 238n
Carrasco, Davíd, 217n
Casas, Bartolomé de Las, xiii, xvii, xix, xxin, 8, 11, 20–23, 24n, 29–30, 32–40, 42, 46–48, 62, 96, 99–100, 141, 181–96, 197n–198n, 216, 218n, 224–25, 243, 264–69
Casas, Ignacio de las, 24n
Castañeda, Felipe, 4–5, 197n
Castañeda Delgado, Paulino, 197n
Certeau, Michel de, 87n
Cervantes, Miguel de, 12, 28, 36
Charles II, 77, 81–84
Charles III, 229
Charles V, 34, 185
Chilam Balam, 59, 68n
Chimalpahin, Domingo Francisco, 54, 72–73, 269–70
Christian, William, 242, 259n
Clark, Stuart, 105
Clendinnen, Inga, 215
Codex Xolotl, 165
Codex Telleriano-Remensis, xv
Códice de Santiago Tlacotepec, 162
Códice franciscano, 169
Códice Magliabechi 67n
Colegio Imperial de Santa Cruz de Tlatelolco, 53

Collins, Adela Yarbro, 60, 68n
Combés, Francisco de, xviii; 137–54, 155n
Cooper, Frederick, 237n
Coronil, Fernando, 234
Cortés, Hernán, 33, 39, 43, 47, 73, 78–79, 87n, 165, 168, 185, 206–7, 209–11, 214–15, 217n–18n, 236, 243,
Cortés, Rocío, 67n
Cruz, Francisco de la, 8, 24n
Cummins, Tom, 76, 160
Curcio-Nagy, Linda, 75–76

Dallmayr, Fred, 146
Darian-Smith, Eve, xxin
Dean, Carolyn, 76, 160
Deleuze, Gilles, 259n
Derrida, Jacques, 217, 263–64, 266
Descartes, René, 17, 23n
Díaz, Juan, 203, 205
Díaz del Castillo, Bernal, 33–34, 88n, 210–12, 215–17n, 218n, 243
Douglas, Eduardo de Jesús, 165
Drake, Francis, 34, 102 fig.2
Durán, Diego, 59, 68n
Dussel, Enrique, x, 17, 195, 196
Duverger, Christian, 217n

El Alaoui, Youssef, 6, 24n
Encomienda, xi, 13, 73, 168–69, 172–73, 225
Eximiae devotionis, xii

Fanon, Frank, 32
Fernández Christlieb, Federico, 67n
Fernández de Oviedo, Gonzalo, 203, 205, 217n
Figgis, John, 244, 258n, 259n
Fitzpatrick, Peter, xxin
Flores Hernández, Benjamín, 30
Florescano, Enrique, 217n
Foucault, Michel, 12
Foz y Foz, Pilar, 223, 232, 234
Fuchs, Barbara, 143

García Zambrano, Ángel, 67n
Gaudio, Michael, 112n

Geertz, Clifford, 75
Gibson, Charles, 74, 76, 87n, 88n, 112n
González, Alonso, 163, 166, 167–68, 174
González Echevarría, Roberto, 36
González-Holguín, Diego, 119, 133n
González Torres, Yolotl, 217n
Gramática de la lengua, x
Green, L. C., xi
Grijalva, Juan de, 203–4, 206, 217n
Groessen, Michiel van, 112n
Grosfoguel, Ramón, 198n
Gruzinski, Serge, 67n, 68n, 133n, 243, 249, 259n
Guardino, Peter, 238n
Guattari, Felix, 259n

Hakluyt, Richard, 97, 100–4, 106, 108, 112n
Hale, Charles, 238n
Haley, Richard, 67n
Harriot, Thomas, 98–100, 102–4, 106, 108, 112
Hegel, 24n–25n
Hernández de Córdoba, Francisco, 206
Hill, Ruth, 226, 230

Imperium, x–xi
Inter caetera bull, xi, 94, 99, 111n, 183, 197n
ius gentium, xiii, 183, 188,
ius naturae, xiii

Jackson, Robert, 226, 238n
James I, 104
Jáuregui, Carlos, 187, 197n
Jenkins, Richard, 224
Joaquin, Nick, 258n, 259n
Julius II, xii

Kamen, Henry, 140
Kellog, Susan, 86n, 174
Klapisch-Zuber, Christiane, 173
Klor de Alva, José Jorge, xiv, 67n
Kranz, Travis Barton, 86n
Krug, Frances, 73, 86n

León Pinelo, Antonio de, xxin
Leyes de Burgos, xi

INDEX 277

Lockhart, James, xvii, 52–55, 67n, 68n, 72–74, 85–86n, 87n, 160, 168, 174–75
Lodares, Juan R., 155n
Lopes Don, Patricia, xviii, 67n
López de Gómara, Francisco, 209–10, 218n
López de Legazpi, Miguel, xxi*n*, 240, 248–49
López de Palacios Rubio, Juan, x–xii
Loyola, Ignacio de, 23n, 25n, 155n

MacCormack, Sabine, xv, 133
Magellan, Ferdinand, xxi*n*, 138
Majul, Cesar Adib, 139, 140, 142, 149
Maldonado-Torres, Nelson, ix–x
Mariscal, George, 186
Marrero-Fente, Raúl, xiv, 111n, 197n, 198n, 225
Marshall, John, 93, 111n
Martínez, María Elena, 225, 237n
Martínez Baracs, Andrea, 72, 74, 86n, 87n
Martínez-San Miguel, Yolanda, 237n
Mather, Cotton, 108–9
Mayuga, Silvia, 254
McAndrew, John, 169
Mede, Joseph, 105–6, 108, 112n
Memmi, Albert, 31–32
Mondzain, Marie-José, 247–49
Montesinos, Antonio de, xi, 197n
Morga, Antonio de, 138
Motolinía, Toribio de, 59, 68n, 185
Muldoon, James, x, xiii, 30, 111n
Muñoz Camargo, Diego, 78, 86n
Muriel, Josefina, 235 fig.1, 238n

Nandy, Ashis, xvii, 30–32, 34, 40, 47
Nebrija, Antonio de, x
Noguez, Xavier, 162, 165–66, 168

O'Hara, Mathew, 223, 227–28
Olko, Justyna, 87n
Osowski, Edward, 79–80

Pagden Anthony, 7, 111n, 112n, 188, 207–8, 214–15
Paz, Fray Matías de, 193
Pereña, Luciano, 23–24n
Pizarro, Francisco, 47

Phelan, John Leddy, xxi*n*, 140, 142, 145
Philip II, xvii, 29
Philip IV, 81, 82, 83, 84
Poma de Ayala, Felipe Guaman, 29, 30, 32–33, 35–39, 42–47, 120, 133n, 237n
Purchas, Samuel, 106

Quiahuiztlan, 71, 82, 85
Quijano, Aníbal, xvi, xxn, 265

Rabasa, José, xi, xv; 66n, 206, 224, 268
Ralegh, Walter, 97, 99, 100, 103, 104
Rama, Ángel, 53
Ramírez, Susan E., 133n
Ramírez de Arrellano, Joaquín, 232–33
Ramos, Demetrio, xxi*n*
Recopilación de leyes de los reynos de las indias, 80, 87n
Requerimiento, x–xii, xxi*n*, 185, 198n
Reyes García, Luis, 52, 54–55, 67n, 72, 86n, 87n
Romano, Ruggiero, 67n
Romero Galván, José Rubén, 76, 87n
Rowlandson, Mary, 108
Royal Patronage of the Indies, xi–xii
Ruiz de Alarcón, Hernando, 110, 112n
Ruiz Medrano, Ethelia, xv, 86n, 160, 162, 164, 166, 167

Sahagún, Bernardino de, 59, 62, 68n
Salomon, Frank, 133n
Santa Cruz Pachacuti Yamqui Salcamaygua, Joan de, 120
Santos, Joel R. de los, 141
Schmitt, Carl, xi, 23n, 244, 245, 246, 259n, 265
Schussler, Elizabeth Fiorenza, 68n
Selwyn, Jennifer, 6, 24n
Sepúlveda, Juan Ginés de, xix, 38, 181–96, 197n
Smith, John, 106, 107 fig. 4, 108
Solórzano y Pereira, Juan, xxi*n*, 30
Spivak, Gayatri Chakravory, 266, 269
Sticca, Sandro, 259n
Suárez, Francisco, xiii

Távarez, David, xiv, 67n, 209, 214, 242
Taylor, Diana, 75, 81, 217n
Taylor, Gerald, 130, 132n, 133n
Tenochtitlan, 61–62, 64–65, 68n, 72, 160, 165, 210–11, 215–16, 243
Terra nullius, 94, 110, 111n
Thomas, Keith, 97
Todorov, Tzvetan, 59, 68n
Townsend, Camilla 52, 54, 71, 73, 86n
Treaty of Tordesillas, xi, xxn, 94
Turner, Edith, 259n
Turner, Victor, 259n

Universalis Ecclesiae regimi, xii

Vacuum domicilium, 96, 111n
Vargas Machuca, Bernardo, xvi, xvii, 27–47, 264
Viana, Don Francisco Leandro de, 257

Villoro, Luis, 193
Vitoria, Francisco de, xiii, 94, 96, 111n, 141, 193, 196, 197n, 208, 225, 243–44

Warner, Marina, 259n
Weber, David, xvii
Wey-Gómez, Nicolás, xx*n*
White, John, 100, 101, 102, 104
Whitener, Brian, 25n
Williams, Raymond, 258n

Ybarra, Patricia, 81, 83, 87n, 88n

Zapata Mendoza, Juan Buenaventura, xvi, xvii, 71–87
Zavala, Silvio, xxi*n*, 182–83, 198n
Žižek, Slavoj, 25n
Zorita, Fray Antonio, 164

VOLUMES IN THE HISPANIC ISSUES SERIES

40 *Coloniality, Religion, and the Law in the Early Iberian World*
   edited by Santa Arias and Rául Marrero-Fente
39 *Poiesis and Modernity in the Old and New Worlds*
   edited by Anthony J. Cascardi and Leah Middlebrook
38 *Spectacle and Topophilia: Reading Early (and
   Post-) Modern Hispanic Cultures*
   edited by David R. Castillo and Bradley J. Nelson
37 *New Spain, New Literatures*
   edited by Luis Martín-Estudillo and Nicholas Spadaccini
36 *Latin American Jewish Cultural Production*,
   edited by David William Foster
35 *Post-Authoritarian Cultures: Spain and Latin America's Southern Cone*,
   edited by Luis Martín-Estudillo and Roberto Ampuero
34 *Spanish and Empire*, edited by Nelsy Echávez-Solano
   and Kenya C. Dworkin y Méndez
33 *Generation X Rocks: Contemporary Peninsular Fiction, Film, and
   Rock Culture*, edited by Christine Henseler and Randolph D. Pope
32 *Reason and Its Others: Italy, Spain, and the New World*,
   edited by David Castillo and Massimo Lollini
31 *Hispanic Baroques: Reading Cultures in Context*,
   edited by Nicholas Spadaccini and Luis Martín-Estudillo
30 *Ideologies of Hispanism*, edited by Mabel Moraña
29 *The State of Latino Theater in the United States: Hybridity,
   Transculturation, and Identity*, edited by Luis A. Ramos-García
28 *Latin America Writes Back: Postmodernity in the Periphery
   (An Interdisciplinary Perspective)*, edited by Emil Volek
27 *Women's Narrative and Film in Twentieth-Century Spain:
   A World of Difference(s)*, edited by Ofelia Ferrán and Kathleen M. Glenn
26 *Marriage and Sexuality in Medieval and Early Modern Iberia*,
   edited by Eukene Lacarra Lanz
25 *Pablo Neruda and the U.S. Culture Industry*, edited by Teresa Longo
24 *Iberian Cities*, edited by Joan Ramon Resina
23 *National Identities and Sociopolitical Changes in Latin America*,
   edited by Mercedes F. Durán-Cogan and Antonio Gómez-Moriana
22 *Latin American Literature and Mass Media*,
   edited by Edmundo Paz-Soldán and Debra A. Castillo

21 *Charting Memory: Recalling Medieval Spain*, edited by Stacy N. Beckwith
20 *Culture and the State in Spain: 1550–1850*,
    edited by Tom Lewis and Francisco J. Sánchez
19 *Modernism and its Margins: Reinscribing Cultural Modernity from Spain and Latin America*, edited by Anthony L. Geist and José B. Monleón
18 *A Revisionary History of Portuguese Literature*,
    edited by Miguel Tamen and Helena C. Buescu
17 *Cervantes and his Postmodern Constituencies*,
    edited by Anne Cruz and Carroll B. Johnson
16 *Modes of Representation in Spanish Cinema*,
    edited by Jenaro Talens and Santos Zunzunegui
15 *Framing Latin American Cinema: Contemporary Critical Perspectives*, edited by Ann Marie Stock
14 *Rhetoric and Politics: Baltasar Gracián and the New World Order*,
    edited by Nicholas Spadaccini and Jenaro Talens
13 *Bodies and Biases: Sexualities in Hispanic Cultures and Literatures*,
    edited by David W. Foster and Roberto Reis
12 *The Picaresque: Tradition and Displacement*, edited by Giancarlo Maiorino
11 *Critical Practices in Post-Franco Spain*,
    edited by Silvia L. López, Jenaro Talens, and Dario Villanueva
10 *Latin American Identity and Constructions of Difference*,
    edited by Amaryll Chanady
 9 *Amerindian Images and the Legacy of Columbus*,
    edited by René Jara and Nicholas Spadaccini
 8 *The Politics of Editing*, edited by Nicholas Spadaccini and Jenaro Talens
 7 *Culture and Control in Counter-Reformation Spain*,
    edited by Anne J. Cruz and Mary Elizabeth Perry
 6 *Cervantes's Exemplary Novels and the Adventure of Writing*,
    edited by Michael Nerlich and Nicholas Spadaccini
 5 *Ortega y Gasset and the Question of Modernity*, edited by Patrick H. Dust
 4 *1492–1992: Re/Discovering Colonial Writing*,
    edited by René Jara and Nicholas Spadaccini
 3 *The Crisis of Institutionalized Literature in Spain*,
    edited by Wlad Godzich and Nicholas Spadaccini
 2 *Autobiography in Early Modern Spain*,
    edited by Nicholas Spadaccini and Jenaro Talens
 1 *The Institutionalization of Literature in Spain*,
    edited by Wlad Godzich and Nicholas Spadaccini

www.ingramcontent.com/pod-product-compliance
Lightning Source LLC
Chambersburg PA
CBHW051210300426
44116CB00006B/509